THE TORAH'S VISION OF WORSHIP

OVERTURES TO BIBLICAL THEOLOGY

EDITORS

WALTER BRUEGGEMANN
Columbia Theological Seminary, Decatur, Georgia

JOHN R. DONAHUE, S.J.
Jesuit School of Theology at Berkeley, California

SHARYN DOWD
Lexington Theological Seminary, Lexington, Kentucky

CHRISTOPHER R. SEITZ
University of St. Andrews, Scotland

THE TORAH'S
VISION OF WORSHIP

Samuel E. Balentine

FORTRESS PRESS
MINNEAPOLIS

For my students at BTSR,
who have shared the vision
and shaped the journey

The Torah's Vision of Worship

Cover image: Palestine. Megiddo. Four-horned incense altar, limestone, Iron Age IIA, 10th century B.C.E. Courtesy of the Oriental Institute of the University of Chicago.
Cover and book design: Joseph Bonyata
Typesetting: Peregrine Graphics Services

Library of Congress Cataloging-in-Publication Data
Balentine, Samuel E.   (Samuel Eugene),   1950-
    The Torah's vision of worship   /   Samuel E. Balentine.
        p.   cm. — (Overtures to biblical theology)
    Includes bibliographical references and indexes.
    ISBN: 0-8006-3155-2 (alk. paper)
        1. God—Worship and love—Biblical teaching.   2. Worship in the Bible.
3. Covenants—Biblical teaching.   4. Bible.   O.T.   Pentateuch—Theology.
5. Bible.   O.T.   Pentateuch—Criticism, interpretation, etc.   I. Title.   II. Series.
BS1199.L67B35   1999
296.4'9—dc21   99-12063
                                                                                        CIP

The paper used in this publication meets the minimum requirements of American National Standard for Information Sciences—Permanence of Paper for Printed Library Materials, ANSI Z329.48-1984.

Manufactured in the U.S.A.   AF 1-3155
    02   01   00   99   1   2   3   4   5   6   7   8   9   10

CONTENTS

EDITOR'S FOREWORD

O LD TESTAMENT STUDIES ARE MARKED AT THE PRESENT TIME BY enormous ferment. Two dimensions of that ferment are particularly pertinent to the present volume. First, there is immense generativity concerning method. What we are able to see is that the long unchallenged dominance of historical criticism has been broken, so that many other approaches can now be undertaken with a reasonable claim to legitimacy. It is not at all clear how these various newer methodological concerns will shake down, if indeed any methodological consensus will emerge beyond a dazzling pluralism. Second, among those who continue to ask historical (and historical critical) questions, there is a powerful tendency to pull the dating of almost every document in the Old Testament much later, contrary to the earlier impetus of Albrecht Alt and William Foxwell Albright of situating everything as early as possible. Specifically, scholars are now much inclined to date a great deal of the material as late as the Babylonian period of Judean history, and the Persian period is now being increasingly treated as a primally generative period for the literature of the Old Testament. Of course, such matters are deeply contested, and we are far from any redefined consensus on the historical questions.

In light of the new stirrings in the discipline, Sam Balentine has written a remarkably suggestive book that is well situated in the context of the new emergents in the field. Balentine bases his study of the Torah (Pentateuch) on the judgment that it is framed in the Persian period and is reflective of the delicately nuanced status of the Jerusalem community in the face of imperial policy. That policy, unlike the earlier practices among the Assyrians and Babylonians, was not only to allow local religious options, but to encourage such activity and to preempt local practice as a concentration of regional power that was submissive to and reliant upon Persian support and legitimacy. Thus Israel's liturgic-theological response to its situation in a Persian environment is one that deals with "internal uncertainty and external Persian direction."

In that context, Balentine understands the worship life of Judaism in Jerusalem as a mix of subservience and assertion that seeks to formulate and generate a distinct faith identity for the community, to enact a liturgical "world" in which Jewish identity is viable and makes sense. Methodologically, Balentine's work has most in common, in Old Testament studies, with the early work of Sigmund Mowinckel who insisted that the liturgy was generative of social reality. Balentine, however, does not appeal to the underdeveloped claims of Mowinckel, but appeals to more current anthropological work, namely that of Mary Douglas, Victor Turner, and especially Clifford Geertz. These scholars have seen that public religious activity in worship is not nonsensical as it may appear to an uninformed outsider, but is a meaningful, generative activity that legitimates a socioreligious context that is not anywhere outside the liturgic community legitimated or sustained.

It is evident in such a project that Balentine has broken decisively with the history-of-religion approach of H. H. Rowley and Hans-Joachim Kraus (even in their attempt to be theological), and still vigorously reflected in the more recent work of Rainer Albertz. Balentine's work, after a historical judgment about the Persian period, is primally concerned with the "substitute world" that is being enacted through these texts in something like a liturgical setting. Such a perspective that concerns "the social construction of reality" is particularly suited to the Persian period that operated with a dialectical practice of supervision and autonomy. It was exactly such a context that permitted Israel to enact a counter-imagination in the service of a counter-identity.

Though he does not labor the larger architectonic pattern, Balentine's hypothesis has its immense power because he is able to see the whole of the Torah in a patterned coherence. He sees the Sinai tradition at the center of the Torah as a covenantal practice of vocation, with the formation of the Tabernacle as "world building" and priests as the agents to sustain that new world. That Sinai practice of world building looks back to the Genesis traditions that have sabbath at the core, the creation materials that are concerned with world building and community formation, so that creation and Sinai are intentionally linked in the generation and maintenance of a peculiarly YHWH-intended world.

On the far side of Sinai, Balentine understands the book of Deuteronomy as "boundary literature" that looks into the future with a "vision of governance that is meant to be" and that is "imminently attainable." Thus the Torah ends at the boundary with an "interim liturgy that awaits completion." It would be fair to term this vision of the Torah as "eschatological," as long as that is not taken as a long-term, dogmatic project, but is seen as a future-generating activity wherein the hopes of Israel are quite concrete and immediate.

When one remembers the old scholarly accounts of Israelite worship and their endless catalogues and inventories of practices, it is clear that Balentine has profoundly advanced our understanding by seeing the wholeness and dynamic of the text that reflects in turn the wholeness of liturgic vision and the dynamic of actual worship.

After Balentine has shown himself to be a remarkably sensitive reader of texts with full command of a vast store of secondary literature, the concluding section of the book exhibits him, as well, as an acute theological interpreter concerned with the contemporary scene of faith.

In the end, Balentine's theological interest does not stay in the ancient Persian world. He reads the text "as Scripture." And since he has seen the "boundary" literature looking to an alternative world, he asks of the Torah our own belated questions of hope. He takes the question from T. S. Eliot's presentation of the end as a "whimper" and not "a bang," a sad, sorry, quiet failure. From Eliot, Balentine engages Richard Friedman's notion of the growing, increasing, irreversible hiddenness and silence of God in the Old Testament, a theme on which Balentine himself has done important research. Eliot's question and Friedman's scholarly exposition are matched in Balentine's conclusion by a lingering over John Updike's *In the Beauty of the Lilies,* a novel in which Updike considers a concrete case of the withdrawal of God from human experience. Balentine draws us very close to how the world is lived in such awesome absence at the turn of the millennium.

In the end, of course, Balentine will not yield to silence. For that reason he understands, with attention to the suggestion of Jacob Neusner on Jewish imagination, that Torah is an act of counter-imagination that refuses to give in to the world of absence and silence. Balentine observes that this counter-world that is a habitat for faith is centered in the "sabbatical principle." This centering is an affirmation of a world still coming, but a world peopled with the holiness of the God of Israel. Living in the present toward the future is a daring "as if." But then, that is how the people of this text have always lived, differently, within every empire.

Balentine models a new way of scholarship that builds powerful connections between the critical task and the hermeneutical capacity of the text. In the end he is not interested in methodological considerations. He makes good use of new methods with great interpretive sensitivity. His focus finally is upon the theological claim of the text. I anticipate that his book will be a baseline for future theological work in the Torah, work rooted critically but in close touch with the lived crisis of our own world.

Walter Brueggemann

ABBREVIATIONS

AB	Anchor Bible
BA	*Biblical Archaeologist*
Bib	*Biblica*
BZ	*Biblische Zeitschrift*
CBQ	*Catholic Biblical Quarterly*
CQR	*Church Quarterly Review*
EvTh	*Evangelische Theologie*
HBT	*Horizons in Biblical Theology*
HUCA	*Hebrew Union College Annual*
Int	*Interpretation*
IOS	*Israel Oriental Society*
JAOS	*Journal of American Oriental Studies*
JBL	*Journal of Biblical Literature*
JSOT	*Journal for the Study of the Old Testament*
JSOTSup	Journal for the Study of the Old Testament Supplement Series
JTS	*Journal of Theological Studies*
NIB	*New Interpreter's Bible*
OBT	Overtures to Biblical Theology
OTS	*Oudtestamentische Studiën*
PSB	*Princeton Seminary Bulletin*
RB	*Revue biblique*
SBL	Society of Biblical Literature
ST	*Studia Theologica*
TBT	*The Bible Today*
TD	*Theology Digest*
TLOT	*Theological Lexicon of the Old Testament*
TToday	*Theology Today*
USQR	*Union Seminary Quarterly Review*
VT	*Vetus Testamentum*
WW	*Word and World*
ZAW	*Zeitschrift für die alttestamentliche Wissenschaft*

PREFACE

THIS IS NOT THE BOOK I SET OUT TO WRITE. I HAVE TAUGHT A COURSE ON worship in ancient Israel off and on through the years, and each time I have been reminded that there is not adequate treatment of the subject in print that I could assign as a text. My conviction that the situation should be remedied pushed me finally to draft the first outlines for this project. My original objective was to provide a basic update of the subject that would have followed the history-of-religion approach modeled by Hans-Joachim Kraus, although I hoped to supplement this with a modest theological perspective that might suggest an overall framework for understanding general issues. This objective was gradually discarded for several reasons, none of which I foresaw when I started.

First, I began to realize that it was not the disparate details of Israel's worship that I needed to describe. Instead, I found myself wanting to understand the fundamental objectives of Israel's worship, which the various rites and practices may have served. I eventually conceptualized these objectives with the rubric of the Torah's "vision" of worship. When I completed that part of the work (part 2 of this book), I thought the manuscript was finished.

Second, this vision of Israel's worship gradually pushed me to ask a range of other questions, landing me far outside the lines of my first-draft projections. Where did this vision originate? What context(s) did it address? What were the historical, political, and social factors that shaped its formulation? Such questions led me eventually to look to the Persian period and to reflect on how this world, which by all accounts provided the setting for the Pentateuch's canonization, may have contributed to the vision I had discerned. Although I am keenly aware of my limitations in this area, I have tried to give a brief account of what I have learned in what is part 1 of this book: "The World That Shaped the Torah's Vision."

Third, the tension created by the juxtaposition of parts 1 and 2 made it imperative for me to rethink the theological perspective of the Torah's vision of worship that I had once been content to let stand in undisturbed isolation. Was Israel's worship an accomodation to the regnant powers that defined its given existence? Or did its worship have the capacity to sustain a vision of another world and a different identity that was more attuned to God's creational design? Part 3 of this book is my attempt to answer these questions.

The long and winding journey toward the completion of this book has been shaped in important ways by a number of persons who have kindly offered the benefit of their counsel. I am especially grateful to Terry Fretheim and Walter Brueggemann, both of whom responded to early drafts with cautious encouragement and leading questions that helped me to realize my first thoughts ought not be my last thoughts. Most of all, I am deeply indebted to my students at Baptist Theological Seminary at Richmond, to whom this book is dedicated. Over the years, they have listened patiently as I bootlegged the developing argument into numerous classes. When they read this final version, I hope they will see how much I have learned from their comments and questions.

This is not the book I set out to write. But the reasons I have given above do not tell the full story of why this is so. Almost ten years ago, I resigned from my previous teaching post in the midst of a denominational-political controversy that, for all I could see, threatened to shut down my call to ministry. In a letter to my colleagues and friends, I tried to explain my decision and the grief that it carried. The words that best described my despair at the time were those I learned from the prophet Ezekiel: "The days are long, and every vision has perished" (12:22). On this side of my immersion into the Torah's vision of worship I now know, with Ezekiel and his forebears, that the summons to be "a priestly kingdom and a holy nation" (Exod. 19:6) remains alive and well, even in exile. For the gift of my journey from then to now, this book is but a down payment.

PROLEGOMENA

1.
WORSHIP AS A SUBJECT
IN OLD TESTAMENT STUDIES

ALMOST A FULL GENERATION HAS PASSED SINCE THE LAST COMPREHEN-
sive treatments of worship in the Old Testament were published. H.-J.
Kraus's *Gottesdienst in Israel (Worship in Israel)*, which first appeared in 1954,
introduced a brief period when this subject emerged as a principal concern.[1]
Over the next fifteen years, significant studies were offered by R. de Vaux,
H. H. Rowley, and W. Harrelson.[2] By the end of the 1960s, few would have
quibbled with U. Simon's observation, in reviewing the 1965 English translation of Kraus, that "Worship is nowadays no longer just a department in
Old Testament studies, but without a doubt the master-key."[3]

Since Harrelson's 1969 publication, however, the subject of "worship" in
ancient Israel seems largely to have faded from Old Testament studies. One
can still find discussion of selected aspects of Israel's worship, for example
the sacrificial system[4] or the temple and its cult.[5] But when one looks for
the kind of comprehensive assessments of worship that characterized the
generation of Kraus and his peers, nothing comparable emerges. Indeed,
even the general synopses of Israel's worship that were once standard

---

1. H.-J. Kraus, *Worship in Israel: A Cultic History of the Old Testament*, G. Buswell trans.
(Oxford: Basil Blackwell; Richmond: John Knox, 1965), is a translation of the 1962 revised and
enlarged edition; the book was first published in 1954.

2. R. de Vaux, *Ancient Israel*. Vols. I, II, trans. J. McHugh (New York: McGraw-Hill, 1961);
H. H. Rowley, *Worship in Ancient Israel* (London: SPCK, 1967); W. Harrelson, *From Fertility
Cult to Worship* (New York: Doubleday, 1969).

3. U. Simon, "Old Testament Cultus," *CQR* 168 (1967), 111.

4. Note especially the significant contributions of J. Milgrom, e.g., *Studies in Levitical Terminology: The Encroacher and the Levite. The Term 'Aboda* (Berkeley: University of California
Press, 1970); *Cult and Conscience: The Asham and the Priestly Doctrine of Repentance* (Leiden:
E. J. Brill, 1976); *Studies in Cultic Theology and Terminology* (Leiden: E. J. Brill, 1983); *Leviticus
1–16*, AB (New York: Doubleday, 1991).

5. E.g., M. Haran, *Temples and Temple Service in Ancient Israel* (Oxford: Clarendon, 1978).

features in Bible dictionaries and handbooks are now either subsumed under other subjects or lacking altogether.[6]

In 1969, Harrelson observed that a re-examination of Israel's worship could help with the problems confronting the community of faith in an "ecumenical and post-Christian age."[7] Given the perceived secularism that characterized the 1960s, Harrelson argued that a study of Israel's worship could contribute toward restoring the quality of relationship between God and humankind, and toward restoring and reappropriating God's design for the world.[8]

This need for a re-examination is no less pressing now, as we enter a new millennium bereft of certainties that our predecessors enjoyed. One no longer speaks of a "post-*Christian*" world; even this vestige of religious consciousness seems to claim far too much. This is now a post-*modern* world, defined more by intellectual, spiritual, and moral ambivalence than by faith assertions, whether Christian, Jewish, or otherwise. It is a world advanced and sustained as never before by technology and its by-products and yet at the same time a world that seems to many to be void of any transcendent meaning that may guide human accomplishments toward a construction of life that offers peace and justice to all peoples. As R. Friedman recently suggested, the legacy of the twentieth century is a prevailing conviction that God has simply "disappeared."[9]

With Harrelson, I believe that a study of ancient Israel's worship may offer a meaningful word in a world where much is askew. My thesis, which must be substantiated in the following chapters, is that the Torah conveys a "vision" of worship. It portrays worship as a principal means by which a community of faith (or a community *seeking* faith) attains clarity about God, God's design for the world, and the role of humankind in implementing and sustaining the world of that design.

I do not believe, however, that this vision of worship can be fully discerned simply by walking in the footsteps of those who charted the course for previous generations. The world has changed significantly; hence the argument for the relevance of Israel's worship must now be made on different grounds. Further, the ways we read and appropriate Scripture have undergone dramatic changes. The collapse, or at least the weakening, of

6. *The Anchor Bible Dictionary*, vols. 1–6 (New York, London: Doubleday, 1992), has no entry on worship in the Old Testament.

7. Harrelson, *From Fertility Cult to Worship*, xi.

8. Ibid., 93–99.

9. R. E. Friedman, *The Disappearance of God: A Divine Mystery* (Boston, New York, Toronto, London: Little, Brown and Company, 1995); reissued as *The Hidden Face of God* (San Francisco: HarperCollins, 1997).

traditional historical-critical methods has invited a range of new approaches to biblical texts and new possibilities for constructive theological interpretation. I suggest, in tracing the Torah's "vision" of worship for the modern world, that traditional concerns with the "history" of Israel's worship must now be enlarged with new perspectives that make clearer the sociological context in which and for which these texts have been shaped.

As an introduction to that discussion, I offer first a "study of the study" of worship in Old Testament scholarship.[10] How (and why) has worship been studied in the past, and why does it no longer appear as a prominent subject in Old Testament studies? How (and why) may this subject be retrieved as a vital component in a theological discourse fitted for the twenty-first century?

I do not propose a comprehensive review of the discussion of this subject. In a previous work, I detailed the history of scholarship with respect to "prayer," and much of that discussion remains relevant for the present investigation of worship.[11] Moreover, Kraus has provided a basic historical survey of the study of Old Testament worship through 1962.[12] I will simply review the foundations that Kraus and others have provided, then bring the discussion up to date with some broad summary discernments that situate my own approach within the context of the scholarly discussion.

The History Paradigm

With few exceptions, the study of worship in the Old Testament has been dominated by a history-oriented paradigm, developed most fully by J. Wellhausen and the "history of religions" school. In a strict sense, the dominance of this approach was confined to roughly fifty years, from the latter half of the nineteenth century to the early decades of the twentieth when World War I brought radical changes in the world and, not coincidentally, to the landscape of biblical scholarship. With the study of worship, however, Wellhausen's approach has continued to provide the primary interpretive paradigm for virtually every significant treatment throughout the twentieth century, including those of Kraus, Rowley, and Harrelson.

10. On the need for a "study of the study," that is, for critical reflection on the philosophical, cultural, and political contexts that shape biblical scholarship, see J. Rogerson, "Philosophy and the Rise of Biblical Criticism: England and Germany," in *England and Germany: Studies in Theological Diplomacy*, ed. S. W. Sykes (Frankfurt: Peter Lang, 1982), 63–79. Rogerson subsequently offered a thorough treatment of these matters with respect to nineteenth-century biblical scholarship in England and Germany in *Old Testament Criticism in the Nineteenth Century: England and Germany* (Philadelphia: Fortress, 1985).

11. S. E. Balentine, *Prayer in the Hebrew Bible: The Drama of Divine-Human Dialogue*, OBT, (Minneapolis: Fortress, 1993), 246–59.

12. Kraus, *Worship in Israel*, 1–25.

J. Wellhausen and the History of Religions Approach

Building on the work of his predecessors in the field of historical criticism—especially de Wette, Vatke, and Graf—Wellhausen set himself the task of reconstructing the genetic development of Israel's history. For Wellhausen, the key to this history was the development of the religion of Israel, hence he began his influential study, *Prolegomena to the History of Ancient Israel* (1878), with a section entitled "History of the Ordinances of Worship,"[13] essentially a history of Israel's worship.

This history addressed four specific aspects of Israel's worship: the place of worship, sacrifice, the sacred festivals, and the cultic personnel (the priests and the Levites). With each aspect, he traced the successive stages through which Israel's religion had developed, and associated those stages with their respective literary traditions in the Pentateuch: JE (Jehovist), D (Deuteronomy), and P (Priestly). In Wellhausen's periodization of history, JE corresponds with the earliest stage of Israel's religion, when worship is spontaneous and natural. The D tradition corresponds with the Deuteronomic Code, the first edition of which emerged in connection with the Josianic reformation (622 B.C.E.). This marks a second stage in Israel's religion, when worship is centralized in the one place chosen by God (cf. Deut. 12:10-14) and the ordinances fall under greater institutional control. The Priestly tradition marks the third and final stage in the historical development of Israel's religion, the post-exilic period. At this stage, the priestly establishment emerges as firmly in control of a comprehensive ritual and legal system. It is this priestly system of religion that becomes the authoritative mechanism of governance in a post-exilic theocracy.

Wellhausen's discussion of the sacred festivals illustrates the development in Israel's religion that he discerned. He distinguished three stages with differing cultic regulations concerning the annual festivals. The first stage is represented by the JE calendar (Exod. 34:18-26; 23:14-19), which assumes that the annual festivals originated as simple offerings of first-fruits in dutiful thanksgiving for the bounty of the land. In its earliest form, Wellhausen argued, Israel's religion was tied firmly and quite naturally to agrarian concerns. In his words:

> The blessing of the land is here the end of religion. . . . It has for its basis no historical acts of salvation, but nature simply, which, however, is regarded only as God's domain and as man's field of labor, and is in no manner itself deified. . . . In accordance with this, worship consists simply of the thanksgiving due for the gifts of the

13. J. Wellhausen, *Prolegomena to the History of Ancient Israel* (Gloucester, Mass.: Peter Smith, 1973 [1878]), 15–167.

soil, the vassalage payable to the superior who has given the land and its fruits.[14]

The Deuteronomic cultic calendar (Deut. 16) marks the transition to the second stage in the development of Israel's religion. In addition to commanding a centralization of the annual festivals in the "place that the Lord will choose" (vv. 2, 6, 7, 11, 15, 16), Deuteronomy 16 makes a connection between what had formerly been nature festivals and specific historical events, principally the exodus from Egypt. Thus, for example, the instructions concerning Passover: "Observe the month of Abib by keeping the passover for the LORD your God, for in the month of Abib your God brought you out of Egypt by night" (16:1; cf. v. 12). Wellhausen interpreted this second stage as the beginning of a process of the "denaturalization of the feasts."[15] He states:

> It is in Deuteronomy that one detects the first perceptible traces of a historical dress being given to the religion and worship, but this process is still confined within modest limits. The historical event to which recurrence is always made is the bringing up of Israel out of Egypt, and this is significant in so far as the bringing up out of Egypt coincides with the leading into Canaan, that is, with the giving of the land, so that the historical motive again resolves itself into the natural.[16]

With the Priestly calendar (Num. 28–29) the process of denaturalizing the festivals reaches its climax. The verification that the process is complete comes in three ways according to Wellhausen. First, the offerings of the first-fruits, once an integral part of the harvest cycle, are separated from the natural circumstances in daily life that had inspired them and become instead simply dues paid to the priests. As such they are "degraded into mere 'exercises of religion'" and become "petrified remains of the old custom."[17] Second, the festivals are no longer dated in conjunction with the agricultural cycles of the year, but become fixed according to the phases of the moon. Thus they lose their connection with the natural occasions in which they had originated (e.g. planting, harvesting), and are transposed into the "fixed and uniform regulation of the cultus."[18] Third, in addition to the three annual festivals, which had been "denatured," the priestly

14. Ibid., 97.
15. Ibid., 102.
16. Ibid., 92.
17. Ibid., 100.
18. Ibid., 101.

calendar introduces two new "ecclesiastical" days—New Year's Day (Num. 29:1-6) and the Day of Atonement (Num. 29:7-11)—both of which reflect the distinctive religious interests of the priests. With respect to the Day of Atonement, the holiest day of the year in the priestly calendar, Wellhausen observed:

> Nothing could illustrate more clearly the contrast between the new cultus and the old; fixing its regard at all points on sin and atonement. . . . It is as if . . . men had felt themselves not as in an earlier age only momentarily and in special circumstances, but increasingly, under the leaden pressure of sin and wrath.[19]

It should be clear from the citations above that Wellhausen had little appreciation for the Priestly materials.[20] As we shall see, this anti-Priestly bias has remained a sad characteristic of Protestant biblical scholarship throughout much of the twentieth century.

The appearance of the history of religions approach declined markedly after World War II, as it began to be eclipsed by the "golden age" of Old Testament theology.[21] Nevertheless, those few that were written continued to address Israel's religion much along the lines developed by Wellhausen. Representative of such works are the histories by H. Ringgren and G. Fohrer.[22]

In both these histories the main interest lies in tracing the genetic development of Israel's religion from its earliest manifestations in the pre-state period to its later forms in the exilic and post-exilic periods. Both give pride of place to the monarchical period. Ringgren devotes approximately two-thirds of his book to the period of the monarchy; the pre-Davidic period and the exilic/post-exilic periods together, by contract, comprise only one-third of the discussion. Fohrer's discussion is somewhat more balanced, but, with about one-half of the book devoted to the monarchy, it is clear that he too considers this period to be the apex in Israel's religious development.[23] In this connection, both Ringgren and Fohrer cite the con-

---

19. Ibid., 112.

20. There is a growing bibliography on Wellhausen's negative attitude toward the Priestly literature and Judaism in general. For a collection of essays, see *Semeia* 25 (1982).

21. For an assessment of this period (1930–1960) with respect to the study of prayer, see Balentine, *Prayer in the Hebrew Bible*, 230–37.

22. H. Ringgren, *Israelite Religion*, trans. D. E. Green (Philadelphia: Fortress, 1966); G. Fohrer, *History of Israelite Religion*, trans. D. E. Green (Nashville: Abingdon, 1972).

23. For a critique of histories that typically privileged the monarchical period over other periods, particularly with reference to the inadequate treatment of the exilic and post-exilic periods, see R. Albertz, *A History of Israelite Religion in the Old Testament Period, Vol. 1: From the Beginnings to the End of the Monarchy*, trans. J. Bowden (Louisville: Westminster/John Knox, 1994), 9–12.

tributions of the writing prophets to this most formative period in Israel's history. In Fohrer's judgment, it is the prophets who mark the transition in Israel from "early religion to a fully developed high religion" that is "superior" to previous movements.[24]

H.-J. Kraus and the Form Critical Approach

In his review of the history of the study of worship, Kraus concluded that Wellhausen had successfully used the literary sources of the Old Testament to grasp and describe the historical development of Israel's religion "in a most comprehensive and logical manner."[25] Nonetheless, Kraus argued, if the contemporary generation of scholarship was to capitalize on Wellhausen's contribution, it must make corrections and modifications in two principal areas. First, it must avoid Wellhausen's reliance on Hegelianism,[26] the philosophy of history that assigns ideas to stages in an idealistic process of development that moves from primitive to mature. Second, it must supplement the understanding of Israel's worship that resulted from Wellhausen's source criticism with perspectives based on newer approaches to biblical studies, such as tradition-history and form criticism.[27]

These "course corrections" proved to be of enormous importance in the study of Israel's worship.[28] In the first instance, over against the notion that Israel's cultic tradition could simply be consigned to a late Priestly enterprise, Kraus called on the work of S. Mowinckel to enlarge the concept of Israel's cultic life.[29] With Mowinckel, Kraus embraced a more dynamic understanding of cult as the enactment of a sacred "drama that manifests reality."[30] On the one hand, such an understanding of cult pushes our knowledge of Israel's religion back into an era before the formation of the texts as we have them. Israel's cultic tradition may be seen, therefore, to connect positively to ancient Near Eastern mythical traditions (e.g., the Babylonian New Year Festival) that conceive and propagate universally applicable truths about life in the cosmos. On the other hand, when cult is

24. Fohrer, *History of Israelite Religion*, 290.

25. Kraus, *Worship in Israel*, 6; cf., 19.

26. Ibid., 19–20.

27. Ibid., 20–24.

28. So constructive and convincing were Kraus's observations that one reviewer concluded that form criticism should now be acknowledged as the only effective approach to this subject. In his words, "It should go without saying that without such a methodology one cannot hope to grasp the significance of Israel's worship or the character of its many literary precipitates" (J. Muilenburg, review of H.-J. Kraus, *Worship in Israel: A Cultic History of the Old Testament*, USQR 22 [1967], 277).

29. Kraus refers especially to Mowinckel's *Psalmenstudien II: Das Thronbesteigungsfest Jahwäs und der Ursprung der Eschatologie* (1922). See *Worship in Israel*, 14–16.

30. Kraus, *Worship in Israel*, 9.

understood as a dynamic reality, then cultic or ritual texts can no longer be assigned exclusively to one era or to one tradent group on the historical continuum. Even when cultic texts may be assigned with confidence to a relatively late literary source—for example, the Priestly tradition—the possibility remains that they have retained something of their older, more archaic origins.

In the second instance, Kraus's form critical approach enabled him to move beyond Wellhausen's preoccupation with literary origins and putative authors. With Gunkel, Kraus was able to focus on the regularly recurring occasions for worship in Israel—for example, "settings in life" that call forth praise or lamentation.[31] Building on the work of A. Alt, G. von Rad, and Mowinckel, Kraus was able to show that not only isolated cultic acts but also whole festivals, such as the Feast of Passover and of Unleavened Bread and the great Autumn Festival, could be illumined through form critical investigations.[32] In this regard Kraus could argue, following the lead of de Vaux, that whatever the connections might be between Israel's cultic traditions and those of its ancient Near Eastern neighbors, its worship was peculiarly based on regularly recurring events within Israel's history, not simply on common myth and ritual patterns shared in the ancient world.[33]

Notwithstanding these important advances in focus and methodology, Kraus's approach to the worship of ancient Israel retained a decidedly historical orientation. As the subtitle of his book indicates, his goal was to write "A Cultic History of the Old Testament." Towards this end, Wellhausen's outline of the historical development of Israel's religion—now supplemented by form critical discernments—provided the foundation for Kraus's work.

His indebtedness to Wellhausen is clear in both the design and the substance of his book. The four specific aspects of Israel's worship identified by Wellhausen—the place of worship, sacrifice, the sacred festivals, and the cultic personnel—also provide the principal foci for Kraus. He begins with a discussion of the cultic calendars and the main festivals listed in them,

---

31. Ibid., 11.

32. Ibid., 11–14.

33. The issue for Kraus was posed with a question: Should scholars focus on the *phenomenology* of the cult or on the *history* of the cult? The phenomenological approach, which Kraus identified with the myth and ritual school associated with S. H. Hooke and others, tended in his judgment to disregard the historical context of relevant biblical data. The historical approach to Israel's cultic institutions, which offers a necessary corrective to the cult-myth theories, is ably modeled in Kraus's judgment by R. de Vaux's *Ancient Israel: Its Life and Institutions* (1961).

then proceeds to fit these into a general chronological sequence.[34] Next follows a chapter on the cultic officials, with particular attention to the history of the priesthood and the historical connection between the priests and the prophets.[35] A further chapter focuses on the different "central" sanctuaries in early Israel and the particular cultic traditions associated with each one.[36] The final chapter addresses what for Kraus is the most formative stage in the development of the Israelite cultus: the state sanctuary in Jerusalem and the particular traditions concerning the election of David and the Royal Festival of Mt. Zion.[37] Within this last chapter, Kraus includes a brief discussion (seven pages) of the post-exilic cultic traditions.

Worship in the Context of Old Testament Theology

The most substantive discussions of worship in the 1960s and 1970s were not in histories of religion but in works that were more intentionally concerned with the theology of the Old Testament. The two most important of these for the task at hand are H. H. Rowley's *Worship in Ancient Israel* (1967) and W. Harrelson's *From Fertility Cult to Worship* (1969).

Rowley traced the development of Israel's worship from the patriarchal age to the days of the synagogue and the New Testament. In this historical presentation, his approach remained consonant with previous studies of worship, concentrating on the period of the monarchy, specifically on the temple and its place in Israelite worship. This focus on worship in the temple, broadly construed to include sacrifice, prophecy, and psalmody, takes up more than half the book.[38]

Rowley's contribution is distinctive not simply for his reliance on Wellhausen, but also for his primarily theological interests. He is concerned to trace a different kind of development in Israel's worship, one that is not only historically evolutionary—in Fohrer's terms, evolving from "early" to "high" or "superior" religion—but theologically progressive. In Rowley's estimation, Israelite religion "progressed" from ritual acts of worship, such as the sacrifices offered in the temple, to spiritual ones, such as the prayers offered in the synagogue when the rituals of sacrifice were no longer possible.

---

34. Kraus proposes the following historical development: 1. sabbatical year, 2. Sabbath, 3. the three annual festivals (Unleavened Bread, Weeks, Autumn Festival), and 4. later, post-exilic festivals (Hanukkah, Purim); *Worship in Israel*, 32, n.16.

35. Ibid., 93–124.

36. Shechem, and covenant law traditions; Bethel, and the ancestral traditions; Gilgal, and the traditions of land settlement; ibid., 125–78.

37. Ibid., 179–236.

38. Rowley, *Worship in Ancient Israel*, 71–212 (chap. 3–6).

This discernment of a theological development in Israelite religion provides the foundation for Rowley's assessment of the importance of Old Testament worship for Christianity. In his concluding chapter, "The Forms and the Spirit," he identifies two elements of "spiritual worship" bequeathed to the church by the synagogue: prayer, and the exposition of Scripture.[39] In the case of the former, he argues that the ritual dimensions of prayer (for example, animal sacrifice) "perished" with the loss of the temple, but prayer "survived" in the synagogue in spiritualized forms (for example, as a "sacrifice of praise"). As a "sacrifice of the spirit," prayer continued to nourish spiritual life in Judaism and in Christianity even without the accompanying temple rituals. In sum, Rowley concludes, "the spirit without the ritual act could suffice."[40]

With respect to the exposition of Scripture, Rowley discerned a somewhat different legacy. In the synagogue, there was the reading of the Law and the Prophets. This was a new medium for sustaining the spiritual dimension of worship that had had no place in the temple. It was this practice that Jesus subsequently modeled as a means of applying Scripture to his own day (cf. Luke 4:21). In this manner, Rowley suggested, it could be said that "the Synagogue gave the Church the sermon as an instrument of worship."[41] In sum, just as the spiritual dimension of prayer could be "divorced" from the ancient rituals that had perished, so Jesus showed that the teachings of the Law and the Prophets could be "divested" of their ancient settings and refitted with new meanings in a new day.[42]

Rowley presented his understanding of the importance of Israelite religion for Christian worship in an irenic and generally nonpolemical manner.[43] Nonetheless, he self-consciously approached his subject from the confessional perspective of Christianity. At the very outset of the book, he made clear the theological premise that guided his entire discussion:

> It will be observed that I have defined my subject as "The Forms and Meaning of Worship in Ancient Israel." For it is quite insufficient to pay attention to the forms alone. The quality of worship is to be found in the spirit even more than in the forms, for worship belongs to the heart rather than to the act.[44]

39. Ibid., 246–71.
40. Ibid., 246.
41. Ibid., 270.
42. Ibid.
43. The following admonishment to his readers concerning the spiritual riches of the Old Testament is typical of Rowley's judicious approach: "We should also remember with humble gratitude that this great and enduring organ of worship was bequeathed to us and to Judaism by that ancient Israel we too often deprecate." Ibid.
44. Ibid., 3.

For Rowley, the true quality of worship resides in the spiritual meaning that infuses the ritual, more than in the ritual itself. With reference to the particulars of worship, Rowley values spirit over form, sermon over sacrifice, ethics over ritual, the prophetic over the priestly. In such valuations there is no mistaking a certain Christian (and Protestant) bias.

Harrelson's assessment of Israel's worship continued—with Kraus and Rowley—to draw upon the basic deposits of the historical paradigm provided by Wellhausen. Like his predecessors, Harrelson addressed the issues of cultic calendars and sacred festivals, cultic personnel, and cultic sacrifices. Furthermore, even though he did not propose to write a history of worship, he did discern in Israel's religion a development beyond the practices that prevailed in the religions of other peoples. On the historical continuum, Israel's religion advanced beyond the fertility rites that characterized worship in neighboring cultures to a demythologized understanding that related fertility motifs directly to the salvation history of YHWH.[45] The title of his book, *From Fertility Cult to Religion,* suggests this evolution.

But like Rowley, Harrelson's objective was primarily theological, not merely historical or descriptive. He was self-consciously concerned to connect Israel's worship to contemporary issues facing the community of faith in an "ecumenical and post-Christian age."[46] In Harrelson's judgment, the world he addressed had moved from a religious age to a secular age. In this age, a "complex, technological, urbanized culture" appeared to render immaterial—if not completely erroneous—religious perspectives on the world, the nature and destiny of humanity, and the values and evils of contemporary society.[47] For such an age, Harrelson argued, a re-examination of Israel's worship offers both a necessary perspective and an urgent summons.

Israel's worship provides a clarifying perspective because it sees the world as the place where creation theology is articulated. In marked contrast to previous studies of Israel's worship, Harrelson began his discussion with a substantive treatment of cosmology, the "Israelite World View."[48] In a world gone awry, the particulars of worship—the place, the rituals, the times, the personnel—may compel little interest unless the world in which they can and should have meaning can be clarified. Harrelson suggested that Israel's worship sought and attained such clarity about the world by giving a large place to creation theology.[49] Through an assortment of

45. Harrelson, *From Fertility Cult to Worship,* 12–15, 67–71.
46. Ibid., xi.
47. Ibid., xiii.
48. Ibid., 1–18.
49. Ibid., 81–99.

narratives, songs, and liturgical texts, the cult was the occasion for returning symbolically to primordial time, to the primal assertions of Genesis 1: God created the world, brought order to disorder, established a divine purpose for the cosmos that is secure and sustainable, and created humankind in the divine image with the responsibility and the capacity to fulfill God's creational design for the cosmos. In sum, worship for Israel "was a means for the restoration and reappropriation of the world order."[50]

Worship that serves such a purpose, Harrelson contended, has direct relevance for the world he was addressing. With a theological sharpness seldom encountered in previous studies of Israel's worship, Harrelson made his case as follows:

> For what are we most intent upon when we worship God in terms derived from biblical faith? We are concerned most with this world that God has created. We want to see the chaos of our world and of our individual lives given order, straightened out, set right. We want to be reminded of the beauty of the earth made whole. . . . We want, in short, to receive our world as well as our individual lives as gifts from God's hands, and to be pressed out into this world to take responsibility for maintaining it, subduing it, directing it towards ends that make for life and wholeness.[51]

Israelite worship does not just offer the modern world a clarifying perspective, it also sustains an urgent summons to live in accordance with God's primordial design for the universe. In this connection, Harrelson noted that the cult was the place for the presentation of Torah.[52] Through ancient rituals of blessing and cursing (for example, Deut. 27:15-26), the steady proclamation of the Ten Commandments, and the enactment of Torah liturgies (for example, Psalms 15, 24), the cult kept worshipers reminded of the Creator God's summons to justice and righteousness. Ethical and moral imperatives sustained the world that God created. To embrace them in obedience is to direct one's life toward personal and cosmic fulfillment. To ignore them is to diminish one's life and imperil God's design for the cosmos.

Harrelson judged this connection between Israelite worship and Torah also to be directly relevant for his readers. He suggested that if the church should commit itself to Torah as a central part of its worship of God, it would be committing itself to concrete actions that would sustain and restore God's creation, even in a secular age which may seem to have out-

---

50. Ibid., 93.
51. Ibid., 98–99.
52. Ibid., 121–36.

grown any need of religion. The community of faith would, in effect, be saying before God:

> God, help us . . . to give ourselves to thee and to our fellow men in such devotion to thy holy and righteous will that we shall not sin against thy holiness by bigotry, violation of the person of our brothers, contempt for honesty, or *any other acts that produce a twisted and perverse world.*[53]

The survey thus far has noted a number of emphases and characteristics of the "history paradigm" that dominated the study of Israelite worship from Wellhausen to Harrelson. These may now be summarized as follows:

1. Beginning with Wellhausen, the primary emphasis has been on tracing the genetic development of Israel's religion from early forms to late forms. In Wellhausen's basic historical outline, the development was from "natural" or "spontaneous" religious acts to formalized "ritual" practices.

2. With the advent of form criticism there emerged a consistent preoccupation with individual "forms" or features of Israelite worship—for example, the basic types of sacrifice, the major sacred festivals, the different cultic calendars. By and large, discussion of these features seldom moved beyond traditional questions concerning form and setting in life. Mowinckel's work on cult as a dynamic reality was a notable exception to this practice. But here, too, the restraints imposed by form criticism were believed to be crucial, lest—as Kraus warned—an interest in the phenomenology of cult supplant more substantive concerns with history.

3. On the historical continuum outlined by Wellhausen, the consistent tendency has been to evaluate the Jerusalem cultus or the monarchical period as the high mark in Israelite religion. By contrast, the early period of Israelite history (generally, everything pre-monarchical) and the late period (exilic, post-exilic) have been regarded typically as either too obscure (that is, historically unverifiable) or too unrepresentative of Israel's true religion (that is, "mere 'exercises of religion'") to warrant more than cursory discussion.

4. Ritual and liturgical texts, in essence anything that on literary grounds would be assigned to the Priestly tradition, have been consistently devalued or dismissed. Wellhausen is an early and influential model of this disparagement of the Priestly tradition, but he is by no means the lone example. Although there are important exceptions to Wellhausen, it has become increasingly clear that modern biblical study has harbored an insidious

---

53. Ibid., 136 (emphasis added).

Protestant bias that is not only anti-ritual, but at its worst, anti-Jewish as well.[54]

The Collapse of the History Paradigm

In the last generation the study of Israel's worship has faded. No longer the "master-key," it seems hardly present at all among Old Testament issues and topics. In part, this diminished interest is linked to the demise of the historical paradigm that has been its interpretive lifeline since its inception.

Assaults on the historical paradigm for biblical interpretation have been underway since at least the late 1970s.[55] More recently, L. Perdue has concluded that we stand on the threshold of a new era, having witnessed the "collapse of history" as the primary category for understanding and appropriating the biblical witness.[56] Perdue has chronicled and critiqued this collapse, focusing on Old Testament theology and how it may be redefined and revived in light of current developments in the discipline. His general assessment of both the problems and the possibilities that confront contemporary biblical scholarship is pertinent to our task of understanding the study of worship in this new interpretive context.

Perdue identifies the following five reasons for the collapse of history and historical methods as the dominant paradigm in biblical interpretation:[57]

1. The appropriateness and the adequacy of the historical-critical method, grounded in philosophical positivism, has been challenged by other methods of study with quite different philosophical and theological foundations. The canonical approach to Scripture, for example, proposes

---

54. For a review of the devaluation of ritual in biblical studies as undertaken especially by Protestant scholars, see F. H. Gorman Jr., "Ritual Studies and Biblical Studies: Assessment of the Past; Prospects of the Future," *Semeia* 67 (1994), 13–36.

55. B. S. Childs, an early and enormously influential critic of history's hegemony in biblical study, articulated the basic challenge succinctly in *Introduction to the Old Testament as Scripture* (Philadelphia: Fortress Press, 1979). He said: "Having experienced the demise of the Biblical Theology movement in America, the dissolution of the broad European consensus in which I was trained, and a widespread confusion regarding theological reflection in general, I began to realize that there was something fundamentally wrong with the foundations of the biblical discipline. It was not a question of improving on source analysis, of discovering some unrecognized new genre, or of bringing a redactional level into sharper focus. Rather, the crucial issue turned on one's whole concept of the study of the Bible itself. I am now convinced that the study of the Bible and its theological use as religious literature within a community of faith and practice needs to be completely rethought. Minor adjustments are not only inadequate, but also conceal the extent of the dry rot" (p. 15).

56. L. G. Perdue, *The Collapse of History: Reconstructing Old Testament Theology,* OBT (Minneapolis: Fortress, 1994).

57. Ibid., 7–11.

that the meaning of biblical texts is found within the boundaries of the text itself, not in the mind of the putative author or in some reconstructed original historical context. Social science approaches may build on the philosophical framework of conflict models (usually Marxist or neo-Marxist) to describe Israel's social system. Literary approaches, broadly conceived in terms of a variety of foci—for example, the narrative world of the text or the rhetoric of the text—seek meaning not in ancient contexts but in contemporary ones that bring reader and text into immediate engagement. The very fact that these and other new approaches now claim a seat at the table of biblical scholarship means that the historical-critical method can no longer monopolize the interpretive agenda.

2. Contemporary theological discourse has also become considerably more diverse. The old paradigms that seemed to forge a consensus—liberalism, neo-orthodoxy—can no longer command the support they once received. The horizons of contemporary theology must now be reconceived in terms of a wide range of new concerns and issues, for example: feminism, ecology, ethno-religious warfare. Such concerns, in turn, address new questions to the biblical text and contribute further to the need for new reading strategies.

3. The epistemological claims of the Enlightenment that produced and informed historical criticism have broken down. The argument increasingly heard in contemporary circles is that we have moved from the "modernity" of the Enlightenment period, with its emphasis on scientific positivism, to a postmodern era that resists such claimed "objectivity." The legacy of the Enlightenment was a supreme confidence in the power of reason and rational inquiry to master the world in all its variety. One part of this legacy was the certainty that a "right reasonable religion"[58] could be constructed from the universal truths disclosed by history. Historical criticism confidently asserted its unique access to these universal truths as preserved in Scripture. But in the aftermath of two world wars, the Holocaust, and the ongoing barbarity that humans have directed toward one another and toward the cosmos, Enlightenment claims have now only a "lacquered depth."[59] Historical criticism has neither adequately disclosed nor effectively evoked the "true religion" that it claimed as its goal.[60]

---

58. Cf. I. Barbour, *Issues in Science and Religion* (San Francisco: Harper and Row, 1966), 34–64. I am indebted to F. H. Gorman's use of Barbour in his discussion of the place of ritual in Enlightenment thinking ("Ritual Studies and Biblical Studies," 17–18).

59. The phrase is from G. Steiner's *In Bluebeard's Castle: Some Notes towards the Redefinition of Culture* (New Haven: Yale University Press, 1971), 60. He uses it to describe the empty claims of Western civilization in the wake of two world wars.

60. For further discussion of biblical study in the interpretive context of postmodernism that is critical of older paradigms, see, G. Phillips, "Exegesis as Critical Praxis: Reclaiming His-

4. There has been an increasing dissatisfaction with the descriptive approach to the Bible and its theology in favor of interpretive models that are more intentionally reflective and constructive. A purely descriptive approach is not only epistemologically questionable, it also severely disengages the text from contemporary culture and its concerns. It may describe details of religion or religious practice in their ancient setting, but in so doing it also creates a distance between the biblical world and the world of the modern reader, and does nothing to bridge that gap. If there is no connection between past and present for the contemporary Bible reader, then there can be little hope that faith as described in the biblical world will intersect authentically with the faith required for the modern world.

5. Finally, Perdue observes that practitioners of the history paradigm tended to operate in insular intellectual contexts. Typically there was little or no serious conversation with work in other fields, such as contemporary theology, ethics, cultural anthropology. Thus, important contemporary issues were either ignored or inadequately addressed, and the intellectual inquiry of biblical scholarship appeared to claim exemption from critical evaluation outside its own academic discipline. For any intellectual inquiry to claim an exclusive role in speaking to and for the human situation is naive. More importantly, it is potentially dangerous. As Perdue notes in a trenchant reference to the Nazi period: when any theology or ideology claims exemption from critical scrutiny, it is susceptible to the demonic.[61]

If the collapse of the history paradigm identifies the crucial problem confronting contemporary biblical interpretation, it also invites new and critical reflection about the way biblical study may be done in the future. Perdue notes the development of a number of new approaches to biblical study variously focused on liberation, creation, canon, feminism, story, and imagination. While these approaches differ in their respective methods and emphases, collectively they share a common foundational assertion: the history paradigm must at least be supplemented (some would say replaced) by a paradigm that takes seriously the text itself. Reality, Perdue affirms, is both historical and linguistic: "To deny one in favor of the other or to privilege one while subordinating the other runs counter to what is fundamentally true about what it means to be human. Thus *history and text belong together*."[62]

tory and Text from a Postmodern Perspective," *Semeia* 51 (1990), 7–49; F. Burnett, "Postmodern Biblical Exegesis: The Eve of Historical Consciousness," *Semeia* 51 (1990), 51–80; W. Brueggemann, *Texts Under Negotiation: The Bible and Postmodern Imagination* (Minneapolis: Fortress, 1993).

61. Perdue, *Collapse of History,* 11.
62. Ibid., 302 (emphasis added).

Perdue reviews a number of studies that reflect the contemporary shift in biblical scholarship away from the history paradigm as traditionally conceived, to fresh perspectives that reconstrue and enlarge it. Although his discussion is directed toward a reassessment of Old Testament theology, much of what is going on in that field is relevant to reconceiving the study of Israelite worship.

The following are examples of recent work that develops important new directions in the study of worship. Most are discussed by Perdue; a few others are included because they are relevant to the subject of worship. All are grouped according to the rubrics proposed by Perdue: first those that reconstrue the understanding of *history*, then those that enlarge the understanding of history with new perspectives on *text*.

History and Creation

When history collapses as the dominant paradigm for discerning meaning, new perspectives must be sought. Perdue notes a renewed interest in cosmology during the last generation of biblical scholarship. Whereas once it may have been sufficient to look for meaning *in history*, it now seems imperative to inquire whether there is some cosmic meaning or design *above and prior to history* that offers a more primary context for meaning. He states:

> In some important sense, the understanding of human nature, history, and redemption are defined by the meaning of cosmology, even as the meaning of cosmology is defined, at least in part, by reference to these other theological themes.[63]

In sum, the collapse of the historical paradigm pushes the interpretive task back to the primordial ground of history, to creation itself.

Perdue cites several recent significant presentations of creation theology. Their common agenda—the relationship between *history and creation*—invites a rethinking of the hermeneutical context in which the worship of ancient Israel has meaning. The works are those of R. Knierim, J. Levenson, and F. Gorman.

Knierim has suggested that in Hebraic thought history is subordinate to cosmos.[64] The central theological assertion of the Old Testament, he

---

63. Ibid., 115. See further the recent essay by W. Brueggemann, "The Loss and Recovery of Creation in Old Testament Theology," *TToday* 53 (1996), 177–90. He discusses both the advantages and the risks that attend the paradigmatic shift toward creation as the horizon of meaning for biblical faith.

64. R. Knierim, "Cosmos and History in Israel's Theology," in *Werden und Wirken des Alten Testaments* (Göttingen: Vandenhoeck and Ruprecht, 1980), 59–123; "The Task of Old

argues, is "the universal dominion of Yahweh in justice and righteousness."[65] This assertion holds together two fundamental claims. First, the
primary domain of God's sovereignty is the universe, the cosmos, not history. Human history, a part of which is Israel's history, derives meaning
from its relation to the created order of the world, not vice versa. The
Hebrew Bible asserts that history is the venue in which God's cosmic
designs for creation are carried out.[66] As Perdue puts it, "The ultimate goal
of history is to achieve harmony with God's good creation."[67]

The second fundamental claim is that God's primordial design for the
cosmos is defined by "justice and righteousness." With H. H. Schmid,[68]
Knierim notes that creation is endowed with a primal justice and righteousness, a fundamental concept of order that embraces all aspects of reality—cosmic, social, and moral. God alone establishes the cosmic order,
and God acts to sustain the cosmic design toward its ultimate fulfillment.
Nonetheless, in the specific arena of history, humans have important
responsibilities to actualize the cosmic order through patterns of behavior
that support rather than subvert God's intentions. In Knierim's words,
"History fails or is justified to the extent that it is in step with the just and
righteous order of the world."[69]

The second author, Levenson,[70] is also concerned with the just and
righteous order of the world. Whereas Knierim focuses on the *order* of the
cosmos, Levenson reflects on its *fragility*. The context for his reflection is
the Jewish Holocaust, an experience of evil in history that poses serious
questions for belief in a just and righteous world. He argues that there is an
abiding tension in Israel's creation theology between the mastery of God

Testament Theology," *HBT* 6 (1984), 25–57. For Perdue's review of Knierim's contribution, see
Collapse of History, 125–28.

65. Knierim, "The Task of Old Testament Theology," 43.

66. Knierim makes the case as follows: "Yahweh is not the God of creation because he is the
God of the humans or of human history. He is the God of humans and of human history
because He is God of creation. For the Old Testament, just as for the New Testament, the most
universal aspect of Yahweh's dominion is not human history. It is the creation and sustenance
of the world. This aspect is at the same time the most fundamental because creation does not
depend on history or existence, but history and existence depend on and are measured against
creation" (ibid., 40).

67. Perdue, *Collapse of History,* 127.

68. H. H. Schmid, *Gerechtigkeit als Weltordnung: Hintergrund und Geschichte als alttestamentlichen Gerechtigkeitsbegriffes* (Tübingen: J. C. B. Mohr, 1968); *Altorientalische Welt in der
alttestamentlichen Theologie* (Zurich: Theologischer Verlag, 1974).

69. Knierim, "Cosmos and History," 94.

70. J. D. Levenson, *Creation and the Persistence of Evil: The Jewish Drama of Divine
Omnipotence* (San Francisco: Harper and Row, 1988). For Perdue's discussion of Levenson, see
Collapse of History, 122–24.

on the one hand and the vulnerability of creation to chaos on the other. He then shows how the liturgy of the cult, as preserved in the Priestly tradition, enabled Israel to mediate between these tensions. Through sabbath observance, temple building, and the rituals of cultic worship, the community of faith affirmed God's dominion over creation and liturgically enacted the defeat of chaos and the restoration of the world to God's ordered design.

With respect to the study of worship, Levenson's positive assessment of the Priestly tradition is a most important contribution. In contrast to the disparagement of this tradition by Wellhausen and others, Levenson shows that ritual texts should not be devalued and simply assigned a marginal role in the construction of Hebraic theology. Instead, the practice of cult may be seen as a faithful response to God's command, an act of obedience that God judges to be crucial for the development and implementation of creation's design. Levenson makes the case as follows:

> [I]t is through the cult that we are enabled to cope with evil, for it is the cult that builds and maintains order, transforms chaos into creation, ennobles humanity, and realizes the kingship of the God who has ordained the cult and commanded that it be guarded and practiced.[71]

Levenson's work is but one of several indications that the Priestly tradition and ritual texts are being examined in new ways and increasingly are being accorded a more prominent role within biblical studies. Of particular note is F. Gorman's *The Ideology of Ritual.*[72]

Moving beyond more traditional approaches, Gorman draws on the work of cultural anthropologists like C. Geertz and V. Turner to show that all ritual is a form of "social drama" that is meaningfully integrated into a specific worldview. It is this worldview that gives rise to ritual acts and words, and in turn is shaped by them. Gorman shows that Priestly rituals are shaped by a Priestly worldview: the world is created and designed by God with an order and a purpose. Priestly rituals are structured to be attentive to this creational order. Liturgically and imaginatively, worship rituals serve three purposes: 1. to "found" or "establish" on earth certain "moments

---

71. Levenson, *Creation and the Persistence of Chaos*, 127.

72. F. H. Gorman Jr., *The Ideology of Ritual: Space, Time, and Status in the Priestly Theology* (Sheffield: JSOT Press, 1990). See further R. Cohn, *The Shape of Sacred Space: Four Biblical Studies* (Chico, Calif.: Scholars Press, 1981); G. Anderson, *Sacrifices and Offerings in Ancient Israel: Studies in Their Social and Political Importance* (Atlanta: Scholars Press, 1987); P. Jensen, *Graded Holiness: A Key to the Priestly Conception of the World* (Sheffield: JSOT Press, 1992); R. D. Nelson, *Raising Up a Faithful Priest: Community and Priesthood in Biblical Theology* (Louisville: Westminster/John Knox Press, 1993).

of origin" that can be traced to God's cosmic design (for example, Lev. 8–10: the institution of priesthood); 2. to "maintain" the creational order and keep it from falling into disorder (for example, Lev. 11–15: the rituals for distinguishing between the "clean" and the "unclean"); 3. to "restore" God's creational intentions when they are abused or neglected (for example, Lev. 16: the Day of Atonement). In short, Israel's ritual system is grounded in creation theology. In this sense, Israel's worship should be construed as a liturgical means of "world construction."[73]

The Move from History to Text

With the collapse of the history paradigm has come the move to reconceive history in terms of creation theology. The shift in the interpretive agenda is towards the search for the worldview, the cosmology, that provides the context for meaning in history. While this shift leads to a more balanced view that makes history *and* creation two important poles of biblical interpretation, it has not produced an *alternative* to the history paradigm. It simply subordinates historical (human) time to "cosmic time."[74]

Perdue, however, identifies a development in biblical studies that has produced alternatives to the history paradigm and to historical criticism: *the move from history to text*.[75] This development should not be treated in isolation from the movement toward history and creation considered above. Instead, we must allow for some overlap between a variety of new approaches, some more oriented toward the "historicality" of the biblical world, others more focused on the "linguistic worlds of the Bible."[76] Generally, the former tend to be descriptive, the latter more constructive. But these characteristics should not be applied rigidly.

In reviewing new work that focuses on the linguistic worlds of the Bible, I depart somewhat from Perdue's survey and identify instead three general categories: the canonical reality of the text; the social reality of the text; and the rhetorical reality of the text.

1. By "canonical reality" I refer to the goals and methods of the canonical approach to Scripture identified initially with B. S. Childs.[77] The general characteristics of this approach have drawn wide attention and substantive

---

73. Gorman, *The Ideology of Ritual,* 59.

74. Perdue, *Collapse of History,* 154. The reference to "cosmic time" comes from Perdue's review of Knierim's work; see ibid., 127.

75. Ibid., 153.

76. Cf. ibid., 304.

77. See especially: *Introduction to the Old Testament as Scripture* (Philadelphia: Fortress, 1979); *Old Testament Theology in a Canonical Context* (Philadelphia: Fortress, 1985); *The New Testament as Canon: An Introduction* (Philadelphia: Fortress, 1985); *Biblical Theology of the Old and New Testaments: Theological Reflection on the Christian Bible* (Minneapolis: Fortress, 1992).

critique from a variety of quarters. It is not necessary to reproduce that discussion here.[78] I note simply that for Childs the context for biblical meaning is not primarily history but canon. It is the Word *within the canonical text* that is authoritative and revelatory, not the historical or social particularities that may lie behind the text and have influenced its development from origin to canonization. For Childs, the final form of the text preserves and discloses a canonical reality that is theologically normative for the faith community. It is only the canonical reality that attains the privileged status of "Scripture."

Childs's approach to canon is somewhat static and locates meaning primarily in the final form of the text itself. Others have developed a more dynamic model of canon that emphasizes the ongoing interaction between community and text.[79] Of special interest in this regard is P. D. Hanson, whose canonical assessment of "community" in the Bible gives a prominent place to the role of worship.[80]

Hanson traces the biblical notion of community to the exodus traditions, specifically to the Yahwistic memory of God's gracious deliverance of Israel from Egyptian slavery. From the earliest traditions in the Bible he discerns a notion of community that is defined by a triad of interrelated qualities: righteousness, compassion, and worship.[81] Righteousness and compassion are qualities of God that people called of God are to imitate in both their personal conduct and their institutional structures. Righteousness is God's universal standard of justice; the people manifest it by strict obedience to the statutes and ordinances that order life in accordance with this standard. Compassion is the quality of God that tempers justice with mercy; the people, being delivered from bondage, manifest it by devising systems of justice that do not enslave.

Hanson argues that in Israel's triadic notion of community, worship was the linchpin that held righteousness and compassion in healthy and constructive tension.[82] Without a commitment to righteousness, compas-

---

78. Perdue's overview offers a clear treatment of the major issues, along with relevant bibliography; see *Collapse of History*, 154–96.

79. See especially J. A. Sanders: "Adaptable for Life: The Nature and Function of Canon," in *Magnalia Dei: The Mighty Acts of God*, ed. F. M. Cross, et al. (Garden City, N.Y.: Doubleday, 1976), 531–60; *Canon and Community: A Guide to Canonical Criticism* (Philadelphia: Fortress, 1984); *From Sacred Story to Sacred Text* (Philadelphia: Fortress, 1987).

80. Hanson, *The People Called: The Growth of Community in the Bible* (New York: Harper and Row, 1986). The methodological presuppositions for Hanson's interactional model of canonical interpretation are outlined in his *Dynamic Transcendence* (Philadelphia: Fortress, 1978), 46–94.

81. Hanson, *The People Called*, 70–78.

82. Ibid., 73–75.

sion may slide toward sentimental permissiveness that encourages social chaos. Without compassion, the desire for social order may harden into judicial systems that lack a heart. As Hanson puts it, "Only in worship of this unique God, Israel believed, could righteousness and compassion intertwine as strands of one life-enhancing pattern."[83]

Hanson shows that this concept of community was not static but dynamic. It was "tested and refined" throughout Israel's history in numerous ways: for example, by royal ideology and prophetic critique, by the crisis of exile and the competing plans for restoration offered by the "visionaries" (the followers of Second Isaiah) and the "pragmatists" (the Zadokites). Through the twists and turns of history, however, the Yahwistic notion of a community defined by righteousness, compassion, and worship was sustained. It is this developing notion of community that constitutes the canonical reality for Hanson.

Especially pertinent here is the suggestion that the biblical vision of community was and is nurtured through worship. By liturgical recitation and confession, the example of the dramatic interplay of God's righteousness and compassion is kept alive. In worship, righteousness and compassion become the "holy fascination"[84] that enables people to engage life as agents of God's purpose in the world. In this sense, Hanson argues that worship for the contemporary believer, as for the ancient Israelite, possesses a generative force. Not only does it preserve the memory of God's actions in history for successive generations, it also has the capacity to summon forth ever new efforts at recapturing the biblical vision that people are called to imitate.

2. The social reality of the text differs significantly from the canonical reality. The canonical approach locates meaning primarily within the boundaries of the canon itself, typically with little or no attention to historical or social factors. As a result, the "canonical reality" of Israel's religion is presented as virtually self-generated, or, to use theological terms, God-generated. It derives from a transcendent realm beyond or above history: God enters into history and directs it according to divine purposes. Perdue notes, however, that a renewed interest in social scientific methods of biblical study has brought a serious challenge to the notion that the Bible's "canonical reality" is somehow *sui generis*, that it can simply be abstracted from the network of contributing historical and cultural factors.

In one respect the social scientific approach is directly related to the historical paradigm: it seeks to reconstruct the social history of Israel that lies behind the biblical text and in turn provides its framework for mean-

83. Ibid., 74.
84. Ibid.

ing.[85] Typically, it functions descriptively in that it identifies and illumines the social organization of ancient Israel. This approach is represented most influentially by the work of N. K. Gottwald. His contribution, which will be summarized shortly, provides a general context for understanding how social scientific methods may impact on the study of Israel's worship.

In another respect, however, social scientific approaches go beyond the historical paradigm. They help us to understand not only that social patterns shaped the biblical text and its depiction of Israel's religion, but also that the text itself conveys *a religious perception of reality that may in turn shape social structures and their functions*. With this latter emphasis, social science models move away from being merely descriptive and invite theological reflection on religion's role in the social construction of reality. I note especially the recent work by J. Berquist, *Judaism in Persia's Shadow*.[86] Although his focus is neither on the Pentateuch nor on worship, he provides a heuristic interpretive model for reflecting on the dialectic of society and religion.

Gottwald, through a number of highly influential works, has endeavored to show that the biblical text, like all texts, is a complex social construction.[87] It reflects, legitimates, endorses, even criticizes the social systems within which it originates. The picture of Israelite religion that is preserved in the text, therefore, cannot be simply removed from its social matrix and presented as an abstract system of beliefs and practices, as Wellhausen and others were inclined to do. The task instead is to connect Israel's religion with the values and interests of the persons or institutions that produced it.

Gottwald focuses on early, pre-monarchical Israel: specifically, the period of the intertribal confederacy (1250–1050 B.C.E.). He discerns here an Israelite *social system* that was characterized by sociopolitical egalitarianism,[88] and an Israelite *religion*, "mono-Yahwism," that sanctioned a social order in which all participate equally in the production and consumption

---

85. Note that Perdue includes the social scientific analysis within his general survey of approaches that continue the historical paradigm; see *Collapse of History*, 69–109.

86. J. L. Berquist, *Judaism in Persia's Shadow: A Social and Historical Approach* (Minneapolis: Fortress, 1995).

87. See especially N. K. Gottwald, *The Tribes of Yahweh: A Sociology of Liberated Israel, 1250–1050 B.C.E.* (Maryknoll, N.Y.: Orbis Books, 1979); *The Hebrew Bible—A Socio-Literary Introduction* (Philadelphia: Fortress, 1985).

88. In his words, "a self-governing association of economically self-sufficient free farmers and herdsmen constituting a single class of peoples with common ownership of the means of production vested in large families" (*The Tribes of Yahweh*, 613). Such an arrangement represented a revolutionary movement that provided a radical alternative to the hierarchical systems of domination in the Canaanite city-states.

of natural goods.[89] The critical issue for Gottwald is the relationship between Israel's social structure and its religion. Does social structure determine or create religion, or does religion determine or create social structure?

In response to this question, Gottwald adopts a structural-functional model for social organization that understands religion and society to be interdependent and reciprocal. In theory the functional model does not focus on the question of priority (Which comes first, society or religion?). Instead, as Gottwald takes care to demonstrate, it focuses on the interrelations between society and religion.[90] After carefully stipulating this interdependence, however, Gottwald ultimately concludes that Israelite social arrangements have priority over Yahwistic religion.[91] The causal flow is from social relations to religious symbolization. In other words, social egalitarianism provided the "initiating motive and energy" that produced the innovations of Yahwist religion.[92] Then, and as a consequence, Yahwist religion served powerfully to sustain the foundational egalitarian social system. In short, religion is ideology. It serves and sustains the interests of the sociopolitical structure in which it arises.

Gottwald's proposals have elicited a huge response, both pro and con. Perdue has summarized and commented on most of the major areas of debate.[93] I will not reproduce that discussion, but one issue has special significance for the task at hand.

Perdue notes that the major theological liability in Gottwald's materialist approach is the loss of transcendence. In Perdue's assessment, Gottwald's argument in effect "makes God a social symbol with no existence outside the matrix of communal life."[94] In such an arrangement religion is reduced to ideology, and theology is reduced to social ethics. In both instances the reduction serves the interests of the particular social groups who control the means of production.

Gottwald does not deny that his approach moves in these directions. In his words, "The cultural-material directive is to press the religious data back

89. For Gottwald's summary of the characteristics of mono-Yahwism, see ibid., 614–15.

90. As he puts it, mono-Yahwism was "dependably related" to the rise and maintenance of sociopolitical egalitarianism, such that any strengthening or weakening in this social arrangement "enhanced the probability" of a comparable alteration in Israel's religion (ibid., 611–18). And vice versa, communal egalitarianism was "dependably related" to religion, so that any material alterations in Israel's religious concepts or institutions "enhanced the probability" that social arrangements would be comparably impacted (ibid., 618–21).

91. Ibid., 642–49.

92. Ibid., 643.

93. Perdue, Collapse of History, 99–108.

94. Ibid., 105.

to their social base."[95] But in his model of early Israelite society, the social control of religion is not a negative phenomenon. He envisions an interdependence between society and religion that rewards both managers and the managed in ways that are mutually agreeable and fulfilling. The "managers" of this social order are Israelites (and proto-Israelites) who, for the two hundred years in question, worked to facilitate a network of egalitarian power relations. The extended families and tribes who comprise the "managed" society are Israelites (and proto-Israelites) who have entered into a consensual agreement with those who control the means of production.

In this arrangement, the initiative lies within the Israelite social order, and the response comes from the religion of Yahwism, which is organically rooted in this social order. Yahwism's response provides what Gottwald calls "a feedback loop."[96] The terminology derives from feedback devices or "servomechanisms," such as safety valves or thermostats, that regulate a machine or a process. Such devices help maintain a constant value within an agreed-upon range of values. The switch for the feedback device is triggered automatically by a closed-loop information and response system in which the machine and the feedback device are part of one and the same instrument.[97]

As mentioned earlier, J. L. Berquist has employed social scientific methods to address another period in Israel's history when this relationship appears to be very different from what Gottwald describes. In *Judaism in Persia's Shadow,* Berquist contributes to the increasing shift of emphasis in biblical study away from the history of pre-exilic Israel and toward the sociology of the Second Temple period.[98] A number of factors have contributed to this shift,[99] but the most pertinent is that a good deal of the Bible attained final or near-final form during this period. Of principal importance for the focus here is the canonization of the Pentateuch, which was worked out in several stages during the Persian period. Berquist's socio-historical examination of this period, therefore, helps indirectly to illumine the social reality that underlies the Torah's canonical presentation of worship in Israel.

95. Gottwald, *The Tribes of Yahweh,* 645.

96. Ibid., 642–49.

97. See Gottwald's extended footnote on "feedback devices," ibid., 786, n. 569.

98. One indication of the increasing importance of this period is the work associated with the SBL's "Sociology of the Second Temple" consultation group. See P. R. Davies, ed., *Second Temple Studies I: Persian Period* (Sheffield: JSOT Press, 1991); T. Eskenazi and K. H. Richards, ed., *Second Temple Studies II: Temple Community in the Persian Period* (Sheffield: JSOT Press, 1994).

99. See, for example, the summary discussion provided by Davies, "Sociology and the Second Temple," *Second Temple Studies I,* 11–15.

Berquist's study is framed by two questions. First: How did Persia's transformation of Judah into Yehud, a Persian colony, affect Yehud's ideology, self-understanding, religion, rhetoric? Second: How did Yehud's identity—as a Persian colony *and* as a people of God—serve both to maintain and to resist the society in which it took shape?[100] In framing the issues this way, Berquist invites exploration of the tension between the *sociopolitical conditions imposed on Yehud from outside* and the *religious traditions to which Yehud/Judah was heir from the inside.* The dialectic between society and religion that he envisions is more complex than what Gottwald identified in early Israel. Berquist puts the central issue succinctly: "Were the chief factors that caused or contributed to Yehud's specific character internal or external?"[101]

Berquist begins with the external factors. Yehud existed as a Persian colony, a secondary state created and controlled by Persian imperial politics. As such, Yehud was permitted a measure of freedom and self-maintenance, so long as nothing compromised Persia's realization of the maximum benefit from Yehud's natural resources. In short, Persia's political policies were designed to create a colony that would cooperate with the empire's objectives.

To induce and sustain this mutually beneficial relationship, Persia used a number of mechanisms for social control and political maintenance. Of these, three are of particular significance for a consideration of the Torah's vision of worship: 1. *Symbols and stories of cosmic order* (for example, creation stories), which from the empire's perspective encouraged subject citizens to accept and maintain their current social existence as a harmonious part of the larger cosmic design;[102] 2. *The codification of local law,* which enhanced the colony's sense of self-governance, at the same time ensuring that their identity remained within the confines of Persia's ideological perameters;[103] and 3. *The construction and maintenance of regional cult sites* (for example, the temple in Jerusalem), which provided a physical and religious symbol for the colony's self-definition, and at the same time provided the imperial government an administrative center through which it not only collected taxes and distributed revenue, but it also helped to shape the "ritual world" celebrated in Yehud in accordance with the political reality desired by the state.[104]

---

100. Berquist, *Judaism in Persia's Shadow,* iv.
101. Ibid., 9.
102. Ibid., 134–35.
103. Ibid., 138–39.
104. Ibid., 135, 140–43.

Given Persian hegemony, it was at least theoretically *possible* that such external controls could completely determine Yehud's life. Berquist shows, however, that Yehud was also heir to its own rich traditions and that these too played a formative role in shaping its distinctive character. In describing Yehud's social organization, he supplements the structural-functional model (which informs his discussion of Persia's social control) by drawing upon a symbolic interaction model.

He notes, with C. Geertz and others, that religion functions within culture to provide a system of symbols by which practitioners create order and meaning.[105] Religious conceptions of reality may endorse or legitimate existing (or imposed) worldviews, but they may also oppose or resist them and assert alternative ones. As Geertz put it, religion has the capacity to create new worlds of meaning and to clothe these worlds with "such an aura of factuality" that they elicit belief and commitment even beyond the empirical realities of everyday life.[106]

Berquist suggests that the assertion of an alternative social reality came from various quarters in Yehud.[107] He does not cite the Pentateuch among his examples of alternative visions of reality. In general he understands the canonization of the Pentateuch as illustrating how Persia controlled Yehud. By promoting the standardization of Pentateuchal law, "Persia not only promulgated a law for Yehud to obey but presented a story that defined who Yehud was."[108] In this assessment, Berquist's discernment of the priority of social reality over religion does not differ substantially from Gottwald's conclusion concerning the sociopolitical dynamics that controlled the intertribal period. The "initiating motive and energy" that produced the Pentateuch was Persian politics, not Israelite religion.

Still, Berquist has opened the door on another possibility concerning the relationship between social reality and canonical reality. If religion does indeed function not only as a servomechanism to existing social arrangements, but also as a signifier of new and alternative social realities that have what Geertz called "an aura of factuality," then the Pentateuch's function in

---

105. Ibid., 247–48.

106. C. Geertz, "Religion as a Cultural System," in *The Interpretation of Cultures: Selected Essays* (New York: Basic Books, 1973), 90, 109–18. See further Berquist, *Judaism in Persia's Shadow,* 247.

107. Berquist suggests that it came from various sources: the sages and the wisdom tradition, where dissent literature like Job and Qoheleth fostered theological argumentation concerning the justice of the world; apocalyptic visionaries, like those represented in Zech. 14, Isa. 24–27, and Daniel, whose rhetoric was of violence and social separation; and short stories and narratives that depicted fictional worlds where heroes of faith emerged victorious, like Ruth and Esther. See his discussion in *Judaism in Persia's Shadow,* 131–232.

108. Ibid., 138–39.

society can be conceived differently than Berquist has done. As a Persian-sponsored document, the Pentateuch surely functions in ways that are at least ideologically acceptable to the empire. But as the embodiment of a distinctive religious perspective, it may do more. It may instruct in matters of faith that move the human community, in Geertz's words, "beyond the realities of everyday life to wider ones which correct and complete them."[109]

3. How do religious perspectives move "beyond the realities of everyday life to wider ones which correct and complete them"? From a cultural anthropological perspective, Geertz has observed that religion is a system of sacred symbols that serve as "vehicles for a conception" of meaningful existence.[110] Such symbols provide models *of* and *for* reality. As models *of* reality, they conceptualize it in a way that makes reality apprehensible, that shapes *what is* so it conforms to *what is already established*. For example, a house that is built can be said to model, or make apprehensible, the reality of the house already established in the blueprint. Symbols also serve as models *for* reality. Here, they construct or create reality in accordance with the reality envisaged in the model—the blueprint is a symbol that makes real the house that is yet to be built. As a system of sacred symbols, religion may both shape itself (conform) to the existent social reality and shape social reality (make it conform) to itself.[111]

Geertz recognizes that religious symbols or models come in a variety of forms. Any object, act, or event may be a vehicle for conception. One such vehicle, which Geertz recognizes but does not specifically discuss, is the linguistic model of and for reality.[112] I refer to this linguistic model as "rhetorical reality."

Perdue notes that in the move from history to text, biblical scholarship has come increasingly to focus on rhetorical reality. He calls particular attention to approaches to Scripture that operate with a hermeneutic of "imagination."[113] He notes that imagination operates at two primary levels: "common imagination" typically offers conventional understandings of what is real and experienced; "creative imagination" offers constructive, often nonconventional, understandings of what is perceived as real but does not exist. Religious imagination operates primarily at the second level.[114]

109. Geertz, "Religion as a Cultural System," 112.
110. Ibid., 91.
111. Ibid., 92–93.
112. Ibid., 94.
113. Perdue, *Collapse of History*, 263–98.
114. Ibid., 265–69.

A hermeneutic of religious imagination understands that the narratives and poems of the Bible have been shaped by the creative imagination of authors, editors, and redactors. It also stresses that the rhetoric of texts may engage the imagination of hearers, readers, and interpreters in a way that compels them not only to enter into the canonical and social world of the ancient text but also to shape a present world so it conforms to the reality envisaged in the text.[115] In short, the rhetoric of the text has the capacity not only to describe a reality that exists (or existed in the past), but also to summon into existence a reality that does not yet exist but remains possible.

Perdue notes that W. Brueggemann, more than any other contemporary Old Testament scholar, has modeled a hermeneutic of imagination in his approach to Scripture. He calls attention especially to Brueggemann's programmatic essays that are specifically concerned with reconceiving the task of Old Testament theology.[116] For my purposes here, I focus on a recent work that is more generally concerned with the importance of imagination for the contemporary interpretive task, *Texts Under Negotiation: The Bible and Postmodern Imagination.*

In the postmodern world, Brueggemann asserts, the task of biblical interpretation must be both descriptive and constructive. It must focus not only on the "facticity" behind the text—long the objective of traditional historical approaches—but also on the "perspective" within the text. For this latter task, the formative work is done through newer approaches to Scripture that focus on rhetoric: specifically, the recognition that speech is decisive for reality. With language humans have the capacity to portray, imagine, and authorize perspectives of reality that make sense out of the experiences of life.[117]

The rhetoric of the Bible has this capacity. It provides imaginative construals of reality—what Brueggemann calls "counterimagined worlds" or "proposed worlds"—that offer alternatives to "presumed worlds." Brueggemann acknowledges that such imagined worlds cannot be proven or absolutely established. They are not scientifically or objectively demonstrable, but they can be tested for truth nonetheless. Their validity, he suggests, resides not in their logic or their facticity but in their capacity to move those who embrace them to the expenditure of their lives.[118]

115. Ibid., 285.

116. Especially W. Brueggemann: "A Shape for Old Testament Theology, I: Structure Legitimation," *CBQ* 47 (1985), 28–46; "A Shape for Old Testament Theology, II: Embrace of Pain," *CBQ* 47 (1985), 395–415. See also the collection of Brueggemann's essays in P. Miller, ed., *Old Testament Theology: Essays on Structure, Theme, and Text* (Minneapolis: Fortress, 1992).

117. Brueggemann, *Texts Under Negotiation*, 12–18.

118. Ibid., 10.

Brueggemann does not address the subject of worship in the Hebrew Bible as such. But he does argue that the Bible has the capacity to fund new construals of the reality about God, the world, and the human community. In a postmodern era when old certitudes may have failed, such imaginative construals disclose a powerful vision, a "vision that affirms that the future is not yet finished."[119] In this general way, then, Brueggemann has contributed to the changing hermeneutical landscape of biblical studies within which the Torah's "vision" of worship can be addressed.

From History to Vision:
A New Interpretive Context for the Study of Worship

Perdue concludes his survey of the study of Old Testament theology with a chapter entitled "From History to Imagination: Between Memory and Vision."[120] The title summarizes the shift he has traced in biblical theology during the last century, in essence a move away from traditional historical paradigms for interpretation to newer ones that endeavor to reimagine and revisualize the meaning of ancient texts for a contemporary world. I suggest that the *movement from history to vision* is also an apt description of a new interpretive context in which the importance of Israelite worship can be reassessed.

For at least a century—from Wellhausen to Harrelson—the historical paradigm has provided the primary interpretive approach to Israel's worship. This approach has contributed in important ways to our understanding of the worship data preserved in the Hebrew Bible. Not only has it provided foundational perspectives on the historical context of Israel's various religious rites, practices, and institutions, it has also established the critical distance that exists between the world of the ancient text and the world of the modern reader.[121] Such contributions can be and should continue to be reassessed in light of new developments. But they cannot be ignored, and they should not be simply displaced.

The collapse of the history paradigm, however, shifts the interpretive context, not only for biblical theology but for the study of worship as well. The study of Israel's worship, I suggest, needs also to be illumined by new approaches that move our understanding beyond historical insight to constructive theological appropriation. Both the scope and the design of the study I offer here seek to acknowledge the importance of this shift and to contribute to it.

119. Ibid., 40.
120. Perdue, *Collapse of History*, chap. 9, pp. 263–98.
121. Cf. ibid., 304.

The Scope of the Present Study

First, with respect to subject matter, I offer here a study of *worship* in the Hebrew Bible not of Israelite *religion*. The two are not identical. The study of Israelite religion has enjoyed an influential role in the history of biblical scholarship during the last century, and deservedly so. But almost since its inception, the history of religions approach has steadfastly restricted itself to an investigation of information in the text that might be objectively correlated with verifiable times, places, names, and practices.[122] As a result, much light has been shed on, for example, the history of the sacrificial system,[123] or of certain religious institutions, like the priesthood.[124]

But this approach typically has given little, if any, attention to broader theological issues. What, for example, is the theology of sacrifice? What does the particular offering of, say, the "communion sacrifice" communicate about God and the ones who offer it? What is the theology of priesthood? It is one thing to trace the genealogy of the Aaronide or Zadokite lines of priests, but another to inquire about the ministry of priesthood.[125] The subject of worship necessarily extends beyond the history of rites and rituals, beyond the analysis of religious technique and practice. It includes an effort to discern the theology that underpins those rites and practices and gives them meaning.[126]

---

122. See, e.g., O. Eissfeldt's classic distinction between the "history of religion" approach, which concerns itself properly with *knowledge,* and the "Old Testament theology" approach, which concerns itself properly with questions of *faith* and *believing:* "The knowing mind is conscious that in spite of all its efforts it cannot reach out beyond the limited world of space and time; Faith knows itself laid hold upon by an eternal reality . . ." ("Israeltisch-jüdische Religionsgeschichtliche und alttestamentliche Theologie," *ZAW* 44 [1926], 1–12); the quotation is taken from J. Hayes and F. Prussner, *Old Testament Theology: Its History and Development* (Atlanta: John Knox, 1985), 159.

123. E.g., G. B. Gray, *Sacrifice in the Old Testament* (Oxford: Clarendon, 1925); R. Dussaud, *Les origenes cananeenes du sacrifice israelite* (2nd ed.; Paris: Leroux, 1941); R. Rendtorff, *Studien zur Geschichte des Opfers in alten Israel* (Neukirchen-Vluyn: Neukirchener 1967).

124. E.g., A. H. J. Gunneweg, *Leviten und Priester* (Göttingen: Vandenhoeck and Ruprecht, 1965); R. de Vaux, *Ancient Israel: Religious Institutions,* vol. 2 (New York, Toronto: McGraw-Hill, 1965), 345–405; A. Cody, *A History of Old Testament Priesthood* (Rome: Pontifical Biblical Institute, 1969).

125. On this and other related issues, see the helpful discussion in Nelson, *Raising Up a Faithful Priest.*

126. After years of virtual neglect, there are now signs that the history of religions genre may be revived, but along different lines. In particular, R. Albertz has offered a major new effort that proposes to combine, for the first time, traditional history of religions concerns with a social and political history of Israel. See *A History of Israelite Religion in the Old Testament Period.* Volume I: *From the Beginnings to the End of the Monarchy* (Louisville: Westminster/John Knox, 1994); *A History of Israelite Religion in the Old Testament Period.* Volume II: *From the Exile to the Maccabees* (Louisville: Westminster/John Knox, 1994).

Second, I have restricted this study of Israelite worship to what can be discerned within the Pentateuch. Thus what I offer falls far short of the more comprehensive studies of Kraus and Rowley that were so influential for a previous generation. I have settled for this restricted analysis primarily for two reasons. From a practical perspective I have had to concede that a study of Israelite worship warrants a far more extensive treatment than the present format allows. I propose in due course to offer such a study in which I will extend my understanding of the Torah's vision of worship to the Prophets and the Writings.[127] Even so, restricting the present study to the Torah serves a useful theological purpose. I believe that within the Hebrew Bible the Torah constitutes the founding vision of God and of God's design for the world and for humankind. This vision, as I hope to demonstrate, winds its connective tissue throughout all of Scripture, both Old and New Testament, in such a way that its witness is essential to comprehending the nature and purposes of God.

But I see a more important theological reason for calling special attention to the Torah. It is precisely this part of the biblical canon that Christians have too often labeled as merely "the Law" that has been superseded by the grace of Christ. From this perspective the Torah becomes at least obsolete, if not directly obstructive to the new revelation of the gospel in Christ. The reasons for Christian neglect and disparagement of the Torah are many and complex, but the study of Israelite religion in the last century has contributed at least indirectly to this situation.[128] By affirming the importance of the Torah's vision for all peoples of faith, I hope to encourage a substantive dialogue between Christians and Jews that might bind both in a shared journey towards the fulfillment of God's ultimate plan for the world.

The Design of the Present Study

This study takes seriously the recognition that reality is both historical and linguistic. Therefore, the task of presenting Israel's worship is both descriptive and constructive. It requires an understanding of the "historicality" of the Torah within the context of the biblical world, *and* it requires an imaginative construal of the "linguistic realities" of the Torah—canonical, social, and rhetorical—that invite and enable an effective theological appropriation of the biblical witness. Specifically, the study has three characteristics.

127. I have tentatively outlined this as "The Vision Fractured: Broken Covenant, Shattered Kingdom, Destroyed Temple," and "The Vision Reclaimed: Between Torah Piety (Psalms) and Temple Piety (Chronicles)."

128. See further the discussion below, chap. 3, pp. 70-73.

1. The study focuses on the final form of the Pentateuch, what some would call the "canonical reality" of the Torah. I prefer the expression "Torah's vision" and will explain in chapter 3 what I mean by it. Briefly, my principal focus is not on the literary traditions that comprise the Pentateuch—Wellhausen's J, E, D, and P—but on the final mosaic to which each has contributed. I suggest that the Torah's aggregate vision, a melding of originally separate details concerning ancient Israel's worship, conveys both a summons and a challenge that is far more than the sum of its individual parts.[129] This aggregate vision will be unfolded in part 2.

2. The study addresses the social reality that generated the final form of Pentateuch by focusing on the strategies and policies that guided Persian imperial politics. I regard the canonical reality of the Torah's vision to be powerful and theologically instructive. But I also acknowledge that this collage of texts called the Pentateuch does not constitute "a photograph of social reality." It is instead, as Gottwald and others have seen, a complex social construction that was *generated* by such reality.[130]

Berquist has shown that Persian control in Yehud was manifest not only in the funding and maintenance of the Second Temple, but also in the assembling of the Pentateuchal materials into their "official" and "constitutional" form.[131] In this respect, the "initiating motive and energy" that produced the Torah was, as I have already suggested, Persian politics, not Israelite religion. I have therefore prefaced the discussion of the Torah's vision with a brief overview of the world of Persia that shaped and authorized that vision (chap. 2).

3. Finally, this study pays attention to the larger reality that is encoded in the Torah's vision, the reality generated by Israel's unique religious perspective regarding God and the world of humankind. Although the social and political reality of the Achaemenid Empire provides a necessary context for reflecting on the Torah's vision, it is instructive to remember that the Torah conveys a *religious* perspective of reality, not only or simply a historical or social one. Such a perspective, although certainly shaped by the Persian system, does not function to describe it completely or to endorse it wholly. Religious perspectives, as Geertz has shown, have the capacity to

129. On the literary and theological issues involved in designating the final collection of narratives and laws within the Pentateuch as "Torah," see F. Crüsemann, "Der Pentateuch als Tora. Prolegomena zur Interpretation seiner Engestalt," *EvTh* 49 (1989), 250–67; *The Torah: Theology and Social History of Old Testament Law* (Minneapolis: Fortress, 1996), 329–32.

130. For this particular language, see R. P. Carroll, "Textual Strategies and Ideologies in the Second Temple Period," *Second Temple Studies: Persian Period*, 114, n. 2.

131. For a discussion of the Pentateuch as a "constitutional document" authorized by Persian policies, see J. Blenkinsopp, *The Pentateuch: An Introduction to the First Five Books of the Bible* (New York: Doubleday, 1992), 239–42.

shape social reality and to bring it into conformity with a larger reality that corrects and completes it. In this sense, religion has the capacity to keep alive the vital distinction between the "real" and the "really real."[132]

I express this attention to the larger reality in two ways. First, I look closely at the world encoded within Israel's rituals (chap. 6). The world of ritual, as Gorman has shown, is a "world of gestural construal" where alternative worlds are embodied and enacted in consecrated behavior.[133] Words and speech are part of the ritual world, but only a minor part. The message is in the action, in the liturgical embodiment of the reality about the world God has created.

Second, and more generally, I recognize the decisive power of rhetoric to fund imaginative construals of alternative worlds. With Brueggemann, I am persuaded that the Bible, and in particular the Torah, preserves for the community of faith an enormously rich reservoir for a "counterimagination of the world." I address the "rhetorical reality" of the Torah's vision throughout this study and particularly in part 3. There I focus on Santayana's observation that the power of the religious perspective resides not only in its ability to shape the present world but also in its capacity to propose "another world to live in."[134]

---

132. Geertz, "Religion as a Cultural System," 112.

133. Gorman, "Ritual Studies and Biblical Studies," 22.

134. G. Santayana, *Reason in Religion*, quoted in Geertz, "Religion as a Cultural System," 87. A fuller citation of the quote is instructive: "Thus every living and healthy religion has a marked idiosyncrasy. Its power consists in its special and surprising message and in the bias which that revelation gives to life. The vistas it opens and the mysteries it propounds are another world to live in; and another world to live in—whether we expect to pass wholly into it or no—is what we mean by religion."

PART ONE

THE WORLD THAT SHAPED
THE TORAH'S VISION

2.

PERSIAN POLITICS
AND THE SHAPING
OF THE PENTATEUCH

THE FINAL FORM OF THE PENTATEUCH CONVEYS A RELIGIOUS PERSPEC-
tive on worship in Israel. This perspective is clearly important and
theologically instructive for the community of faith. It is, nevertheless, a
literary construct, a textual profile, not simply, or even necessarily, a historical description. The serious reader will therefore probe for further
information. Did a community defined by worship in the manner
described by the Pentateuch actually exist? Could such a community have
existed, or should it have existed? These questions shift the inquiry from
theology to sociology. The issue is not simply what the biblical view of
worship in the Pentateuch *is*, but rather *why* these books present this particular view. The answer requires investigating the social, economic, and
political circumstances that shaped the world of the Pentateuch and its literary tradents.

It is generally agreed that the Pentateuch achieved its final form during
the two centuries (539–333 B.C.E.) when Jews were subject to Persian rule. It
has been easier to come to this general conclusion, however, than it has
been to explain the circumstances and events that precipitated the canonization. With the collapse of Wellhausen's documentary hypothesis (JEDP),
recent work in Pentateuchal criticism has largely abandoned the search for
continuous pre-exilic narrative sources that cover the entire range of the
Pentateuch. The current discussion now focuses more on exilic and post-
exilic combinations of what are broadly classified as Priestly and non-
Priestly materials.

Two redactional theories dominate the present debate; neither thus far has
established itself as the consensus view. R. Rendtorff has argued that the overarching redaction that created the Pentateuch was accomplished by an exilic
Deuteronomic editor, with relatively minor additions from a post-exilic

Priestly source.[1] J. Blenkinsopp, on the other hand, has called attention to the preponderance of legal and ritual materials in the final form of the Pentateuch, roughly more than one-third of the entire narrative. The importance accorded these materials in the Pentateuch's final version, he argues, makes it more likely that the principal redaction has been effected by the Priestly tradition, which he dates to the early post-exilic period.[2]

For my purposes here, it is not necessary to decide for one or the other of these theories, although I believe Blenkinsopp's proposal has much to commend it. More important is the growing recognition that the combination of Priestly and non-Priestly materials into a final, canonized form of the Pentateuch cannot be explained exclusively in terms of literary history, as if writers or editors were working in a cultural cocoon. The political and sociological conditions that defined Yehud during the Persian period must also be taken into account. In this respect it becomes increasingly clear that the canonized Pentateuch, whether edited principally from a D perspective or a P perspective, was ultimately the product of *both internal Jewish incentives and external Persian directives*.

We may speculate that, internally, priestly and nonpriestly Jewish groups during the Persian period shared a number of interests and goals (as well, of course, as many substantive differences). Both groups likely had vested interests in the formation of a new nonmonarchical Jewish community under Persian rule. Both would have looked to the Torah of Moses, the constitutive authority for the pre-state period, as a foundation for this community. And both likely would have been concerned to build a community with a strong sense of social solidarity and self-identity, if only to improve the Jewish prospects for living well on their own land during this time of foreign rule. These and other shared objectives would have been important internal incentives for different Jewish groups to work toward a common history of early Israel as a foundation document that would help secure the survival of the community under Persian rule.[3]

---

1. R. Rendtorff, "Pentateuchal Studies on the Move," *JSOT* 3 (1977), 2–10, 43–45 (VTSup 28 [1975], 158–66); *The Problem of the Process of Transmission in the Pentateuch* (Sheffield: JSOT Press, 1990 [1977]); *The Old Testament: An Introduction*, trans. J. Bowden (Philadelphia: Fortress, 1986), 157–64]). J. Van Seters has proposed an important variation on this theory, arguing for a primary editing by an exilic J source whose context is pre-P and post-D. *Prologue to History: The Yahwist as Historian in Genesis* (Louisville: Westminster/John Knox, 1992); *The Life of Moses: The Yahwist as Historian in Exodus-Numbers* (Louisville: Westminster/John Knox Press, 1994).

2. J. Blenkinsopp, *The Pentateuch: An Introduction to the First Five Books of the Bible* (New York: Doubleday, 1992), 19–28, 229–43; "Introduction to the Pentateuch," *The New Interpreter's Bible*, Vol. 1 (Nashville: Abingdon Press, 1994), 305–18.

3. See further E. Blum, *Studien zur Komposition des Pentateuch* (Berlin: Walter de Gruyter, 1990), especially 345–60; and F. Crüsemann, "Der Pentateuch als Tora. Prolegomena zur Interpretation seiner Endgestalt," *EvTh* 49 (1989), 250–67; idem, *The Torah: Theology and*

And yet, even with such internal incentives, the biblical witness itself suggests that the directive to assemble and promulgate Pentateuchal law came from outside the Jewish community. According to Ezra 7, the Persian king Artaxerxes (probably Artaxerxes I) commissioned Ezra in the seventh year of his reign (458 B.C.E.) to return to Jerusalem to teach the "law of the LORD" in Israel (7:10). Ezra's royal commission, according to the biblical account, involved three responsibilities. First, he was to investigate the religious situation in Judah and Jerusalem to see that cultic practices were brought into harmony with "the law of your God, which is in your hand" (7:14). Toward this end he was to convey imperial contributions intended to make possible a full and proper service of worship (7:11-20). Second, he was to convey the king's directive to the treasurers in the province that they provide supplementary financial assistance for Ezra's mission through the collection of local taxes and duties. The temple personnel were to be exempt from such taxes (7:21-24). Finally, he was to appoint magistrates and judges who would implement the "laws of your God" throughout the province, punishing nonobservance with appropriate legal penalties (7:25-26).[4]

The biblical perspective is intent on showing that God is the ultimate authority behind Ezra's mission. It is God "who put such a thing as this into the heart of the king to glorify the house of the LORD in Jerusalem" (Ezra 7:27). Even so, the text does not ignore the existence of another reality in Yehud. The people are charged to obey "the law of your God *and the law of the king*" (v. 26). The "and" envisions two *complementary* authorities that exercised power in Yehud: YHWH, the God of the ancestors, and the Persian emperor.

From a religious or confessional perspective, we may be inclined to weight the former of these authorities more heavily than the latter. Indeed, a good deal of contemporary theological reflection on the Pentateuch gives little or no attention to the significance of Persian hegemony. But the text itself suggests a broader perspective. It suggests that both the directives of God *and* the directives of the Persian king were instrumental in defining the world of Yehud. It is the meaning of this "and" that opens up

Social History of Old Testament Law, trans. A. W. Mahnke (Minneapolis: Fortress, 1996), 339–49; R. Albertz, *A History of Israelite Religion,* vol. 2: *From the Exile to the Maccabees* (Louisville: Westminster/John Knox, 1994), 466–93.

4. The authenticity of this Aramaic text continues to be debated. Was there in fact a Persian decree that mandated or authorized Ezra's mission, or is the biblical account only a theological invention? Although the evidence may not allow for a final resolution of this question, there is a growing recognition that what is reported here is generally consistent with standard Persian policy. The major issues and the contrasting arguments are succinctly presented in Crüsemann, *The Torah,* 334–39.

new possibilities for understanding the Persian world that shaped the Torah's vision.[5]

Persian Imperial Politics

J. L. Berquist has suggested that the formative social dynamics of the Persian Period may be illumined by a sociological analysis of empires and their colonies.[6] Drawing upon the work of S. Eisenstadt, B. Price, R. Thapar, and others, Berquist examines the development of "secondary states" within conditions imposed by foreign imperial domination. The data show that empires typically develop and administer power within a socially and institutionally differentiated network of relationships that comprise a "core" and a "periphery."[7]

The core constitutes the empire's central base of power. It encompasses the institutional center, that is, the capital city or province in which the central government bureaucracy is located. It includes the elite citizens of the society who have both the opportunity and the power to exploit the natural and political resources that the empire controls. It also includes the ideological center, from which flow the mental and symbolic values (for example, beliefs, philosophy, world view) that are designed to shape the empire distinctively. In sum, "The core identifies the locations of greatest power and privilege, whether measured in terms of politics, economy, military, or ideology."[8]

The core of an empire chooses the degree of sovereign control it exercises over its peripheral areas. The control may be absolute or limited, depending on the needs and objectives of the empire. Some circumstances may require that the empire maximize its control over colonial resources, for example, in offensive or defensive military engagements. In other circumstances, the empire may advance its agenda more effectively by granting some measure of autonomy to its colonies, for example, in the collection of local taxes. In all circumstances, however, ultimate power resides within the imperial center of the empire. The degree of benevolence is entirely the empire's choice.

The peripheral areas of an empire are typically designated as colonies or secondary states. In terms of geography, social and political organization,

---

5. On the general issues that support understanding the Pentateuch as a product of the Persian period, see, for example, Blenkinsopp, *The Pentateuch*, 239–42; Albertz, *A History of Israelite Religion*, Vol. II, 466–70; Crüsemann, *The Torah*, 329–39.

6. J. L. Berquist, *Judaism in Persia's Shadow: A Social and Historical Approach* (Minneapolis: Fortress, 1995), 241–55.

7. Ibid., 245–47.

8. Ibid., 246.

and general ideological parameters, secondary states are created by the imposition of a foreign imperialism. The empire establishes the geographical boundaries of the territories it captures from others or carves out of its existing holdings. The empire designs the governance of its colonies and enforces such governance with irresistible military force. The empire determines and/or permits the basic values and beliefs that define a colony as either cooperative and obedient or defiant and rebellious.

Within the conditions imposed by imperial authorities, secondary states typically possess a derivative power to define themselves. Since they do not control the "hard" resources of power—material and economic resources, political organization, military force—colonies turn more to symbolic forms of power and self-definition. In this connection, Berquist notes particularly that religion often flourishes within secondary states for multiple reasons.[9] From the point of view of the imperial center, a colony's religious practices may effectively serve political interests. Its rites and rituals may be used to inculcate a view of the world that legitimates present political arrangements as part of a larger sacral design. Such politicization of religion is particularly effective when religious leaders hold their institutional position in the local cult by imperial appointment. From the point of view of the colony, religion offers symbolic conceptions of order and meaning that enable a community to survive otherwise intolerable situations without directly challenging imperial power.

This sociological grid of the dialectical relationship between empires and colonies offers a heuristic model for assessing the data about Yehud during the time of the Persian Empire.[10] For two centuries (539–333 B.C.E.) Yehud existed as a Persian colony, one of twenty provinces created by the administrative reorganization of the Persian Empire implemented by Darius I. In the Persian system, ultimate power belonged to the emperor and

9. Ibid., 244.
10. The literature on Persian administrative practices in Yehud continues to expand. For discussions with particular emphases on socio-political issues, see M. A. Dandamaev, *A Political History of the Achaemenid Empire* (Leiden: E. J. Brill, 1989); P. Frei and K. Koch, *Reichsidee und Reichsorganisation im Perserreich* (Freiburg, Göttingen: Universitätsverlag/Vandenhoeck & Ruprecht, 1984); H. Kreissig, *Die sozialökonomische Situation in Juda zur Achämenidenzeit* (Berlin: Akademie, 1973); H. Sancisi-Weerdenburg, ed., *Achaemenid History I: Sources, Structures, and Synthesis* (Leiden: Nederlands Instituut voor het Nabije Oosten, 1987); H. Sancisi-Weerdenburg and A. Kuhrt, eds., *Achaemenid History IV: Centre and Periphery: Proceedings of the Gröningen 1988 Achaemenid History Workshop* (Leiden: Nederlands Instituut voor het Nabije Oosten, 1991); E. Stern, "The Persian Empire and the Political and Social History of Palestine in the Persian Period," *The Cambridge History of Judaism: Vol. 1, Introduction, The Persian Period*, eds. W. D. Davies and L. Finkelstein (Cambridge: Cambridge University Press, 1984), 70–87.

was centralized in the bureaucracy of the imperial government, first in Ecbatana, then in Susa, and later in Persepolis. Colonies such as Yehud were governed by local administrators appointed by the emperor, usually ethnic Persians whose loyalty to the crown extended an official Persian presence throughout each colony.

In most cases, the colonies were permitted a measure of freedom and self-control, so long as nothing compromised Persia's realization of the maximum benefit from its provincial holdings. In this respect, the destiny of each colony rested on compliance with two essential restrictions: they must maintain political and economic loyalty to the Persian Empire, and they must sustain sufficient political stability and internal social control so as not to present a threat to their overlords.[11] Colonies willing to submit to these conditions could reasonably expect limited opportunities not only to survive but to prosper.

Within this general framework of governance, the balance between Persia's control and Yehud's limited autonomy shifted over time in direct proportion to Persia's changing political objectives.[12] Persia's first two emperors, Cyrus (539–530 B.C.E.) and Cambyses (530–522 B.C.E.), focused primarily on the military expansion of the empire's boundaries, first with the defeat of Babylon, then of Egypt. Hence their direct involvement in the administration of Yehud was minimal. In general, the relationship between the imperial center and the peripheral colony was little different than it had been under Babylonian rule, with one important exception. By decree of Cyrus (the so-called "Edict of Cyrus"; cf. Ezra 1:2-4; 6:3-5) Jews were given permission to emigrate from Babylon to Yehud and were authorized to rebuild the temple and restore Jewish religion in Jerusalem.

The immediate impact of this decree may have been only slight, for emigration to Yehud proved in fact to be slow and sporadic, and the temple was not finally rebuilt until the reign of Darius I, some eighteen years after the authorization had been given. Nonetheless, with Cyrus there began a gradual shifting of the population of subject people from the center of the empire to its peripheries. In Yehud this policy resulted in a growing tension between emigrants and natives and a consequent fracturing of the community as different Jewish groups began to vie for influence and power

11. On the restrictions placed on Yehud as a "secondary state," see Berquist, *Judaism in Persia's Shadow*, 131–37, 233–37, 243–48. See further P. Frei, "Zentralgewalt und Lokalautonomie im Achämenidenreich," *Reichsidee und Rechsorganizatio*, 7–43.

12. In what follows I offer only a brief summary of certain major events during the Persian Period, in general focusing on the dialectic of imperial-colonial relations as discussed by Berquist (*Judaism in Persia's Shadow*, 23–127). On the history of Yehud in the Persian Period more generally, see the standard literature.

within the province.[13] Over time those groups that expressed conscious loyalty to the Persians, especially the priests, would gain special positions of privilege and authority.

The third Persian emperor, Darius I (522–486 B.C.E.), instituted the most formative changes in Yehud, concentrating on organizational and administrative matters to maximize the empire's profit from its various holdings. Internally he strengthened the imperial bureaucracy, now centralized in Susa. Externally, he devolved power to local leaders who were loyal to the Persian crown, who administered the twenty provinces of the empire.

Two aspects of this devolution of power were of particular significance in Yehud. First, as part of a general policy to standardize the legal base of the empire, Darius charged officials in the provinces to codify extant legal traditions, which then became part of imperial law. It is reasonable to speculate that the canonization of Pentateuchal law in Yehud is related to this charge. Second, as part of a general policy to support and maintain local cult establishments, Darius ordered and funded the rebuilding of the Jerusalem temple. His motives were more political than religious: regional temples served the empire as civic and administration centers and thus helped to secure the stability of the provinces. (I will return to both these means of Persia's decentralized control of Yehud in the next section.)

Xerxes (486–465 B.C.E.) and his son Artaxerxes I (465–423 B.C.E.) brought the Persian Empire to its halfway point. Persia's continuing wars on the western front against Egypt and Greece dominated the political strategy of the empire during this period, and Yehud was caught in the middle of changing objectives. Xerxes continued the Greek wars, but against increasing odds. As income from taxes and trade steadily declined, he sought to offset the drain on the imperial treasury by reversing Darius's policy of funding local cults. The impact in Jerusalem on temple maintenance and on the temple personnel who provided local

---

13. The multiple theological/power groups vying for control in the post-exilic period have been variously described, often with bipolar models pitting priestly (theocratic, hierocratic) parties against prophetic (eschatological, egalitarian) parties. Cf. O. Plöger, *Theocracy and Eschatology*, trans. S. Rudman (Richmond: John Knox, 1968); P. D. Hanson, *The Dawn of Apocalyptic: The Historical and Sociological Roots of Jewish Apocalyptic* (Philadelphia: Fortress, 1979); "Israelite Religion in the Early Postexilic Period," in *Ancient Israelite Religion*, eds. P. D. Miller, et al. (Philadelphia: Fortress, 1987), 485–508. Recent discussions have tended to resist narrow delimitations for these various parties, but continue to propose a dialectical view of post-exilic politics. J. Berquist (*Judaism in Persia's Shadow*), as has been noted, focuses on the dialectics of imperial and colonial politics. See further Albertz, who focuses on the dialectic of "splintering and union," and "integration and disintegration," particularly in terms of the convergence of "official religion" and "personal piety" (*A History of Israelite Religion*, Vol. II, 437–522).

leadership was significant. Priests lost not only their financial support but also their base of authority.[14]

In the first half of his reign, Artaxerxes I sought to strengthen Yehud as a military outpost for the ongoing wars against Egypt and Greece. He increased fortifications in Jerusalem, reinstated funding for the temple, and sought to maintain the loyalty and security of the province through the influence of local administrators.[15] The reform efforts by the two Persian appointed governors, Ezra and Nehemiah, attest to such policies.[16] In the second half of his reign, however, when the threat from the Egyptians and Greeks had lessened, Artaxerxes I returned to Xerxes' policy of diverting funds from the colonies to the imperial treasury.

The extant sources of information concerning the latter half of the Persian Empire (423–333 B.C.E.) are limited, making it difficult to describe precisely the impact of imperial politics on Yehud during this period. Berquist suggests the following general scenario.[17] The empire experienced a continuing decline in both economic and political power, owing primarily to the growing control of trade and commerce by Greece. Persia's administration of Yehud seems to have remained basically unchanged, with local governors and priests, loyal to the empire, providing leadership in the service of royal objectives. Economically, the diminishing tax base of the empire likely resulted in increased taxation of Yehud and the other colonies, thus continuing the policies of Xerxes and Artaxerxes I to deplete colonial resources for the sake of the imperial core. At the same time, however, Persia's ability to enforce taxation would have been considerably weaker as its general imperial rule began to fade. As Persia's control mechanisms began to break down, Yehud's relative autonomy increased, not only in economic matters, but in religious ones as well. In this connection Berquist notes that there emerged a greater variety and pluralism in Yehud's practice of religion.

---

14. On Xerxes' withdrawal of imperial funding for the temple and its effect on the realignment of Yehudite society, see Berquist, *Judaism in Persia's Shadow*, 91–94.

15. Ibid., 108–9.

16. The dates for Ezra and Nehemiah are open to question, since the biblical text (cf. Ezra 7:7-8; Neh. 1:1; 2:1; 5:14) does not specify which Artaxerxes either of them served: Artaxerxes I (465–423 B.C.E.), Artaxerxes II (404–359 B.C.E.), or Artaxerxes III (359–338 B.C.E.). The preponderance of the evidence supports the view that the governorships of both Ezra and Nehemiah are best explained against the backdrop of the reign of Artaxerxes I. Berquist summarizes the general issues (*Judaism in Persia's Shadow*, 110–11). For further discussion see J. Blenkinsopp, *Ezra-Nehemiah* (Philadelphia: Westminster, 1988), 139–44; H. G. M. Williamson, *Ezra and Nehemiah* (Sheffield: JSOT Press, 1987), 55–69.

17. Berquist, *Judaism in Persia's Shadow*, 120–27.

To summarize, Persian imperial politics were designed to create Yehud as a colony that would cooperate and advance the empire's goals. In this sense, Yehud's "world" was defined and imposed by the Persians. Persian control fluctuated over time, but the empire consistently held the balance of power. Whatever identity and life Yehud might construct for itself internally, it did so only with the permission, if not the explicit direction, of its Persian overlords. To insure that Yehud did not overstep the boundary between external directive and internal incentive, Persia utilized mechanisms for the social control and political maintenance of its subject citizens. We turn now to these control mechanisms.

Imperial Mechanisms for Social Control

Once an empire establishes its coercive dominance of a foreign colony or province, it typically moves to put in place a number of interrelated mechanisms designed to insure its possession and control of the conquered territory. In Yehud, Persia employed such mechanisms.[18] One was the process of militarization. By garrisoning imperial troops at strategic locations, Persia not only intensified a military presence within the colony, it also secured vital trade routes, thus protecting investments in the local economy and maximizing royal profits. Another important mechanism for control was the process of immigration. Persia authorized and funded the immigration of Jewish exiles and Persian officials to Yehud. These immigrants were distinct both culturally and ethnically from the native population. Their presence served both to decentralize former arrangements of power and to create new social hierarchies through which Persia could extend and sustain its influence.

In addition to these mechanisms, empires also extend their control and maintenance of subject citizens by symbolic means. A military presence in a colonial outpost may be a first and necessary means of establishing control, but it is also costly. For an empire to maintain itself over a long time span, its military and structural controls are more effective when combined with mechanisms that provide ideological justification for compliance with imperial designs. Berquist has noted that Persian imperialism utilized several symbolic means for extending its authority in Yehud.[19] Of

18. K. G. Hoglund has identified four imperial mechanisms of control: ruralization, commercialization, militarization, and ethnic collectivization. See "The Achaemenid Context," in *Second Temple Studies: 1. Persian Period*, ed. P. R. Davies (Sheffield: JSOT Press, 1991); *Achaemenid Imperial Administration in Syria-Palestine and the Missions of Ezra and Nehemiah* (Atlanta: Scholars Press, 1992). In what follows I have modified Hoglund's description slightly to speak more generally about "immigration" rather than "ruralization."

19. Berquist, *Judaism in Persia's Shadow*, 133–44.

these, the following are of particular relevance for understanding the Persian world that shaped the Pentateuch: creation stories and symbols of cosmic order; codified law and symbols of political reality; regional cult centers and symbols of ritual legitimation.[20]

Creation stories

Persia required Yehud to maintain an internal order that would maximize the empire's benefit from the colony's goods and services. One means of constructing order on earth was through symbols that conceptualized contemporary social and political realities in terms of a larger cosmic harmony. In the ancient Near East a primary vehicle for such conceptualizations was the creation story.

The extant creation stories from Mesopotamia, Egypt, and Syria-Palestine reflect the distinctive emphases of their respective cultural environments. Nevertheless, these various cosmogonies share a number of important assertions about the world and humankind's place within it.[21] 1. The cosmos is described as an ordered, carefully designed whole, all parts of which have been created by and remain under the control of divinity. 2. Neither the cosmos nor humanity comes into existence by chance or without purpose; a creator god(s) is directly responsible for the existence of both. It is therefore the divine intention that establishes order, meaning, and purpose in the world. 3. Creation describes not only the primordial order and meaning of the cosmos, but also the proper and perpetual order that is required to sustain the creator's design. Basic to this assertion is the understanding that creation is endowed with a fundamental order that embraces all aspects of reality—social, political, religious—and humans are expected to live in harmony with this order, not to subvert it. In sum, ancient Near Eastern creation stories typically conceptualize the world as divinely ordered and purposefully structured. This symbolic picture intends to encourage praise of the creator deity as well as affirmation of the creator's established role for humankind within the world.

It is significant that the Pentateuch, the canonized form of which emerged in Yehud during the Persian Period, begins with an account of creation. The Pentateuch actually preserves two creation stories: the first (Gen.

20. For a preliminary treatment of these issues, particularly with respect to the influence of Persian politics on the canonical frame of the Writings (Psalms, 1 and 2 Chron.), see S. E. Balentine, "The Politics of Religion in the Persian Period" in *After the Exile: Essays in Honour of Rex Mason*, eds. J. Barton, D. Reimer (Macon, Ga.: Mercer University Press, 1996), 129–46.

21. For discussion of these and other common assertions in ancient Near Eastern cosmogonies, especially with respect to the ethical and moral actions they authorize, see D. A. Knight, "Cosmogony and Order in the Hebrew Tradition" in *Cosmogony and Ethical Order*, eds. R. W. Lovin, F. E. Reynolds (Chicago: University of Chicago Press, 1985), 138–44.

1:1-2:4a), a priestly account; the second (Gen. 2:4b-25), a non-priestly version that is traditionally associated with the J or Yahwistic tradition. While these two accounts may have originated separately, the canonical text places them side by side as part of a coherent whole. This arrangement likely reflects a final editing from the Priestly perspective, a point not without significance given the important status the priests enjoyed during the Persian period. Since I will discuss the creation texts in some detail in chapter 4, I limit my comments here to general observations concerning their symbolization of a cosmic order that may work in favor of Persian imperialism.

The symbolic world of Genesis 1 is understood to be created and ordered by God. Each day in the primordial sequence establishes a place and a role for everything in creation, according to the divine master plan. The focus is on the cosmic order: the separation of light from darkness, water from dry land, land and sea animals from human beings. Everything in creation has its designated boundaries and responsibilities. Humans are placed by God at the apex of the social hierarchy. Blessed by God, they are given the responsibility of moving the whole of creation, without confusion or conflict, towards its designated fulfillment within the larger cosmic design. This story of creation climaxes on the seventh day, which in the priestly tradition becomes foundational for the Sabbath day and the rituals of worship. It is, in sum, a symbolic picture of a world where religion and the priestly cult is preordained by God as the highest purpose of creation.

The world conceptualized in Genesis 2 augments this picture of cosmic harmony with a more specific perspective on humankind's earthly responsibilities. The divine purpose for the human being is to "work/serve" (*'ābad*) the land and to "protect" (*šāmar*) it (Gen. 2:15). Though this primary task is not different from Genesis 1, its fulfillment is explicated with different verbal images. In 1:26, humans are commissioned to exercise "dominion" (*rādah*) over creation—language that conveys the image of a king's power to govern and rule. But in 2:15, "dominion" over the earth is envisioned not as royal power but as human servanthood.[22] Here, humans realize their full potential by placing themselves in the service of the good of creation.

Several features of these two Pentateuchal creation stories have particular usefulness for the Persian agenda in Yehud. First, their final editing was probably from a Priestly perspective, and in Yehud the priests enjoyed the endorsement of the Persian government. The high priest was appointed by the Persians, and temple personnel who were loyal to the empire served in

---

22. See further the discussion below, chap. 4, p. 86.

positions of authority and influence. One would expect that under such circumstances the priests—in assembling a creation story that emphasizes the order and stability of the world, servanthood as a means of fulfillment, and worship rather than politics as the goal of creation—would not be unaware that they were serving the interests of both the Jewish community and its Persian overlords.

Second, the social and political order envisioned in these creation stories encourages Yehud toward a self-understanding that would not be inconsistent with Persian objectives. The symbolic picture connects the world as experienced in Yehud with God's primordial plan. The cosmic order, and within it a social hierarchy, is divinely sanctioned. It ascribes to the human community a carefully limited understanding of power and responsibility: humans are servants, called to work/serve the land and to protect it, all for the good of the whole earth. In a Persian world, one can expect that any creation story that defines its believers as "servants" of the land would advance imperial strategies for the production and consumption of colonial resources. As Berquist puts it:

> God's control of the world and God's desire that each human take a divinely ordained place within that world offer dominant themes that reflect the Persian desire for a harmonious, integrated society that would honor its own limits and live within the empire as productive contributors to the greater welfare of the whole.[23]

Finally, the creational foundation for the sabbath day also conveys an important symbolization of the world. Under the direction of the priests—who are agents of God *and* stewards of imperial policy—the observance of the sabbath emerged as a key component in Yehud's religious and economic self-definition. As a *religious symbol,* observing the rituals of sabbath calls the community of faith to image God by resting from work and celebrating God's design for creation.[24] As a *political symbol,* sabbath provides imperial overseers an opportunity to connect the religious practices of their subjects to the desired cycles of work and production. In short, sabbath observance may combine religion and politics in ways that serve the empire.[25]

The Codification of Law

A second means of symbolically extending Persian control in Yehud was the codification and promulgation of native law. The Persians did not pro-

---

23. Berquist, *Judaism in Persia's Shadow,* 139.
24. For further discussion see below, chap. 4, pp. 89–93.
25. On sabbath as a political symbol, see Berquist, *Judaism in Persia's Shadow,* 143.

duce a uniform legal code of their own for the whole empire. Instead, the general policy seems to have been to encourage the colonies to codify their own legal traditions, which might in turn be incorporated into "the king's law" and administered with imperial force. By providing imperial authorization for local legal practices, the Persians not only participated directly in the internal affairs of their subject citizens, they also insured that imperial interests would not be threatened by the "self-administration" permitted in their colonies.

The picture is somewhat ambiguous, but evidence indicates that such a practice was utilized throughout the empire's colonies. In particular, Darius I gained a reputation as the great "lawgiver" for his efforts to codify traditional laws in Babylon and Egypt.[26] Although there is no direct evidence that this practice was followed in Yehud, it is reasonable to suppose that Persian policy influenced the codification of Jewish law and therefore the canonization of Pentateuchal law.[27] The reference to "the law of the king" in Ezra 7:26 certainly points in this direction. A reasonable hypothesis is that Darius I authorized the assemblage of Pentateuchal law in Yehud as part of general Persian policy, and that the mission of Ezra mandated by Artaxerxes represents a further phase in the consolidation of Jewish legal traditions.[28]

From this perspective, the Pentateuch, the constitutive "torah" in Yehud, may be viewed as the product of both internal and external factors. It represents an internal synthesis of traditional laws and customs that provided Yehud a sense of cultural and religious identity. It also represents an essential aspect of imperial control, a standardized law that was approved, implemented, and enforced in the service of Persian political objectives. Berquist's description is particularly apt:

26. Cf. A. T. Olmstead, *A History of the Persian Empire* (Chicago: University of Chicago Press, 1948), 119–34.

27. The evidence comes especially from the Behistun inscription, in which Darius boasts of his legal accomplishments in Babylon, and from a Demotic papyrus, which describes Darius's authorization of a commission to codify Egyptian law. On the importance of this evidence with reference to the canonization of the Pentateuch, see Blum, *Studien zur Komposition des Pentateuch*, 345–60; Blenkinsopp, *The Pentateuch*, 239–42; Albertz, *History of Israelite Religion*, Vol. II, 467–68; Crüsemann, *The Torah*, 337–39; Berquist, *Judaism in Persia's Shadow*, 54–55, 137–39.

28. Ezra 7:25 indicates that Ezra was to appoint magistrates and judges "who know the laws of your God" and that these laws were in turn to be taught to those "who do not know them." The implication seems to be that while something new is being commissioned, the contents of the laws were already known, at least in principle. As Crüsemann has put it, "How ever this law might have looked; how much it was like the finished Pentateuch; it was out of this law that what we know as the Pentateuch developed near the end of the Persian period" (*The Torah*, 339).

Persia not only promulgated a law for Yehud to obey but presented a story that defined who Yehud was. This external definition rhetorically limited Yehud's own self-understanding and kept it within certain ideological confines.[29]

The Construction and Maintenance of Regional Cult Centers

Throughout the Persian Empire, local temples—with their own land, work force, and capital—served the empire in a role comparable to that of modern banks and credit unions.[30] Besides supervising religious practices, local cult centers also collected taxes, advanced loans, and were regional distribution centers for goods and commerce. The priesthoods that served these cult centers were under the supervision of imperial authorities whose responsibility was to see that the local temple, whatever its internal religious value to the community, advanced the empire's economic and political objectives.

In a suggestive proposal that is drawing increasing attention, J. Weinberg has argued that Yehud provides a model example of the Persian's use of local cults to develop a new type of sociopolitical organization called the "citizen-temple community."[31] Such communities came into existence, he suggests, with "world empires" of the first millennium B.C.E. that sought to develop an effective fusing of local institutions with a centralized imperial bureaucracy. This was accomplished by merging regional temples and their personnel, which originally enjoyed local autonomy and privileges, with civic leaders whose status and economic power derived from the private sector. Out of this merger arose a coalition of local leaders, from both the private and the communal sectors of the economy, with mutual financial interests. Weinberg theorizes that the Persians encouraged such a coalition in Yehud, modifying it for their own purposes by appointing loyal temple personnel, and funding it out of the royal treasury. The result was a citizen-temple community that gave its members a system of limited self-governance while providing the Persians with a means of externally controlling the community's political, social, and economic development.

Debate concerning the value of Weinberg's interpretive paradigm for the temple remains very much in the fore of contemporary studies of the

29. Berquist, *Judaism in Persia's Shadow*, 138–39. For specific examples of how the Persian legal system may provide the background for understanding the structural and theological distinctives of the Pentateuch, see Crüsemann, *The Torah*, 349–65.

30. The analogy is from J. Blenkinsopp, who provides examples of regional temples and their function in the Persian administration system, with supporting bibliography. See "Temple and Society in Achaemenid Judah," *Second Temple Studies: 1*, 23–26.

31. For a collection of Weinberg's essays on this subject, see J. Weinberg, *The Citizen-Temple Community*, trans. D. L. Smith-Christopher (Sheffield: JSOT Press, 1992).

Persian period.[32] In no small measure this is because the evidence that a citizen-temple community actually existed in Yehud is circumstantial. There are no definitive legal or economic texts that describe the Persian administration of the temple in Jerusalem, and the relevant biblical texts are obviously not designed to provide this information.[33]

Nonetheless, the biblical texts do provide a general picture suggesting that the standard Achaemenid policy toward local cults operated in Yehud as well.[34] Ezra 1–6 reports that Cyrus mandated the rebuilding of the Jerusalem temple (1:2-4) and paid for the cost of the construction out of the royal treasury (6:4). Among those who returned to Jerusalem in response to Cyrus's initiative were Zerubbabel, the Persian-appointed governor, and Yeshua (Joshua) the high priest (2:2), both of whom provided leadership in the initial stages of the rebuilding project (3:1-13). Owing to local opposition (4:1-23), the completion of the temple was delayed until the sixth year of the reign of Darius I, who renewed the original mandate, complete with imperial funding (5:3—6:15). Once completed, the temple certainly provided for a renewal of worship in Jerusalem, but the biblical evidence also suggests a commercial dimension. Nehemiah 13 describes the measures taken by Nehemiah, an appointee of the Persian emperor, to gain control of the collections and disbursements that funneled through the temple's treasury.[35]

Given the biblical data and the growing body of information concerning standard Achaemenid policy, it is reasonable to suppose that in Yehud, as throughout the empire, the Persians viewed the maintenance of the local cult as an important means of imperial governance. Three particular aspects of the temple as a mechanism for social control may be cited: the temple as administrative center, as a religious center, and as the locus of regional power.

---

32. The impact of Weinberg's thesis concerning the role of the temple in the Persian period can be seen from the collection of essays in *Second Temple Studies: 1* and *Second Temple Studies: 2. Temple Community in the Persian Period*, eds. T. Eskenazi and K. H. Richards (Sheffield: JSOT Press, 1994). Note especially Blenkinsopp, who supports a qualified version of Weinberg's citizen-temple model ("Temple and Society," 22–53).

33. Weinberg responds to the problem concerning the gap between a proposed theory and scientifically demonstrated reality in "The Postexilic Citizen-Temple Community: Theory and Reality," *The Citizen Temple-Community*, 126–38.

34. See the general discussion of biblical literature dating to the reign of Darius I in Berquist, *Judaism in Persia's Shadow*, 61–81.

35. In addition to the standard commentaries, see, for example, J. Schaper, "The Temple Treasury Committee in the Times of Nehemiah and Ezra," *VT* 47 (1997), 200–206; "The Jerusalem Temple as an Instrument of the Achaemenid Fiscal Administration," *VT* 45 (1995), 528–39.

As an administrative center, the Jerusalem temple represented an official Persian presence in Yehud. Unlike the Solomonic Temple, which was funded by the royal government, the Second Temple was funded largely by the Persian treasury (cf. Ezra 6:4,8-9; 7:15,20-22; 8:25,33). Moreover, financial support for the maintenance of the temple could be increased or limited, depending on whether the government wished to strengthen or reduce the temple's role in the imperial design for Yehud. For example, Darius I and Artaxerxes I, who used Yehud as a strategic outpost in military campaigns against Egypt, strengthened the temple's administrative efficiency through imperial donations.[36] But Xerxes, who was concerned with decreasing nationalistic sentiments in the colonies, reduced the funding for the temple.[37]

As a religious center, the temple provided the imperial government with the opportunity to use it's own perception of reality to shape the "ritual world" celebrated in Yehud.[38] Not only could the government require that sacrifices and prayers for the imperial rulers be incorporated into the liturgy (cf. Ezra 6:10), but its funding of temple enterprises meant that every religious act had a potential political dividend. This is because ritual, as Berquist notes, builds a sense of solidarity and consensus that is based more on emotional ardor than on intellectual assent.[39] Each time the community gathered in worship, therefore, it recognized at least tacitly its debt of gratitude to its Persian benefactors. Such a mixture of emotions and desires meant that religious ritual could collapse into political ritual. The devotion offered to God would not necessarily interfere with obedience to, or at least compliance with, Persian objectives. Indeed, it might encourage them. The ritual of sabbath observance for example, provided opportunity for worshipers to offer thanks to God *and* (implicitly) to the Persian authorities who permitted scheduled times of rest from the normal routines of work.[40]

As the locus of regional power, the temple not only symbolized imperial designs for the political and social hierarchy that Persia desired in Yehud, it advanced them. Through the appointment of the High Priest and the temple personnel—plus selective support of a strata of educated, urban

36. Cf. Berquist, *Judaism in Persia's Shadow*, 60–63, 111–16.

37. The Book of Malachi suggests that reduced funding for the temple contributed to an intense internal debate concerning the maintenance of worship in Yehud. On Malachi against the backdrop of Xerxes' policies, see ibid., 94–101.

38. D. Kertzer has shown that ritual effectively serves political agendas, especially those of new regimes seeking to legitimate and enhance their authority. *Ritual, Politics, and Power* (New Haven/London: Yale University Press, 1988).

39. Berquist, *Judaism in Persia's Shadow*, 142.

40. On sabbath as a political and religious symbol, see ibid., 143.

elite with vested interests in a local, semi-autonomous system of governance—the Persians developed a coalition of loyal power within the temple. This had at least two important consequences.

First, it introduced and strategically supported a non-monarchic temple cult.[41] In contrast to the religious situation in monarchic Israel, temple leadership in Yehud owed its position and hence its loyalty not to a local king but to a foreign emperor. If it was to continue to enjoy its privileges, the temple had to organize itself politically to maintain the status quo distribution of power, not to subvert it.

Second, the practice of religion that the temple supervised carried the stamp of official approval.[42] The official religion in Yehud was the religion sanctioned by the priestly establishment and indirectly by their Persian sponsors. To observe the ordinances of the temple was to comply with the objectives of the empire, and so to participate in its economic and political rewards. But to withhold obedience from the temple establishment—for example, by refusing to pay the stipulated tithes and offerings—was to oppose the government, becoming a target for its formidable powers of retribution. As the mediator of official religion, the temple's responsibility was to broker imperial threats and promises in such a way that people and empire were joined in a common task that was mutually beneficial.

One further issue needs to be addressed with respect to the temple as a means for social control. The Pentateuch speaks of a tabernacle, not a temple. Thus Persian support for the rebuilding of the Jerusalem temple might appear on first examination to contribute little to the present discussion. On this matter two comments are in order.

First, Persian policy should be considered in broad terms as focused on the maintenance of the cult and its rituals, not simply on the physical reconstruction of a sacred site. It is clear that the Pentateuch places

---

41. Ibid., 81.

42. Cf. ibid., 64–65. It is wise not to regard "official religion" in Yehud as a simple, uniform construct. Berquist has noted the "institutionalized pluralism" in colonial Yehud but concludes that with the support of the Persians the priests gradually increased their influence until they were able to "capture" the religion of Yehud (ibid., 155–58). The groups that may have comprised the social-religious nexus in Yehud have been described in different ways. Albertz identifies three rival interests that contributed to official Yahwism: Deuteronomistic theology; priestly reform theology; and exilic prophecies of salvation (*A History of Israelite Religion*, vol. 2, 437–93). Crüsemann suggests two basic groups: the "free farmers," (that is, the landed aristocracy) and the cultic personnel (*The Torah*, 340–43). It is likely that no one of these groups had sufficient political power to impose its religious or social agenda as *the* official one. With the canonization of the Torah, however, a compromise was reached between the priestly and non-priestly groups on the official and normative document for Yahwism. Although this did not eliminate rival schemes, it would surely have shifted the balance of influence to those who aligned themselves with the priests and their Persian sponsors.

considerable emphasis on ritual laws—laws that provide for that very maintenance. Indeed, in the Pentateuch's final form, such ritual and moral instructions make up about one-third of its total narrative.[43] Moreover, from that same priestly (Persian-sponsored) perspective, the prescriptions for the reconstituted worship in Jerusalem derive from the plan of creation itself, which includes the sabbath observance. Thus the construction of the holy place—whether at Sinai or Jerusalem—serves to complete God's design for creation.[44] Inasmuch as the Persians targeted the cult in Jerusalem as a mechanism for social control, their sponsorship of the Pentateuch and its ritual instructions offered a means of overseeing Yehud's blueprint for the implementation of their policy.

Second, for all the attention that the Second Temple usually attracts in treatments of the Persian Period, it is perhaps surprising how little specific information about it is given in the biblical text.[45] The Edict of Cyrus (Ezra 6:3-5) stipulates that the temple is to be rebuilt but provides only a general account of its appearance. Prophetic texts from the Persian Period, especially Haggai and Zechariah 1–8, provide additional insight but once again do not provide anything like a detailed description.[46] Ezekiel 40–48, a precursor to the Persian Period prophetic texts, offers considerably more information about the temple, but this text is represented as Ezekiel's vision for the future, not as a literal description of an existing structure.

Nowhere, then, does the biblical text give any detailed information about the restored temple's structure or function in Yehudite society. Instead, wherever this temple becomes the subject of intensive concern in literature from the Persian Period, the imagery that is used comes from traditions canonized in the Pentateuch, specifically from the priestly account of the tabernacle that was constructed at Sinai (Exodus 25–31, 35–40).

43. On the structural and theological significance of the prominence of these laws in the Pentateuch, see Blenkinsopp, *The Pentateuch*, 31–53.

44. On the literary and symbolic connections between Solomon's Temple and the tabernacle, see J. D. Levenson, *Sinai and Zion: An Entry Into the Jewish Bible* (San Francisco: Harper and Row, 1985), 142–45.

45. R. Carroll has argued that most texts that mention the Second Temple actually only describe a "textual" or "midrashic" temple, not a specific or actual temple ("So What Do We Know About the Temple? The Temple in the Prophets," *Second Temple Studies: 2. Temple Community in the Persian Period*, ed. T. Eskenazi and K. H. Richards [Sheffield: JSOT Press, 1994], 34–51).

46. Cf. D. L. Peterson, "The Temple in Persian Period Prophetic Texts," *Second Temple Studies: 1*, 125–44; D. J. A. Clines, "Haggai's Temple: Constructed, Deconstructed, and Reconstructed," *Second Temple Studies: 2*, 60–87; P. Marinkovic, "What Does Zechariah 1–8 Tell Us about Building the Temple?" *Second Temple Studies 2*, 88–103.

Particularly interesting in this connection are 1 and 2 Chronicles, which date to the latter half of the Persian Period. They present the temple and its cult as the institutional center of communal life. Nearly half (43 percent) of this rewrite of Israel's early history focuses on the reigns of David and Solomon, and especially on their roles in the preparation and building of the temple (1 Chron. 10 to 2 Chron. 9). It is striking, however, that the temple Chronicles describes is not the Second Temple, which presumably had already been rebuilt, but the Solomonic Temple, *which recalls the plan of Moses*. In fact, Chronicles places that plan, understood to have been passed from Moses to David to Solomon, at the center of the world it describes.[47] The point I make here is simply that the Pentateuch, even though it does not speak of the temple directly, nevertheless addresses issues relating to the cult and its maintenance that both the Persians and the citizens of Yehud recognized as important for their objectives.

In summary, the religious perspective conveyed by the final form of the Pentateuch is a literary construct. Recognition of this fact does not negate its theological importance for the community of faith (as I will show in succeeding chapters), but it does mean that the biblical portrait cannot be simply equated with historical fact. As R. Carroll has put it, "texts are not photographs of social reality."[48]

Behind the final form of the Pentateuch is the reality of Persian hegemony. In this respect, the sociological data available to us suggests that the catalyst for Yehud's self-definition was as much the Persian imposition of social and political directives as it was the internal convictions of a fervent faith. The biblical vision of the Pentateuch, therefore, for all its theological merit, was to a significant degree the result of Yehud's willingness to concede its limitations and adjust its religious ideals to the realities of life in the Persian Empire.

---

47. Like Moses, David received a plan *(tabnît)* from God for the design of the holy place and its furnishings (1 Chron. 28:11-19; cf. Exod. 25:9). Moreover, David supervised the collection of the building materials, recruited the workers (cf. 1 Chron. 22), and organized the temple personnel (cf. 1 Chron. 23–26). As Joshua succeeded Moses and completed what he had initiated, so, Chronicles suggests, Solomon succeeded David and placed the construction of the temple at the center of his royal responsibilities. I have discussed these matters in more detail in "'You Can't Pray a Lie.' Truth *and* Fiction in the Prayers of Chronicles," in *The Chronicler as Historian*, eds. M. P. Graham, K. G. Hoglund, and S. L. McKenzie, (Sheffield: Sheffield Academic Press, 1997), 246–67.

48. R. P. Carroll, "Textual Strategies and Ideology in the Second Temple Period," *Second Temple Studies: 1*, 114, n. 2.

3.

THE TORAH AS VISION

In *A WHOLE NEW LIFE*, REYNOLDS PRICE REFLECTS ON HIS TEN-YEAR battle with the cancer that invaded his body and grew up his spinal column like an eel.[1] The cancer's assault was massive and relentless. Once it had penetrated his body's defenses, he was powerless before its steady march toward takeover and control. He survived, although with a paralysis that bears witness to his war, and he now enjoys what he self-consciously describes as a new and better life.

On the other side of his battle with cancer, from the "far side of catastrophe,"[2] where life is marked by both inalterable limitation and relentless yearning, Price offers three survival steps for all who may be victims of similar physical or psychic takeovers. First, grieve hard and for a decent time over whatever parts of your old self you have lost. Next, check the grief. Finally, "find your way to be somebody else, the next viable you."[3] Such is the advice of one who learned to look his real self square in the eye and say, "Reynolds Price is dead. Who will you be now?"[4]

Price's personal struggle to create a new life for himself offers a heuristic analogy for reflecting on the struggle that defined the community of faith in the Persian Period.[5] After nearly fifty years of Babylonian exile and domination, submerged in what would be two centuries of intrusive control by the Persian Empire, the community in Yehud had reason to concede that the old, pre-exilic way of being Israel was dead. What used to be the kingdom of Israel had become a secondary state, a political entity created by Persian takeover and governed by Persian policies. Persia designed Yehud to function as a controlled environment, with limited opportunities

1. R. Price, *A Whole New Life* (New York: Atheneum, 1994).

2. Ibid., 180.

3. Ibid., 183.

4 .Ibid., 184.

5. I used this analogy previously in discussing the influence of Persian politics on the shaping of the canonical frame of the Writings. Cf. S. E. Balentine, "The Politics of Religion in the Persian Period," in *After the Exile: Essays in Honour of Rex Mason,* eds. J. Barton and D. Reimer (Macon, Ga.: Mercer University Press, 1996), 129–46.

for self-definition, so long as nothing compromised Persia's realization of its own goals and objectives. In sum, whatever life the community in Yehud built for itself, it had to be viable in relation to Persia's imperial control.

The Pentateuch provides an important perspective on the life that Yehud built for itself during the Persian Period. Shaped in important ways by the social and political realities of the Persian world, the Pentateuch's final form may be regarded as a Persian sponsored "constitutional document" that served as an important means of imperial control in Yehud.[6] This is the hard datum of historical reality. It cannot simply be dismissed or ignored as if it has no bearing on the meaning the Pentateuch conveys. The urgent task for the community in Yehud was to survive—not in some abstract, imaginary world, but in the real world of the Persian Empire. The task was to create a "viable self," a community that could exist meaningfully in the environment in which it was placed. Given these dynamics—foreign domination and the imperative to survive—accepting Persia's directive to codify the Pentateuchal laws would require that Yehud construct its new and viable self as part of a compromise with imperial authority.[7]

Even so, it is instructive to remember that the Pentateuch candidly offers a religious perspective, not simply a historical or social one. This religious perspective, what I refer to as the Torah's "vision," does not ignore the reality of Persian domination, but neither does it accept it as final or ultimate. Instead, the Torah's vision construes another world to live in, a "proposed world"[8] designed and ordered by God. The Torah asserts that if this world does not yet exist, it remains nevertheless credible and possible.

Before outlining the Torah's vision, it will be useful to lay a foundation for reflecting on what is meant by the term "religious perspective." There are of course any number of perspectives by which humankind seeks to construe meaning in the world, and we may be confident that neither in Yehud nor in modern society would the religious view enjoy an unchallenged authority. Nonetheless, religion does have a peculiar orientation to life that enables it to speak in the marketplace of competing ideas with a distinctive voice.

6. Cf. J. Blenkinsopp, *The Pentateuch: An Introduction to the First Five Books of the Bible* (New York: Doubleday, 1992), 239–42.

7. See chap. 2, 47–56. For discussion of the compromises that the community in Yehud had to make if it was to accept the limited chances the Persians offered for sharing in a new beginning, see further R. Albertz, *A History of Israelite Religion in the Old Testament Period*. Vol. II: *From the Exile to the Maccabees*, trans. J. Bowden (Louisville: Westminster/John Knox, 1994), 443–50; F. Crüsemann, *The Torah: Theology and Social History of Old Testament Law,* trans. A. W. Mahnke (Minneapolis: Fortress, 1996), 345–49.

8. W. Brueggemann, *Texts Under Negotiation: The Bible and Postmodern Imagination* (Minneapolis: Fortress, 1993). See the discussion of Brueggemann above, chap. 1, 31–32.

C. Geertz has suggested that religion's capacity to create meaning in life derives from its power to tune human actions to an envisioned cosmic order, then to project images of this cosmic order onto the plane of every-day human experience.[9] A key for discerning how this is accomplished lies in the definition of religion itself. In Geertz's view, religion is "(1) a system of symbols which acts to (2) establish powerful, pervasive, and long-lasting moods and motivations in men by (3) formulating conceptions of a general order of existence and (4) clothing these conceptions with such an aura of factuality that (5) the moods and motivations seem uniquely realistic."[10]

Geertz elaborates on each of these five features, showing that religion plays an important and indeed determinative role in the shaping of meaning. The following observations may be singled out for particular review:[11]

1. Religion is a system of symbols—linguistic, gestural, material, etc.—that provides models *of* and *for* reality.[12] As such, it not only renders a reality that already exists apprehensible, it also renders an alternative reality that does not yet exist conceivable and attainable.

2. A religious perspective induces in believers enduring moods and motivations that keep them focused on the vision. Such dispositions do not guarantee that the reality envisioned becomes an actuality, but they do effect a "chronic inclination" towards the vision that provides stability and meaning in the interim between conception and fulfillment.[13]

3. Religion and its sacred symbols affirm transcendent truths that offer meaning and order in the midst of chaos. While religious truths do not serve *only* in such situations, Geertz is intent to show that the problem of suffering (or more generally, the problem of evil) represents both the critical challenge and the acute need for meaning that transcends present (dis)order. The challenge, minimally, is to affirm that "God is not mad."[14] The acute need is not so much to avoid suffering, as to find a way to comprehend it and cope with it as part of a meaningful existence. As Geertz puts it, religious perspectives of truth offer to those able to embrace them a way of making "physical pain, personal loss, worldly defeat, or the helpless contemplation of others' agony something bearable . . . something, as we say, sufferable."[15]

9. C. Geertz, "Religion as a Cultural System," in *The Interpretation of Cultures: Selected Essays* (New York: Basic Books, 1973), 90.

10. Ibid.

11. For the full discussion, see ibid., 90–123.

12. Ibid., 93–94.

13. Ibid., 96.

14. Ibid., 99. Here Geertz quotes the dictum of Salvador de Madariaga.

15. Ibid., 104.

4. The religious perspective is a faith perspective; its "truth" must be believed before it can be known.[16] This is no reason to value it less than historical or scientific construals of the world. On the contrary, it is distinguished from these others precisely because it claims to move "beyond the realities of everyday life to wider ones which correct and complete them."[17] The critical demarcation (as noted in the previous chapter) is between the "real" and the "really real."[18]

Geertz gives special attention to the role religious ritual plays in clothing the "really real" with "an aura of utter actuality."[19] Ritual generates, reinforces, and sustains religious conviction. "In a ritual, the world as lived and the world as imagined, fused under the agency of a single set of symbolic forms, turn out to be the same world."[20]

5. The religious perspective, for all its focus on the "really real," cannot create a cultural vacuum where believers live in unchallenged fidelity. Social and political realities necessarily impinge on religious convictions, if only because when the ritual ends the worshipers must return to their everyday world. Commonsense modes of discernment require that this world be recognized as simply "given." Religion may invite believers to return to that world as courageous agents of change and transformation, but it cannot pretend that the world outside the sanctuary does not exist or has no relevance. In fact, this movement back and forth between the religious perspective and what Geertz calls the "common-sense perspective" defines an essential pattern in society.[21] By repeatedly crossing the boundary between the world as religiously conceived and the world as politically given, one's understanding of both the sacred and the secular changes, enlarges, and sharpens.

The religious perspective that Geertz describes is, I suggest, what the Torah offers in regard to the reality of Persian hegemony. But it also asserts that this reality can—indeed should—be seen as only partial; there is a wider reality, a larger transcendent truth that corrects and completes it. In the Torah's vision, the truth about God's ultimate intentions for the cosmos and for humankind is generated, sustained, and actualized through worship. For a preliminary sketch of how this journey from the "real" to the "really real" is imagined in Hebraic tradition, I turn now to the Torah's vision of worship.

16. Ibid., 110.
17. Ibid., 112.
18. Ibid.
19. Ibid.
20. Ibid. On this understanding of ritual and its importance for appropriating priestly ritual in the Hebrew Bible, see the discussion below, chap. 6.
21. Ibid., 119–23.

The Torah's Vision: An Overview

In the Hebrew Scriptures the Torah conveys a vision of worship that summons the community of faith to its most distinctive way of being the people of God in the world. In broad terms this vision comprises three essential affirmations: 1. the summons to worship inheres in the liturgy of
creation; 2. worship is itself a primary means of honoring, sustaining, and
restoring God's creational design for the world; and 3. for a people called
into relationship with God, worship is at the heart of community building
and world construction. Each of these affirmations requires further
exposition.

The Torah asserts that a summons to worship inheres
in the liturgy of creation

From the external perspective of the Persians, traditional creation stories,
carefully managed, may provide a symbolic means of legitimating status
quo systems of power and management. From an internal religious perspective, however, the Torah's assertion that the world is created, ordered,
and purposefully designed by God invites a community of faith to wider
horizons of meaning.

In the Torah's vision, the world is created as part of a grand, cosmic
liturgical celebration. The liturgy culminates on the seventh day (Gen. 2:1-
3), the primordial foundation for the institution of the Sabbath day (cf.
Exod. 31:12-17). This day marks the intersection of God's creative design in
the heavens and God's creative hopes for humankind on earth. After six
days of God's creative work, the seventh day *celebrates* the goodness and the
stability of the world that God has called into being (Gen. 1:1-31), and it *prepares* humankind for its divine commission to be co-creators with God in
the world that God has designed. God is, of course, supreme Creator, but
the Torah's vision is clear that God also places before humankind opportunities to participate with God in acts of "creaturely creativity."[22] To cite but
one example, God creates the animals, the human being names them, and
God accepts the human decision (Gen. 2:18-23). As T. Fretheim has put it,
"Creation is process as well as punctiliar act; it is creaturely as well as
divine."[23]

The liturgy of creation, however, is more candid than to suggest that
worship joins God and humankind in perfect harmony. The world God
creates is a fragile one, open to the best and the worst that humankind may

22. T. E. Fretheim, "Creator, Creature, and Co-Creation in Genesis 1–2," *Word and World*,
Supplement Series 1 (1992), 18.
23. Ibid.

contribute. Thus it is vulnerable not only to human distortion but also to divine anguish. In a world that is no longer "very good," a real world where human corruption rouses divine heartache (Gen. 6:5-7), an act of worship once more signals both an ending and a new beginning. Noah's altar, the first mentioned in Genesis, marks the recession of the flood waters and the uncovering of a cleansed earth (Gen. 8:20). Noah's rite of speechless thanks marks the transition in God's heart from pain to promise. A new world emerges, this one founded on a cosmic covenant (Gen. 9:8-11) that announces God's relentless intentions to stay in relationship with the created order.[24]

The Torah envisions worship as a principle means of creating and recreating God's design for the world

While Persian policy may have sought to expropriate the worship center for socioeconomic objectives that would advance the empire, the Torah envisions the sacred place as a center for a different agenda. In the tabernacle and in the worship associated with it, the Torah conceives the community of faith as empowered to create a ritual world of space, time, and status that mirrors God's cosmic designs.[25] Corresponding to the number seven in the liturgical drama of creation, the instructions for building the tabernacle are conveyed in seven speeches (Exod. 25–31), the implementation of these instructions is carried out by seven acts of Moses (Exod. 40:17-33), the instructions for sacrificial activities are reported in seven speeches (Lev. 1–7), and the duration of important rituals, including the ordination of the priests, is seven days (Lev. 8:33).

It is not just that the tabernacle and its rituals correspond to God's created order. The Torah also understands Israel's ritual world to have the capacity to sustain and, if necessary, to restore God's design for creation.[26] For example, the prescriptions for daily, monthly, and annual offerings in Leviticus 23 (cf. Num. 28–29) not only reflect the natural rhythm built into creation, their observance also serves ritually to actualize that rhythmic order in everyday life. In like manner, the ritual for the Day of Atonement

24. Note the repetition of the promise "never again" (Gen. 8:21 [2x]; cf. 9:11, 15). On God's "cosmic covenant" see R. Murray, "Prophecy and the Cult," in *The World of Ancient Israel: Sociological, Anthropological, and Political Perspectives*, ed. R. E. Clements (Cambridge: Cambridge University Press, 1989), 209–10; idem., *The Cosmic Covenant: Biblical Themes of Justice, Peace and the Integrity of Creation* (London: Sheed and Ward, 1992).

25. Cf. F. H. Gorman Jr., *The Ideology of Ritual: Space, Time, and Status in the Priestly Theology* (Sheffield: JSOT Press, 1990).

26. Gorman has shown that just as it is appropriate to speak of the narrative world created by narrative texts, so it is useful to think of the "ritual world" that is created and enacted in ritual texts; ibid., 14–18.

(Lev. 16) seeks both to address and repair the breakdown in divinely established distinctions of holy/profane, pure/impure, and order/chaos.[27] As the Torah understands creation to be the context within which God summons forth the liturgy of worship, so its concomitant focus on the tabernacle suggests that worship is itself an important constitutive act that sustains and reclaims God's intentions for the created order.

The Torah understands worship to be at the heart of community formation and world building

The Persian strategy may have been to use cultic centers to develop a social hierarchy of power that was committed to the imperial agenda. But in the Torah's vision, religious imperatives summoned the community of faith to social and political structures that were defined by quite different commitments.

When Israel leaves Sinai for the land of Canaan, it departs as both a covenant community (Exod. 19–24) and a worshiping community (Exod. 25–Num. 10:28). In a word, it is a community constituted by its commitment to "covenant holiness." Such a community, the Torah asserts, is commissioned to love God absolutely and to live by that love. At the same time, by departing Sinai, Israel also becomes a community on the move. It is a community on a journey *away from* the sacred mountain where covenantal obedience and ritual holiness might enjoy an unthreatened harmony, and *towards* the land of Canaan, where the obstacles to realizing covenant holiness in concrete terms will be significant indeed.

In the Torah's vision, the book of Deuteronomy provides the charter for Israel's journey from Sinai to Canaan. Encamped in the plains of Moab, the community of faith finds itself on the border between past and future, between God's vision for them as a people and their actualization of this vision in the real world of Canaan. For the journey that lies ahead, Moses recalls the Sinai experience in order to review one last time the critical role that worship will play in their constitution as a people of God. He begins with a recapitulation of the religious imperatives conveyed through the "decrees" (that is, the Decalogue, Deut. 5:6-21), then outlines in the "statutes and ordinances" (Deut. 12–26) the constitutional formation of the structures of society. Both the religious imperatives and the political and social concerns that will define the body politic are to manifest the community's exclusive loyalty to God. To cite but one part of the relevant evidence, both the "decrees" and the "statutes and ordinances" begin with First Commandment concerns: "you shall have no other gods before me" (Deut. 5:7; cf. 12:1—13:8).

27. Cf. ibid., chaps. 3 and 7.

In short, the biblical witness understands Moses to have summoned forth a new community in which the Torah's vision generates an ever-renewing covenant that binds together God, humankind, and cosmos (Deut. 27:1—30:20). Just as in primeval days, so forever after, the community of faith must decide whether to live in harmony with this vision or in opposition to it. And just as it was "in the beginning," the choice remains a crucial one. It is the choice between "life and death, blessings and curses" (Deut. 30:19).

The Torah's vision of worship as outlined above may be conceptualized in various ways. If one approaches the Pentateuch in its "narrative integrity" (what R. Alter refers to as its "composite artistry"),[28] then the Torah in its final form gives pride of place to the events that transpire at Sinai, specifically those reported in Exodus 19 through Numbers 10. This report of Israel's constitution as both a covenant community (Exod. 19–24) and a worshiping community (Exod. 25–Num. 10) comprises slightly less than half the total text of the Pentateuch.[29]

As figure 3.1 illustrates, the Sinai pericope records two revelations to Israel: God's revelation from the mountain (Exod. 19–40), and God's revelation from the tabernacle (Lev. 1–27). From the perspective of the Torah, the first revelation belongs to the past, the second belongs to the present and the future. The revelation from the mountain of Sinai is preliminary and foundational; the revelation from the tabernacle is decisive for the ongoing life of Israel.[30] In other words, in its final arrangement into five books, the Torah focuses the community of faith on the instructions contained in the third book, the book of Leviticus. In this conceptualization, the Pentateuch presents worship as the goal of creation.[31]

Another conceptualization, which supports a similar understanding, is to imagine that the three essential affirmations discussed above are in a triangular relation (see figure 3.2).

At the apex of the Torah's vision is *worship*, especially as it unfolds in the events at Sinai recorded in Exodus 19 through Numbers 10. This extended account describing the creation of Israel as both a covenant community and a worshiping community is linked inextricably to two other poles.[32]

28. R. Alter, *The Art of Biblical Narrative* (New York: Basic Books, 1981), especially chap. 7.

29. Cf. R. Knierim, "The Composition of the Pentateuch," in *Society of Biblical Literature 1985 Seminar Papers*, ed. K. H. Richards (Atlanta: SBL, 1985), 396.

30. Cf. Ibid., 405.

31. Blenkinsopp, *The Pentateuch*, 47, 221. See further Knierim, "The Composition of the Pentateuch," 405: "The Sinai-pericope aims at the book of Leviticus. This book is the center of the Pentateuch."

32. Hanson has discussed Israel's notion of community as a triad of righteousness, compassion, and worship. Although his concern is somewhat different from mine, he understands

FIGURE 3.1
The Centrality of the Sinai Pericope in the Torah's Vision[*]

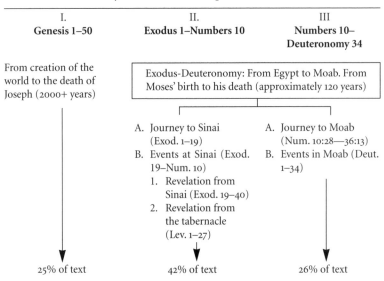

I. Genesis 1–50	II. Exodus 1–Numbers 10	III Numbers 10– Deuteronomy 34
From creation of the world to the death of Joseph (2000+ years)	Exodus-Deuteronomy: From Egypt to Moab. From Moses' birth to his death (approximately 120 years)	
	A. Journey to Sinai (Exod. 1–19) B. Events at Sinai (Exod. 19–Num. 10) 1. Revelation from Sinai (Exod. 19–40) 2. Revelation from the tabernacle (Lev. 1–27)	A. Journey to Moab (Num. 10:28—36:13) B. Events in Moab (Deut. 1–34)
25% of text	42% of text	26% of text

* For this outline of the literary units of the Pentateuch ,see Knierim, "The Composition of the Pentateuch," 395–415. I have modified slightly Knierim's proposal.

On the one hand, the Torah establishes a number of verbal and thematic links between Genesis 1–2 and the Sinai pericope, where Israel's construction of the sanctuary and the ritual world it serves is presented as the completion of the work begun in creation.[33] Just as the Spirit of God hovered over the formless void (Gen. 1:3), so the Spirit of God breathed life into those crafting the tabernacle (Exod: 31:3). Just as God finished the work of

worship to be the essential link in this triad, unifying the two polarities of righteousness and compassion into one "life-enhancing pattern." *The People Called: The Growth of Community in the Bible* (San Francisco: Harper and Row, 1986), 70–78, passim. The quotation appears on 74. See further the discussion of Hanson in chap. 1, 23–24.

33. The literary and conceptual links between the Priestly creation account and the Sinai pericope have often been noted, e.g. J. Blenkinsopp, "The Structure of P," *CBQ* 38 (1976), 278–83; *The Pentateuch*, 218; J. Kearney, "Creation and Liturgy: The P Redaction of Ex 25–40," *ZAW* 89 (1977), 375–78; M. Fishbane, *Text and Texture: Close Readings of Selected Biblical Texts* (New York: Schocken Books, 1979), 11–13; N. Lohfink, "Creation and Salvation in Priestly Theology," *TD* 30 (1982), 4–5; V. Hurowitz, "The Priestly Account of the Building of the Tabernacle," *JAOS* 105 (1985), 21–30; J. D. Levenson, *Creation and the Persistence of Evil* (San Francisco: Harper and Row, 1988), 218; J. G. Gammie, *Holiness in Israel,* OBT (Minneapolis: Fortress, 1989), 14–20; F. H. Gorman Jr., *The Ideology of Ritual*, 39–60; T. E. Fretheim, *Exodus* (Atlanta: John Knox, 1991), 268–72. See further the discussion below, 80–93.

FIGURE 3.2

Worship
(Exod. 19–Num. 10)

Cosmic order
(Genesis 1–2)

Community/
world building
(Num. 11–Deut. 34)

creation (Gen. 2:2), and blessed the seventh day (Gen. 2:3), so Moses finished the work of the tabernacle (Exod. 40:33) and declared it worthy of blessing (Exod. 39:43). The tabernacle, then, is the "one spot in the midst of a world of disorder where God's creative, ordering work is completed according to the divine intention just as it was in the beginning."[34]

On the other hand, the Torah also presents worship as the principal means through which God's creative design for the world is established, sustained, and restored. Though the *summons* to worship inheres in the liturgy of creation, the *act* of worship is an extension of God's creative work into the community-building and world-building that uphold the order of creation. Thus in Moses' final address to a people preparing to enter Canaan (Deut. 5–26), he turns once more to the Sinai liturgy for the founding principles that are to define Israel's body politic. The Torah's vision is that the tabernacle stands at the center of the community of faith, defining its internal cohesiveness and directing its journey into the complex world beyond. As T. Fretheim has observed, both the ark and the tabernacle are portable sanctuaries for Israel in the midst of a world of sin and chaos, and both of them bring Israel safely through a dangerous passage to a new place of being in the world.[35] Note also that both the ark and the tabernacle mark this new beginning with an act of worship.

A number of observations emerge from this sketch of the Torah's vision of worship. First, the three essential affirmations discussed above correspond generally to the previously identified Persian mechanisms for social and political control in Yehud: creation stories; the codification of ethical and ritual law; and the construction and maintenance of cultic sites. How these foci may have served imperial objectives was discussed in chapter 2 and should be assumed here in principle as the "given" sociopolitical reality behind the authorized and canonized form of the Pentateuch. I do not suggest that each

34. Fretheim, *Exodus*, 271.
35. Ibid., 269.

of these emphases within the Pentateuch is created by the Persians, nor that in each case the Persian influence can be specifically identified in the way the themes have been presented in the biblical text. I argue only that the Torah's composite vision of worship cannot be explained exclusively in terms of circumstances and events intrinsic to the Jewish community.[36]

Second, this sketch of the Torah's vision of worship (as well as the more extensive discussion that follows in part 2) focuses not on the historicality of the world behind the biblical text but on the linguistic world within the text. The primary emphasis is on the capacity of the Torah's vision to generate, in the midst of the realities constructed by Persian hegemony, new construals of the reality about God, the world, and humankind. The objective of this study is to analyze how major worship emphases that are embedded deep within Israel's own traditions and history were incorporated through various redactions into an aggregate vision that has validity and power in the world of Yehud and beyond.

Third, other important foci in the Pentateuch could justifiably be added to this discussion of the Torah's vision of worship. The one part of the canon most obviously under-represented in the present study is Genesis 12–50. Apart from discussing Genesis 15–17, which treats Abraham and Sarah as important paradigms for worship,[37] I chose not to focus on the ancestral narratives. I made this decision in part because "the religion of the patriarchs" has long been a central focus in studies of Israelite worship, so the ground has been well covered, at least from a historical-critical perspective.[38] From a canonical standpoint, however, the Torah's central focus is not on the ancestors—as significant as they are in the Pentateuchal narrative—but on the Sinai pericope (Exod. 19–Num. 10), where literary and thematic emphases trace Israel's foundational story back to creation and forward to Moab.

More importantly, this study shifts the focus to the themes of creation, law and covenant, and tabernacle because these Pentateuchal emphases may be readily integrated with the growing body of sociological data that clarifies Persian imperial policies. It is precisely this backdrop of tension between internal religious incentives and external political controls that invites theological reflection on the Torah's vision of worship as a model *of* and *for* the world.

Finally, it is important to emphasize once more that the Torah's presentation of Israel's worship is truly a literary construct, a theological *vision*. The three essential affirmations discussed above, as well as the various con-

---

36. Cf. Blenkinsopp, *The Pentateuch*, 239.
37. See below, chap. 4, 100–116.
38. See above, chap. 1, 5–16.

ceptualizations that serve to bring them into focus, emerge from a collage of texts traditionally distinguished with the labels J, E, D, and P. Each of these texts, and the literary traditions they represent, lends its own bit of truth to the mosaic of the eventual vision. But the aggregate vision is more than the sum of its individual pieces.

There is in fact no material evidence that the vision of worship preserved in the Torah actually functioned in Israel exactly as it is described in the text. The Persian Period is the sociopolitical context that gave rise to the canonization of the Pentateuch, but that does not mean the Pentateuch's characterization of worship describes what actually existed in Yehud. In fact, the Pentateuch does not purport to describe the Persian Period at all; its focus instead is on the early history of Israel, from creation to Moses. One could expect the citizens in Yehud who received the Pentateuch as the normative account of Israel's foundational story to recognize that there was a large gap between life during the days of the ancestors and life as they experienced it in a Persian colony.

I suggest that for these ancient recipients of the story (and for modern ones as well), the Torah presents a vision of worship grounded in authorized memories of the past, yet still awaiting its full realization in history. Such a gap between vision and actuality recalls the words of T. S. Eliot:

> *Between the idea*
> *And the reality*
> *Between the motion*
> *And the act*
> *Falls the Shadow* [39]

Between the Idea and the Reality

If the church is to reclaim the Torah's vision of worship from the shadows that fall across the gap between texts and reality, it must make certain changes in the way it approaches Hebrew Scripture, particularly the ritual texts that play such a prominent role in the Pentateuch. I suggest that two matters require urgent reappraisal. The first is primarily theological: How does the biblical witness describe what it means to be a people of God? The second is primarily methodological: How is one to read and interpret ritual texts?[40]

---

39. T. S. Eliot, "The Hollow Men," *Collected Poems 1909–1962* (New York: Harcourt, Brace & World, Inc., 1970), 81–82.

40. See further the methodological comments above, chap. 1, 32–36.

1. *Torah or Law?* In Hebraic tradition the first five books of Scripture are recognized primarily as Torah. The theological perspective is that these books offer foundational "instruction" from God (in Hebrew, *tôrāh*) that enables those who receive it and obey it to become the covenant people of God. Commandments that require obedience are an essential part of this *tôrāh*, as the statutes and ordinances revealed to Moses at Sinai make crystal clear. But these requirements are part of a larger story that chronicles God's relentless love for creation and for humanity; hence from the Hebraic perspective, *tôrāh* is received as a great gift from God, without which covenant partnership could not happen. J. Levenson, from a Jewish perspective, describes the Torah's importance for faith in terms of its ever-renewing summons and sustenance:

> There is, therefore, no voice more central to Judaism than the voice heard on Mt. Sinai. Sinai confronts everyone who would live as a Jew with an awesome choice, which, once encountered, cannot be evaded—the choice of whether to obey God or to stray from him, of whether to observe the commandments or to let them lapse. Ultimately the issue is whether God is or is not king, for there is no king without subjects, no suzerain without vassals. In short, Sinai demands that the Torah be taken with radical seriousness. But alongside the burden of choice lies a balm that soothes the pain of decision. The balm is the history of redemption, which grounds the commandments and insures that this would-be king is a gracious and loving lord and that to choose to obey him is not a leap into the absurd. The balm is the surprising love of YHWH for Israel, of a passionate groom for his bride, love ever fresh and never dulled by the frustrations of a stormy courtship. Mount Sinai is the intersection of love and law, of gift and demand, the link between a past together and a future together.[41]

Christians have typically taken a quite different approach to these books, viewing them, with the apostle Paul (for example, Gal. 3), as deadening law, not enlivening *tôrāh*, as a vehicle of curse, not blessing, and as something old and temporary that has now been superseded and replaced by the grace of Christ. Within Protestantism especially this negative view of "the Law" is associated with the idea that it was principally the priests in ancient Israel who were preoccupied with legalistic matters. The Protestant preference is for "prophetic religion." In terms of Reformation theology, the bias favors word over sacrament, faith over works, the grace-filled response to the Spirit over legalistic obedience to the law.

---

41. J. D. Levenson, *Sinai and Zion: An Entry Into the Jewish Bible* (San Francisco: Harper and Row, 1985), 86.

The reasons for this neglect and disparagement are many and complex, and I do not propose a detailed discussion here. But there can be no denying that the study of Israelite religion in the last century has contributed at least indirectly to a general unwillingness among Christians and others to regard the Torah as having a significant claim on the community of faith outside Judaism.

The direction for much of Protestant thinking about these matters was set by J. Wellhausen at the beginning of critical biblical scholarship in the late nineteenth century.[42] Wellhausen traced the origin of the Priestly texts (P) to the post-exilic period when, in his view, the priests took over the reins of religion from the prophets. Through their mistaken and excessive focus on rituals, the priests falsified and corrupted the authentic faith of Israel. In Wellhausen's view, Israel's authentic religion deteriorated into Judaism, a pale reflection of its former self, a lingering "ghost" of a body that had died.[43]

The influence of Wellhausen's negative assessment of the post-exilic period in general and of the Priestly tradition in particular is evident in the history of scholarship. Note the consistent tendency in studies of Israelite religion to view the monarchical period (the period of the prophets) as the setting for Israel's "high" religion, and everything else as either early and primitive or late and defective. In such "objective" assessments, as I have already suggested, there is no mistaking a certain Christian and decidedly Protestant bias.[44]

Wellhausen's influence has not been limited to the guild of biblical scholarship. Latent within his view of Priestly texts is a more serious disparagement of Judaism that has infected the very heart of the church. One particularly instructive early example of this infection is J. Colenso's 1873

42. The influence of Protestant bias in biblical scholarship has now been well documented. See, for example, J. H. Hayes and F. Prussner, *Old Testament Theology: Its History and Development* (Atlanta: John Knox Press, 1985), 274–75. For a Jewish perspective, see the collection of essays in J. D. Levenson, *The Hebrew Bible, the Old Testament, and Historical Criticism* (Louisville: Westminster/John Knox, 1993).

43. Note, e.g., the following quotes from Wellhausen's *Prolegomena to the History of Israel* (Gloucester, Mass.: Peter Smith, 1973). Concerning Priestly ritual: "The law thrusts itself in everywhere; it commands and blocks up the access to heaven; it regulates and sets up limits to the understanding of the divine working on earth. As far as it can, it takes the soul out of religion and spoils morality" (509). Concerning the written Torah as a measure of a dead religion: "Yet it is a thing which is likely to occur, that a body of traditional practice should only be written down when it is threatening to die out, and that a book should be, as it were, the ghost of a life which is closed" (405). These and similar disparaging observations about the religion of Judaism by Wellhausen and others are the subject of strong critique by J. D. Levenson in *The Hebrew Bible*, 1–32.

44. See above, chap. 1, p. 8, 12–13, 15–16.

Lectures on the Pentateuch and the Moabite Stone.[45] Colenso's work is espe-cially pertinent because, as the Bishop of Natal, he writes with the expressed intention of informing lay readers about the more important results of Pentateuchal criticism in his day. His goal is to educate those in the church "who desire to impart to their children an intelligent knowledge of the real nature of these books, which have filled all along, and still fill, so prominent a part in the religious education of the race."[46]

In Colenso's view, the most important product of Pentateuchal criticism is the "death-blow" it struck to the whole sacerdotal system conveyed by the Levitical laws in the Books of Exodus, Leviticus, and Numbers.[47] This ritu-alistic system, Colenso argues, is not of Mosaic origin—that is, of divine ori-gin. It imparts instead only the late, fictitious "pretensions of the very numerous body of priests, lording it over the consciences of the compara-tively small number of devoted laity."[48] To this Priestly "fraud," Colenso applies the words of Zechariah 13:3, "you speak lies in the name of the LORD." These "lies" have far-reaching and evil consequences for Christianity.[49] In Colenso's view, once the sacerdotal yoke was fastened upon the neck of the people,

> . . . true spiritual life became at last deadened in them, and so, when the Great Prophet came, they blinded their eyes and stopped their ears, that the Truth might not reach them, and the multitude urged on by the priests cried "Crucify him! Crucify him!," and "the voices of them and of the chief priests prevailed."[50]

Colenso's pointedly negative characterizations of the Priestly legacy— "pretensions," "fraud," "lies"—and his easy transition from the priests who perpetrated the corruption of the Old Testament to those who instigated the crucifixion of Jesus, presents all too clearly the sad rupture in the church's relationship with Judaism. The most extreme and tragic manifes-tation of this fracture in the communities of faith is the church's complic-ity in interpreting the Jewish legacy to the world not as blessing to be received and embraced with gratitude, but rather as a "question" that prompted the sick of soul to seek a "final solution."[51]

---

45. J. Colenso, *Lectures on the Pentateuch and the Moabite Stone,* 2nd ed. (London: Long-mans, Green, and Co., 1873).
46. Ibid., vii.
47. Ibid., 373.
48. Ibid.
49. Ibid., 346.
50. Ibid., 374. The biblical citation is from Luke 23:23.
51. Since the 1960s, the literature calling for a reassessment of Jewish-Christian relations has grown to enormous proportions. For a discussion that engages most of the relevant

In view of this sad legacy from some of the previous work on Israelite religion, one objective of the present study is to summon the church to a reappraisal of the Torah's importance for the community of faith, both Jewish and Christian. The biblical summons is to become a "priestly kingdom and a holy nation" (Exod. 19:6) that is committed to realizing the creational design for the whole of the cosmos "on earth as it is in heaven" (Matt. 6:10).

For this mission, the Torah's vision of worship is vitally important. But to receive this vision, we must open ourselves to the rich legacy of the Priestly tradition as preserved in the Pentateuch. We must be willing to receive this gift as *tôrāh,* as God's foundational instructions for covenant partnership. If the church is to embrace this gift fully, as an authentic expression of the biblical faith bequeathed to it, then a first step might be the ritual act that is perhaps most distinctive in Priestly theology: the painful and transforming act of confession and repentance.

2. If the church is to orient itself anew to the Torah's vision of worship, it must do more than revise its view of how the biblical witness describes what it means to be a people of God. It must make a second adjustment: it must learn *how to read ritual texts and how to appropriate ritual theology.* Much of modern critical biblical study, especially as practiced by Protestants, has displayed a negative, often hostile, attitude toward ritual. Reformation theology and the epistemological assumptions of the Enlightenment combined in different ways to identify ritual as a primitive form of religious expression that focused on body rather than soul, prescribed rules, often irrational, rather than free and reasoned ethical behavior. With the collapse of Enlightenment paradigms of investigation, however, recent studies concerning the nature and character of ritual have opened new possibilities for reassessing the importance of the ritual literature in the Bible.[52]

F. Gorman has shown that it is not sufficient to read ritual texts with the same methodologies normally applied to narrative texts. With ritual texts the focus cannot be exclusively on the *text*—that is, on the author, setting, form, or transmission of the linguistic message—for this too often disregards the meaning of the *ritual* that the text conveys. Ritual texts require ritual analysis, not just textual analysis. As Gorman puts it, "The world of ritual is a world of gestural construal, a world enacted, a world bodied

bibliography, see C. M. Williamson, *A Guest in the House of Israel: Post-Holocaust Theology* (Louisville: John Knox, 1993).

52. For a survey of the place of ritual in the history of biblical study, see F. H. Gorman Jr., "Ritual Studies and Biblical Studies: Assessment of the Past; Prospects for the Future," *Semeia* 67 (1994), 13–35. This entire issue of *Semeia* is devoted to ritual studies and includes a helpful annotated bibliography of seminal works.

forth, a world that exists in anticipation of ritual and a world that is actualized and brought forth in, by, and through the ritual itself."[53] The interpreter of ritual texts, therefore, must broaden the exegetical task beyond traditional historical-critical concerns. What is required is an imaginative construal of both the rituals described in the text—how they might have been enacted, how enactment might have functioned in society—and the worldview within which the rituals have meaning.[54]

Such a view understands ritual as both a symbolic action and a mode of theological reflection. As symbolic act, ritual has the capacity both to *mirror* and to *transform* a society's worldview and ethos. In this connection Gorman locates Priestly rituals within the larger context of Priestly creation theology.[55] This theology asserts that God has endowed creation with a recognizable order and structure. Priestly rituals assume the reality of this order and seek both to reflect it and to enact it symbolically—for example, by correlating the divinely established boundaries between order and disorder with ritually observed distinctions between the holy and the common, the clean and the unclean. Priestly rituals do not simply reinforce existing assumptions about order and structure. They also alter established ways of seeing and living in the world by providing models for beliefs and behavior that have the potential to bring the regnant social order into conformity with God's design. For example, the annual purgation of the sanctuary on the Day of Atonement (Lev. 16) symbolically restores both the individual and the world to the founded order of creation.[56] In short, rituals are never merely formal actions, offered simply for the sake of the acts themselves. They are a means of "world construction,"[57] a means of enacting, maintaining, and where necessary recreating the world of God's design.

53. Ibid., 22.

54. Gorman recognizes that the use of imagination in reconstructing ancient rituals is both required and problematic. On the one hand, biblical scholars are *interpreters* of *texts*. They can neither participate in the ritual they study nor observe it directly. From this perspective they can do little else but *imagine* how a ritual may have been enacted and how it may have functioned. On the other hand, fieldwork studies and ethnographic methods developed by anthropologists offer valuable data that can be utilized by biblical scholars in cross-cultural research. When ritual study becomes an interdisciplinary endeavor, therefore, imaginative construal of ancient priestly rituals need not be fanciful or capricious. See further, "Ritual Studies and Biblical Studies," ibid. 20–22; J. J. Pilch, "Response to Frank H. Gorman Jr. 'Ritual Studies and Biblical Studies,'" *Semeia* 67 (1994), 38–39.

55. Gorman, *The Ideology of Ritual*; idem, "Priestly Rituals of Founding: Time, Space, and Status," in *History and Interpretation: Essays in Honour of John H. Hayes*, eds. M. P. Graham, W. Brown, and J. K. Kuan (Sheffield: JSOT Press, 1993), 47–64.

56. On Priestly rituals that serve to "found," "maintain," and "restore" the created order, see the discussion below, chap. 6, 150–65.

57. Gorman, *The Ideology of Ritual*, 59.

But religious rituals are more than symbolic acts of social construction. They are also a primary means by which a community of faith engages in theological reflection. On this point, Gorman has called attention to an important contribution that ritual can make to traditional, especially Protestant, ways of doing theology. He observes that "human existence is marked as much by enactment as by thought and reflection."[58] Protestant theology has typically favored more cognitive approaches to religious truth, emphasizing mind over body, rational thought over prescribed action.[59] In this cognitive realm religious practitioners learn to be at home with the abstract world of theological ideas and inner spirituality. Ritual, however, invites "embodied" reflection. The knowing and the learning come from performing the ritual act itself. In ritual activity, persons take a concrete stand in the world, and by engaging in very specific "flesh and blood" acts, they engage *mind and body* in a drama of teaching and learning. In this sense, rituals may be understood as a liturgical form of exegesis, a way for the community gathered in worship to strive for clarity in its thinking *and* in its execution of God's design for the world.

Summary

R. Price observed that in his struggle to create a new self within his given world, what he most needed to read was some story, however distant, that might parallel his situation. He needed "some honest report from a similar war, with a final list of hard facts learned and offered unvarnished."[60] We might expect that, for the citizens of Yehud, the Torah offered just such a report of "hard facts learned." The political reality was that Yehud was a Persian colony, subject to the imposition of alien directives backed up by imperial power. The canonized Pentateuch, assembled and promulgated with support from the Persian Empire, is but one evidence of the Persian influence on the internal matters of Yehud.

And yet the Torah also conveys a vision not confined by such "hard facts." In various ways, the Torah asserts that the reach of Persian politics was not the same as its grasp.[61] The Torah conveys a vision of worship grounded in the liturgy of God's creative acts, and fitted for constructing

58. Gorman, "Ritual Studies and Biblical Studies," 24.

59. On the specific ways the Protestant Reformation functioned to produce an ideological perspective that was hostile toward ritual, see ibid., 14–20.

60. Price, *A Whole New Life*, 181.

61. For an assessment of the fundamental distinction between the ideal political ambitions and agendas of rulers and the ends actually accomplished, see C. Geertz, "Politics Past, Politics Present: Some Notes on the Uses of Anthropology in Understanding the New States," *Interpretation of Cultures*, 327–41.

another world in which God's cosmic commitments might be celebrated, sustained, and restored. It is a vision that emerges out of a concrete world of cultural and social determinants, yet a vision that the community of faith may regard as inviolable by the dissonant realities of any historical period.[62] It is a vision that births the historical community of faith called Israel, and that summons all who would embrace the biblical testimony into a shared community of faith. Commitment to this vision, the Torah asserts, holds out the real hope that the world as designed by God and the world as lived in may indeed one day be the same world. This Torah vision, sketched here only in brief terms, will be the subject of part 2.

62. Cf. Geertz, "Religion as a Cultural System," 112.

PART TWO

THE TORAH'S VISION:
"YOU SHALL BE FOR ME
A PRIESTLY KINGDOM
AND A HOLY NATION"

4.

CREATION'S LITURGY
AND THE COSMIC COVENANT

T HE TORAH'S VISION BEGINS WITH A PICTURE OF GOD, THE WORLD, AND
humankind that derives from a time before there was an Adam and Eve
or an Israel, before there were earthly kingdoms ruled by Canaanites, Babylonians, or Persians. It is a vision of a world in which every object and
every person exists in happy accord with God's grand creational design.
When the exigencies of history and the frailties of human nature distort
this design and threaten to nullify its importance, the Torah's vision will
continue to beckon towards possibilities that transcend those limitations
and failures. Whether at Sinai or in the plains of Moab, in Jerusalem or in
Yehud, the people defined by this vision are to know that the world God
created remains possible and attainable.

The Torah's vision begins with the liturgy of creation. In Genesis 1–2 this
liturgy proclaims that the world God brings into being is an *orderly world,*
created and shaped by God's purposive design, a *ritual world* in which the
liturgy of creation might be sustained (Gen. 1:1—2:4a), and a *relational
world* in which God invites humankind to share responsibility for the
maintenance, development, and restoration of God's purposive designs for
the universe (Gen. 2:4b-25). In the liturgy of Genesis 1–2, the crucial intersection between the ordered world *qua* ritual world and the relational
world is the seventh day (Gen. 2:1-3). Foundational for the precept of the
sabbath, this day marks the merging of God's creative design in the heavens and God's creative hopes for humankind on earth. It is the day on
which the work of "the heavens and the earth . . . and all their multitude"
(Gen. 2:1) receives God's blessing.

The liturgy of creation, then, is the summons to celebrate and participate in the ordered, ritual, and relational world that God calls into existence. But it is also the proclamation that the world of God's design and
hopes is a *fragile world,* open to the best and the worst that the human partner brings to God's designs. In Genesis 6–9 the Torah's vision acknowledges

that humankind's wickedness can evoke God's grief (Gen. 6:5-6); that human disorder can subvert God's orderly cosmos (Gen. 6:5—8:19); and that nothing short of a cosmic commitment from God is sufficient for restoring the world to God's creative designs (Gen. 9:8-11). In the midst of such a candid vision, the Torah inserts a pointed reminder of the importance of worship: God restores the cosmic order, but Noah's act of worship (Gen. 8:20-21) marks the transition in God's heart from pain to promise.

With the cosmic order restored, the Torah's vision turns to restoring the relational world of God's creative design. Just as Noah marks the transition to God's cosmic covenant, so Abraham and Sarah serve as the conduit for God's renewed commitment to partnership with humankind. And just as Noah's ritual of speechless thanks serves as the catalyst for divine commitment, so the range of responses offered by Abraham and Sarah—submission and protest, laughter and liturgy—anticipates both the promise and the plight of the journey that lies ahead.

The following pages discuss in detail four aspects of the Torah's vision: the liturgy of creation, the cosmic commitment of God, the everlasting promise of relationship, and the paradigms of worship represented by Noah and Abraham and Sarah.

Genesis 1–2: The Liturgy of Creation

Traditional critical interpretations of Genesis 1 and 2 have focused on the stylistic and theological differences between the Priestly account (1:1–2:4a) and the Yahwistic account (2:4b-25). These differences are widely recognized and need not be listed here. It is sufficient to summarize the general consensus by observing that the Priestly text operates mostly on a vertical axis and focuses on God's unassisted creation of the entire cosmos, including human beings. The J account, by contrast, traverses primarily a horizontal plane and concentrates on God's intimate creation of humankind and more specifically on the foundational relationships of human existence. In short, the emphasis in Genesis 1 is on God and the cosmos, in Genesis 2, on human existence within God's world.[1]

In the Torah's aggregate vision of creation, however, the critical differences noted above are allowed to stand side by side. They are not collapsed into a single, conflated version, as happens, for example, in the two accounts of the flood, nor are they isolated one from another, as is the cus-

---

1. D. A. Knight summarizes: "In the one [Genesis 1], we see the cosmos in its fullness and breadth; the other [Genesis 2] portrays human existence in its complexity and depth" ("Cosmogony and Order in the Hebrew Tradition," *Cosmogony and Ethical Order*, eds. R. W. Lovin and F. E. Reynolds [Chicago: University of Chicago Press, 1985], 144).

tom in critical study. Instead, the two accounts, with their distinctive perspectives on God, cosmos, and human existence, are allowed to interact with one another.

The composite vision of Genesis 1–2 is greater than the sum of its individual parts.[2] It is a vision that celebrates both the boundaries between heaven and earth and the relational ties that join the two. It is a celebration of both the meticulous order of the cosmic design, and of the manifold ways that order yields to interplay, precision to change, divine fiat to human response. Together, Genesis 1 and 2 celebrate the Hebraic vision of a God who moves between the "heavens and the earth" (2:1) so that there might be a reciprocal movement between the "earth and the heavens" (2:4b). In the composite vision that connects God, cosmos, and humankind, the critical intersection occurs on the seventh day (2:1-3), which celebrates the possibility that the grandeur of God's cosmic designs may be matched by the commitment of creation to live in harmony within God's world. This aggregate vision may be conceptualized as follows:

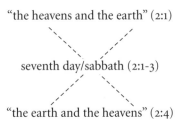

"the heavens and the earth" (2:1)

seventh day/sabbath (2:1-3)

"the earth and the heavens" (2:4)

Several aspects of this aggregate liturgy of creation require further exposition.

A Liturgy of Order, Not Origin

The liturgy of creation celebrates the order, more than the origin, of the cosmos. Both creation accounts affirm that the entire cosmos and everything within it has its ultimate origin in God: "In the beginning God" (Gen. 1:1); "When YHWH made" (Gen. 2:4b). Apart from this central, yet rather

---

2. A number of studies, seeking to explicate a canonical perspective on Gen. 1 and 2, have drawn attention to the semantic and theological links between the P and J creation accounts. For what follows, I have found particularly instructive a number of studies by T. E. Fretheim: *The Suffering of God*, OBT (Philadelphia: Fortress, 1984), 72–75; "The Reclamation of Creation: Redemption and Law in Exodus," *Int* 45 (1991), 54–65; "Creator, Creature, and Co-Creation in Genesis 1–2," *Word and World*, Supplement Series 1 (1992), 11–20. Fretheim's several probes find their fullest exposition in his commentary, "Genesis," *The New Interpreter's Bible*, vol. 1 (Nashville: Abingdon, 1994). See further, M. Welker, "What Is Creation? Rereading Genesis 1 and 2," *TToday* (1991), 56–71, on whom Fretheim relies in part.

oblique, assertion that God stands at the beginning of all that comes into existence, the biblical creation stories have little interest in delving into the mystery of ultimate origins. There is no concern with the time before this God or the time before the creation that God summoned forth.[3] Rather, the overriding concern is with the order and harmony of God's creation at the beginning of time. The concern to present creation as orderly and harmonious is expressed in several ways. The structuring of the process into a pattern of seven parts emphasizes the central idea of symmetry and perfection. There are seven (Hebrew) words in the opening announcement (1:1), seven succeeding sections delineating God's creative acts (1:3-5, 6-8, 9-13, 14-19, 20-23, 24-31; 2:1-4a), seven repetitions of the "Let there be" formula for effecting creation (1:3, 6, 9, 11, 14, 20, 24) and seven proclamations of divine approval: "it was good" (1:4, 10, 12, 18, 21, 25) and "it was very good" (1:31).[4]

Within this seven-part structure, as Westermann notes, is a sequence of divine "command accounts": introduction ("And God said"), command ("Let . . ."), completion of the creative act ("And it was so"), evaluation ("it was good"), and temporal framework ("And it was evening").[5] By divine fiat the process of creation unfolds, with each day's events presented more expansively than the preceding day's. The progressive movement peaks on the sixth day, which requires the most elaboration of all (1:24-31).

Within this seven-day pattern, there is an inner symmetry and a hierarchical ordering that further emphasize the design and perfection of God's creation. The events unfold in parallel groups of three days each.[6] On days

3. Regarding the Hebrew Bible's disinterest in pushing beyond the basic facts of God's creation, S. Talmon observes that in Jewish thinking the first word of the creation stories offers both an invitation and a guide for interpreting these texts: "In reply to the question why does the Hebrew Bible begin with the second letter of the alphabet, the *bet* in the initial word *běrēšît,* it is stated: the *bet* is 'open' on its left side, but 'closed' on its right. This implies (for the Hebrew reader) that one may investigate what follows upon the first letter of the creation story, but one should refrain from exploring what precedes it. The Sages do not delve into questions about [what] was before the world was created. They never ask 'what is above, what is beneath, what was before time was created, what will be thereafter?'" (*m. Hag.* 2.1; *t. Hag.* 2.1 177c) ("The Biblical Understanding of Creation and the Human Commitment," *Ex Auditu* 3 [1987], 107).

4. The heptadic pattern in Gen. 1, and its structural and theological importance for the P creation account, is frequently noted. See, for example, C. Westermann, *Genesis 1–11: A Commentary* (Minneapolis: Augsburg, 1984), 88–90; N. M. Sarna, *The JPS Torah Commentary: Genesis* (Philadelphia, New York, Jerusalem: The Jewish Publication Society, 1989), 4; U. Cassuto, *A Commentary on the Book of Genesis, Part I: From Adam to Noah* (Jerusalem: Magnes, 1978), 12–15.

5. Westermann, *Genesis 1–11,* 84.

6. The inner symmetry of the six days of creation is widely recognized, with some variations, by a number of commentators; e.g., Cassuto, *A Commentary on the Book of Genesis: Part*

FIGURE 4.1
In the beginning God . . .

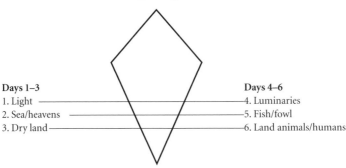

Days 1–3   Days 4–6
1. Light —————————————4. Luminaries
2. Sea/heavens ————————————5. Fish/fowl
3. Dry land—————————————6. Land animals/humans

Day 7   The sabbath of God

1–3 God performs three acts of division and separation that summon into existence the basic elements of the created order: Day 1, the separation of light from darkness (v. 4); Day 2, the separation of the waters under the firmament from the waters above the firmament (v. 7); Day 3, the separation of the dry land from the waters under the firmament (v. 9).[7] On days 4–6 God summons forth the appropriate objects and life forms that will inhabit the respective elements of the created order: Day 4, the heavenly bodies that augment the boundaries between light and darkness, day and night (vv. 14-18); Day 5, the water and air creatures that populate heaven and sea (vv. 20-21); and Day 6, the land animals and humankind, whose domain is the dry land (vv. 24-26). The culmination of creation is the seventh day, a day set off from the previous six days of work. It is a day of divine rest and cosmic celebration occasioned by the completion of "the heavens and earth . . . and all their multitude" (2:1).

The structure of the text resembles a diamond shape (figure 4.1), with God at the initial and culminating points, and the six days of creation in perfect symmetry with each other.

In each group of days (1–3, 4–6) there is both a horizontal symmetry and a vertical hierarchy. The symmetry shows the connection of the created order to its respective life-forms and objects (light-luminaries; sea/heavens-

I, 16–18; Fishbane, *Text and Texture*, 10–11; Blenkinsopp, *The Pentateuch*, 60–61; Sarna, *Genesis*, 4.

7. The specific term used in days one and two to describe the act of separation, *bādal*, is lacking in the account of day three, although it is likely implied there. See Westermann, *Genesis 1–11*, 86–87, 120–21.

fish/fowl; land-creatures). The hierarchy shows God's relationship with heaven, earth, and humankind.[8]

A Liturgy in Celebration of Division, but Not Estrangement

In the liturgy of creation, God's orderly and harmonious world rests on the basic ideas of division, separation, and distinction. Three basic acts of separation distinguish light from darkness, heavens from the earth, terrestrial waters from dry land. Implicit also is God's act of separating order and chaos, distinguishing man and woman, and dividing ordinary days from days—six days of work from a seventh day that is "sanctified" or "set apart" (qādaš).

In this conceptualization of creation, the Torah's vision proclaims that God has endowed the cosmos with certain divisions and boundaries that are essential to observe and maintain if the created order is to continue as God intends. When these are not recognized, when the order inherent within creation is breached or broken, then creation is threatened with confusion, perhaps even with collapse.

In this sense, as H. H. Schmid has recognized, there is a close relationship between the cosmic order and the ethical-social order of creation.[9] In the Torah's vision of creation, as in most other ancient Near Eastern cosmogonies, the order God endows on the cosmos extends to all aspects of life. In Schmid's words, "Law, nature, and politics are only aspects of one comprehensive order of creation."[10] In Israel, the divine ordering of creation at the cosmic level endows the social order of human existence with a corresponding ethic of "righteousness" (ṣedeq/ṣĕdāqāh). Just as the cosmos is ordered into a harmony of divisions and boundaries, so, in Israel, to be "righteous" means to do justice to the harmony inherent in the cosmic order.

In the Hebrew Bible, one usually associates the summons to righteousness with the prophets. But as Fretheim has observed, the cosmos is itself endowed with "creational demands" that summon Israel to join with God

---

8. Cf. Sarna (Genesis, 4) for a somewhat different conceptualization of this hierarchical ordering.

9. See H. H. Schmid, Gerechtigkeit als Weltordnung: Hintergrund und Geschichte als alttestamentlichen Gerechtigkeitsbegriffes (Tubingen: J. C. B. Mohr, 1968); idem, "Creation, Righteousness, and Salvation: 'Creation Theology' as the Broad Horizon of Biblical Theology," in Creation in the Old Testament, ed. B. W. Anderson (Philadelphia: Fortress; London: SPCK, 1984 [1973]), 102–17. See further the very helpful survey of the cosmogonic basis for ethics by Knight, "Cosmogony and Order," 133–57, and the discussion of the role of the heavenly council in its specific association with cosmogonic order in P. D. Miller, "Cosmology and World Order in the Old Testament. The Divine Council as Cosmic-Political Symbol," HBT 9 (1987), 53–77.

10. Schmid, "Creation, Righteousness and Salvation," 105.

in actualizing on earth the cosmic harmony of God's intent.[11] The commands to "Be fruitful and multiply, . . . fill the earth and subdue it" (Gen. 1:28) and "to work it and watch over it" (Gen. 2:15) envision a world where human initiative and God's design coincide, where Israel joins with God in maintaining *and developing*[12] what God has created.[13] Israel's ethic, therefore, is grounded not on asceticism or removal from the created order, but on immersion within this created order for the sake of cosmic harmony and justice on earth.[14]

In view of God's endowment of the cosmos with orderly divisions and boundaries, it is important to stress that in the liturgy of creation *division does not mean estrangement*. Here the aggregate vision of Genesis 1–2 helps to correct a misdirected assumption about God's designs for the created order. Treated separately, Genesis 1 and 2 have traditionally been construed as affirmations of two ideas: God's independent (or, in religious terms, transcendent) and unassisted creation of the world (Genesis 1); and humankind's dependent and totally passive receipt of divine imperatives (Genesis 2). Such a reading presumes that God's design for the world entails a complete and impenetrable wall of separation between God and creation. God is sovereign Creator; everything that God creates, human beings included, is merely the recipient of divine initiatives. As M. Welker has noted, such a reading of the creation texts has fortified, especially in the Judeo-Christian traditions of Western culture, a "simple pattern of power."[15] God holds all power, creation is designed merely as the object of God's power.

In the vision of Genesis 1–2, however, such a simple view of God's cosmic design is inadequate. Close attention to creation's liturgy makes it clear that in the world God creates, God chooses to remain open and responsive to acts of "creaturely creativity."[16] God and creation are portrayed as engaged in a relationship of mutual creativity: God separates and divides (1:4, 7), *and* the firmament, which God has already created, also engages in

11. Fretheim, "The Reclamation of Creation," 363.

12. When God evaluates the world as "good" (*ṭôb*), this assessment does not imply an abstract, fixed idea of perfection or completion. As Westermann has noted, the word *ṭôb* is used throughout the Hebrew Bible primarily with a functional sense, i.e. "good for . . ." (*Genesis 1–11*, 166–67); cf. Knight, "Cosmogony and Order," 145. Fretheim has expanded on this understanding by stressing that in God's "good" world, God assigns an important role to humankind in "bringing the world along toward its fullest possible potential" ("Creator, Creature, and Co-Creation," 15); cf. "The Reclamation of Creation," 358.

13. On this point see especially, Welker, "What Is Creation?" 60–64.

14. Fretheim, "The Reclamation of Creation," 362.

15. Welker, "What Is Creation?" 59.

16. Fretheim, "Creator, Creature, and Co-Creation," 18; cf. Welker, "What Is Creation?" 62.

acts of separation (1:6; cf. 1:18); God rules, *and* the heavenly bodies rule in their respective domains (1:16); God brings forth by divine fiat (1:11, 24), *and* the plants, animals, and human beings bring forth out of their own capacity to reproduce (1:12; cf. 1:22, 28).[17]

Genesis 1 and 2 also portray humankind as having a distinctive participation in the creative process. Fretheim has been particularly attentive to the creative role assigned to human beings in God's cosmic design.[18] Two "creational demands" commission human beings to the task of being God's co-creators. The first (1:26-28) assigns to humankind, and only to humankind, the task of "imaging" God in the world (v. 26),[19] then develops this task with reference to creaturely "dominion" over the earth's resources (*rdh*; vv. 26, 28). The language of dominion, as is now widely recognized, conveys the notion of a king's power and responsibility to secure the safety and welfare of his subjects.[20] By analogy, humans are commissioned to act like God, that is, to display the right combination of royal power and gentle compassion so that whatever has been entrusted to them might prosper and realize its fullest potential.

With the second command (2:15) God gives to humankind the responsibility "to till" or "to serve" *('ābad)* the ground and "to keep," "guard," or "protect" *(šāmar)* it. While the responsibility is much the same as in the first command—to care for and develop the earth—its actualization is somewhat different. In the first instance, humans image God as kings; in the second, they image God as "servants," as those who place themselves at the service of the good of creation. In its pre-creation state, the earth lacked such servants (cf. 2:5). Only when God summons forth the servants, and only when the servants take up their commission, can the earth attain its maximum potential.[21]

Coupled with these creational demands, humans also image God in the act of naming (2:18-23).[22] God names the day, the heavens, the earth, and the sea (1:5, 8, 10), thereby determining their essential natures and calling them into harmony with their unique relationships to the Creator. Just so,

---

17. Cf. Welker, "What Is Creation?" 62.

18. See the bibliography cited above, n. 2.

19. Brueggemann suggests that Gen. 1:26 is to be interpreted as a "counter-assertion" to the temptation to idolatry. There is only one way in which God determines to be imaged in the world: through humankind. (*Genesis: A Bible Commentary for Teaching and Preaching* [Atlanta: John Knox, 1982], 32).

20. In addition to the standard commentaries, see, for example, J. Limburg, "The Responsibility of Royalty: Genesis 1–11 and the Care of the Earth," *WW* 11 (1991), 124–30; idem, "What Does It Mean to `Have Dominion Over the Earth'?" *Dialogue* 10 (1971), 221–23.

21. Cf. Fretheim, "Creator, Creature, and Co-Creation," 15.

22. Ibid., 15–19.

God relinquishes the creative act of naming to human beings when it comes to determining their essential relationships with other living creatures.[23] Where human relations are concerned, the text portrays God as presenting various possibilities and leaving their naming to the creative decision of the human being. What the human being decides, God accepts, even if it means that God must continue to present new possibilities for companionship until the human being decides what is most appropriate.[24]

In these several ways, then, the liturgy of Genesis 1–2 affirms that God has endowed creation with categories that are internally differentiated but also interdependent.[25] It is a liturgy that celebrates order, not estrangement. The cosmic order of Genesis 1 clearly affirms that God has freely crafted a world that is "very good" for the accomplishment of the divine will. It clearly affirms that in this created world, God has installed divisions and boundaries that order and sustain God's designs. Genesis 2 asserts with equal clarity that God has endowed the cosmos with a divine imperative: "heaven and earth . . . and all its multitude" should live in harmony with God's creative design. Within that design is clearly a hierarchical ordering, a preeminence of status and power, of autonomy and holiness, that resides in God to a degree not manifest in creation. But just as clearly, Genesis 1 and 2, in their aggregate vision, celebrate the connectedness of God and creation, the cooperation of the Creator with that which is creaturely, and the divine commitment to adjust cosmic designs in keeping with God's ongoing interaction with the world.

In this ordered and relational world, the seventh/sabbath day crucially intersects God's creative hopes and humankind's creative possibilities. This day marks simultaneously an ending and a beginning, a bridge between God's first and second creational demands (1:26; 2:16-18)—the day of rest for God and all God's creation that signals the transition between imaging God's creative act as royalty and imaging it as servant. To this seventh/sabbath day—and the ritual world for which it is foundational—the discussion now turns.

---

23. Blenkinsopp has noted that divine naming ceases after the earth comes into being, thereafter to be assigned to humans as part of the task of "subduing and dominating." (*The Pentateuch*, 60).

24. Fretheim notes (contra P. A. Trible, *God and the Rhetoric of Sexuality* [OBT; Philadelphia: Fortress, 1978], 94–105) that "naming," especially where *'ādam* names the woman (Gen. 2:23) does not imply the authority or the domination of male over female ("Creator, Creature, and Co-Creation," 17); cf. G. Ramsey, "Is Name-Giving an Act of Domination in Genesis 2:23 and Elsewhere?" *CBQ* 50 (1988), 24–35.

25. On this point see especially Welker, "What Is Creation?" 64–69.

A Liturgy Foundational for a Ritual World

The discussion thus far has repeatedly used the words "liturgy" and "ritual" to describe the Torah's vision of creation. The assumption behind this description must now be spelled out. In what sense is it appropriate to speak of creation as a liturgy or as a "ritual world"?

In pursuit of this question, I am indebted to the work of F. Gorman.[26] Building on the work of cultural anthropologists such as M. Douglas, C. Geertz, and others, Gorman focuses on the "ideology" of rituals by concentrating on their sociocultural contexts. Such an approach has two distinct advantages over most previous efforts to interpret the ritual texts in the Hebrew Bible.

First, it helps to clarify ritual as something more than simply a formal rite or practice, and show instead that it is a *symbolic act of social construction*.[27] In Gorman's approach the interpretive interest in ritual shifts from the usual preoccupation with the *text* that conveys the ritual—for example, its presumed author or historical setting—to the *ritual* itself, and more specifically, to the world of meaning that shapes and is shaped by the ritual.[28] In religious societies, this world of meaning is the particular view of the world order and the particular system of conduct that is understood to be congruent with that order and necessary for its continuance.[29] Ritual, then, becomes a primary means not only of maintaining and sustaining the order of the world, but also, when necessary, of repairing and restoring that world order when it is broken or distorted.[30] Inasmuch as the Torah begins with the enunciation of a distinctive world order in which God's crowning act of creation is the seventh/sabbath day, it anticipates that the ritual of worship, in whatever specific forms it might be manifest, will be empowered both to sustain and to redeem the world of God's design.

The second advantage of Gorman's approach is that he has shown ritual to be a *primary means for a community of faith to do theology*, not simply a symbolic act of social construction.[31] Ritual goes beyond being a series of social acts that identify primary societal structures and the meanings people or communities give them. It is a means of seeking clarity with respect to God, the world God has created, and human existence within this world.

---

26. F. H. Gorman Jr., *The Ideology of Ritual: Space, Time, and Status in the Priestly Theology* (Sheffield: JSOT Press, 1990). Other helpful studies of Israelite ritual include: M. Haran, *Temples and Temple Service in Ancient Israel* (Oxford: Clarendon, 1978); P. P. Jensen, *Graded Holiness: A Guide to the Priestly Conception of the World*, JOSTSup 106 (Sheffield: JSOT Press, 1992).

27. Gorman, *Ideology of Ritual*, 22–25; cf. 59.

28. Ibid., 15.

29. Ibid., 16–18.

30. Ibid., 28–30.

31. Ibid., 59–60.

Here Gorman's view of ritual as "act" or "performance" helps to make clear that what takes place in ritual is at heart an interaction between the one(s) offering the ritual and the one(s) for whom or to whom it is offered.[32] Ritual is a form of communication. Something is articulated, something is heard and received. In ritual, the lines of interaction are multiple and complex. There is an interaction between the world of meaning that gives rise to the ritual, and the performative act that seeks to respond meaningfully to that world. There is an interaction between theological assertions and assumptions about the world God has created, and theological reflections and critiques about the world as experienced. And most dramatically, in the ritual world there is an interaction between God and humankind.

In all these interactive junctures the drama of ritual can be a means of establishing, sustaining, and, when necessary, transforming the status[33] of the persons and the objects who make up the ritual world, including God. The drama of ritual, thus conceived, is no less than the drama of dialogue with God. In a world order where God elects to be present both as Creator and as Interactor with creation, the ritual holds out the possibility for theological reflection of the most consequential sort.

Gorman's proposal that ritual is both a means of world construction and theological reflection fortifies the suggestion that Genesis 1–2 constitutes a "liturgy of creation." The most distinctive and obvious feature of this liturgy is its arrangement of the creation into a heptadic pattern, a liturgical week,[34] crowned by the seventh/sabbath day. The structuring of the creative process into a seven-part schema has been noted above. The climax of this heptadic pattern occurs in the seventh section (2:2-3a), which is devoted to the seventh day. The heart of this section, as Cassuto has seen, contains three parallel lines of seven words each. Each line has two parts, the first of which ends with the expression "the seventh day." Cassuto's translation shows this emphasis nicely:[35]

> And since God was finished on the seventh day / with His work which He had done,
>
> He abstained on the seventh day / from all His work which He had done.
>
> So God blessed the seventh day / and hallowed it.

---

32. Ibid., 20–22.

33. On the concern with "status" within a ritual system, see ibid., 59.

34. Blenkinsopp, *The Pentateuch*, 61.

35. Cassuto, *Genesis: Part I*, 61. Cf. J. D. Levenson, *Creation and the Persistence of Evil: The Jewish Drama of Divine Omnipotence* (San Francisco: Harper and Row, 1988), 67.

It is the seventh day, then, that holds the key to the liturgy of creation. But note that the Torah's language at this point focuses on the *seventh day* (*yôm hašĕbîʿî*), not strictly on the sabbath (*šabbāt*). The institution of the sabbath comes clearly into view only at Sinai (Exod. 20:8-11), at which time the observance of the seventh day as the sabbath day becomes the crowning act of the construction of the tabernacle (Exod. 31:12-17).[36] Genesis 1–2 is but the overture to the sabbath institution, the constitutive vision that understands sabbath to be rooted in God's cosmic design.[37]

A good deal of biblical interpretation evaluates the seventh day as an ending point in God's creative acts, a kind of climax that is marked by rest, solemnity, and divine remoteness. The oft-quoted comments of R. Pettazzoni, who has analyzed the motif of the "rest" of creator gods in ancient Near Eastern cosmogonies, is typical of this view:

> It may . . . be the case that the *otiositas* ["rest," "leisure"] itself belongs to the essential nature of creative Beings, and is in a way the complement of their creative activity. The world made and the cosmos established, the Creator's work is as good as done. Any further work on his part would be not only superfluous but possibly dangerous, since any change in the cosmos might allow it to fall back into chaos.[38]

As Levenson has noted, such an interpretation leaves the impression that on the seventh day God withdraws "in a state of mellow euphoria, benignly fading out of the world that he has finished and pronounced to be 'very good.'"[39]

In the Torah's liturgy of creation, however, the seventh day represents a much more dynamic interchange between God and creation than is usually noticed. In the aggregate vision of Genesis 1–2, the seventh/sabbath day marks simultaneously both an ending and a beginning. The diagram below (figure 4.2) helps to conceptualize the important transitional role assigned to sabbath in God's created order.

36. This and other connections in the Torah's vision between the creation of the world and the creation of the sanctuary will receive further attention in chap. 5.

37. Levenson notes that although the word "sabbath" is lacking in the Genesis account of creation, the *idea* of sabbath is very much present in the theology of the creation. He observes that throughout the Hebrew Bible, whenever the sabbath is mentioned, it is defined as the seventh day. With this opening statement of the seventh day as the foreword to the Torah's vision, "[i]t is fair to say that the text of the Hebrew Bible in the last analysis forbids us to speak of the theology of creation without sustained attention to the sabbatical institution" (*Creation and the Persistence of Evil*, 100).

38. R. Pettazzoni, *Essays on the History of Religions* (Leiden: Brill, 1954), 32. For discussion and critique of Pettazzoni's comments with respect to the biblical creation accounts, see Westermann, *Genesis 1–11*, 167–69; Levenson, *Creation and the Persistence of Evil*, 109–11.

39. Levenson, *Creation and the Persistence of Evil*, 109.

FIGURE 4.2

The divine work of creation (Gen. 1:1-31)	⟷	Seventh day/sabbath (Gen. 2:1-4a)	⟷	All new and future creations (Gen. 2:4b-25)
"the heavens and the earth" (2:4a)		The transition between the end of God's work of creation and the beginning of creaturely creativity		"the earth and the heavens" (2:4b)
		"God rested from all the work which he had creatively made (*bārā' 'elōhîm la 'ašôt*)"[1] (2:3)		

1. For this translation, see Cassuto, *A Commentary on the Book of Genesis. Part I*, 60.

Certainly the seventh day marks a culmination in the divine creation process. It is a day "hallowed," that is, "set apart" *(qādaš)* or lifted up from the previous six days by a number of distinctions. It is a day of "rest," not a day of work. On the seventh day there is no divine activity, apart from the "special form of inactivity which is the biblical sabbath."[40] It is a day totally blessed, endowed with a sanctity that distinguishes it from the blessing common to the specific works of creation on the fifth and sixth days.[41] Unlike the previous days, the seventh day is simply announced.[42] There is no mention of morning or evening, no mention of a beginning or an ending. The suggestion is that the primordial seventh day exists in perpetuity, a sacred day that cannot be abrogated by the limitations common to the rest of the created order.[43]

But for all its hallowed distinctiveness, the seventh day is as much the liturgical beginning-point of creation as it is its culmination. The seventh/sabbath day is, as previously noted, the bridge between what has been and what is to be. It stands at the intersection between heaven and earth (Gen. 1:1-31) and what will subsequently happen on earth (Gen. 2:4b-25). It

40. N-E. A. Andreasen, *The Old Testament Sabbath: A Traditio-Historical Approach* (Missoula, Mont.: SBL, 1972), 185–86; cf. Levenson, *Creation and the Persistence of Evil*, 110–11.

41. Cf. M. Fishbane, *Text and Texture: Close Readings of Selected Biblical Texts* (New York: Schocken Books, 1979), 9.

42. Cf. Levenson, *Creation and the Persistence of Evil*, 109.

43. On the speciality of the seventh day's blessing, see Westermann, *Genesis 1–11*, 171–72; Sarna, *Genesis*, 14; Cassuto, *Genesis: Part I*, 64–68.

hinges the two creational demands of God: humankind's stewardship of the earth's resources in royal terms (Gen. 1:28) and the summons to be servants (Gen. 2:15). It marks the point where God rests from the divine activity of naming and relinquishes the responsibility for earthly naming to humankind.

One further indication of the way the seventh/sabbath day prepares for new beginnings is the suggestive phrase: "God rested from all that he had creatively made." The words "creatively made" are conveyed by a combination in Hebrew of two verbal forms: *bārā'* ("create") and *'āśah* ("make"). The first is the verb that in Hebrew is reserved for God's special acts of creation. It always occurs with God as the subject of the action. In the Priestly account of Genesis 1:1—2:4a, this verb, *bārā'*, frames the creation (cf. 1:1 and 2:3) as the series of wondrous works that only God can bring into existence.[44] The second verb in 2:3, *'āśah,* is the common word for human making. Elsewhere in the creation account God is described as engaging in the everyday act of making that is common to humankind,[45] but this is the first time the verb is used as a virtual synonym for *bārā'*. Cassuto has captured the symmetry implied here with the suggestion that this verse speaks of "an act of creation that is also a 'making.'"[46]

Genesis 2:3 suggests that when, on the seventh/sabbath day, God rests from a divine creating that is also a making, it is not in order to retire from the world, but rather to wait expectantly—with "the heavens and the earth . . . and all their multitude"—for the subsequent acts of human making that will bring about new and future creations. This sabbatical symmetry between God's creation and humankind's re-creation is captured nicely in a Jewish interpretation of the text. N. H. Sarna notes that Ibn Ezra and Radak understood the verb *'āśah* in Genesis 2:3 to mean that God rested from all the work that God created in order "[for man] to [continue to] do [thenceforth]."[47]

In the Torah's vision, the liturgy of creation is rooted in the stability of the created order. It is a liturgy that endows humankind with the responsibility and the capacity both to sustain the created order and to restore its creational harmony when necessary by acts of "making" that are also acts of "creating." The crucial moment in this primordial liturgy comes when God rests from divine creativity and relinquishes earthly dominion to those

44. Cf. Cassuto, *Genesis: Part I*, 69–70.

45. Cf. Gen. 1:7, 16, 25, 26. Fretheim sees in the use of *'āśah* with reference to God as "maker" another example of the relational character of God. As he puts it, "the creative activity of God is not thought to be without analogy in the human sphere" ("Creator, Creature, and Co-Creator," 14).

46. Cassuto, *Genesis: Part I*, 70.

47. Sarna, *Genesis*, 15.

commissioned to image God on earth as royal servants. On the primordial sabbath day, the cosmic design has been established, blessed, and secured. All that remains is for human possibilities to join with divine hopes in the creation of an ongoing liturgy that will sustain on earth God's cosmic pronouncement: "very good."

A Fragile World, an Earthly Altar, a Cosmic Commitment

The world God pronounces "very good" remains nevertheless a fragile world. There is a kind of cosmic fragility inherent in the created order; with all its boundaries and divisions, its categories and separations, it is a world susceptible to chaos. When the work of creation is complete, there is still light *and* darkness, day *and* night. As J. Levenson has shown, Israel's liturgy of creation affirms that God *confines* chaos, not that God *eliminates* it.[48]

Woven into this cosmic fragility and contributing to it is the fragility that exists on earth as humankind strives to realize its creational harmony with God. Genesis 3–6 offers two paradigms for the human disorder that subverts the orderly relationships God prescribes: the relationship between man and woman in their small community (Gen. 3:1-24); and the relationships of humankind in its larger communities (Gen. 6:1-4; cf. 11:6-7).

The subversion of the relationship God intends between man and woman

Genesis 1 mostly emphasizes God's orderly division of the cosmos into light and darkness, heaven and earth, waters and dry land. It stresses the demarcations that give meaning to God's cosmic design. Only when this creation account reaches its climax, with the creation of humankind (1:26-28), is the emphasis on differentiation set aside. In humankind, God desires to create likeness or sameness,[49] a being "in the image of God" that will properly embody the foundational relationship God intends for the human order.

In Genesis 1 the foundational relationship for the human order is presented as the relationship between male and female. The key terms in Genesis 1:27 are *zākār* ("male") and *nĕqēbāh* ("female"). P. A. Bird has shown that these terms are biological, not sociological. That is, male and female are distinguished one from another in terms of their sexuality, not in terms of their social status. Male and female alike are accorded what Bird calls an

48. Levenson, *Creation and the Persistence of Evil*, 14–25.

49. Cf. D. N. Fewell, D. M. Gunn, *Gender, Power, and Promise: The Subject of the Bible's First Story* (Nashville: Abingdon, 1993), 23.

"ontological equality" before God.[50] Both are created in the image of God; both are blessed by God; both are commissioned with the creational demand to "be fruitful and multiply," to "fill the earth and subdue it." There is no suggestion that male and female are to be estranged from one another (or from God), no implication that in God's design human relationships should be flawed by inferior qualities such as domination or hierarchy.

In Genesis 2 the dynamics of human relationship are envisioned somewhat differently, although the founding principles as set forth in Genesis 1 are not substantially changed. In Genesis 2 different words for the human species are employed that bring more clearly into focus the relational aspects of being male and female. The terms 'îš, ("man") and 'iššāh, ("woman") are sociological, not biological.[51] They describe the relationship, the companionship that may be enjoyed by "man" and "wo-man." Woman is created of the same bone and flesh as man. She is "taken away from"[52] man, and man "leaves" parents behind in order to be reunited with that which makes him fully human. The vision in Genesis 2, like that of Genesis 1, is one of a relationship of equality, not of dominance or subservience. Two persons are created from one, and two persons cleave for reunion with a mutual devotion and passion that images the yearning that humankind has for God.[53] The stress is on the passion that binds woman and man together, not on the functions that divide them.[54]

As the story of human relationships unfolds, however, it becomes clear that the vision of neither Genesis 1 nor Genesis 2 will prevail uncontested on earth. In Genesis 3 the relationship between man and woman deteriorates from one of partnership and companionship to one of dominance and subordination. It is clear that the fracturing of the relationship is a

50. P. A. Bird, "Genesis I–III as a Source for a Contemporary Theology of Sexuality," *Ex Auditu* 3 (1987), 35. See further "'Male and Female He Created Them': Gen. 1:27b in the Context of the Priestly Account of Creation," *HTR* 74 (1981), 129–59; "Sexual Differentiation and Divine Image in the Genesis Creation Texts," *Image of God and Gender Models in Judeo-Christian Tradition*, ed. K.E. Borresen (Oslo: Solum Forlag, 1991), 11–34. The first two articles are reprinted in Bird's *Missing Persons and Mistaken Identities*, OBT (Minneapolis: Fortress, 1997).

51. Ibid., "Genesis I–III," 38.

52. For this translation of *luqoḥāh* in Gen. 2:23 and its significance for reconstructing the character of "woman" in a less ideological/patriarchal way, see M. Bal, *Lethal Love: Feminist Literary Readings of Biblical Love Stories* (Bloomington: Indiana University Press, 1987), 117.

53. The word in Gen. 2:24, "cleave/cling" *(dbq)* is used in the Hebrew Bible with reference both to the "yearnings" present in interhuman relationships (Ruth 1:14) and to those expressed by humans to God (e.g. Deut. 4:4; 11:22; 30:20). See further, Sarna, *Genesis*, 23 and 354, n. 32.

54. Cf. Bird's comment: ". . . the account in Genesis 2 subordinates function to passion. The attraction of the sexes is the author's primary interest, the sexual drive whose consummation is conceived as a re-union" ("Genesis I–III," 38).

subversion of God's creational design for humankind. And it is clear, despite much traditional commentary that seeks to lay all blame on the woman,[55] that both male and female have transgressed the divine boundaries for human relationship. As a consequence both are estranged from God, hence from the source of their harmony with one another. For the man *('ādām)* this is manifest in separation from the ground *('ădāmāh)* out of which he was created and on which he depends for his livelihood (3:17-19). For the woman *('iššāh)* the separation is from man *('îš)*, from whom she was created and on whom she depends for the work of procreation (3:16-17).

The subversion of the relationship God intends in the larger community of humankind

The rupture of the cosmic order that is manifest in the smallest community of man and woman (Gen. 3:1-24) escalates to its farthest dimensions in the corruption of the larger community. Especially in the mythic account of Genesis 6:1-4 it becomes clear that the boundaries between God and creation, even as far as the celestial world of heavenly beings, have been obliterated. Whatever else this strange account intends to convey,[56] its report of the intercourse between the "sons of God" and the "daughters of humans" underscores the collapse of the distinctions between the divine and the human spheres.

It is interesting that in the Torah's vision the transgressions of man and woman and of humankind uses similar language. In both cases the transgression is linked with the abrogation of the boundaries between God and creation. Just as man and woman succumb to the temptation to "become like God" (Gen. 3:5, 22), so does the larger community yield to the opportunity to circumvent the boundaries of human mortality in order to "live forever" (6:3; cf. 3:22). In both cases the order of the cosmos is subverted. In Westermann's words, it is "the overpowering force of human passion that brings people to overstep the limits set for them."[57]

---

55. Feminist and other ideological re-readings of Gen. 3 offer a much needed correction to traditional approaches which too often have distorted the text and its theology in keeping with personal or cultural biases. See, e.g., Trible, *God and the Rhetoric of Sexuality*, 72–143; Bal, *Lethal Love*, 104–32; D. J. A. Clines, *What Does Eve Do to Help? and Other Readerly Questions to the Old Testament* (Sheffield: JSOT Press, 1990), 25–48; F. Landy, *Paradoxes of Paradise: Identity and Difference in the Song of Songs* (Sheffield: Almond, 1983), 183–265. For a general discussion of these matters and much helpful bibliography, see further, Fewell, and Gunn, *Gender, Power, and Promise*, 22–38, 196–97 (bibliography).

56. For the history of interpretation, see Westermann, *Genesis 1–11*, 365, 379–81.

57. Ibid., 381.

The strategic placement of Genesis 6:1-4 just before the flood narrative (Gen. 6:5—8:22) prepares the way for God's reassessment of the cosmic design. What God "saw" (rā'āh)[58] upon completion of the primordial week was judged to be "very good" (1:31). Now, in the aftermath of ten generations of creaturely distortion, what God "saw" (rā'āh 6:5, 12) was a world corrupted by an all encompassing human wickedness and violence (6:5; cf. v. 12).[59] God responds by executing a judgment of catastrophic proportions: creation is uncreated and the cosmos is returned to primordial chaos.

But the Torah's vision asserts that the breakdown in the human heart (6:5) also occasions a breaking of the divine heart (6:6). And though God moves decisively to reverse the plan for relationship with humankind,[60] the change of course fills God with grief and pain. God is "grieved" to the heart (wayyit 'aṣṣēb 'el libbô), an expression that recalls both the anguish (bĕ'ēṣeb) of childbirth that God had imposed on the woman (Gen. 3:16) and the toil (bĕ 'iṣṣābôn) with which man is consigned to work the ground (Gen. 3:17). If the world itself is fragile, susceptible to the best and the worst that the created order brings to it, so in an analogous way, God elects to be open to the fragility of relationship with humankind. The God who presides with ultimate authority over the cosmos is at the same time a God who chooses to be vulnerable to the best and the worst that humankind may bring to the divine-human relationship.[61]

In a fragile world no longer "very good," the anguish of God prepares for the most radical turn of events in the Torah's vision. But before the flood waters are released, God singles out Noah, a man "righteous" and "blameless" (Gen. 6:9). Such qualities mark him as one who embodies both the cosmic justice (ṣaddîq) and the ritual purity (támîm) that God endowed upon primordial creation. Noah is to build an ark, a kind of "cosmos in

58. The expression "And God saw" is used repeatedly in Genesis 1, and elsewhere, to convey divine investigation and appraisal (cf. Westermann, *Genesis 1–11*, 410; Sarna, *Genesis,* 47).

59. Three words are central in God's appraisal of creation's distortion: "evil" (rā') twice in 6:5; "corrupt" (šaḥat) in 6:12 and repeatedly in this chapter; "violence," "lawlessness" (ḥāmās) in 6:13.

60. On the use of the verb niḥam in 6:6 to indicate a genuine change of direction on God's part, see T. E. Fretheim, *The Suffering of God,* OBT (Philadelphia: Fortress, 1984), 104–26; "The Repentance of God," *HBT* 10 (1988), 47–70.

61. On the construal of God in Gen. 6:5-8, T. Mann comments: "Here the depiction renders a character whose pathos matches his indignation—indeed, a God who is vulnerable to human unrighteousness, who can be hurt by human sin. Consequently, we cannot construe the flood as the heartless and brutal act of an uncaring deity. Here there is a tragic element even in the inner life of God, for in order to restore his creation to its original goodness he must all but destroy it" (*The Book of the Torah: The Narrative Integrity of the Pentateuch* [Atlanta: John Knox, 1988], 22).

miniature,"[62] according to God's specifications (Gen. 6:14-16). This ark will carry to safety Noah and his family and the requisite male and female exemplars of the animal kingdom (Gen. 6:19-20; 7:1-5). Together they will provide the nucleus for a new world: Noah, the new Adam; they, the progenitors of a renewed creation. One additional announcement from God prepares Noah for the journey ahead: "I will establish my covenant with you" (Gen. 6:18). It is the first occurrence of the word "covenant" *(bĕrît)* in the Hebrew Bible.

In Genesis 6, the notion of covenant is only introduced. The details are delayed until Genesis 9, at which point, in the aftermath of the flood, the cosmic significance of God's promise comes more clearly into focus. The story of God's re-creation of the world order (Gen. 9:1-17) unfolds in two stages.[63] The first stage (9:1-7) repeats the primordial blessing of 1:28 as well as its creational command (9:1). The same command reappears in verse 7, an indication that God's intent for the post-flood world is to re-establish the rhythms of the creational order, with some modifications and new restrictions.[64]

The second stage of the re-creational process (9:8-17) extends God's intentions for the cosmos beyond anything previously envisioned in the liturgy of creation. Seven times God speaks of a unilateral covenant with Noah and with every living creature (9:9, 11, 12, 13, 15, 16, 17). It is an "everlasting covenant" *(bĕrît 'ôlām;* 9:16) that signals God's relentless commitment to relationship with creation. "Never again" (vv. 11, 15) shall God undo creation with a retributive response to the failings of humankind.[65] The sign of this commitment is the rainbow whose unfailing appearance assures humankind and reminds God that as long as the earth shall last, God's promise shall be in place.

Several features of this covenant commitment warrant close attention. First, God announces this covenant in the midst of a real world that manifests all too clearly the fragility of the cosmic plan. This is not the world of Eden, where all is "very good." This is the world "east of Eden," where human

---

62. Fishbane, *Text and Texture,* 30.

63. For the structure of Gen. 9, see Westermann, *Genesis 1–11,* 461.

64. Gen. 9:3 provides for the eating of meat, an innovation that goes beyond Gen. 1:27. Gen. 9:4-6, then, provides two additional restrictions concerning the eating or the shedding of blood. For further discussion, see the standard commentaries, e.g. Westermann, *Genesis 1–11,* 464–68; Cassuto, *A Commentary on the Book of Genesis: Part Two: From Noah to Adam* (Jerusalem: Magnes, 1984), 126–29.

65. Brueggemann suggests that such a divine promise severs the one-to-one connection of guilt and punishment. In the post-flood world, death and destruction are not eliminated, but they are removed from the sphere of God's retributive anger and rejection. From this point, the relationship between creator and creature is based not on retribution but on God's unqualified grace *(Genesis,* 84).

wickedness and violence have distorted God's designs and subverted creation's harmony. Second (and connected with the first observation), the covenant God makes is unconditional and unilateral. It imposes on humankind no obligations, no conditions for the divine promise to be realized. All the initiative and all the responsibility rest on one side of the partnership: God's. Indeed, throughout this narrative God is the only one who speaks. No response is asked from or given by those who are the recipients of God's largesse. Third, this covenant extends God's promise to all that God re-creates in the post-flood world. Envisioned here is a cosmic promise that endows in perpetuity God's creational intentions for every living creature.

The importance of this cosmic covenant in Genesis 9 has been under-appreciated. Biblical studies of covenant have usually been preoccupied either with the semantics of the word "covenant" or with the political and historical models for covenant,[66] especially the covenant traditions associated with Moses and Abraham. In the Torah's vision, however, it is this cosmic covenant, with its unilateral and unconditional commitment from God, that provides the framework for all that follows in the post-flood world.[67] Both the perpetual covenant offered unconditionally to Abraham (Gen. 17:7, 13, 19) and the Sinaitic covenant that specifies the requirements of Israel's obedience (Exod. 19–24), are set within the larger creational purposes of God announced in Genesis 9.[68] As R. Rendtorff has seen, this cosmic covenant in effect serves as a structuring concept for both the primeval history in Genesis 1–11 and the Sinai story in Exodus 19–34.[69]

The importance of the cosmic covenant highlights a further aspect of God's restored relationship with creation—one especially significant for this study. Though the text is clear that it is God who "remembers" Noah and the animals (Gen. 8:1), thereby initiating the act of divine restoration even before the chaotic waters begin to recede, a critical turning point occurs when God's internal deliberations actualize a new relationship with

66. For a survey of these issues, see, e.g., E. W. Nicholson, *God and His People: Covenant and Theology in the Old Testament* (Oxford: Clarendon, 1988); R. Davidson, "Covenant Ideology in Ancient Israel," *The World of Ancient Israel: Sociological, Anthropological, and Political Perspectives*, ed., R. E. Clements (Cambridge: Cambridge University Press, 1989), 323–47.

67. R. Murray, *The Cosmic Covenant: Biblical Themes of Justice, Peace and the Integrity of Creation* (London: Sheed and Ward, 1992).

68. Fretheim has suggested that it is the covenant with Abraham that has a "positive *creational* effect" on the Sinaitic covenant, which he interprets to be a "vocational covenant with those who are already God's people" ("The Reclamation of Creation," 360–61). I suggest, however, that in the Torah's vision it is the "cosmic covenant" of Gen. 9 that has the "creational effect" on those that follow.

69. R. Rendtorff, "Covenant as a Structuring Concept in Genesis and Exodus," in *Canon and Theology: Overtures to an Old Testament Theology*, OBT (Minneapolis: Fortress, 1993), 125–34.

70. Westermann (*Genesis 1–11*, 461) notes that there is a "cumulative emphasis" in the J and

the fragile world. And it is precisely at this juncture that the Torah's vision locates Noah and the first clearly identified act of worship in the Hebrew Bible.

The transition occurs in Genesis 8:20-22. On critical grounds this text is usually identified with the J source and interpreted as the conclusion of the Yahwistic flood account. The Priestly source, with which it may be contrasted, does not reach its conclusion until 9:19. In the aggregate account of the flood, however, it is 8:20-22 that marks the crucial intersection between the subsiding of the waters (8:6-18) and God's restoration of the created order (9:1-17).[70]

On exiting the ark, Noah's first act is to build an altar to YHWH (the first one mentioned in the Hebrew Bible) and to offer sacrifices. The scene describes an act of worship that combines both ritual and spontaneity. There is an altar, but it rests on common ground; there is a whole burnt offering of ceremonially clean animals but no priest to mandate or to supervise its implementation.[71] Instead, Noah's offering is presented as a natural and immediate response of thanksgiving to God that emerges out of the concrete experience of having been delivered from the consuming waters of the flood.[72]

Noah's spontaneous ritual of speechless thanks has an enormous effect on God. Where before there was grief in God's heart (Gen. 6:6), now there is a new resolve (8:21). The new movement within God is conveyed by both negative and positive resolutions. Twice God determines to turn away from previous decisions (8:21): "I will not again curse. . . ."; "I will not again destroy. . . ." The first commitment refers back to the curse put in place in Gen. 3:17[73] and signals God's intention from this point forward not to curse, ever again (*'ôd*), the ground (*'ădāmāh*) because of the transgressions of humankind (*'ādām*). The second commitment refers to God's previous decision to destroy the world by flood, signaling God's new resolve, never again (*'ôd*), to smite every living thing with universal catastrophe. To these negative resolutions, which turn God away from previous actions, is added a further resolve that moves God positively to restore what had been undone. The rhythmic interchange between the seasons, times, and temperatures that had been obliterated with the flood are once again (*'ôd*) to be initiated (8:22).

P conclusions to the flood narrative. The promise in 8:21 that there shall never again be a flood corresponds with the promise in 9:8-17 of an "everlasting covenant"; the promise in 8:22 for the restoration of the rhythmic orders of life corresponds with the covenant blessing of 9:1-7.

71. See Lev. 1 for the ritual details surrounding this kind of sacrifice in the Hebrew Bible.

72. Cf. Westermann, *Genesis 1–11*, 453; Cassuto, *Genesis: Part II*, 117; Sarna, *Genesis*, 59.

73. Cf. Cassuto, *Genesis: Part II*, 119–20; Westermann, *Genesis 1–11*, 454–56.

God does not announce these resolutions to anyone. They are envisioned only as internal decisions, judgments wrought in the heart of God that await implementation. A promise of covenant had been announced (Gen. 6:18), and its actualization will be fulfilled (9:8-17). In between the promise and its enactment, the fragile cosmos is submerged and prepared for renewal.

It is striking that even after the flood's cleansing waters, there is little to suggest that creation is genuinely renewable. When the waters subside, the heart of humankind remains as flawed by the tendency to evil *(yēṣer lēb)* as before (cf. Gen. 6:5; 8:21). Besides Noah—and with him the new possibilities for justice and purity—little else seems to have changed. At this critical juncture, with promise and fulfillment suspended in the divine process of deliberation, the drama of the story invites the question, "What will be God's next move?"

Precisely at this point, the Torah's vision locates the first altar, the first act of worship, the first thanksgiving in celebration of a God committed to deliverance, even in a broken world. In the aftermath of Noah's offering, the first words God addresses to the surviving humankind are words of blessing and commission. Henceforth, the cosmic covenant will secure the possibility that God's creational designs may yet be realized in a fragile world. And henceforth, in this fragile world, the context most suited for enacting and restoring the cosmic covenant will be worship.

From Cosmic Covenant to Everlasting Covenantal Relationship

In its vision of the post-flood world, the Torah connects God's "everlasting covenant" *(bĕrît 'ôlām)* with the cosmos (Gen. 9:16) to God's "everlasting covenant" *(bĕrît 'ôlām)* with Abraham (Gen. 17:7, 13, 19). The first covenant signals God's unilateral commitment to restore creational harmony to a fragile world. The second signals God's intent to restore the relationship between God and humankind, a relationship now centered specifically in Abraham and Sarah, the ancestors of the special people called Israel. In this second extension of God's covenantal intents, as in the first, worship plays an integral role.

To examine worship's role in the extension of God's everlasting covenantal relationship to Abraham and his descendants, I turn specifically to Genesis 15–17. At the outset two preliminary observations concerning these texts are pertinent to the present task: their literary coherence; and the social reality that underlies their aggregate vision.

1. In terms of literary coherence, Genesis 15–17 clearly presents issues that reflect different historical settings and different ideological and theological interests. The promises of land and progeny (chap. 15–16) likely derive from the J source, dated conservatively to the time of the monarchy, or to the exilic period, and have been converted for special use in the ancestral narratives. The rite of circumcision, used to distinguish the community of Abraham from all other peoples, identifies chapter 17 with the Priestly interests that emerge out of the exilic period. The usual line of interpretation separates Genesis 15–16 from Genesis 17 in order to locate their respective interests within these putative historical contexts.[74]

But the final form of the Torah melds these distinct historical perspectives into a coherent whole. Genesis 15–17 presents a composite account of God's covenant with Israel's first family. Though announced and executed personally with Abraham (15:18; 17:7), this covenant must be worked out in the midst of family strife, where Abraham is practically a bystander to the more important struggle over social status that dominates the relationship between Sarah and Hagar (Genesis 16). It is the combined contributions of Abraham and Sarah—their willing submission to God's intention for them (e.g., 15:6; 17:3) and their strong need to question and to manage God's design (e.g., 15:2; 16:2, 5)—that precipitate the execution of the covenant in Genesis 17. In the composite account of these events, God establishes new identities for both of them (17:5, 15), indicating that both are integral to the implementation of the "everlasting covenant" (17:7, 13, 19).

2. In terms of the social reality underlying the aggregate account, it must be kept in mind that the Torah's vision of God's commitment to relationship with humankind, like its vision of the world God created, looks to a time in the honored past when life was governed by realities that may be different from those that presently exist. In the ancestral period, the primary social reality was the small family unit *(bēt 'āb)*, not the state or the sociopolitical stratifications that it served.[75] Within that unit, matters of religion and worship typically consisted of personal acts of piety, fully integrated into ordinary life experiences. The ancestral world had altars and various other special religious places, but it lacked central religious institutions that

---

74. For the source, critical decisions, see the standard commentaries.

75. On the social reality of the ancestral period vis-à-vis religious expression, see Westermann, *Genesis 12–36*, 110–11; R. Albertz, *A History of Israelite Religion in the Old Testament Period*, vol. 1, 29–39 (Philadelphia: Westminster, 1994). For a model study of the socio-political bases of Israel's religion, although without significant attention to the ancestral period, see D. A. Knight, " The Social Basis of Morality and Religion in Ancient Israel," in *Language, Theology, and the Bible: Essays in Honor of James Barr*, eds. S. E. Balentine, J. Barton (Oxford: Clarendon, 1994), 151–69.

existed independently of the family's personal domain. Though its religious language nurtured the sense of a personal relationship with the deity, in practice the discourse with God was modeled on the rhetoric common to interpersonal conversation.[76] In the family setting, the father carried out what would later be called the priestly functions (for example, offering sacrifice, communicating the blessing). Beyond him, there was as a rule no officially designated religious spokesperson or mediator whose presence was required for an act or expression of worship. In all these ways, the "ritual" of worship in the ancestral period was fully integrated into a way of life governed by the everyday needs and experiences of the family.

The account of Genesis 15–17 is consistent with the governing social reality of the ancestral period. This small cross-section of the Abraham narratives offers a glimpse into the inner-workings of a family unit. Abraham is the father figure and the principle character in the events reported. But Sarah also has a role in this family, as does Hagar, and their interpersonal relationships are all part of the family dynamic.

Moreover, the perspective on worship that these texts convey is also congruent with what might be expected in the ancestral period. Interspersed throughout chapters 15 and 17 are expressions and acts that have a formal connection with established rituals.[77] Yet the formality of ritual is subsumed in the narrative of the family's experience, at the center of which is the decidedly common familial confrontation between Abraham and Sarah and Sarah and Hagar. In other words, acts and expressions of worship, like the family dynamic out of which they are offered, are a complex intermixing of piety and worldliness. In the aggregate vision of Genesis 15–17, it is this fusion of life and worship that moves Israel's first family

---

76. On the linkage between ordinary interhuman discourse and the language of prayer, see E. S. Gerstenberger, *Der bittende Mensch* (Neukirchen: Neukirchener Verlag, 1980), 18–20, 127; M. Greenberg, *Biblical Prose Prayer as a Window to the Popular Religion of Ancient Israel* (Berkeley: University of California Press, 1983), 19–37; A. Aejmaelaeus, *The Traditional Prayer in the Psalms* (Berlin/New York: Walter de Gruyter, 1986), 88–91; S. E. Balentine, *Prayer in the Hebrew Bible: The Drama of Divine-Human Dialogue*, OBT (Minneapolis: Fortress, 1993), 64–71; P. D. Miller, *They Cried to the Lord: The Form and Theology of Biblical Prayer* (Minneapolis: Fortress, 1994), 32–48.

77. For example, Abraham's gesture of falling to the ground on his face (17:3,17) is a typical act of submission and reverence, as Westermann puts it, a "bodily expression of 'Amen'" that is common in ritual settings (cf. Lev. 9:24; Westermann, *Genesis 12–36*, 260). The language in 15:6, "and the Lord reckoned it to him as righteousness," has been traced to a cultic setting where it refers to a priest's acknowledgment of a ritually correct sacrificial offering (cf. Westermann, *Genesis 12–36*, 223). Similar cultic settings would appear to underlie other expressions such as "Do not be afraid" (15:1) and "blameless" (17:1; cf. Gen. 6:9). The cutting of the sacrificial animals (15:9-10) and the circumcising of the foreskin of the penis (17:9-14) also connect with established ritual ceremonies.

along the path toward the "everlasting covenant" with God. To explicate this point, I now turn to a more focused discussion of these particular texts.

Genesis 15:1-21

Two concerns important to the Torah's vision of worship in the ancestral period are introduced for the first time in Genesis 15: God's covenant with Abraham, and Abraham's dialogue with God.

In 15:18 the word "covenant" occurs for the first time in the ancestral stories. The context is God's solemn promise to Abraham of descendants (vv. 1-6) and land (vv. 7-21). This promise is enacted by a ceremonial rite in which the contracting parties pass through the halves of sacrificial animals (vv. 9-10, 17). In the ancient world, such a ceremony is commonly associated with the binding promises that are exchanged between the contracting parties. By passing through the animals, they invoke upon themselves the fate of the slain animals should they fail to abide by their agreement. In Genesis 15, however, the only one passing through the covenant pieces is God—symbolized by the "smoking fire pot" and the "flaming torch" (v. 17). Unilaterally and unconditionally, God assumes responsibility for the promises extended to Abraham.

In several respects, this covenant with Abraham extends and sharpens God's cosmic covenant announced in Genesis 9. In both instances, God is the initiator of the covenant and is solely responsible for its implementation. As Noah responds to God's initiative with a ritual offering of thanks, so Abraham responds obediently to God's instructions to prepare the sacrificial animals. As the covenant with Noah is cosmic in its scope, so the promises to Abraham reach out beyond his person: his progeny will be as innumerable as the stars of the cosmos (v.5); the boundaries of the land he is promised are more extensively envisioned than anywhere else in the Torah (15:18-21).[78] In sum, this first occurrence of the notion of covenant in the ancestral narratives concretizes God's cosmic promises in the specific human family of Abraham and his descendants.

There is, however, one important difference between the cosmic covenant and the covenant with Abraham. Whereas Noah offers a ritual of speechless thanks to God (Gen. 8:20), Abraham engages God in substantive dialogue. The Torah reports that Abraham, like Noah, builds altars and calls on the name of the Lord (Gen. 12:7, 8; 13:4, 18). But the first actual words of Abraham to God occur in Genesis 15, precisely at the intersection between God's unconditional promises and Abraham's halting trust in them.

The structure of Genesis 15 locates the covenant within the context of a dialogue between Abraham and God. Twice God initiates the conversation

---

78. Cf. Sarna, *Genesis*, 117–18.

with an "I am" saying, the first time (v. 1) to convey the promise of progeny (*'anōkî*), the second (v. 7) to introduce the promise of land (*'ănî yhwh*). And to each divine address, Abraham responds with an invocation of God that introduces a prayer of lament (vv. 2-3, 8). The invocations are identical: "O Lord God" (*'ădōnāy yhwh*). The word *adonay* is common in non-religious settings with reference to the "master" or "lord" who has the superior status in a master-servant relationship. Given this background, it is possible that Abraham's invocation is purposely phrased to convey an appropriate reverence and respect for God.[79]

The substance of Abraham's responses, however, suggests that reverence, if such is the manner in which Abraham approaches God, does not prohibit protest and questioning. God's opening words to Abraham (v. 1) convey general promises of assurance ("Do not be afraid") and protection ("I am your shield"). But Abraham's first response counters God's general assurances with specific complaint and protest (vv. 2-3): "what will you give to me . . . I am childless . . . you have not given to me children." In the context of a family's most urgent need to procreate itself, a barren father laments that general words of assurance are insufficient comfort.[80] Abraham's lament invites a further promissory word from God (vv. 4-5), following which Abraham moves from complaint to acceptance of God's assurances (v. 6).

A second round of the dialogue also begins with a word of promise from God (v. 7), now focused on the land that Abraham and his descendants will inherit. Once again, Abraham responds with a question: "How shall I know that I am to possess it?" (v. 8). It is to this question that God responds with the ceremony enacting an unconditional commitment to secure the promise, against all odds, in the fullest way imaginable.

In Genesis 15 God's covenantal promises merge with Abraham's prayers. The unconditional commitment on God's part to secure divine intentions, irrespective of any response Abraham or his descendants might offer, invites and responds to the candid participation of one who would shape what he can only receive as divine gift. In short, Genesis 15 announces that God's cosmic design for order without estrangement, for divine creation that summons forth "creaturely creativity," has begun to take shape in the specific family of Abraham and his descendants.

Genesis 16:1-16

In the midst of two grand accounts of God's covenantal intentions for Abraham and his descendants (Gen. 15 and 17), Genesis 16 presents a can-

---

79. Ibid., 111.

80. Westermann notes that the word used in 15:2 to describe Abraham's childlessness, *'ărîrî*, is used only of the husband (*Genesis 12–36*, 219).

did description of the way human conflict may ensnare and distort the divine plan. The text shifts its focus twice: first (vv. 1-6) from Abram to Sarai, then from Sarai to Hagar; next (vv. 7-14) from all three family members to God. Through a triangle of human relationships, the divine hopes and plans are passed between husband and wife, wife and servant, and finally, servant and God. At each step, there is cruelty and affliction, pain and sorrow. By the story's end, all parties to the covenantal promises, including God, are affected.

The point of departure for this story is Sarai, not Abram. Genesis 15 described Abram's perspective on childlessness and his response to it in the face of divine promises. Genesis 16 now presents the woman's perspective on barrenness and her response to it. Whereas the barrenness of the two is similar, they deal with it differently. Both understand that God is implicated in their plight. Abram had charged God by saying, "*You* have not given to me children" (15:3). Sarai states even more frankly" *The* LORD has kept me from bearing children" (16:2). Abram is gifted with a vision from God, a word that addresses him and invites his response. But Sarai receives no such word and therefore proceeds on her own initiative to address the situation with the resources available to her.

Sarai resorts to a widely known and legally accepted custom by instructing Abram to take her maidservant Hagar as his concubine.[81] In this situation a common practice is also a successful one, for Hagar conceives the child that both Abram and Sarai had hoped for. But now the situation begins to deteriorate. Hagar shows contempt *(qālal)* for Sarai (v. 4), which Sarai interprets as an act of violence *(ḥāmās)* towards her that requires legal redress (v. 5).

Sarai makes her appeal for justice with a standard legal formula: "The Lord judge between me and you" (v. 5). The appeal is directed specifically to Abram, who in the family context is expected to adjudicate the matter fairly. But indirectly, Sarai's appeal is to God, who she believes is responsible for her barrenness.[82] From Sarai's perspective, she has entered into a just arrangement with Abram and her servant, and she has been victimized. She appeals to God, the ultimate Judge, to enter into this dispute on her side.

This web of human conflict leaves no innocent parties. Sarai regards her maidservant as little more than a possession, an object to be bartered on

---

81. For discussion of the relevant parallels, see J. Van Seters, *Abraham in History and Tradition* (New Haven: Yale University Press, 1975), 68–71; idem, "The Problem of Childlessness in Near Eastern Law and the Patriarchs of Israel," *JBL* 87 (1968), 401–8; T. L. Thompson, *The Historicity of the Patriarchal Narratives* (Berlin: Walter de Gruyter, 1974), 252–69; Westermann, *Genesis 12–36*, 239; Sarna, *Genesis*, 119.

82. Cf. J. G. Janzen, *Genesis 12–50: Abraham and All the Families of the Earth* (Grand Rapids: Wm. B. Eerdmans, 1993), 43.

the market in order that she might "build" *(bānāh)* for herself a family with children. Having condemned Hagar for her attitude, Sarai afflicts her *('ānāh)* with a measure of cruelty that anticipates the Egyptians' oppression of the Hebrews. For her part, Hagar sees her elevation in status as an occasion for belittling her mistress and for flaunting a social victory at Sarai's expense. [83] Eventually, though, Hagar must flee *(bārāh)* for her life, just as Israel will flee from Pharaoh.[84] Finally, Abram is a passive accomplice to this exchange of affliction and contempt. He does not adjudicate the matter in favor of Sarai. He does not protest Sarai's abuse of another human being. Instead, he abdicates responsibility in favor of allowing the unequal power struggle between mistress and servant to run its course: "Your servant is in your power; do to her as you like" (v. 6).

This conflict takes on heightened tension in vv. 7–14 where the focus shifts from Abram and Sarai to Hagar and God. Just as God's promises become ensnared in the machinations of Abram and Sarai, so here, divine plans for the covenant with Abram and his descendants must take account of a new situation in the human community. Hagar is a foreigner, a servant, a woman, and an afflicted human being. How does the divine plan for a covenant community apply to someone such as herself?

On the one hand it is clear that Hagar is more than an object to God. She is a person, marked by suffering and sorrow, who is sought out by God for special treatment. She is the first person in the Bible to receive a visitation by one of God's heavenly messengers (16:7). For the first time in this story she is addressed by name, and she alone in this story speaks directly to God. She is the only person in the Hebrew Bible who names God (v. 13). She receives from God (v. 10) the same unconditional promise of innumerable descendants that Abram had been given; indeed, she is the only woman in the Bible to receive this promise.[85] Crowning all these indicators of God's special esteem for Hagar is the announcement that she will be the mother of Ishmael (which means "God hears") because God has heard and responded to her affliction (v. 11).

On the other hand, God's unconditional promises to Abram clearly applies differently to Hagar and her descendants. Having fled from affliction (v. 6) and been sought out by a God who hears and responds to the

---

83. Cf. Janzen, *Genesis 12–50,* 42. For other possible interpretations of Hagar's response to her pregnancy, see the discussion in K. Darr, *Far More Precious Than Jewels: Perspectives on Biblical Women* (Louisville: Westminster/John Knox, 1991), 135–38.

84. Trible, "Hagar, the Desolation of Rejection," *Texts of Terror: Literary-Feminists Readings of Biblical Narratives,* OBT (Philadelphia: Fortress, 1984), 13; cf. Darr, *Far More Precious than Jewels,* 138.

85. Cf. J. A. Hackett, "Rehabilitating Hagar: Fragments of an Epic Pattern," in *Gender and Difference in Ancient Israel,* ed. P. Day (Philadelphia: Fortress, 1989), 15.

afflicted (v. 11), she is told to return to Sarai and submit herself once more to affliction (v. 9). Further, though the son born of Hagar's affliction will bear God's name, Ishma*el*, thus partaking of God's identity, he is destined for a life of strife with "his hand against everyone, and everyone's hand against him" (v. 11).[86]

By the end of chapter 16, some things are clear about the post-flood human community with which God intends to be in covenant relationship. It is a community where human beings have the capacity to be cruel and abusive of one another; where human beings may elect to acquiesce to the abuse of other human beings, rather than to protest; where affliction is a way of life, which in some instances seems inexplicably to be sanctioned by God; where some in the community that bears the identity of God are destined for strife and isolation.

What is not yet clear is how the promises of God announced to Abraham in chapter 15 can be enacted in such a world of affliction and sorrow. Just as in the aftermath of the flood it was an "everlasting covenant" that signaled God's relentless commitment to proceed with the divine plan, so, according to Genesis 17, an "everlasting covenant" announces that the promises of God will not be thwarted, not even in a world of affliction and sorrow.

Genesis 17:1-27

In Genesis 15, it is the divine promise of progeny (vv. 1-6) and land (vv. 7-21) that dominated the interchange between God and Abraham; the covenant that enacted these promises is mentioned but once (15:18). In Genesis 17, these emphases are reversed. Now the idea of covenant dominates God's discourse with Abraham (the word *běrît*, "covenant," occurs 13 times); the promises of posterity and land are subordinate to this primary concern. In a world of affliction and sorrow, embodied in the conflicted lives of Abram, Sarai, and Hagar, something more than children and possessions is required if the creational vision of a community on earth to image God is to be realized. According to Genesis 17, nothing short of a divine commitment to an "everlasting covenant" with Abraham and Sarah and their descendants will suffice for God's purposes.

In the transition from "covenant" (Gen. 15:18) to "everlasting covenant" (Gen. 17:7, 13, 19), certain features of the divine plan remain the same while

---

86. H. Orlinsky has suggested that the Hebrew expression '*al pěnê* in the last clause of v.11 may be translated "alongside of," rather than, as traditionally rendered, "at odds with," thus the translation "He shall dwell alongside of all his kinsmen" (so NJPS). Such a translation suggests that Ishmael's destiny is to live in harmony with, not in hostility towards, his own kindred (*Notes on the New Translation of the Torah* [Philadelphia: Jewish Publication Society, 1969], 90), See further, Sarna, *Genesis*, 121; Janzen, *Genesis 12–50*, 45.

others become clear for the first time. God's intent to be in covenant with humankind remains central. God's general commitment to sustain the cosmos, transmitted through Noah, is reiterated in God's specific commitment to Abraham to sustain in perpetuity a community of faith on earth. In the cosmos, as in the human community, God is ever the initiator of covenantal decisions, Creator of the world and Creator of the design for relationship with the world.

Moreover, God's covenantal intentions consistently include the desire to remain open and responsive to the contributions of humankind. In the aftermath of the flood, Noah's ritual of thanks reaches to God's very heart (Gen. 8:20-21), and what follows is God's re-creation of the world (9:1-16). In the post-flood world, Abraham receives God's promises and responds to them with questions and affirmations (15:2, 6, 8). With Sarah, Abraham ventures to enact divine plans in ways that engage and entangle God in the web of human frailty. As chapter 17 makes clear, even as God responds to these developments with renewed and strengthened covenantal commitments, Abraham continues to offer God that unique mixture of reverence and incredulity (17:3, 17) that so defines the human character. In the Torah's vision, *all* these endeavors to contribute to God's covenantal intentions—the liturgy of ritual and of life—constitute acts of worship that help establish and sustain God's cosmic purposes.

But the "everlasting covenant" in Genesis 17 also clarifies God's covenantal intentions in important new ways. Three new features in particular may be cited.

A new identity for all the parties involved

Not only Abram and Sarai, but God too has a new identity disclosed. The vision granted to Abram begins with a familiar term: "I am God Almighty" (*'ēl šadday*). The Priestly tradition uses this term to identify the God of the ancestors (cf. Exod. 6:3). Throughout that tradition, the term is always associated with the divine promise of land and progeny (e.g., Gen. 28:3-4; 35:11; 48:3-4).[87] This is also true of its use in Genesis 17, but here the rhetoric of disclosure adds a new dimension to the identity of God Almighty. Thus,

> v. 1: *I* am *God Almighty* (*'ănî 'ēl šadday*)
> v. 2: And I will put *(wĕ'etnāh)* my covenant between me and you,
> and I will make you exceedingly numerous *(wĕ'arbeh)*
> v. 4: *I*, behold, *my covenant* with you (*'ănî hinnēh bĕrîtî 'ittāk*)

---

87. The studies of this term are extensive. For a survey of the relevant issues, see Westermann, *Genesis 12–36*, 257–58; Sarna, *Genesis*, 384–85.

Between the two "I" disclosures (vv. 1, 3), God's identity is unfolded with two first-person verbs ("I will put," "I will make numerous"). The God of familiar promises, El Shaddai, is now identified as the God of covenant relationship. God's intentions are not just to create a numerous people but to create a covenant between God and people. It is this covenant "between me and you" (v. 2; cf. vv. 7, 10, 11) that is central to God's new disclosure to Abram. From this point forward God's identity can only fully be known in relationship to Abram and his descendants.

The strongest expression of the divine commitment to covenant relationship occurs in verse 7. Westermann has noted that the language of this verse conveys the idea that an institution is emerging.[88] The covenant is "set up," "founded," "established" *(qûm)* as something God intends will endure forever *(bĕrît 'ôlām)*. What is institutionalized is not some social or political structure, but the idea of relationship.[89] God announces that through this "everlasting covenant" there will exist in perpetuity a binding relationship between God and those who enter into the community of Abram and Sarai.

If God is in some way redefined by this commitment to the covenant relationship, so too are Abram and Sarai. Abram will henceforth be known as Abraham (v. 5). The new name clearly refers to an expanding destiny. To the old name, "Abram," which means something like "exalted father," is added a new syllable, *hām*, presumably connected with the word *hāmôn*, "multitude," which appears twice in the immediate context. The apparent meaning is that Abraham is to become the "father of a multitude of nations" (vv. 4, 5).

But here as elsewhere in the Hebrew Bible, the conferring of a new name marks a new era in the life of the individual, a transition from what used to be to what will newly emerge. In the context of Genesis 17, we may understand that Abraham's new name anticipates changes more significant than merely the increase in his sexual potency. As the father of a multitude, Abraham will enjoy the privileged status of a male in a patriarchal society. But as the discourse between God and Abraham unfolds, it also becomes clear that Abraham must learn to relinquish the status quo privileges of his maleness to the unpredictable ways of God. He will be the honored father through whom the sons of Israel will come, but the rights of primogeniture that he assumes will be transferred automatically through him to the seed

---

88. Westermann, *Genesis 12–36*, 262.

89. On the debate within biblical scholarship between viewing the covenant as a theological idea or as a social institution, see Nicholson, *God and His People*. Nicholson argues—rightly, I believe—that in the Old Testament, covenant is a distinctive theological idea with important sociological consequences.

of his firstborn will be subverted. The mantel will pass not to Ishmael, as Abraham pleads, but to Isaac, the son born of Sarah (vv. 18-19).[90]

For Sarai too there will be a new identity (v. 15). Henceforth she will be Sarah, one associated with "princes, rulers" *(śar[r])*. In the context of the immediate promise, Sarah will become a "mother of nations": "she shall give rise to nations; kings of people shall come from her" (v. 16). But as with Abraham, so the text invites us to understand that Sarah's transformation exceeds a simple move from barrenness to fertility. Sarah is blessed by God (v. 16), just as Abraham has been blessed (e.g., Gen. 12:1-3), preparing her for an integral role in the covenantal community. And just as Abraham must learn to relinquish the status quo privileges of his maleness, so Sarah must learn that in the community God calls forth, status quo gender roles will be reformulated.

A mutual commitment

God's first-person commitments—"*I* am God Almighty" (v. 1), "*I*, behold my covenant" (v. 4)—require a response from Abraham: "and *you* shall keep my covenant" (v. 9). Towards this end God's second address to Abraham conveys instructions for observing the rite of circumcision (vv. 9-14). These instructions comprise the first commandment *(mitzvah)* in the Torah that is directed explicitly to Abraham and his descendants.[91] Like the creational commands in God's primordial design (cf. Gen. 1:26-28; 2:15), these first commands summon the community of Abraham to recognize that response is indispensable to the "I-you" relationship God intends.

The practice of circumcision is common among many peoples. It typically enacts a social rite of passage associated either with puberty or marriage.[92] In Genesis 17, however, circumcision conveys a religious commitment more than a social transition. It is a "sign" *('ôt)* of the covenant (v. 11), just as the rainbow in Genesis 9:12. But unlike the rainbow, for which God is solely responsible, circumcision is a sign that human beings must perform. Whereas God *establishes (qûm)* the covenant with Abraham unilaterally (v. 7), Abraham and his ancestors must choose either to *keep* it *(šāmar)* or to breach it *(pārar)* it (vv. 9, 14).

Envisioned is an unconditional commitment on God's part that is entrusted to the best and the worst the human partner may offer in response. Human partners may "break" the covenant with God, and as a

---

90. Cf. Janzen, *Genesis 12–50*, 49–50.

91. Cf. Sarna, *Genesis*, 125.

92. For a survey of the history of this rite, see Westermann, *Genesis 12–50*, 265. For a brief history of the observance of the ritual among Jews, see Sarna, *Genesis*, 385–86.

consequence remove themselves from the covenantal relationship.[93] But God does not "break" the covenant,[94] even when it is violated or abandoned by human failure, for God has established it as "everlasting." Circumcision is the sign that the human community desires to commit itself to God in a relationship of comparable loyalty and intensity. As the everlasting covenant commits God to an *unending* pursuit of relationship with humankind, so circumcision marks the bodily organ that generates human life with an *ineradicable* sign of the commitment to obedience.

Note that the ritual of circumcision recalls the summons to worship that inheres in the liturgy of creation. Newborn males are to be circumcised on the eighth day (v. 12), that is, after the child has completed the first seven-day cycle of his life. On the child's eighth day, the day after his first sabbath day, life in the community of Abraham begins with a ritual of commitment to God.[95] In the primordial design, the sabbath day sanctifies the transition between God's creative acts and the responding efforts of humans to join God in the ongoing work of creation. In Abraham's community, the eighth day of life begins with a rite of sanctification that marks the human endeavor to remain ever faithful in the ongoing work of covenantal partnership with God.

Shaped by a spirit of inclusion

The discourse in this chapter is between God and Abraham; in this sense, the promises and commands are transmitted primarily in conventional

93. Sarna notes that there are thirty-six occurrences of the formula "shall be cut off" (v. 14) in the Torah. In most cases, as here, the verb occurs in a passive form that leaves the agent of the verbal action unspecified. Where the agent is mentioned, as in Lev. 20:1-6, it is God, not humans, who executes the decision to remove perpetrators of the covenant. Sarna concludes, "Certainly, the general idea is that one who deliberately excludes himself from the religious community cannot be a beneficiary of the covenantal blessings and thereby dooms himself and his line to distinction" (*Genesis*, 126).

94. In the Hebrew Bible God is never the subject of the verb "break," *(pārar)* when the reference is to breaking the covenant. Israel can and does break God's covenant on many occasions, but according to the Hebraic perspective on God's commitments, God will never break the divine covenant with humankind. See further the similar assessment offered by Rendtorff, "Covenant as a Structuring Concept," 131.

95. It is clear that as a ritual of commitment to God, circumcision is limited in its applicability. Its deficiencies as an act of worship have been justifiably noted by those who are sensitive to its obvious exclusion of women (e.g., H. Eilberg-Schwartz, ed., *People of the Body: Jews and Judaism from an Embodied Perspective* [Albany: State University of New York, 1992], 23–24). Janzen has proposed that Gen. 17 presents circumcision in such a way as to subvert its conventional patriarchal associations (*Genesis 12–50*, 50–51). Without dismissing the limitations inherent in this masculine metaphor for covenant, I want to observe that the "everlasting covenant" marked by this eighth-day ritual is nonetheless shaped by a spirit of inclusivism. See the discussion below, 111–13.

guise: from God to patriarch. The blessings of Sarah and Ishmael, however, extend this community beyond conventional gender restrictions, beyond conventional tribal boundaries, beyond the social hierarchies that would divide the slave and the citizen.

Sarah's blessing from God (17:15-16) is the first occurrence in this chapter of the verb "bless" (*bārak*), and the first time in the ancestral narratives that God's blessing is conveyed to and through a woman. Heretofore the blessing that has guided these ancestral stories is that given to Abraham in Genesis 12:1-3. With Genesis 17 we are invited to understand that Sarah becomes more than a full partner with her spouse in the blessing of God. Her blessing, like that of Abraham, bestows upon her a progeny of "nations" (v. 16; cf. 12:2). Beyond this, she possesses a regal destiny; from her progeny will come forth "kings of peoples" (v. 16). Abraham apparently finds Sarah's blessing incredulous—but his laughter discloses how far he is from understanding the radical inclusiveness of God's intentions.

God also blesses Ishmael (v. 20), though making a distinction between him and Isaac, the special bearer of the covenant. Yet the blessing that accrues to Ishmael is clearly formulated to include him and his descendants in God's creational design in two pointed ways. First, though the blessings extended to Abraham and Sarah (vv. 2, 6, 16) recall the vocational mandate of 1:28 only in part, with Ishmael the full blessing resides: "I will bless him and make him fruitful . . . and I will make him a great nation." Second, Ishmael is, like Sarah, the progenitor of a noble lineage ("father of twelve princes," cf. Gen. 25:12-16). As Janzen has discerned, such rhetoric serves to "balance the particular covenant in Isaac with the general creation blessing in Ishmael."[96]

To summarize, in both the primordial world and the ancestral world the Torah envisions the covenant to be the context for God's commitment to humankind. The everlasting covenant that was extended to creation through Noah finds specific embodiment in the everlasting covenant promised to the community of Abraham and Sarah. Both in the cosmos and in the earthly community, God's covenantal intentions are enacted, sustained, and restored within the context of worship. Whether it is manifest as the speechless thanks of Noah's altar ritual or the common discourse that Abraham and Sarah offer in the ritual of their lives, the Torah's vision asserts that God remains ever desirous of and receptive to the acts and words of worship that bind together heaven and earth. Indeed, in Noah and in Abraham and Sarah, the Torah understands that from the beginning Israel's journey with God has been shaped by paradigms of worship that

---

96. Janzen, *Genesis 12–50*, 52.

invite reflection and emulation. It is to these early paradigms of worship that the discussion now turns.

Paradigms for Worship

With the first *act* of worship (Noah, Gen. 8:20) and first *words* of worship (Abraham and Sarah, Gen. 15-17), the Torah begins to unfold its vision of the indispensability of worship for the realization of God's creational and covenantal designs for humankind. Whenever the people of God find themselves submerged in a world where creation and covenant are in jeopardy—whether in Canaan, Babylon, or Yehud—the memories of these ancestors of faith will be instructive. As a conclusion to this chapter on "beginnings," it is appropriate, therefore, to look more closely at these foundational models for Israel's worship.

The account of Noah's sacrifice in Genesis 8 anticipates a primary means of worship that will subsequently receive detailed elaboration in the Sinai pericope, the subject of the next chapter. But several general observations are pertinent at this juncture, especially because this brief text reveals more than it actually declares.

First, Noah's act of worship combines ritual and spontaneity. The mention of altar and sacrifice suggests the formality of ritual that one normally associates with fully developed priestly institutions. At this stage in the Torah's vision, however, there are no priests to supervise the sacrifice, and no sanctioned altars on which the sacrifice must be offered. Noah simply responds to God out of his own initiative and according to his own resources. It is the picture of an unmediated, unsupervised interchange between Creator and creature, a distinctly non-priestly view of worship.

Noah's worship includes no words; it achieves its effect with unembellished ritual act. Thus ritual, in and of itself, has the capacity to communicate with God. In fact, not only does Noah never speak to God, he never speaks at all in the entire story. Yet the story recognizes that through his acts Noah distinguishes himself as "righteous" and "blameless" before God (cf. 6:9). In part this assessment is justified by Noah's glad obedience to God's commands to build the ark and to prepare for its embarkation. But the assessment is also fortified by Noah's spontaneous act of speechless worship. The "pleasing odor" of his offering (v. 21) is what marks the transition in God's heart from pain to promise (vv. 21b-22). Without a word ever passing between Noah and God, obedience and ritual convey the requisite justice and purity that God desires in order to restore the creational design.

It is also significant that the first act of worship is an offering of thanksgiving. Some commentators suggest that Noah's sacrifices are designed to secure either God's forgiveness for the past or God's blessing for the future.[97] In other words, this first act of worship would serve Noah's self-interests as a means for "receiving" something from God. But Cassuto sees no need to impute to Noah such ulterior motives: "When a person has been saved from a terrible danger, or has escaped from a general catastrophe, his first reaction is to give thanks to him who saved him or helped him to escape."[98] Noah's first act of worship is occasioned by God's grace, not by any self-conscious desire to appease or to persuade.

Abraham and Sarah also model a dimension of worship that will continue to be of central importance to the ongoing story of Israel. The distinctive witness of the ancestral narratives is that the beginnings of the people of Israel are not in formal institutions, whether religious or political, but in the personal and intimate realities of family life. In such a setting, worship may involve rituals, like circumcision, that are woven into the fabric of everyday life experiences. But above all, this worship conveys to God the complex fusion of piety and worldliness that is typical of the family dynamic.[99]

Abraham and Sarah are key paradigms for this part of the Torah's vision of worship. Abraham offers to God a faith marked by both protest and submission, both incredulous resistance and glad acquiescence. In Hebraic tradition Abraham emerges as the "father of faith," the first in the Torah to merit the positive assessment that "he believed the LORD" (15:6).[100] And yet the Torah announces at the outset that even for Abraham the journey towards faith is surrounded by lament. Abraham's first recorded words to God convey a question filled with both anguish and reproach: "O Lord GOD, what will (can) you give to me. . . ? (15:2). And even after God responds with words of reassurance that seem to move Abraham from doubt to acceptance, his next words continue to question the very promise that he has decided to believe: "O Lord GOD, how shall I know. . . ? (15:8). With such questions Abraham becomes the first exemplar of the strong lament tradi-

97. For a survey of representative opinions, see Westermann, *Genesis 1–11*, 452–53.

98. Cassuto, *Genesis: Part Two*, 117.

99. On the religion of the ancestors, especially as newer sociological analyses have clarified the distinctions between family piety and the piety of corporate entities like the state, see Westermann, *Genesis 12–36*, 110–11. Particularly helpful on this matter have been the several studies of Westermann's student R. Albertz: *Weltschopfung und Menschenschopfung. Untersuchung bei Deuterojesaja, Hiob und den Psalmen* (Stuttgart: Calwer, 1974); idem, *Personliche Frommigkeit und offizielle Religion* (Stuttgart: Calwer, 1978). In his most recent work, Albertz describes the personal piety of the ancestors as "pre-cultic," "pre-political," and "pre-moral"; *A History of Religion*, vol. 1, 29–40.

100. Westermann has shown that the representation of Abraham as the "father of faith" is a later theological reflection that likely derives from the period of the monarchy; *Genesis 12–36*, 222, 230–31.

tion in Hebraic piety that comes to the fore with Moses, Samuel, Jeremiah, and a host of others, especially those whose anonymous legacy is preserved in the Psalter.[101]

Moreover, Abraham's piety is a candid mixture of reverence and resistance. In a gesture of reverent submission, he receives the promises of God by falling on his face (17:3); confronted with the great gap between God's promises and his expectations, he falls on his face and laughs (17:17). In place of silent acceptance, Abraham now offers his first petition: "O that Ishmael might live in your sight!" (v. 18). The petition places Abraham at odds with God's promise that the fortunes of his progeny rest with the child to be born from Sarah, not with Ishmael.

God's promise subverts the social convention of primogeniture that is central to Abraham's honored status in a patriarchal society. The child who carries the divine blessing is not *Abraham's* firstborn, Ishmael, but the firstborn of *Sarah and Abraham*. Abraham petitions God to sustain the status quo, but God responds negatively, announcing that divine plans will not be bound by the conventions of Israel's first ancestor. With Abraham's petition and God's response to it, the Torah's vision acknowledges that the life of faith is often a struggle between self-interest and God's transforming purposes.

Sarah too is a central model for the piety of those who come forth from her womb. She speaks out of the context of violence and oppression. Indeed, the violence *(ḥāmās)* of which she complains (16:5) invokes the memory of the violence in primordial times that subverted God's cosmic plans and prompted the judgment of the flood (6:11-13).[102] Like the cosmos, Sarah has suffered a violation, and like the cosmos, she yearns for a divine intervention that will restore justice. Her words (16:5) mark the first time that the Torah's vision includes a prayer for justice: "May the Lord judge *(šāpaṭ)* between you and me."

Sarah's prayer is couched in the typical language of legal appeal. She makes an accusation ("the violence done to me"), offers evidence to substantiate her charge (Hagar's "contempt"), and demands a decision in her case.[103] Ostensibly this is a family matter, a conflict between Sarah and Hagar, and by extension between Abraham and Sarah. Hence Sarah appeals to Abraham to resolve it fairly.

---

101. See further, Balentine, *Prayer in the Hebrew Bible,* 146–88.

102. The word "violence" *(ḥāmās)* connotes a general sense of "lawlessness," often in association with violent acts involving the shedding of blood; cf. Westermann, *Genesis 1–11,* 415–16; Sarna, *Genesis,* 51.

103. Cf. Westermann, *Genesis 12–36,* 241.

But we are also invited to understand that Sarah perceives in this intrafamily strife a matter requiring God's intervention. Because God had closed her womb (16:2), Sarah resorted to the custom of the times to provide the child that would restore her status in the community and provide the appropriate way for Abraham's line to continue. But now, despite Hagar's child, Sarah is not only barren; she is also an object of shame. Janzen has proposed that in a patriarchal world Sarah might well have suspected that both Abraham and his God would be on the side of Hagar in this dispute. Thus, Janzen suggests, with this appeal Sarah is in effect challenging the "patriarchal God to be her God in her own right."[104]

Such a prayer for justice on behalf of the disadvantaged is crucial in the Torah's unfolding vision of Israel's piety. Abraham himself will exhibit similar concerns in his interchange with God concerning Sodom and Gomorrah (Gen. 18:22-33), and Moses will sustain the tradition on numerous instances on behalf of those who make their way from Egypt under his direction.[105] For both Abraham and Moses, as for the numerous ones after them who will continue insisting that justice be part of the equation between God and people, Sarah is the exemplar of faith.

104. Janzen, *Genesis 12–50*, 43.
105. See further, chap. 5, 140-45.

5.

THE LITURGY
OF COVENANT

A MONG THE EARLIEST TEXTS OF THE HEBREW BIBLE (E.G, JUDG. 5:5; Ps. 68:9) YHWH is identified as "the One of Sinai" *(zeh sînay)*. The ascription serves as an ancient epithet for God. As J. Levenson has put it, Israel's God is the One "of whom Sinai is characteristic."[1] This identification with Sinai suggests two characteristics of God that are especially pertinent for the concerns of the present chapter.

First, the location of Sinai is finally indeterminate; it lies in the wilderness somewhere between Egypt and Canaan. This elusiveness functions in Hebraic tradition as a symbol of both YHWH's freedom and YHWH's authority. Like Sinai, YHWH's domain is beyond the boundaries of Egypt, of Canaan, of any given regime or state, ancient or modern, that may be located on a map. Like Sinai, YHWH's authority is not confined by, indeed may stand in opposition to, the sovereignty claimed by any earthly kingdom.

Second, Hebraic tradition identifies Sinai not primarily with an earthly place but with a divine act.[2] Sinai is the place of God's salvation: for Moses and the people who flee from the Egyptians (Exod. 19); for Deborah and Barak who defeat the Canaanites (Judg. 5); for Elijah who flees in despair from Jezebel and the putative powers of state-sanctioned Baalism (1 Kings 19). Hebraic tradition asserts that whenever and wherever people encounter the God of Sinai, they will celebrate the memory of the One who rises up against the enemies of the righteous, nullifying their power and preserving the faithful with love and compassion. From their disparate experiences will come a uniform confession: "Blessed be the Lord, who daily bears us up; God is our salvation" (Ps. 68:19).

---

1. J. D. Levenson, *Sinai and Zion: An Entry into the Jewish Bible* (Minneapolis: Winston, 1985), 20.

2. On Sinai as the mountain that signifies God's salvation in the earliest traditions of the Hebrew Bible, see F. Crüsemann, *The Torah: Theology and Social History of Old Testament Law,* trans. A. W. Mahnke (Minneapolis: Fortress, 1996), 31–37.

At the center of the Torah's vision of worship is the God "of whom Sinai is characteristic." That this God and this experience of Sinai is determinative for understanding the Torah's vision is indicated by the disproportionate attention accorded to the Sinai pericope—from Exodus 19 to Numbers 10. These fifty-eight chapters represent roughly 40 percent of the entire Torah story. Herein lies one of the most important anomalies of the Pentateuch. The events that transpire at Sinai occupy just one year out of the 2,706 years that the Pentateuch covers between the creation of the world and the death of Moses in the plains of Moab. In terms of the Pentateuch's own chronology, the year at Sinai might well have been allotted little more than a footnote in the overall story. But the Torah's vision is quite different. In its final arrangement, it understands the year at Sinai to be the constitutive experience in the formation of the community of faith as "a priestly kingdom and a holy nation" (Exod. 19:6).[3]

The centrality of the Sinai pericope for the Torah's vision of worship, however, has typically been lost within the debates over the narrative sources for the Pentateuch. Although Wellhausen's documentary hypothesis can no longer simply be assumed, it remains nevertheless an axiom of critical methodologies that the "covenant" texts (Exod. 19–24) and the "worship" texts (Exod. 25–31, 35–40; Lev. 1–27; parts of Num.) derive from different historical periods and therefore reflect different theological interests. The practical effect of this diachronic approach to the Torah has been to separate the covenant texts from the worship texts, typically assigning both a chronological and a theological priority to the former. Particularly in Protestant biblical scholarship, it has been the notion of covenant, whether assigned to J (JE) or D, that has captured the theological imagination. The distinctively Priestly concerns for ritual and holiness have been regarded by and large as representative of a later, deteriorating period in post-exilic Judaism. In this regard, Wellhausen's shadow, as I have already suggested in the opening chapter, still looms large on the contemporary horizon.[4]

In keeping with the emphases of the study thus far, this chapter will focus on the Torah's *aggregate vision,* not its individual literary strands. In the Torah's vision, covenant and worship are not separate interests of disparate communities of faith, one dominant, the other relegated to the margins. Rather, they are two equally defining characteristics of every community of faith that will enter into Israel's legacy of "covenant holiness." Thus

---

3. On the importance of the "anomalies" in the narrative tempo of the Pentateuch, see J. Blenkinsopp, *The Pentateuch: An Introduction to the First Five Books of the Bible* (New York: Doubleday, 1992), 33–37.

4. See above, chap. 1, pp. 5–16.

the agenda here comprises two objectives. The immediate objective is to uncover within the Sinai pericope the repeating concerns with worship that provide the context for Israel's formation as a covenant community of faith. Toward that end, the focus in this, and the following chapter will be on three major features of the Sinai pericope: covenant as vocation (Exod. 19–24); covenant as sanctuary building and as world building (Exod. 25–40); and "covenant holiness" (Lev. 1–27). The second objective, which I will only introduce at this point, is to reclaim for the church the Hebraic legacy of covenant holiness. Such a reclamation requires that the church be willing to engage in substantive Jewish-Christian conversation.

"A Priestly Kingdom and a Holy Nation": Covenant as Vocation (Exodus 19–24)

Most scholars agree that chapters 19 through 24 of Exodus are a composite to which all the major pentateuchal sources have contributed.[5] In Pentateuchal criticism, the custom has been to isolate the individual sources and their deposits and to focus the interpretive task on the distinct emphases of the separate literary traditions. The Priestly strand, for example, which provides the basic framework of the narrative (Exod. 19:1-2; 24:15-18), reports simply that when Israel arrived at Sinai, Moses ascended the mountain to receive the instructions for building the sanctuary. Subsequent chapters of the P account (Exod. 25–31, 35–40) describe these instructions in considerable detail. As an individual source, P contains no mention of a covenant at Sinai and no reference to the Decalogue or to the statues and ordinances that comprise the Book of the Covenant. The clear emphasis, rather, is on the holy tabernacle and on the holy cult that it serves. When P is isolated from its literary moorings in the Sinai pericope, it can be misread to suggest that the priests, as custodians of the ritual emphases in Israel's life, had little or no interest in the moral exhortations usually associated with covenantal obedience.[6]

---

5. Analyses of the sources comprising the Sinai pericope are readily available in the standard critical commentaries—e.g., B. Childs, *Exodus: A Commentary* (Philadelphia: Westminster Press, 1974). For a recent critique of how the standard approaches have tended to reduce the Sinai pericope to "rubble," in the end destroying the structure of this important text rather than disclosing it, see Crüsemann, *The Torah*, 27–57.

6. It is generally agreed that the only covenants in the Priestly tradition are with Noah (Gen. 9:8-17) and Abraham (Gen. 17:7, 13, 19), and in this tradition the covenant is understood to be unconditional. See J. Blenkinsopp, "Introduction to the Pentateuch," *NIB*, vol. 1 (Nashville: Abingdon, 1994), 316.

The Decalogue (Exod. 20:1-17) and the Book of the Covenant (20:22—23:33), on the other hand, are usually regarded as early legal collections that were originally independent of the Priestly tradition. The history of the transmission of these laws into the Sinai pericope remains a matter of considerable debate. The traditional view understands them to have been shaped for their present context primarily by the early sources J or JE, with only minor expansions or alterations by P and D. An increasingly persuasive alternative hypothesis is that covenant and law are emphases that emerge principally out of the Deuteronomic tradition.[7] With either hypothesis, the implicit judgment is that covenantal obedience at Sinai was construed essentially without the Priestly concern for holiness and ritual.

While maintaining the composite nature of these texts, it is still possible to observe that the Torah's vision of the Sinai event melds into a coherent whole the twin concerns of covenant and holiness. Indeed, the internal dynamics of Exodus 19–24 invite one to understand that precisely in worship are both covenantal obedience and ritual holiness united as constitutive acts of faith. In what follows, I will identify some of the repeating concerns with worship that serve as thematic links within these complex texts—starting with Exodus 19:1-8, then moving on to Exodus 20–24.

Discussion of Exodus 19:1-8 customarily focuses on the "covenant" (bĕrît) that is inaugurated at Sinai (v. 5). Scholars have discerned in the structure of vv. 3b-8 the remnants of a typical covenant ceremony that may have its roots in traditional Near Eastern treaty patterns: a historical prologue announcing God's mighty deeds on Israel's behalf (v. 4); the conditions of the covenant (vv. 5-6); and the people's acceptance of the terms of the covenant (vv. 7-8).[8] Whether assigned to an early source such as E, or interpreted as a later insertion by the D redactor, vv. 3b-8 appear to constitute a distinct literary unit intentionally introducing the covenant that will be formally concluded in 24:3-8.

It is less commonly noted, however, that the Torah conceives the covenant at Sinai to be a part of the same heptadic pattern that informs the

7. E.g., L. Perlitt, *Bundestheologie im Alten Testament* (Neukirchen: Neukirchen-Vluyn, 1969); E. Blum, *Studien zur Komposition des Pentateuch* (Berlin: Walter de Gruyter, 1990).

8. The parallels between Near Eastern suzerainty treaties and the covenant between God and Israel are conveniently summarized in D. J. McCarthy, *Old Testament Covenant: A Survey of Current Opinions* (Richmond: John Knox, 1972); *Treaty and Covenant*, 2d ed. (Rome: Pontifical Biblical Institute, 1978). For a critique of these parallels, see E. W. Nicholson, *God and His People: Covenant and Theology in the Old Testament* (Oxford: Clarendon, 1986), 56–82. Nicholson concludes, rightly in my opinion, that covenant in Israel is more a "theological idea" (albeit one imbued with a social reality) than an "institution," as those who promote the treaty parallels seem to suggest.

liturgy of God's creational design. Exodus 19:1-2 announces that Israel arrives at Sinai "on the third new moon" after the exodus from Egypt. Just as a new moon typically marks a new period of time in the life cycle of nature, so the new moon at Sinai marks a new beginning for the people of Israel. Cassuto has suggested that Israel's arrival at Sinai on the *third* new moon coincides with the beginning of the seventh week after the exodus from Egypt.[9] The seventh week of their journey, like the seventh day in the liturgy of creation, marks a crucial transition in their relationship with God. After six weeks as passive beneficiaries of God's initiatives, Israel's seventh week begins with the announcement that henceforth covenant partnership with God will define the journey. Thus the Torah envisions the Sinai pericope to begin not simply with a traditional covenant ceremony as might be common elsewhere in the ancient world, but with a *liturgy of covenant* that is peculiarly shaped by Israel's understanding of God's cosmic design.

In this liturgy of covenant, the Torah understands that *covenant-making,* from God's perspective, is an act comparable to *world-making.* In each, the first creative act belongs to God. Thus, the covenant at Sinai begins with a recollection of God's gracious acts of deliverance: "You have seen what I did to the Egyptians . . ." (v. 4).

Moreover, God's inauguration of covenant—just like God's creation of the world—finds its ultimate goal in Israel's empowerment to join God in a relationship of creaturely partnership. In the cosmic design of creation, God commissioned humankind to image God as both royal stewards and humble servants.[10]In the liturgy of covenant-making, God concretizes the primordial commission by summoning Israel to a vocation of imaging God on earth as "a priestly kingdom and a holy nation" (v. 6). In other words, the Torah understands that *covenant-keeping,* from Israel's perspective, requires a solemn partnership commitment that places Israel in harmony with the liturgy of creation.

The expression "a priestly kingdom and a holy nation" describes the responsibilities of covenant partnership with a poetic balance that is both careful and dramatic.[11] The parallelism between "kingdom" *(mamleket)* and "nation" *(gôy)* is transparent, both words bringing into view the same basic idea of a community that enjoys some measure of "dominion" or

9. U. Cassuto, *A Commentary on the Book of Exodus* (Jerusalem: Magnes, 1983), 224. Cassuto makes the case as follows: "The mention of the third new moon is not unintentional. Since the Exodus from Egypt, the last two weeks of Nissan and four weeks of Iyyar had passed, and we are now in the seventh week" (224).

10. See above, chap. 4, p. 86.

11. On the variations in the versional treatment of this phrase and its appropriation in the New Testament, see R. B. Y. Scott, "A Kingdom of Priests (Exodus XIX 6)," *OTS* 8 (1950),

"sovereignty."[12] The words "priestly" *(kōhǎnîm)* and "holy" *(qādôš),* while not strictly synonymous, commonly function within the same semantic orbit to describe persons "sanctified," or "set apart" for special service. On a first level then, this parallelism recalls the creational commission to image God in ways that bear a resemblance to both a king's power and a priest's servanthood. As J. Levenson puts it, Israel is summoned to an "aristocracy of humility."[13]

On a second level, however, these terms anticipate that covenant-keeping, while consonant with God's creational designs, nevertheless engages Israel in a vocation that is dramatically discontinuous with the world's politics. In partnership with God, Israel is empowered to become a kingdom of *priests,* not of kings, a kingdom of servants, not of rulers. Their capacity for dominion in God's world resides in their empowerment to serve others, not in any self-assertion of mundane sovereignty. On the one hand, this imagery looks forward to Israel's subsequent transition into statehood and provides a word of warning and caution: do not abuse power; do not equate the prerogatives of statehood with God's covenantal commission for dominion through servanthood. On the other hand, this commission looks backwards from the vantage point of Israel's lost sovereignty under Babylonian and Persian hegemony and offers a word of abiding hope: the people of God are empowered for a dominion that ultimately cannot be negated by the mandates of regnant forces.[14]

The parallelism of the terms "priestly kingdom" and "holy nation" envisions the covenant commission from still another perspective. The Torah's vision elevates what is "priestly" and "holy" to regal status. Whatever is holy and derived from God—which is what the priestly servants mediate through holy ritual—is as crucial for the ministry of dominion as is power and sovereignty. For the community commissioned to image God in the world, the "priestly" and the "holy" are not secondary or marginal concerns. They are primal qualities, without which there can be no authentic consummation of God's covenantal design. A people may claim for them-

213–19. Scott gives special attention to the misuse of the phrase "kingdom of priests," particularly within Protestant theology, to validate the Christian notion of the priesthood of every believer.

12. On this parallelism see especially W. Moran, "A Kingdom of Priests," in *The Bible in Current Catholic Thought,* ed. J. L. McKenzie (New York: Herder and Herder, 1962), 11–17.

13. Levenson, *Sinai and Zion,* 31.

14. Cf. Moran, who observes that Israel's constitution as a "royalty of priests" was not a charter for kingship in the ordinary manner of ancient Near Eastern royalty: "This kingship . . . which is not like that of 'all the nations,' witnesses to the fact that this royalty of priests, like the holy nation, belongs and is subordinate to Israel's invisible king. 'You will be *for me* a royalty of priests and a holy nation'" ("A Kingdom of Priests," 20).

selves a worldly authority. A nation may draw upon its own resources to govern others, for good or for ill. But in the Torah's vision, there can be no fulfillment of the divine purpose for humanity that does not live out of the special communion with God encoded in the "priestly" and the "holy."

Exodus 19:1-8 only introduces the commission to be a covenant community and a priestly community; the requirements follow in the succeeding chapters. Nevertheless, the broad outlines of God's designs are clear. Partnership with God involves obedience to the moral imperatives that may be articulated in covenant statutes and ordinances. *And* partnership with God involves consecration to that which is holy, to that which may be uniquely realized and mediated in worship. The daring assertion of the Torah's vision is that these twin poles of covenant partnership—obedience and consecration—are inextricably linked in God's cosmic design for humanity.

Exodus 20–24 spells out the requirements of the covenantal law and the covenantal holiness just introduced in Exodus 9:1-8. The liturgy of covenant that the Torah envisions continues with the promulgation of the Decalogue (20:1-17) and the Book of the Covenant (20:22—23:33), both of which have invited considerable scholarly analysis.[15] A general consensus now exists regarding the form-critical distinctions between the apodictic laws that comprise the Decalogue and the causuistic laws that dominate in the Book of the Covenant. Moreover, it is generally agreed that the two collections were originally independent of each other and of the Sinai pericope. The track through which they passed into this narrative is disputed, but both collections show signs of Deuteronomic editing.

What has not been sufficiently analyzed is the theological significance of the literary placement of these two law collections within the Sinai pericope. There is much to commend such an analysis. Two observations are particularly pertinent.

First, a number of scholars have noted that when the two law collections are placed side by side, the Decalogue functions as an introduction to the more explicit statutes and ordinances that follow in the Book of the Covenant. G. Mendenhall, for example, has proposed as an interpretive clue the comparison between "legal policy" and "legal technique."[16] By this analogy, the Decalogue may be understood to articulate the basic principles concerning covenant behavior, principles which the Book of the Covenant then expostulates in terms of specific legal implications.

---

15. For a summary of the critical issues, see D. Patrick, *Old Testament Law* (Atlanta: John Knox, 1985).

16. G. E. Mendenhall, "Ancient Oriental and Biblical Law," *BA* 17 (1954), 28; cf. D. R. Hillers, *Covenant: History of a Biblical Idea* (Baltimore: Johns Hopkins Press, 1969), 88.

Second, it has become increasingly clear that in the final arrangement of the Pentateuch, law and narrative are integrated in a way not encountered in the comparable literature of the ancient world. The effects of this integration are significant.[17] It stipulates that "law," whatever its secular or common focus, is a matter of sacred "commandment."[18] Rather than a burden imposed on unwilling recipients by an impersonal authority, it is a gift from a gracious God to a community that gladly receives instructions for furthering a relationship that is of vital importance.

The integration of law and narrative also suggests that divine commandments emerge out of, and address specific situations in, the life experience of the people. As Fretheim observes, law in Israel is not simply a matter of divine revelation.[19] Commandments are spoken into the life of Israel at specific points where there is a need to be especially attentive to the opportunities for accomplishing the will of God. The Torah understands that at Sinai, Israel has come to just such a specific and crucial point in its life with God. Precisely at this juncture between God's deliverance of a people from Egyptian oppression and the people's realization of the divine mandate to become "a priestly kingdom and a holy nation," the Torah asserts that God spoke "all these words" (Exod. 20:1) and all these "ordinances" (24:3).

These observations allow me to push the inquiry one step further. If the two law collections are integrated into the narrative of Sinai events, what is their contribution to this liturgy of covenant? If the Sinai pericope presents the Decalogue as an introduction to the Book of the Covenant, are there internal thematic connections between the two collections that build upon this symbiotic relationship?

With the integration of these law collections into the Sinai episode, the Torah's vision suggests that *covenant-making and covenant-keeping recall and renew God's creational designs.* The Sinai pericope, I have suggested, recalls the heptadic patterning of the creation liturgy. Exodus 19:1 suggests that arriving at Sinai marked an important intersection in the journey of God and Israel. The six weeks of toil since the chaos of Egypt recall the six days of God's labor in the creation of the world.

But at this juncture the narrative tempo of the covenant liturgy changes. The seventh week now becomes the focus of extended reflection; like the seventh day of the primordial week, it is a time for careful deliberation

---

17. For a recent effort to capitalize on the theological significance of the interweaving of law and narrative specifically in the Sinai pericope, see T. E. Fretheim, *Exodus: A Bible Commentary for Teaching and Preaching* (Louisville: John Knox, 1991), 201–7.

18. Cf. Levenson, *Sinai and Zion*, 45–50.

19. Fretheim, *Exodus*, 205.

concerning what lies ahead. In the Torah's vision, this seventh-week deliberation extends for eleven months, after which Israel's passage towards Canaan resumes (cf. Num. 10:11). In essence, the Torah envisions the sojourn at Sinai to be a *sabbath day experience*, a virtual suspension of time to enable the community to reflect on the importance of their covenantal commission to become partners with God.

At Sinai the seventh-week commission to become "a priestly kingdom and a holy nation" is an invitation to receive and embrace the instructions presented in the Decalogue and the Book of the Covenant. These two collections clearly address the requisite societal structures and interpersonal relationships that Israel must create in order to exist as a "kingdom" and a "nation." But the thematic connections between these two collections invite the further understanding that they are also addressed—perhaps principally addressed—to the covenantal commission to become "priestly" and "holy." Towards this end the covenant liturgy presents both the Decalogue and the Book of the Covenant as a *witness to the principal importance of the creational summons to worship God.*

By placing the charge to keep the sabbath at the center of God's instructions (Exod. 20:8-11), the Decalogue (20:1-17) addresses the importance of worship in the life of the community that will leave Sinai. As the heart of God's commandments, sabbath-keeping serves as the vital gateway between commitment to God (vv. 3-7) and commitment to others (vv. 12-17). The Book of the Covenant (20:22—23:33) continues this emphasis, but inverts its rhetorical presentation. In this collection, prescriptions concerning worship and ritual begin (20:22-26) and end (23:10-19) the promulgation, serving to envelop the intervening stipulations concerning societal relations (21:1—23:9).

The centrality of worship in both the Decalogue and the Book of the Covenant is illustrated in Figure 5.1.

The dynamic center of the Decalogue is the fourth commandment. It is the fundamental moral imperative—the principal religious "policy," to recall Mendenhall's language—that defines covenant behavior.

> Remember the sabbath day, and keep it holy. Six days you shall labor and do all your work. But the seventh day is a sabbath to the LORD your God; you shall not do any work—you, your son or your daughter, your male or female slave, your livestock, or the resident alien in your towns. For in six days the LORD made heaven and earth, the sea, and all that is in them, but rested on the seventh day; therefore the LORD blessed the sabbath day and consecrated it. (20:8-11, NRSV)

A number of features underscore this commandment's central importance to the Decalogue. First, the sabbath commandment in the present

FIGURE 5.1

Decalogue	Book of the Covenant
Apodictic stipulations concerning God's exclusive claim on Israel (20:3-7)	Worship free of penultimate concerns (20:22-26)
Sabbath-keeping (20:8-11)	Apodictic/Casuistic stipulations concerning societal relations (21:1—23:9)
Apodictic stipulations concerning interhuman relations (20:12-17)	Worship in the service of others (23:10-19)

configuration is the longest of the Ten Commandments. The otherwise relatively brief, parenetic examples of apodictic law expand here to a more comprehensive form of instruction and commentary. The length of the commandment probably reflects its growth and expansion in the redactional process.[20] Nevertheless, its present shape has an internal coherence that calls attention to its contribution as a unit within the Decalogue. This coherence includes: an *imperative command* to "remember" and "hallow" the sabbath day (v. 8); a description of *how* the command is to be implemented, first in terms of work permitted, then of work prohibited (vv. 9-10); and a commentary on *why* the commandment is to be heeded (v. 11).

Second, the Decalogue links the sabbath commandment explicitly to God's creational design in three ways. 1. Whereas Genesis 2:1-3 refers simply to the "seventh day," the Decalogue reiterates the seven-day pattern of creation and expands upon it by specifying the seventh day as the "sabbath day" (Exod. 20:10, 11). The primordial seventh day is now elevated to a fixed, weekly institution. 2. The commandment to keep the sabbath day holy (*qādaš*), that is, to "sanctify" the day by setting it apart from the other six days, engages the community in an act of imaging God. The subject of the verb *qādaš* is the community of faith in verse 8, but in verse 11 it is God. In Patrick's words, "One might say that God bestows the quality of holiness upon the day, and Israel is called to . . . *join in the sanctifying act.*"[21] 3. The commandment's explicit rationale for remembering the sabbath day is that God created the world in six days and rested on the seventh (v. 11). While sabbath commands elsewhere in the Hebrew Bible contain other motiva-

---

20. For discussion of the basic issues see, e.g., Childs, *Exodus,* 413–17; Patrick, *Old Testament Law,* 49–51.

21. Patrick, *Old Testament Law,* 49–50, emphasis added.

tions for obedience,[22] the Decalogue grounds the exhortation in the sacred reality of the cosmic order. As Fretheim has seen, in the Decalogue "sabbath-keeping is an act of creation-keeping. . . . To keep the sabbath is to participate in God's intention for the rhythm of creation."[23]

A third feature underscoring this commandment's importance to the Decalogue involves how sabbath-keeping enables the covenant community to participate in God's intentions for the rhythm of creation. Recall that in the creation liturgy of Genesis 1–2, the seventh day signals both an ending (of God's creative acts on behalf of the cosmos) and a beginning (of God's partnership with humankind in ongoing acts of creaturely creativity.) The sabbath command commemorates and sustains a similar transition. On the one hand, the internal dynamics of Exodus 20:8-11 explicate sabbath observance with reference to the cosmic rhythm of work that is to proceed and work that is to cease. The work that is enjoined is the work of creation, from God's perspective the "creative making" of "heaven and earth, the sea, and all that is in them" (v. 11; cf. v. 9). From the community's perspective, it becomes the work of sustaining and, where necessary, re-creating the work that God has already wrought. The cessation applies not only to God and humankind, but also to the whole of the created order, as the sevenfold enumeration of living beings in verse 10 indicates.[24]

On the other hand, within the Decalogue as a whole, the sabbath command helps to sustain another important transition between God and humankind. Within the Decalogue, instructions concerning sabbath observance are located precisely at the intersection of the commandments to love God absolutely (Exod. 20:3-7) and the commandments to live in the world with absolute fidelity to the nature and purposes of God (vv. 12-17). As the center around which all commandments converge, the sabbath command stipulates that from this point forward in Israel's journey towards Canaan, there can be no separation between the community's devotion to God and its commitment to the world. Faithfulness to one

---

22. Note especially Deut. 5:13-15, the Deuteronomic version of the Ten Commandments, where sabbath-keeping is grounded not so much in the memory of creation as in the memory of exodus. By this account, to remember the sabbath is to remember that all people, regardless of their social status, need and deserve rest from their labors. It is customary to contrast the ethical-social concerns in this Deuteronomic version of the sabbath commandment with the presumably more theological concerns in the Exodus version (e.g., W. Harrelson, *The Ten Commandments and Human Rights* [Philadelphia: Fortress, 1980], 80). But as the discussion below will stipulate, the Exodus version in fact mediates a theology that summons the community to concretize sabbath observance in interpersonal relationships. See further the discussion in chap. 7, pp. 184–87.

23. Ibid.

24. Ibid.

without faithfulness to the other will not fulfill the divine hopes for covenant partnership with humankind. Only when heaven and earth rest their mutual destinies in the "sanctuary of time"[25] called sabbath, will this partnership be fully realized. In this sense, then, sabbath-keeping is analogous to creation-keeping: it commemorates rest *from* work as the creational, and now the covenantal, means of preparing *for* the work of fulfilling God's ultimate goal for humankind.

Whereas the Decalogue (Exod. 20:1-17) places the concern for worship at the dynamic center of its commandments, the Book of the Covenant (20:22—23:33) begins and ends with basic principles regarding worship, principles which in turn provide the context for the laws governing communal behavior. The thematic coherence between these two law collections should not be missed. The Decalogue prescribes sabbath-keeping as the central imperative that binds together heaven and earth in mutual devotion and commitment. The Book of the Covenant reiterates the principal importance of this religious imperative and explicates it in terms of its consequent ethical and social requirements. This linkage between the two law collections underscores the Torah's vision that at Sinai worship and justice are integrated into the covenantal commission with equal force.

It is clear that the present shape of the Book of the Covenant is the result of a cumulative redactional process over an extensive period of time.[26] Nevertheless, the present compilation has a coherence of its own that underscores its theological function within the Sinai pericope.[27] Figure 5.2 shows this

---

25. Patrick, *Old Testament Law*, 50.

26. A general consensus holds that the collection as it now stands is unevenly divided between two distinct forms of laws. The largest block of laws within the collection, 21:1—22:20, contains case laws (casuistic laws) or "ordinances" *(mišpaṭîm)* which are dominated by an impersonal and conditional "If (when)-then" style. A smaller collection, 22:21—23:9, is apodictic in style and, like the "words" *(dĕbārîm)* or "commands" of the Decalogue, promulgates direct and unconditional personal commands. Case laws are generally regarded to have their origin in the common or "secular" law of the ancient Near East, whereas apodictic laws carry moral imperatives that typically derive their force from a religious authority. While once it was common to regard the apodictic law as unique to Israel, more recent scholarship makes it clear that apodictic law was also known outside Israel. The relationship of these two forms of law to the pentateuchal sources and the date of their inclusion into the Sinai pericope are unclear. Most would agree that the final redaction presumes an agrarian society, thus some time after the settlement in Canaan. For further discussion, see Childs, *Exodus*, 451–64; Patrick, *Old Testament Law*, 63–96; Blenkinsopp, *The Pentateuch*, 197–209.

27. A number of studies have discerned a compositional unity in the Book of the Covenant. E.g., J. Halbe, *Das Privilegrecht Jahwes, Exodus 34. 10-26. Gestalt und Wesen, Herkunft und Wirken in vordeuteronomistischer Zeit* (Göttingen: Vandenhoeck & Ruprecht, 1975); L. Schwienhorst-Schönberger, *Das Bundesbuch (Ex 20,22-23,33). Studien zu einer Entstehung und Theologie* (Berlin: Walter de Gruyter, 1990); Y. Osumi, *Die Kompositionsgeschichte des Bundesbuches Exodus 20,22b-23,33* (Göttingen: Vandenhoeck and Ruprecht, 1991). On the

FIGURE 5.2.
The Book of the Covenant (Exodus 20:22—23:33)

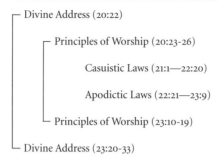

Divine Address (20:22)

Principles of Worship (20:23-26)

Casuistic Laws (21:1—22:20)

Apodictic Laws (22:21—23:9)

Principles of Worship (23:10-19)

Divine Address (23:20-33)

overall structure and will serve as the basis for further comments about the concerns with worship that envelop the Book of the Covenant—rather than the specific laws it promulgates.

In its present shape, the Book of the Covenant presents an assortment of laws and commandments that continue God's seventh-week discourse with Israel at Sinai. The divine address that introduces the collection (Exod. 20:22) serves to connect these words to the instructions begun in 19:3. An epilogue in 23:20-33 concludes the divine address with instructions that focus the community on the forthcoming departure from Sinai and the conquest of Canaan.

At the center of this divine address is a collection of laws, first casuistic (Exod. 21:1—22:20), then apodictic (22:21—23:9), that serve to expand upon the foundational principles of the Ten Commandments. The casuistic laws encompass a wide variety of concerns (for example, slavery, capital offenses, personal injury, property loss) that correspond with those commonly attested in the law codes of the ancient Near East. As a whole, these "common" laws stipulate the basic rights and responsibilities that regulate day-to-day living in every human society. They presuppose an ethical consensus that can be formulated in authoritative law and enforced by civil judiciary systems. In the context of the Sinai pericope, these "secular" laws correspond with God's creational designs for all humankind.[28] Like all ordered societies, Israel is to live in harmony with the common justice that informs and sustains life in any community.

---

importance of attending to the inner structure of the Book of the Covenant as a first step in describing and understanding its function, see further Crüsemann, *The Torah,* 112–15.

28. Cf. Fretheim, *Exodus,* 240–41.

The apodictic laws, by contrast, are principally concerned with ethical and moral issues that derive their authority from Israel's specific relationship with God. They focus on the disadvantaged in society—the widow, the orphan, the poor—persons whose status in life makes them vulnerable to abuse. Their common lot is symbolized by the "resident alien" whose particular needs for justice both introduce (Exod. 22:21) and conclude (23:9) these admonitions.

In most ancient societies, including Israel, the "resident alien" (*gēr*) is the person who lives within the boundaries of the state and hence is expected to conform to its laws, but does not enjoy the full rights of citizenship.[29] All such persons have relatively weak status within the society, making them targets for exploitation. According to these apodictic commandments, just such persons are to be protected. The community that gathers at Sinai must remember that they too were once targets of abuse in a system that disregarded the rights of the "alien" (22:21, 23:9). In this memory they are commanded to display a justice that is consonant with God's special compassion for them (cf. 22:27).

In the final form of the Sinai pericope, the Torah envisions concern for aliens as more than a simple historical reminder of a previous experience. The redactional history of this concern suggests a more complex theological development. It is likely that protection of aliens first becomes an important issue after 722 B.C.E., when the Assyrian conquest of Samaria drove significant numbers of refugees south to Judah. This datum suggests that the main redaction of the Book of the Covenant would have occurred in the late eighth or early seventh century.[30] In this connection Crüsemann has suggested that the Book of the Covenant represents "the most important theological work to come out of the catastrophe of the northern kingdom."[31]

In light of this history, the relocation of the Book of the Covenant within the Sinai pericope suggests that concern for the poor and the weak and the aliens became for Israel both a proleptic *instruction* and an enduring *promise*. As *instruction* the Book of the Covenant warns a future Israel against abusive treatment of aliens within its own borders; such treatment would render the covenant people no more faithful to God's cosmic intentions than the Egyptians. Indeed, by framing the apodictic laws with a concern for the aliens, the Book of the Covenant insists that justice for the socially and politically disadvantaged, no less than love of God, is the

29. On the meaning of *gēr* see R. Martin-Achard, "*Gûr*," *TLOT*, vol. 1, 307–10. See further Patrick, *Old Testament Law*, 86.

30. Crüsemann, *The Torah*, 182–85.

31. Ibid., 197.

essential requirement of covenant fidelity. As *promise* the Book of the Covenant serves to assure all those who may be subject to political control by others—in Israel, Babylon, or Persia—that whenever the weak and the abused cry out for relief, God will surely hear their cry and deliver them (cf. Exod. 22:23).

What is striking about this compilation of laws at the center of the Book of the Covenant is that relevant legal material from extrabiblical sources contains no proper analogy to such a mixing of "secular" and "religious" laws.[32] The Torah's vision is that at Sinai the community of faith receives an unprecedented commission. Their *creational commission* is to live in harmony with the fundamental principles of the cosmic order for humanity. Their *covenantal vocation* is to enact this commission through justice on earth that demonstrates both their responsibility to the world and their commitment to God. In short, they are to unite the secular and the sacred.

This is no easy task. How are they to remain faithful to both their creational and their covenantal commissions without succumbing to the temptation to commit themselves more to the one than the other? The internal dynamics of the Book of the Covenant suggest that the context for realizing this most demanding union of the secular and the sacred is worship.

As Figure 5.2 shows, the entire collection of casuistic and apodictic laws (Exod. 21:1—23:9) is bracketed by prescriptions concerning worship (20:23-26; 23:10-19). This structure suggests that proper relationship with God is the defining concern of Israel's covenantal commission.[33] The first half of these prescriptions (20:23-26) explicates the proper relationship with God in terms of the *object* and the *place* of worship.[34] Whereas the Decalogue states the basic principle that an "idol" *(pesel)* is not to be the object of Israel's worship (20:4), the Book of the Covenant elaborates on this command by specifying that there can be no "gods" *(ĕlōhîm)* manufactured from silver or gold (20:23). A "god" or "God" (the Hebrew word renders

---

32. Cf. Sarna, *Exploring Exodus*, 174.

33. Halbe has argued that exclusive loyalty to God constitutes the original law, what he calls the *Privilegrecht* (the "privilege law"), that is the source model for the Book of the Covenant. He finds the earliest stratum of this law in Exod. 34:11-26 (*Das Privilegrecht Jahwes*, 449–50). Halbe's thesis has certainly not gone unchallenged, especially by those who have long argued that Exod. 34:11-26 represents a late, Deuteronomistic version of covenant-making (e.g., Perlitt, *Das Bundestheologie*, 216–18; cf. Blum, *Studien zur Komposition des Pentateuch*, 68–70). Regardless of the question about date, it is surely significant that both Exod. 34 and the Book of the Covenant introduce individual covenant obligations with instructions concerning altars, idols, and religious festivals.

34. Cf. P. D. Hanson, *The People Called: The Growth of Community in the Bible* (San Francisco: Harper and Row, 1986), 50–51.

both nouns) whose image is constructed from any created substance in the world cannot be a fitting symbol for the Creator of the world who now addresses Moses from heaven.

Exodus 20:24-26 stipulates that the place of worship is also an important concern. Although certain features in this (originally independent) "altar law" remain obscure, the general prescription is clear. There are to be special places in the world where God "comes" to receive the worship of the community and to bestow in special ways the divine blessing (v. 24). These places will not substitute for the reality of God's presence, for they are envisioned as but simple altars of sod or unhewn stone. Nor will they limit God's presence to any one locale, for *God* chooses the places where God will be present to people. Nevertheless, a people committed to absolute fidelity to God and world will not be careless about those holy places where the divine-human encounter is specially accessible.[35]

The second half of these bracketing worship prescriptions (Exod. 23:10-19) addresses the special *times* of worship: first the sabbath year and the sabbath day (vv. 10-13), then the three annual religious "festivals" (vv. 14-19). The sabbath year (the year the land lays fallow) and the sabbath day tie the ritual calendar to the heptadic pattern of God's creational design (six years/days you shall work, but the seventh . . .). The Book of the Covenant stipulates, however, that the ritual observance of God's cosmic design is also the occasion for enacting God's earthly concerns for the poor and the disadvantaged. The fallow year and the sabbath day invite into God's creational care the poor, the resident alien, and the animals, both domestic and wild (vv. 11-12). Just as the ritual calendar integrates cosmic designs with earthly needs for justice, so the seasons of the agricultural year become occasions for celebrating the liturgy of God's life-giving work in creation. Three festivals are designated: Unleavened Bread, Harvest, and Ingathering. No details are provided concerning how or where the community may institute these festivals. The concern at this point, rather, is to

---

35. Crüsemann has argued that having the altar law at the beginning of the Book of the Covenant is a critical clue for dating the Book of the Covenant to the period after the fall of the northern kingdom. During this period the need to distinguish between authentic YHWH shrines and multiple regional shrines would have been pronounced. He states the matter as follows: "It is not the holy place and not even the proper altar with its cult that reveals the presence of God. In spite of, or because of the foreign powers and super-powers in action here, the formulation of verse 24b establishes that it depends upon the wishes of YHWH himself where he will cause his name to be remembered, so that he can appear. *It is he alone, not the Assyrians, the new settlers or the accommodating groups in Judah or Israel who can determine where this will happen.*" (*The Torah*, 174, emphasis added). I suggest that Crüsemann's observation might be extended as a clue not only to the origin of this concern with proper access to God, but also to its subsequent appropriation in Yehud.

recognize that the rhythm of life and nature is a faithful summons to appear "before the Lord GOD" (v. 17).

The epilogue to the Book of the Covenant (Exod. 23:20-33) concludes this part of God's address to Moses. The focus of these verses shifts from Sinai and the promulgation of these laws to the journey that lies ahead once the community departs for Canaan. There is no overt reference to either the casuistic or the apodictic laws that have preceded, hence it is the custom to dismiss these verses as an editorial addition. But Fretheim has rightly seen that in their present context these verses, along with the introductory principles of worship in 20:23-26, provide the basic hermeneutic for interpreting the entire Book of the Covenant.[36]

At issue in the Book of the Covenant is the community's need of the "blessing" of God, not only at this juncture called Sinai, but at every place along the journey toward becoming "a priestly kingdom and a holy nation." Exodus 20:24 announced that God bestows the blessing at special places of worship. The intervening common laws and religious commandments (21:1—23:9) emphasized the need for obedience and consecration, each of which requires careful attention to the *object,* the *place,* and the *times* of worship (20:23-26; 23:10-19). The epilogue now announces that worship of God is not only the key for faithful execution of the covenantal commission, it is also the single most important criterion for possessing the blessing of the land of Canaan. In Canaan as at Sinai, the community is summoned to exclusive fidelity to God: "You shall not bow down to their gods, or worship them. . . . You shall worship the LORD your God, and I will bless your bread and your water" (23:24-25, NRSV; cf. vv. 32-33).

It is fitting, therefore, that in the composite account of Exodus 24, an act of worship provides the context for the covenant ratification. The exchange of God's covenantal commission and the community's vows of obedience is effected by a liturgy (vv. 3-8) that involves a sacred place (altar) and ritual acts (sacrifices and blood). The rite of covenant-making is in turn introduced (vv. 1-2) and implemented (vv. 9-11) as a summons to worship that grants to those assembled an unparalleled intimacy with the presence of God. In the uncompromising language of verse 11: "they beheld God, and they ate and drank."

In fact, Exodus 24 has God addressing Moses twice. The first (24:1), as noted above, summons Moses and those accompanying him to a worship experience in which a ritual act solemnizes and concludes the "sabbath day experience" that had begun in the seventh week after exodus (cf. 19:1-3).

---

36. Fretheim, *Exodus,* 240. Fretheim articulates this hermeneutic as "loyalty and worship"; I agree with his discernment, although I have articulated the matter somewhat differently.

The second divine address (24:12-18) summons Moses to another sabbath day experience. On the seventh day of a new theophany at Sinai (v.16; cf. 19:3), God initiates further deliberations concerning the divine plan for the tabernacle. Once again, the sabbath day experience calls for a virtual suspension of time, here marked as a forty day/night address from God to Moses (v. 18). Just as the requirements for obedience to the moral and religious stipulations of the covenant require careful deliberation, so the requirements of consecration to that which is holy must be undertaken with utmost seriousness.

Covenant as Sanctuary Building and World Building (Exodus 25–40)

I have suggested that in the Torah's vision, covenant-making and covenant-keeping recall and renew God's creational designs. In the seventh week after the exodus from Egypt, God inaugurates a covenant liturgy that corresponds with the creation liturgy and announces the start of a new covenantal commission. To become "a priestly kingdom and a holy nation," the community of faith is summoned to a life shaped by the Decalogue and the Book of the Covenant. The covenant at Sinai also makes clear that the requirements of obedience not only recall the primordial design for an ordered world, they also renew the creational summons to worship God.

The importance of Sinai's covenantal summons to worship God is signaled by the thirteen chapters of detailed instructions regarding the tabernacle and its appurtenances in Exodus 25–31 and 35–40. The sheer volume of this material, which comprises nearly one-third of the book of Exodus, suggests that at least from the narrator's perspective, Israel's experience at Sinai can in no way be regarded as complete without the plans for the tabernacle.[37] Nevertheless, the contribution of these chapters to the Sinai pericope is often undervalued, both in the academy and in the church. Why is this so?

On critical grounds these chapters derive from the Priestly tradition, hence from a post-exilic setting that is incongruous with the period of the exodus. Since the days of Wellhausen, such a judgment has typically supported a negative assessment of the value of this material. At best, these chapters have been thought to provide little more than historical fiction, an idealized retrojection of the Solomonic temple into the Mosaic age. At worst, they have been interpreted as a tendentious rewriting of history that serves only the fraudulent interests of a self-promoting priestly establish-

---

37. Cf. ibid., 263.

ment. In either case, the working hypothesis in critical scholarship has been the assumption that the "historical" experience at Sinai did not include instructions concerning the tabernacle.

On other grounds, all but the most fundamentalist of readers in the church may also have concluded that the rewards for careful attention to the concerns of these chapters are not worth the patience they demand. First, the information regarding the tabernacle and its cultic paraphernalia is given in minute detail and in most cases *twice,* once prescriptively (Exod. 25–31) and once descriptively (Exod. 35–40). Second, even a careful reader soon realizes that the information provided is insufficient to reconstruct exactly the cultic objects that the texts describe. In the words of M. Haran, "We are faced with a unique combination of long-winded description on the one hand and total omission of various particulars on the other."[38]

In view of the tendency to dismiss these chapters, it is important to stress once more that the Torah's aggregate vision is a theological mosaic whose truth is larger than the sum of its individual parts. The texts collected in Exodus 25–31 and 35–40 are of Priestly origin and do reflect historical concerns emerging after the Babylonian conquest. Nevertheless, their present location within the Sinai pericope contributes to and advances the covenant liturgy begun in Exodus 19. In this composite vision, covenant partnership summons the community of faith to a life shaped not just by the earlier noted commandments of law (Exod. 20–23) but by the consecration of the tabernacle as well (25–31, 35–40). To embrace one part of the liturgy without the other does not do justice to the truth of the whole vision.

Moreover, both the inclusion and the omission of detail in these texts are significant indicators of their theological importance. Details concerning the dimensions and compositions of the various ritual objects make clear at least that worship must not be taken lightly. In the Torah's vision, worship that grows out of and embodies true covenant partnership requires more than a random, ad hoc encounter with God. But the omission of a blueprint for the exact replication of the physical objects of worship sounds an equally important caution against misdirected readings. The focus of the texts themselves is not on cubits and figures, numbers and shapes, but rather on the indwelling presence of God that a sanctuary and its holy accoutrements enables a community to celebrate (cf. Exod. 25:8,22; 29:45).[39]

---

38. M. Haran, *Temples and Temple Service in Ancient Israel: An Inquiry into the Character of Cult Phenomena and the Historical Setting of the Priestly School* (Oxford: Clarendon, 1978), 150.

39. Cassuto notes that in the very passages where such details are most noticeably absent, the texts routinely explain that God used a vision to show Moses what he was to make (*Book of Exodus,* 321). In other words, the texts themselves suggest that everything necessary for accomplishing the divine purpose was available to Moses, if not to the reader.

To reclaim the theological significance of these texts within the Sinai pericope, it helps to note that they sustain in important ways the creational imagery that undergirds so much of the covenant liturgy. Hidden correspondences between the tabernacle and the cosmos have long been recognized in both Jewish and Christian interpretation, although too often the symbolical or allegorical approach has dismissed the importance of these texts, rather than confirmed it.[40] Recent scholarship, however, has been particularly attentive to numerous verbal and thematic ties between the tabernacle and creation that may be traced to the texts themselves. These ties may be summarized briefly as follows.

1. The heptadic pattern of the creation account also appears in the instructions regarding the tabernacle.[41] The theophany in which the instructions are disclosed to Moses begins on the seventh day, following six days of preparation for entering into the cloud of divine presence on Mt. Sinai (Exod. 24:16). Instructions for building the tabernacle then unfold through seven speeches from God to Moses, each one distinguished by the introductory formula "The LORD said (*dābar*) [or] spoke (*'āmar*) to Moses" (25:1; 30:11, 17, 22, 34; 31:1, 12). The seventh speech (31:12-17) culminates the instructions for the tabernacle with the divine plans for the sabbath day, just as in the seven speeches in the creational account of Genesis 1:1—2:4a.[42]

In Exodus 35–40 the actual building of the tabernacle begins with instructions concerning the sabbath day (35:2-3), following which the account in these chapters continues with repeated references to work being done "as the LORD had commanded Moses." This phrase is particularly prominent in 40:17-33, where it is repeated seven times to describe the actual erection of the tabernacle by Moses.

---

40. The allegorical approach is operative at least as early as Philo (*De Vita Mosis* 2. 88ff.) and Josephus (*War* 10.55; *Antiquities* 3.77). For further discussion of the history of exegesis, see, Childs, *Exodus*, 547–50.

41. The heptadic pattern in the tabernacle texts has been widely noted. See J. Blenkinsopp, "The Structure of P," *CBQ* 38 (1976), 275–92; J. Kearney, "Creation and Liturgy: The P Redaction of Ex. 25–40," *ZAW* 89 (1977), 375–87; N. Sarna, *Exploring Exodus: The Heritage of Biblical Israel* (New York: Schocken Books, 1986), 213–15; F. H. Gorman Jr., *The Ideology of Ritual: Space, Time, and Status in the Priestly Ritual* (Sheffield: JSOT Press, 1990), 47.

42. Kearney ("Creation and Liturgy") has sought to correlate these seven speeches rather specifically with the acts of creation in the seven days of Genesis 1:1—2:4a. Not all of the correspondences that Kearney discerns have been judged persuasive; see, for example, J. Levenson, *Creation and the Persistence of Evil: The Drama of Divine Omnipotence* (San Francisco: Harper and Row, 1988). Nevertheless, Gorman has noted that the connection between cosmos and cult is important enough to be able to say: ". . . just as cosmos originated with Yahweh, so also the form of sacred space, of cult, originated with Yahweh" (*The Ideology of Ritual*, 47).

FIGURE 5.3

Creation of the World	Construction of the Sanctuary
And God saw everything that he had made, and behold, it was very good (Gen. 1:31)	And Moses saw all the work and behold, they had done it (Exod. 39:43)
Thus the heavens and the the earth were finished (Gen. 2:1)	Thus all the work of the tabernacle of the tent of meeting was finished (Exod. 39:32)
On the seventh day God finished his work which he had done (Gen. 2:2)	So Moses finished the the work (Exod. 40:33)
So God blessed the seventh day (Gen. 2:3)	And Moses blessed them (Exod. 39:43)

2. Additional verbal parallels reinforce the heptadic symmetry between the tabernacle texts and the creation accounts (see Figure 5.3).[43]

3. Besides these verbal parallels, a number of common themes link creation and tabernacle to a shared vision. The liturgy of creation asserts that God's basic acts of separation and division define the boundaries between the holy and the common. The plan of the tabernacle suggests that in worship the community participates in a similar act of dividing and ordering the world according to God's design.

The organizing principle in the tabernacle is the demarcation of sacred space into ordered zones of holiness.[44] From the common world of the camp outside the tabernacle one enters sacred space by passing first into the outer courtyard, then into the Holy Place, and finally into the Holy of Holies. Every aspect of the passage is carefully ordered. Non-priests are permitted in the courtyard but no further. Ordinary priests minister in the Holy Place but may not enter into the Holy of Holies. Only the high priest may minister in the Holy of Holies. The grades of sanctity defined by these zones are reinforced by a comparable ordering of the ritual objects placed within them: the materials used to construct these objects, the craftsmanship required to make them, and the gradations of color they displayed.

43. These parallels are often cited. See, for example, Blenkinsopp, *The Pentateuch*, 218; J. G. Gammie, *Holiness in Israel* (Minneapolis: Fortress, 1989), 14; J. D. Levenson, *Creation and the Persistence of Evil*, 85–86.

44. The seminal discussion of the "grades of sanctity" in the tabernacle belongs to Haran, *Temples and Temple Service in Ancient Israel*, 158–65, 175–88. See further, Sarna, *Exploring Exodus*, 205–6; P. P. Jensen, *Graded Holiness: A Key to the Priestly Conception of the World* (Sheffield: JSOT Press, 1992), 89–114.

Collectively, these parallels envision the construction of the tabernacle to be an intentional complement to God's creational designs for the cosmos. In support of this understanding, J. Blenkinsopp has drawn special attention to the "conclusion formula" in Exodus 40:33, "So Moses finished the work." The parallel between this phrase and the notice in Genesis 2:2 ("God finished the work") suggests that the construction of the sanctuary is indeed a completion of the work begun in creation.[45]

In the Torah's aggregate vision, the tabernacle not only completes the cosmic design, it also reclaims creational intentions from the mire of sin and disobedience. With the tabernacle the community does more than just sustain God's primordial hopes for humankind, it re-creates them. Fretheim has discerned the theological pattern that underlies the present arrangement of Exodus 25–40. It is: creation, fall, re-creation.[46] Three indicators support this judgment and underscore its heuristic value for reclaiming the importance of the covenantal summons to worship.

First, the insertion of the non-priestly account of the golden calf incident (Exod. 32–34) creates an abrupt suspension of the creational designs of Genesis 1–2 recalled in the instructions of Exodus 25–31. Like the primordial subversion of the cosmic design (Gen. 3–6), the golden calf undermines God's intentions for exclusive relationship with the community of faith. The instructions for the tabernacle resume in Exodus 35–40, which announces that the first act in the re-creation of the relationship between God and humankind is the construction of the sanctuary, the "one spot in the midst of a world of disorder where God's creative, ordering work is completed according to the divine intention just as it was in the beginning."[47]

Second, a number of correspondences may be discerned between Moses and Noah and between the tabernacle and the ark.[48] The book of Exodus introduces Moses as the baby who floats on the waters of the Nile in a "basket" of bitumen and pitch (Exod. 2:3-5). The word for "basket" *(tēbāh)* is the same word for "ark" that occurs prominently in the flood narratives of Genesis 6–9. Such a notice identifies Moses in effect as a "new Noah," the one who will deliver his people from the chaos that threatens their destiny as God's special people.[49] Also, Moses' prayers of intercession (Exod. 32–33) resemble Noah's sacrifice (Gen. 8:20-22) in that they address God from a

---

45. Blenkinsopp, "The Structure of P," 278; *The Pentateuch*, 218.

46. Fretheim, *Exodus*, 272, cf. 268–69.

47. Ibid., 271.

48. Ibid., 268–69. I am indebted to Fretheim's basic observations in what follows, although I have modified his discussion in keeping with my own insights.

49. T. E.Fretheim, "The Book of Genesis," *NIB*, vol. 1 (Nashville: Abingdon, 1994), 391; cf. *Exodus*, 38.

world no longer "very good" and they secure from God a renewed commitment to pursue covenantal intentions (Exod. 34; cf. Gen. 9:8-17).[50] Moreover, both Moses and Noah find favor in God's sight (Exod. 33:12-17; cf. Gen. 6:8), receive commands to build a structure, and carry out these commands obediently (Exod. 39:42-43; cf. Gen. 6:22).

Corresponding parallels exist between the tabernacle and the ark. The dimensions of the ark—roughly 450 x 75 x 45 feet (Gen. 6:15)—suggest a floating house rather than a boat, in symbolic terms an inverted temple bearing its passengers safely to shore.[51] The tabernacle, as a portable structure the people carry with them as they journey towards Canaan, is in symbolic terms a "portable Sinai," a mobile home for God in the midst of a people on the move.[52] Finally, both the ark and the tabernacle are "sanctuaries" that provide the prescribed medium by which God and people "move in a secure and ordered way through a world of disorder on their way to a new creation."[53]

The third indicator is that Moses erects the tabernacle on "the first day of the first month" (Exod. 40:2), the same day that the "waters [of the flood] were dried up from the earth; and Noah removed the covering of the ark, and looked . . ." (Gen. 8:13, NRSV). Both events represent a primordial event in the life of the community, the day when a people are given a chance to make a new beginning with God.

These three parallels between creation and tabernacle carry the message that sanctuary building is an act of world building.[54] Just as God designs the cosmos to be an ordered harmony of heaven and earth, so God commands a sacred place on earth where the harmony between the holy and the common may be preserved, sustained, and restored. In the words of J. Levenson:

> The function of these correspondences is to underscore the depiction of the sanctuary as a world, that is, an ordered, supportive, and obedient environment, and the depiction of the world as a sanctuary, that is, a place in which the reign of God is visible and unchallenged, and his holiness is palpable, unthreatened, and pervasive.[55]

---

50. On Moses' prayers as a paradigm of worship, see below, 142-147.

51. Fretheim, "The Book of Genesis," 391; cf. *Exodus*, 268–69.

52. Fretheim, *Exodus*, 274.

53. Ibid., 269. Fretheim speaks of the ark and the tabernacle as means of movement specifically for the "people of God." I have modified this observation to suggest that the movement is God's as much as the people's.

54. Cf. Blenkinsopp, *The Pentateuch*, 62.

55. Levenson, *Creation and the Persistence of Evil*, 86.

Paradigms for Ministry: Prayer as Covenantal Vocation

The Torah's vision of the covenantal liturgy at Sinai portrays prayer as a critical and constitutive act of ministry that opens up new possibilities for God, people, and world. The ongoing theophany (Exod. 19–31) that was preparing the community for life in the presence of God is suddenly interrupted by the report that an unholy golden calf has been fashioned (32:1-6). This event renders instructions for life with a holy God both irrelevant and impossible;[56] the liturgy binding God and people in covenant partnership comes to a tragic and unintended dead end in the smashing of the tablets. Eventually, the tablets will be re-scribed, the covenant renewed, and the building instructions resumed. At a critical juncture between the covenant broken and the covenant renewed the Torah places the prayer of Moses (Exod. 32:7-14).[57]

The Hebrew Bible positions a number of prose prayers strategically within narrative contexts. Although there are differences in detail, such prayers function within literary contexts that typically display three essential features: a crisis erupts in the relationship between people and God; a human responds with a prayer that raises questions about divine justice and/or divine intentions; and the crisis is resolved or explained in a way that the aggregate narrative portrays as the result of a pray-er's engagement with God.[58] In sum, such prayers invite the understanding that God is open and responsive to the contribution that humans may make to the process of divine deliberation.

The crisis that occasions Moses' prayer is the making of the golden calf, the consequences of which are spelled out in God's address to Moses (Exod. 32:7-10). This address begins with a divine imperative, "Go down," that signals an abrupt ending to the lengthy instructions concerning the tabernacle. Next comes an indictment, indicating that God views the golden calf as a violation of the first two commandments. Such apostasy not only abrogates the essential requirements of covenant partnership, it also threat-

---

56. Traditional critical analysis has assigned the bulk of Exod. 32–34 to the early pentateuchal sources (JE), making it a continuation of the basic stratum in Exod. 19–24. Contemporary discussion continues to debate the inner unity of these chapters and how much or how little of the pericope is to be assigned to the Deuteronomistic tradition. There is consensus, however, that Exod. 32–34 is non-priestly and thus effects a break in the otherwise continuous priestly account of 25–31 and 35–40.

57. One indication that Exod. 32–34 combines different traditions is the presence of a number of speeches and prayers offered by Moses to God, some of which stand in tension with each other; cf. 32:7-14, 30-34; 33:12-23; 34:8-9.

58. In addition to Exod. 32:7-14, see, e.g., Gen. 18:22-33; Numb. 11:4-34; 14:11-23; Josh. 7:7-9. For further discussion of these texts, see S. E. Balentine, *Prayer in the Hebrew Bible: The Drama of Divine-Human Dialogue,* OBT (Minneapolis: Fortress, 1993), 118–45.

ens a repetition of the primordial corruption of humankind that had once nullified God's entire creational design. In God's judgment the people "have acted perversely" *(šiḥēt)*. The same root occurs twice in the preface to the flood story: "the earth was corrupt *(nišātāh)*; for all flesh had corrupted *(hišḥît)* its ways" (Gen. 6:12). On that occasion God responded with a comprehensive punishment that signaled the end of creation: "now I am going to destroy them *(mašḥîtām)* along with the earth" (Gen. 6:13).

The verbal and thematic connections between the golden calf and the flood story serve to sharpen the crisis that Moses now faces. Like Noah, Moses finds himself staring into the breach of a world undone, where divine intentions are canceled and the orders of creation yield once more to a sea of chaos. Unlike Noah, however, Moses does not simply acquiesce to God's intentions. Indeed, the text suggests that God anticipates Moses may having something to contribute to the deliberation process.

The key phrase is Exodus 32:10: "Now leave me alone *(hannîḥāh lî—* literally "give me rest"), so that my wrath may burn hot against them." Elsewhere in the Hebrew Bible this language is used with reference to someone who has the power to do something but is asked to refrain.[59] Here in Exodus is the only place where the phrase is used with reference to God. The logic of the text is that God has the power to execute judgment unilaterally, but strangely does not do so without first asking for Moses' silent consent. Given what follows in vv. 11-14, God's request to be left alone seems to anticipate that Moses may respond with a prayer that could alter God's intentions. Targum Onkelos captures the sense of this drama nicely with the paraphrase "Refrain from thy prayer."[60]

Given the people's disobedience and God's clear intent to "consume them" (Exod. 32:10), Moses appears to be faced with but two options. He may yield to God's directive to refrain from speaking, in which case he will become a silent witness to the destruction of a sinful people; or he may respond by accepting God's decision to move into the future without these people, in which case he will be singled out, like Noah, as the one in whom God's future plans will be realized. But Moses dares to pursue a third option.

With a remarkable address that combines accusation and petition (Exod. 32:11-14), Moses implores God to reconsider how the future with this

---

59. The only other case where the exact form occurs is Judg. 16:26, where Samson instructs the guard who has led him into Dagon's temple to leave him alone so that he might feel the pillars of the house. For comparable uses, see 2 Sam. 16:11, 2 Kings 23:18, Hosea 4:17. Most commentators give little attention to this phrase. See, however, the cogent reflections of D. Gowan, *Theology in Exodus: Biblical Theology in the Form of a Commentary* (Louisville: Westminster/John Knox, 1994), 223–24.

60. Quoted from B. S. Childs, *The Book of Exodus* (Philadelphia: Westminster, 1974), 556.

people might unfold.[61] He begins with a twofold repetition of the question "Why?" *(lām[m]āh)*. This language is especially frequent in lament prayers where suppliants raise hard questions about something in the relationship with God that seems very wrong. So, for example, psalms of lament often use *lām(m)āh* to introduce questions concerning God's inexplicable absence (cf. Pss. 10:1; 22:1; 44:24). In other cases, the question concerns innocent suffering (for example, Jer. 15:18; 20:18; Job 7:20) or the perversion of divine justice (for example, Hab. 1:3, 13). For our purposes here, it is significant to note that of all the named persons in the Hebrew Bible to whom such questions are attributed, none figures so prominently as Moses.[62]

The protest conveyed by Moses' questions is heightened by the triple description of God's intentions as "evil" *(r'h)*. In the first instance, Moses attributes such an assessment to the Egyptians: "Why should the Egyptians say, 'With evil intent *(běrā 'āh)* God led them out to kill them . . . and to consume them from the face of the earth'?" (Exod. 32:12). In the second case, Moses repeats the charge himself, petitioning God to "repent concerning the evil toward your people *(wěhinnāhēm 'al hārā 'âh lě 'ammekā)*" (v. 12). A third reference is supplied by the narrator whose summation of this interchange confirms the assessments of both the Egyptians and Moses: "And the LORD repented of the evil *(wayyinnāhēm yhwh 'al hārā 'āh)* that he planned to bring on his people" (v. 14).

Moses' questions are buttressed with three petitions, each directed to God in the same imperative tone that has characterized God's instructions to him (cf. Exod. 32:7). He demands that God: "turn away" *(šwb)* from wrath (v. 12a); "repent" *(hinnāhēm)*, that is, change or reverse the divine decision (v. 12b); and "remember" *(zěkōr)* the promise to secure for Abraham and his ancestors an inheritance in the land of Canaan (v. 13). Coupled with Moses' questions, these petitions present God with three arguments for reconsidering the future possibilities. First, Moses' contends that these people, despite their disobedience, remain "your [God's] people *('ammekā)*" (vv. 11, 12), thus insisting that it is unreasonable for God to abandon

---

61. In the language of v. 11, Moses' prayer seeks to "soften the face of the Lord" *(wayěhal mōše et pěnê yhwh)*. This phrase is typical in contexts that display a set pattern: God's anger is kindled and punishment is threatened; an intercessor "softens" God's face; and divine punishment is withdrawn. For further discussion, see J. Reindl, *Das Angesicht Gottes im Sprachgebrauch des Alten Testaments* (Leipzig: St. Benno, 1970), 175–85.

62. On the distribution and theological significance of *lām(m)āh* in the Hebrew Bible, see S. E. Balentine, *The Hidden God: The Hiding of the Face of God in the Old Testament* (Oxford: Oxford University Press, 1983), 118–19; J. Barr, "'Why' in Biblical Hebrew," *JTS* 36 (1985), 1–33. See further the discussion of this question in Exod. 32:11-14 and other comparable prayers for divine justice in Balentine, *Prayer in the Hebrew Bible*, 118–45.

those whom God has worked so relentlessly to deliver. Second, Moses appeals to God's own reputation among the Egyptians (v. 12). The exodus narratives emphasize that God acted to deliver Israel so that the Egyptians will know that "I am the LORD *(yhwh)*" (Exod. 14:4, 18).[63] This objective will be lost, Moses argues, if God does not reconsider the plans to abandon these people, for the Egyptians and others will surely interpret divine punishment as divine failure. Third, Moses appeals to God's own character. He recalls God's unconditional oath—"You have sworn to them by yourself *(nišba 'tā lāhem bāk)*" (v. 13)—that these people would be multiplied, not eliminated, and that they would inherit the promised land (cf. Gen. 15:5, 18). The violation of this oath, Moses implies, will undermine trust in these promises and in the integrity of the One who has made them.[64]

The narrator of this dramatic interchange reports that God's response to Moses' prayer is immediate and positive. Moses had petitioned God to repent of the evil *(hinnāḥēm 'al hārā 'āh)* that was to be directed against this people (Exod. 32:12), and God does exactly what Moses has asked: "And the Lord repented of the evil *(wayyinnāḥēm yhwh 'al hārā 'āh)*" (v. 14). The notion of divine repentance must of course be carefully nuanced. The language of repentance is ordinarily associated with turning away from sin;[65] since in the Hebrew Bible God's acts and deeds are never assessed as sinful, God never repents of sin. With this crucial exception, however, the idea signified by God "repenting" *(nḥm)* is analogous to the positive openness to change that characterizes God's human counterpart. God is open to change, to reversing divine decisions in keeping with God's ultimate objectives for humankind. In fact, the instances where the Hebrew Bible uses *niḥam* (niphal of *nḥm*) with God as subject suggest that particularly in matters of divine punishment, either intended or actual, God is open to the move from judgment to mercy.[66] This is not to say that judgment is

---

63. Cf. T. E. Fretheim, *Exodus* (Louisville: John Knox, 1991), 285.

64. A number of texts, usually identified with the Deuteronomistic tradition, share one or more of these arguments. The same reasons cited in Exod. 32 occur also in Deut. 9:25-29, although in a different order. The argument that God, not Moses, is ultimately responsible for this people is central in Moses' prayer in Num. 11:11-13. Similar arguments concerning God's reputation among the nations are cited in Josh. 7:9 and in Num. 14:13-19. Such texts suggest a common stock of legitimate reasons that suppliants could use to persuade God to modify or retract plans for divine judgment.

65. The normal word for human repentance is *šwb*, which is used as a synonym with *hinnāḥēm* in Exod. 32:12. In this text both verbs are used with God as subject.

66. Of approximately 30 occurrences of *niḥam* with God as subject, 19 are used with reference to God's changing the mind about some intended or actual judgment of sinful people. For further discussion of repentance as a "controlling metaphor" of God's character, see: T. E. Fretheim, "The Repentance of God: A Key to Evaluating Old Testament God-Talk," *HBT* 10 (1988), 47–70; *Exodus*, 286–87; F. I. Anderson and D. N. Freedman, *Amos*, AB (New York: Doubleday, 1989), 638–79; Gowan, *Theology in Exodus*, 225–26.

eliminated or forgiveness is automatic. Moses' continued intercessions with God at Sinai for the forgiveness of the people (Exod. 32:30-34; 34:9) affirm that God's decisions are sometimes inscrutable and irrevocable. Even so, God's openness to change in response to what humans may bring to the relationship is a central affirmation of the Hebrew Bible.

In the Torah's vision of Sinai's covenant liturgy, this affirmation takes center stage. Moses neither yields to God's instructions to remain silent nor accepts God's decision to move into the future without these people. Instead, he dares to believe that at this critical juncture between the judgment announced and its actualization, faith requires that he challenge God with a "loyal opposition."[67] Moses will not give up on the people God has entrusted to his leadership, even though their sinfulness deserves divine judgment. Instead, he stands before God as an advocate for those who have clearly failed to live up to God's expectations. He will not simply accept that God's decision to judge the people is unalterable and impervious to challenge or change. Instead, he questions God, believing that in a genuine covenant relationship even divine decisions can be reimagined, rethought, recalculated. He will not believe that the future of a people called by God is determined exclusively by human weakness and incapacity. Instead, he prays in the firm conviction that the future remains ever open to God's relentless commitment to love the unlovable, to forgive the undeserving, and to create out of human failure new possibilities for realizing ultimate objectives.

In Hebraic tradition the community of faith remembers Moses' intercession at Sinai as a paradigm for the ministry of prayer. The collection of prayers that comprise the final form of the Psalter's Books I–III (Psalms 1–89) trace a downward spiral from confidence in God's covenantal faithfulness to David and Solomon (Pss. 2, 72), to despair over a covenant "renounced" (Ps. 89:39) and a king "rejected" (Ps. 89:38).[68] With the sustained lament that concludes Book III (Ps. 89:38-51), those who would endeavor to follow the "way of righteousness" (Ps. 1:6) seem to reach a dead end in the anguish of unanswered questions: "How long, O LORD? Will

67. I take this suggestive phrase from G. W. Coats, who uses it to describe Moses as a striking example of how contending with God may be the mark of the faithful servant. See "The King's Loyal Opposition: Obedience and Authority in Exodus 32–34," in *Canon and Authority*, ed. G. W. Coats, and B. O. Long (Philadelphia: Fortress, 1977), 91–107.

68. The basic work that shapes the current discussion of the Psalter's canonical arrangement is G. H. Wilson, *The Editing of the Hebrew Psalter* (Chico, Calif.: Scholars Press, 1985). See further J. C. McCann Jr., ed., *The Shape and Shaping of the Psalter* (Sheffield: JSOT Press, 1993); *A Theological Introduction to the Psalter: The Psalms as Torah* (Nashville: Abingdon, 1993). For commentaries that give special attention to the canonical shape of the Psalms, see: F.-L. Hossfeld and E. Zenger, *Die Psalmen I. Psalms 1–50* (Wurzburg: Echter, 1993); J. L. Mays, *Psalms* (Louisville: John Knox, 1993); J. C. McCann Jr., "The Book of Psalms," *NIB*, vol. 4 (Nashville: Abingdon, 1996), 641–1280.

you hide yourself forever? . . . LORD, where is your steadfast love of old?" (Ps. 89:46, 49, NRSV).

At this critical juncture—when the Davidic monarchy seems to have failed, the steadfast love of God to have waned, and the future of Israel to hang in the balance—the Psalter's Book IV (Psalms 90–106) summons the community of faith back to the memory of Moses. The superscription of Psalm 90 is the only one that bears the name of Moses, and seven of the eight references to Moses in the Psalms occur in Book IV. It is this "Moses-book"[69] that constitutes the "theological heart" of the Psalter.[70] The pivotal memory of Psalm 90 is Moses' intercession with God at Sinai (Exod. 32:11-14), its nucleus recalled in verse 13: "Turn *(šûbāh)* O LORD! How long? Repent *(hinnāḥēm)* concerning your servants!" This plea—not the expressions of God's consuming wrath that preceded it (Ps. 90: 7, 9, 11)—provides the foundation for the petition in verse 14 that the future of this fragile people be secured by God's relentless love *(ḥesed)*.[71] In the Psalter's final ordering of the prayers of Israel, the memory of Moses' daring petition at Sinai instructs the faithful to believe and to live as if the future does indeed belong to the Lord who "reigns" (cf. Pss. 93, 95–99), even in a sinful and conflicted world.[72]

We conclude with an observation from T. Fretheim that returns us to the beginnings of these reflections concerning the ministry of prayer. Commenting on the theological significance of Moses' intercession, Fretheim discerns that God honors human prayer "as a contribution to a conversation that has the capacity to change future directions for God, people, and the world."[73] Here we return to a central truth that stands at the heart of the Torah's vision of what it means to take up the vocation of covenant-making and covenant-keeping. Those who follow Moses' example are entering into the breach between God's hopes and expectations and the chronic failings of humankind. To embark on such a journey, where the stakes are high and the summons is urgent, requires radical faith that the promise of God's hearing is constant.

69. For this characterization, see M. Tate, *Psalms 51–100* (Dallas: Word, 1990), xxvi.

70. Wilson, *The Editing of the Hebrew Psalter*, 215.

71. On the importance of ḥesed in the Psalter, see McCann, "The Book of Psalms," 670–72. McCann notes that the term occurs in all five books of the Psalter, but it is especially frequent in Book V (Psalms 107–50), which contains more than 60 occurrences. This emphasis on God's "steadfast love" in Book V reiterates the centrality of the memory of Moses' prayer for God's love in Psalm 90:14.

72. On the kingship of God as the "root metaphor" of the Psalms, see especially J. L. Mays, "The Centre of the Psalms," *Language, Theology, and the Bible: Essays in Honour of James Barr*, ed. S. E. Balentine, J. Barton (Oxford: Clarendon, 1994), 231–46 (reprinted as "The Center of the Psalms: 'The Lord Reigns' as Root Metaphor," J. L. Mays, *The Lord Reigns: A Theological Handbook to the Psalms* [Louisville: Westminster/John Knox, 1994], 128–35).

73. Fretheim, *Exodus*, 287.

6.

COVENANT HOLINESS

IN THE TORAH'S VISION, THE SEQUEL TO THE ERECTION OF THE TABER-nacle (Exod. 40) is Leviticus, where God continues the instructions of the covenantal liturgy at Sinai. Chapter 1 initiates the address with the words "The LORD summoned *(qārā')* Moses and spoke *(dābār)* to him." Chapter 27 brings the address to its conclusion with similar phrasing, "The LORD spoke *(dābār)* to Moses, saying . . ." In between these framing chapters, the phrase "the LORD spoke to Moses" (or a similar one) appears fifty-six times. It opens seventeen of the twenty-seven chapters. In more than half the cases, it introduces divine words addressed not just to Moses or a select group, but to the entire community of Israel (for example, Lev. 1:2: "Speak to the people of Israel and say to them"). It is proper, therefore, to enter into these continuing words of covenant liturgy by recognizing that, as W. Kaiser has said, "Leviticus, more than any other OT book, claims to be a divine word for humanity."[1]

Such a claim may well strike the average reader of Leviticus as odd. Of all the books in the Hebrew Bible, perhaps none is more routinely dismissed by most Christians as irrelevant, if not pagan,[2] than Leviticus. As T. Mann has observed, "Many a pious vow to read straight through the Bible from cover to cover has foundered on the shoals of Leviticus."[3] Sadly, this neglect and disparagement cannot be judged as benign or innocent. Too often, behind the negative evaluation of ritual laws in the Old Testament there lurks a corresponding lack of regard for the Jews whose identity

1. W. Kaiser, "The Book of Leviticus," in *NIB*, vol. 1 (Nashville: Abingdon, 1994), 987.
2. J. Wellhausen routinely evaluated ritual and cultic laws as the heathen element in the Old Testament that testified to the death of Israelite religion once the controlling reigns of power were seized by the priests. For a critical assessment of Wellhausen's influence in modern scholarship, see J. D. Levenson, *The Hebrew Bible, the Old Testament, and Historical Criticism* (Louisville: John Knox/Westminster, 1993), 1–32.
3. T. Mann, *The Book of the Torah: The Narrative Integrity of the Pentateuch* (Atlanta: John Knox, 1988), 113. Mann summarizes well the typical Protestant response to Leviticus by observing that ritual prescriptions like those cited as a remedy for leprosy (Lev. 14:4-7) conjure up for many the witches' chant in *Macbeth*: "Lizard's leg, and owlet's wing;/For a charm of pow'rful trouble/Like a hell-broth boil and bubble."

and vocation are tied to the cultic and ethical principles that these laws inculcate. When conscience approves the dismissal of a people's sacred scripture, the temptation to discount or even deny the value of the people themselves is not far behind.[4]

The Torah's vision summons the community of faith to a different perspective. It presents Leviticus not only as divine address, but also as the *first* divine address from the new sanctuary, the only specific place on earth said to be "filled up" with the glory of God's presence (Exod. 40:34-35).[5] Thus, the divine pronouncements that sound forth in Leviticus direct the community of faith to the most immediate and intimate discourse from God available in all creation. Such discourse, however challenging it may be to contemporary readers, claims to disclose something of unique importance from God.

It is common to regard Leviticus as a "book of worship," and in such a general designation there lies an important incentive for close attention to these words by the whole community of faith. But Leviticus opens (chap. 1–7) with pronouncements on sacrifice, a decidedly challenging subject for modern readers, particularly for persons whose confessional heritage is in the Protestant tradition. In order to understand sacrifice, we must not isolate it from the larger category of ritual that provides its context. In this connection, the work of F. Gorman is particularly helpful in laying out the ideological and theological framework of ritual.[6]

Building on the work of cultural anthropologists, Gorman shows that all ritual is a sort of "social drama."[7] Symbolic acts and words are performed in a way that is integrally related to a specific worldview, and this worldview gives shape to the ritual and is in turn shaped by the ritual.[8] The

---

4. See, e.g., the candid assessment of E. S. Gerstenberger: "Christian tradition has often arrogantly distanced itself from the sacrificial practices of the Old Testament, and has strictly rejected the ceremonial legislation of the Jews. It has rendered suspicious and disparaged the Jews' entire practice of worship as well as their devotion, and through such religious slander has prepared the ground for discrimination and persecution. Perhaps the annihilation camps of the Nazi period would not have been so easily possible without this sort of centuries-long poisoning of the religious climate and the destruction of the religious souls of the Jewish people. . . . We Christians have thus been horribly ungrateful sons and daughters of our ancestors in faith (or are still). We have been glad to serve as the heirs of our parents in faith—without admitting it either to ourselves or to the world—while delivering them over to constables and henchmen" (*Leviticus: A Commentary* [Louisville: Westminster/John Knox, 1996], 15–16).

5. Cf. Fretheim, *Exodus*, 315.

6. F. H. Gorman Jr., *The Ideology of Ritual: Space, Time, and Status in the Priestly Ritual* (Sheffield: JSOT Press, 1990), see especially chaps. 1 and 2, 13–60.

7. Ibid., 20. Gorman takes the expression "social drama" from the work of V. Turner (e.g., *Dramas, Fields, and Metaphors* [Ithaca/London: Cornell University Press, 1974], 23–59).

8. Ibid., 20; cf. 15.

interpreter of ritual texts must "discover the world view that stands behind the rituals, that gives rise to the rituals, that is enacted and made real in the rituals."[9]

Central to the worldview that underlies the Priestly ritual system are two beliefs.[10] The first is the conviction that world order is brought into being by *God's creational design.* Carefully differentiated categories and boundaries provide for a harmonious relationship between God and all elements in creation. As long as this order is realized and sustained, the world and everything in it prospers. When these divisions do not exist, the created order succumbs to chaos, and the harmony between God and world is ruptured. The second foundational Priestly belief is that *the center of the created order is a ritual order.* This ritual order is manifested in the litany of the primordial week, in which God speaks and brings into existence a cosmic order that finds its culmination in the sabbath day. It is manifested with equal clarity in the liturgy of covenant, in which God speaks and brings into being a cultic order that finds its center in the tabernacle where God resides in the midst of the world.[11] The ritual order, like the cosmic order, establishes boundaries and categories that enable a holy God to dwell in the midst of a world subject to sin and defilement. When these boundaries collapse, God's sacred space on earth is compromised and the harmony between God and world is broken.

Inasmuch as the Priestly world view is decidedly religious, ritual becomes the drama of offering symbolic acts and words to God. It is a way not only of identifying the elements that comprise a structured world, but more importantly, of reflecting on God's creational designs and on how one may live in accordance with these designs.[12] For a people whose worldview begins with God, ritual can never be simply a series of formal actions undertaken for the sake of the acts themselves. Instead, ritual will be a means of communicating with God. It will engage the community of faith in substantive theological reflection concerning the reciprocal relationships between God, world, and humankind.[13]

Gorman demonstrates, therefore, that Priestly rituals are best understood as the meaningful enactment of the ordered and liturgical world of God's creational designs. Just as seven speeches comprise the creation of the world (Gen. 1:1—2:4a) and seven speeches (Exod. 25–31) and seven acts (Exod. 40:17-33) bring the tabernacle into existence, so do seven divine

9. Ibid., 15.
10. Ibid., 39. For Gorman's full discussion of these matters, see 39–60.
11. Ibid., 42–43.
12. Ibid., 15–18.
13. Ibid., 59–60, 230–32.

speeches set forth the instructions for sacrificial activity (Lev. 1–7), and seven acts complete the ordination to priesthood (Lev. 8).[14] In sum, ritual behavior is grounded in creation theology. It is "one means of world construction."[15]

The close of the Sinai pericope sets the stage for Leviticus as ritual instruction for building a holy life in the "profane" world of Canaan. The general picture is relatively simple and straightforward: the community leaves the holy mountain but remains near to God by centering its life on the sacred shrine and the rituals that sustain an ongoing connection with the holy. The redactional history of Leviticus, however, makes this picture much more complex. Textual details show that Leviticus comprises different concerns and emphases that reflect its growth over a considerable period of time. While much remains uncertain about this compositional history, there is broad consensus that the final stage is in the Persian period. Persian hegemony placed Yehud in an actual world where the summons to be holy in the midst of the profane was formidable indeed. The Torah's aggregate vision, which takes final shape within the sociopolitical nexus of Persian domination, announces that it is precisely in this world that Leviticus, with its rituals of world construction, seeks to open up decisively new possibilities for the community of faith.

Gorman identifies three basic types of ritual that convey the Priestly concern to build a world defined and sustained by God's creational intentions: "Founding" rituals, which are designed to establish or "found" some situation or institution; "Maintenance" rituals, designed to maintain the established order and prevent its disorder; and "Restoration" rituals, which seek to restore or repair the order of creation once it has been broken or defiled.[16] These basic types of ritual provide a convenient entry into the first half of Leviticus (chap. 1–16) where the divine address summons forth a "ritual world" in which God's cosmic design can be celebrated, sustained, and restored.

Before exploring each type, it is important to note that the divine word addressed to the community from the newly erected sanctuary summons forth more than just a "ritual world." It also includes engaging in the ritual drama of distinguishing "between the holy and the common, and between the unclean and the clean" (Lev. 10:10). Moreover, it also commands that ritual re-creation of God's cosmic design be manifested concretely in ethical holiness: "You shall not follow the practices of the nations. . . . You shall be holy to me" (Lev. 20:23, 26). Such admonitions anticipate the second half

---

14. Ibid., 49–50.
15. Ibid., 59.
16. Ibid., 54–55.

of Leviticus (chap. 17–26), traditionally called the "Holiness Code," which summons forth a "covenantal holiness" that enacts the ritual world in the real world of everyday life. The summons to ethical holiness will be the focus in the second part of this chapter. In the third part, these two concerns—the priestly world of ritual and the priestly summons to ethical holiness—will provide a basis for theological reflection on the ministry of priesthood.

The Priestly World of Ritual

Founding Rituals

Typically, ritual is understood as a means of regulating or preserving something that already exists, a conserving or maintaining of the societal status quo. Inasmuch as the Priestly ritual system is clearly concerned with the maintenance of creational order, it is often criticized as being an agent of social control.[17] While there is clearly truth in this critique of ritual as a conservative act, it is important to note that ritual also serves as a performative act that is creative. Ritual not only acts to maintain what already exists, it also acts to call something new into being.

Such is the intention of "founding" rituals in the Priestly system. A particularly good example is the founding of worship at the tabernacle in Leviticus 8–10.[18] In the Torah's vision the institution of priesthood marks a "moment of origins"[19] in the covenantal liturgy that is connected to God's cosmic design. With seven speeches God summoned forth creation (Gen. 1:1—2:4a). With seven speeches God gave instructions for the building of the tabernacle (Exod. 25–31). With seven acts of obedience Moses prepared the priestly garments (Exod. 39:1-31) and erected the tabernacle (Exod. 40:19-32), doing it "as the LORD commanded," a phrase that repeats seven times in each case.

---

17. The prophets, for example, frequently protest that sacrifices and offerings are ritual substitutes for justice, mechanisms for maintaining a status quo arrangement of power and politics that favors the priests at the expense of those less fortunately positioned in society's hierarchy (see, e.g., Isa. 1:10-17; Jer. 7:1-15; Hosea 4:4—5:7; Amos 2:6-16; Micah 3:9-12).

18. The connection of Lev. 8–10 with "founding" rituals is made by a number of scholars, e.g. Gorman, *The Ideology of Ritual*, 103–39; R. D. Nelson, *Raising Up a Faithful Priest: Community and Priesthood in Biblical Theology* (Louisville: Westminster/John Knox, 1993), 50–51; J. G. Gammie, *Holiness in Israel*, OBT (Minneapolis: Fortress, 1989), 27–30. For Gorman and most others, the idea of founding rituals is traced to the work done on "rites of passage" by cultural anthropologists such as A. Van Gennep, V. Turner, and E. Leach. For a summary of the major issues see Gorman, *The Ideology of Ritual*, 53–54; J. Milgrom, *Leviticus 1–16: A New Translation with Introduction and Commentary*, AB (New York: Doubleday, 1991), 566–69.

19. Gorman, *The Ideology of Ritual*, 138.

Leviticus 8 continues the litany of divine commands. In announcing that Moses enacted the ritual of priestly ordination, it repeats seven times (vv. 4, 9, 13, 17, 21, 29, 36) the phrase "just as the LORD commanded him" *(ka'ăšer ṣiwwāh yhwh)*.[20] This repetition confirms once again that in the Torah's vision worship is integrally tied to God's primordial design. Creation realizes its goal in worship, just as worship becomes one means of realizing God's creative design for the world.[21]

In Leviticus 8–9 the inauguration of worship at the tabernacle is not only a "moment of origins," it is also a permanent paradigm for the ministry of priesthood. The installation of Aaron and his sons is enacted within the context of the community (Lev. 8:3), an indication that not just the priests but every person in the community is defined by their orientation to the cult.[22] The entire ordination ceremony takes place at the door of the tent of meeting (8:3, 4, 31, 33, 35). At this crucial juncture, between the common space that lies outside the tent and the sacred space belonging to God that lies just inside, the priests undergo a seven-day period of preparation for entrance into the realm of the holy (vv. 32-35).[23]

The priests' passage between the common and the holy is marked by a ceremony of washing, clothing, anointing, and sacrificing (8:6-30). The most distinctive feature in these various ceremonial acts is the offering of the "ram of ordination" (vv. 22-29). The blood of this animal is daubed on the right ear lobes, right thumbs, and right big toes of Aaron and his sons. This ritual is often interpreted allegorically as a religious symbol of the requisite preparation for the service of God. So, for example, "Aaron's ear must be ever attentive to the word of God; his hand ever ready to do the work of God; and his feet ever alert to run in the service of the One who called him."[24] Though such an interpretation is generally useful, it does not adequately explain the function of this daubing rite within the Priestly system as a whole.

---

20. The use of this execution formula, which appears sixteen times in Lev. 8–10, ties the fulfillment of these commands to the instructions given to Moses in Exod. 29–30. On the dependence of Lev. 8 on Exod. 29–30, see Milgrom, *Leviticus 1–16*, 545–49; Kaiser, "The Book of Leviticus," 1056–57; Gerstenberger, *Leviticus*, 99–101.

21. Cf. Gorman, *The Ideology of Ritual*, 104.

22. On *kol hā'ēdāh* ("the whole community," Lev. 8:3) being inclusive of women and children, not just tribal chieftains or adult males, see Milgrom, *Leviticus 1–16*, 498–99.

23. In the Priestly system, seven days is the typical period of enactment for major purification rituals (cf. Lev. 12:2; 14:8; 15:13, 19, 24). It is the necessary time for passage from defilement to purity. See further, Gorman, *The Ideology of Ritual*, 112, 137.

24. Kaiser, "The Book of Leviticus," 1062; cf. K. Elliger, *Leviticus* (Tübingen: J. C. B. Mohr, 1966), 119. Such an interpretation is far from new. See, e.g., the very similar view of S. R. Driver on Exod. 29:20: "The organs of hearing, handling, and walking are touched by the blood, implying that the priest is to have hallowed ears to listen to God's commands, hallowed hands

The only other ritual where blood is placed on the right ears, thumbs, and toes is in Leviticus 14:10-20, the ceremony involving the re-entry of a recovered leper into the camp. The purpose of this rite, expressed in verses 18, 19, 20, is to "cleanse" or "make atonement for" *(kipper)* the leper who is being purified of the disease.[25] This purification permits the leper to return to "life" from a situation that may be likened to death (cf. Num. 12:10-12). The daubing ritual guarantees the leper safe passage between the boundaries of life and death.

Gorman has helpfully suggested that the daubing of the priests similarly provides for their safe passage across the boundaries between the common and the holy.[26] Because the priests have stood in the breach between life and death, they are specially prepared for the ministry of mediation between God and humankind. Indeed, the charge given to the priests in the completion of their ordination ceremony (8:31-36) is that they remain at the door of the tent of meeting (v. 35). Their installation as priests prepares them not only for passing between the dangerous boundaries of the common and the holy, but also of staying within these boundaries,[27] safeguarding the people from the hazards of the holy while at the same time insuring that a safe connection with a holy God will always be attainable (cf. Num. 16:46-48).

The acquired privileges that the priests enjoy carry with them enormous responsibilities to the community on whose behalf they are consecrated for service. Thus, following the ceremony of installation, Moses summons the newly ordained priests to begin their public ministry at the tabernacle (Lev. 9). The inaugural service of regular public worship begins on the eighth day (9:1), or the first day after the sabbath day.[28] The offerings of the preceding days are repeated on behalf of both the priests (vv. 8-14) and the community (vv. 15-21). The purpose of all the offerings is stated clearly: "For today the LORD will appear to you" (v. 4). Three further references to the appearance of the "glory of God" (vv. 6, 23, 24) recall the first time Moses and his companions were granted such a visible manifestation of God's presence on Mt. Sinai (Exod. 24:16-17). Together, these references confirm that on this first day of worship the tabernacle is inaugurated as

to perform his sacred offices, and hallowed feet to tread rightly the sacred places, as also to walk generally in holy ways" (*The Book of Exodus,* 1st ed. [Cambridge: Cambridge University Press, 1911]), 319–20. For further discussion of the debate concerning the meaning of this rite, see Milgrom, *Leviticus 1–16,* 528–29; Gerstenberger, *Leviticus,* 110–11.

25. Cf. Milgrom, *Leviticus 1–16,* 529.

26. Gorman, *The Ideology of Ritual,* 131–35.

27. Ibid., 134.

28. On the eighth day as the paradigm for the inauguration of the worship at the Solomonic temple (1 Kings 8), see Milgrom, *Leviticus 1–16,* 593–95.

the equivalent of Sinai, the one place on earth where God is palpably, visibly present, not just to the priests, but to "all the people" (vv. 23, 24).

Maintenance Rituals

Maintenance rituals are designed both to maintain an already established order and to prevent this order from falling into disrepair. Such maintenance concerns may be easily discerned in two primary areas within the Priestly ritual system: the annual cycle of regularly prescribed holy days (Lev. 23) and the rituals involving the distinction between "clean" and "unclean" (Lev. 11–15).

There are three principal calendrical traditions in the Pentateuch, each reflecting a distinctive context and distinctive emphases. The first is Exodus 23:12-19 (cf. 34:17-26), which focuses on the sabbath day and the three pilgrimage festivals (Unleavened Bread, the Spring Harvest, and Ingathering). The second, Deuteronomy 16:1-17, lists Passover/Unleavened Bread, Weeks, and Booths as the three major festivals when all males are to appear before the Lord in "the place that he will choose" (16:16). The third is Leviticus 23 and Numbers 28–29, which together list all the annual festivals, including the sabbath day, and provide instructions concerning the appropriate sacrifices and rituals that correspond with them. This third tradition, especially Leviticus 23, is where I will focus.[29]

Leviticus 23 may be described as a calendar for the laity.[30] The emphasis is not on the details of the sacrifices to be offered, as in Numbers 28–29, but on the summons simply to remember and observe this liturgical ordering of the year.[31] The calendar divides the year into halves, each with a similar ritual structure.[32] The first half (months 1–6) is the spring of the year (23:4-22), marked by three principal festivals: Passover and Unleavened

---

29. On the role of Num. 28–29 as a "maintenance ritual," see Gorman, *The Ideology of Ritual*, 215–27. Much of what Gorman discerns with respect to these chapters applies as well to Lev. 23.

30. Wenham, *Leviticus*, 300.

31. The relationship between Lev. 23 and Num. 28–29 is complex. Though both reflect Priestly concerns, Num. 28–29 is generally considered the earlier list, associated primarily with the priestly tradition that is responsible for the Holiness Code (Lev. 17–26). This consensus view has been reassessed by I. Knohl, who argues for the priority of the P tradition ("PT," Priestly Torah), which he believes was then edited and revised by the "Holiness School" sometime during the reigns of Ahaz and Hezekiah. In his presentation of this argument, the priority of Lev. 23 over Num. 28–29 is cited as a parade example (*The Sanctuary of Silence: The Priestly Torah and the Holiness School* [Minneapolis: Fortress, 1995], 8–45).

32. The chapter in its present form is a composite, reflecting its growth over time. Note, for example, the two superscriptions (vv. 1, 4) and the two sets of instructions concerning the Festival of Booths (vv. 33-36, 39-43); see further, B. Levine, *Leviticus* (Philadelphia, New York, Jerusalem: The Jewish Publication Society, 1989), 153–54.

Bread (vv. 5-8), Firstfruits (vv. 9-14), and Weeks (vv. 15-22). The second half (months 7–12) is the autumnal period (vv. 23-44), also comprising three major festivals: Trumpets (vv. 23-25) which, in later tradition, is Rosh Hashana, the Jewish New Year (cf. Ezek. 40:1); the Day of Atonement (vv. 26-32); and Tabernacles/Booths (vv. 33-44).

The two halves of the year and their respective ritual observances are introduced as "the appointed festivals of the Lord" that are to be observed by all the people (23:1). But before the first of the appointed festivals is listed, one further introductory statement sets the tone for all that follows: "Six days shall work be done, but the seventh day is a sabbath of complete rest, a holy convocation; ... it is a sabbath to the Lord" (v. 3). Thus the creational design of a "sabbath sequence" introduces and orders the time that the calendar in Leviticus 23 describes. In consideration of this Priestly concern for a ritual ordering of the year, the following three observations are pertinent.

1. The calendar in Leviticus 23 is not designed principally to mark ordinary time, although it serves this purpose. It focuses rather on the recurring ritual times that define the year with respect to God. This emphasis is signaled at the outset by the use of the expression "appointed festivals of the Lord" (23:2). The word *mô 'ădê*, "appointed" or "fixed" festivals, refers to time that is set or designated. The language recalls the primordial actions of God on the fourth day of creation: "Let there be lights in the expanse of the sky to separate day from night; they shall serve as signs for the set times (*mô 'ădîm*)—the days and the years" (Gen. 1:14; Tanakh). Within this creational act there is a coordination, a linkage, between ordinary time—the "days" (*yāmîm*) and the "years" (*šānîm*) that mark the regular movement of the sun, moon, and stars—and the "set times" designated by God for special observance.

Leviticus 23 defines these "set times" as the occasions for the "appointed festivals" of worship. In the Priestly view, these ritual times are built into the created order. They are part of God's creational design. In God's cosmic plan, there is chronological time and liturgical time; there is created order and ritual order. While the "set times" are part of *God's plan,* they nevertheless require *human observance* if they are to fulfill God's intentions. They only become "holy convocations" (*miqrā 'ê qōdeš*), sacred assemblies for worship and celebration, when the human community joins with God to sanctify the ceremony through observance.[33] In this respect, to observe the "appointed festivals" is to remember creation itself, and, in partnership with God, to recall, affirm, and sustain "forever" (*'ôlām;* vv. 14, 21, 31, 41) the cosmic tempo that God has endowed.

33. Cf. Levine, *Leviticus,* 154.

2. To observe the "appointed festivals," however, is to do more than simply remember and sustain *creation*. It is also to remember and image the *Creator*. The spring festivals conclude with the Festival of Weeks (23:15-22), which celebrates the completion of the grain harvest. At this time of ingathering, the community's ritual embrace of creation's bounty intersects with the ethical responsibility to provide for the weaker members of society. They are to leave the edges of the field unharvested, a reserve of grain for those who cannot provide sufficiently for themselves. Why? Because in demonstrating such compassion they image God: "you shall not reap to the very edges in your field, or gather the gleanings of your harvest; you shall leave them for the poor and for the alien: *I am the* LORD *your God*" (v. 22, NRSV).

In similar fashion, the last of the autumn festivals, the Festival of Tabernacles (23:33-44), defines the second half of the year with a commemoration of the time spent in the wilderness. At this pivotal point in the transition to a new year, the community is to remember how they once lived in tents after God delivered them from Egypt. Why this ritual enactment of a time of fragility and dependence on God? Once again the liturgical calendar connects the ritual act to the ministry of imaging God's compassion for all generations of fragile humanity, present and future: "You shall live in booths for seven days . . . so that your generations may know that I made the people of Israel live in booths when I brought them out of the land of Egypt: *I am the* LORD *your God*" (vv. 42-43, NRSV).

3. Perhaps the clearest connection between the liturgical calendar and the Priestly concept of maintaining the world as God designed it is the explicit use of sabbatical imagery. The calendar focuses on the *annual* festivals, yet it is the *weekly* sabbath that provides the model for the year's liturgical order (v. 3). In the primordial week of creation, the seventh day is set apart as holy. It is on this day that creation moves finally from incomplete to complete, from disorder to order, from ordinary time to holy time. This movement toward wholeness is symbolized in the number seven. The seventh day, the sabbath day, undergirds the sabbatical principle that informs the liturgical calendar.

This sabbatical principle is manifested in multiple ways. The principal festivals for the year are seven: Passover, Unleavened Bread, Weeks, the day of solemn rest, Atonement, Tabernacles, and the day after Tabernacles.[34]

---

34. Here I follow a fairly standard listing of the festivals. There is uncertainty concerning some of the details in Lev. 23; e.g., it is unclear whether the expression "day of solemn/complete rest (*šabbat šabbātôn*)" (vv. 3, 32) means an ordinary sabbath day or a special sabbath-like day in addition to the regular weekly observance. Also the phrase "day after the sabbath (*mimmahŏrat haššabāt*)" (vv. 11, 15) is problematic. See further the discussions in the standard commentaries: e.g., Levine, *Leviticus*, 155,158; Wenham, *Leviticus*, 303–4; Kaiser, "The Book of Leviticus," 1156, 1158; Gerstenberger, *Leviticus*, 338–40.

Within these seven ritual occasions, seven days are designated as "holy convocations" *(miqrāʾ qōdeš)*.[35] The major festivals for spring and fall (Unleavened Bread, Tabernacles) comprise a seven-day celebration. The Festival of
Weeks falls at the end of the "seventh sabbath," that is, at the end of seven
weeks, on the fiftieth day (v. 16). Further, the seventh month of the year is
particularly holy to God. Coming at the point where one year ends and
another begins, this month is the occasion for three sacred assemblies: the
Feast of Trumpets on the first day, the most holy Day of Atonement on the
tenth day, and the Feast of Tabernacles on the fifteenth day.

In conclusion, this constant orientation to the sabbatical cycle throughout the calendar year keeps the community of faith reminded of the cosmic
rhythm that sustains the creational order. Each sabbatical observance
recalls the primordial plan, invites the community to reflect on God's
design, and enables them to imitate God's intentions through both their
rituals and their ordering of communal life.

Besides the regularly prescribed holy days, Leviticus is also concerned to
summon forth holiness in the ordinary spheres of everyday life. Toward
this end, chapters 11–15 admonish the community to observe the distinction between "clean" and "unclean." These instructions look back to the
mandate given the priests in Leviticus 10:10: "You are to distinguish
between the holy and the common, and between the unclean and the
clean." At the same time, the instructions anticipate and prepare for the
great Day of Atonement that is described in Leviticus 16. The rituals on that
day are for purging or purifying the sanctuary "because of the unclean-
nesses of the people of Israel" (16:16). Thus the stipulations concerning
"clean" and "unclean" are framed by instructions and rituals that are set
within the context of community worship.[36] Their purpose is to render the
community "clean," that is, fit for worship. Sandwiched between the
instructions for the consecration of the cult and its priests (Lev. 8–10) and
the purification of the sanctuary (Lev. 16), these purity laws in 11–15 teach
that the way one lives outside the sanctuary is also critically important for
worship in the presence of God.

The various categories of clean and unclean things are divided roughly
into five sections, each one marked with a similar conclusion formula,
"This is the law of X" *(zō ʾt tôrat)*.[37] The categories are: clean and unclean

35. The first and last days of Unleavened Bread (vv. 7, 8); Weeks (v. 21); the first day of the
seventh month (v. 24); the Day of Atonement (v. 27); the first Day of Tabernacles and the
eighth day after Tabernacles (vv. 35-36).
36. On the canonical context of Lev. 11–15, see Wenham, *Leviticus*, 161–62; Kaiser, "The
Book of Leviticus," 1074.
37. Cf. Blenkinsopp, *The Pentateuch*, 222. These summative formulas often recapitulate the
title lines of the individual sections, as can be seen by comparing 11:2 and 11:46; 14:2 and 14:54,

animals (11:1-47); the uncleanness of childbearing (12:1-8); the uncleanness of skin diseases and other related impurities (13:1-59); appropriate purification rituals for skin diseases and related impurities (14:1-57);[38] and the uncleanness of genital discharges (15:1-33).

The rationale behind the various categories of clean and unclean is elusive, and numerous efforts to discern foundational principles have met with little or no success.[39] Nevertheless, on a primary level it is becoming increasingly clear that the Priestly impurity system may best be explained as an extension of the Priestly concept of creational order. A number of discernments, buttressed by both the internal dynamics of the biblical text and the external data of social anthropologists, support this understanding.

We begin with the biblical text. Genesis 1 places considerable emphasis on the careful ordering of everything in creation "according to its/their kind," a concern repeated no less than ten times in this creation account.[40] The next most frequent occurrence of this term are in Leviticus 11, where the dietary laws are similarly defined by a concern with categorizing clean and unclean animals "according to its/their kind."[41] The corollary between these two Priestly texts suggests that whatever does not conform to its own kind, to its own category of fellow creatures, is unclean. The emphasis seems to focus on the avoidance of the anomalous. Domestic animals that are "clean"—and therefore edible—are those that walk on split hoofs and chew the cud, such as sheep, goats, and cattle (11:2-3). Those that do not conform to this standard—the camel, the rock badger, the hare, the pig—are unclean (11:4-7). Fish that are "clean" are those that have fins and scales (11:9); water creatures that do not meet these criteria are "unclean"

57; 15:3 (LXX) and 15:33. On the distribution and function of these "Priestly *tôrôt*" in Leviticus and Numbers, see Milgrom, *Leviticus 1–16*, 688.

38. In addition to the stipulations concerning skin diseases, chap. 13 includes regulations concerning impurities in fabrics (vv. 47-59). Chap. 14 extends the purification rituals to address not only impurities in fabrics (vv. 54-57) but also in buildings (vv. 33-53). These additional concerns probably reflect a later stage in the compositional history of the impurity laws; see further Milgrom, *Leviticus 1–16*, 886–87.

39. See Kaiser, "The Book of Leviticus," 1075–76, for a convenient survey of the various theories ranging from Philo's moralistic explanation (the laws were given to encourage self-denial and to discourage self-indulgence) to the twentieth-century scholar W. F. Albright, who championed the hygienic hypothesis (the laws prohibit unclean carriers of disease). See further the numerous important studies by J. Milgrom, whose extensive bibliography and work on this issue are now collected in *Leviticus 1–16*; e.g., 718–36.

40. The key term is *mîn* ("kind, species") which occurs in Gen. 1:11, 12 (twice), 21 (twice), 24 (twice), 25 (three times).

41. There are nine occurrences of *mîn* in Lev. 11:14, 15, 16, 19, 22 (four times), 29.

(11:10-12). Insects that fly and have two legs are "clean," but those that fly and have four or more legs are "unclean" (11:20-23).[42]

This maintenance of recognized boundaries seems to inform other purity laws as well. With respect to the "cleanness" of humans, the integrity of the body's physical boundaries is important. Whenever bodily boundaries are broken or breached, the body is rendered unclean and must be restored to its proper completeness, usually by a process of washing and/or ritual cleansing.[43] So, for example, certain bodily discharges (semen, menstrual blood) represent a breach or leakage in physical boundaries that leaves a person in a temporary state of uncleanness (Lev. 15). The same is true of serious skin diseases that violate the body's integrity with scales, scabs, or other forms of discoloration or dislocation (Lev. 13–14).

Social anthropologist M. Douglas has significantly illumined the biblical rhetoric that links the purity laws to the creational design of Genesis 1.[44] Building on the basic views of E. Durkheim, Douglas notes that in most societies, customs and rituals are a reflection of that society's values and foundational principles. In this connection, she suggests that the taxonomy of sanctioned and forbidden behaviors in Leviticus 11–15 serves to mirror and to maintain the Hebraic sense of cosmic order. Just as Genesis 1 delineates three primary environments within which God orders the elements of creation (earth, waters, and heavens [air]), so Leviticus 11 recalls these three environments and seeks to sustain their creational integrity by identifying animals that do or do not conform to the normative habits of each domain: earth (vv. 1-8); waters (vv. 9-12); and air (vv. 13-25).[45] Douglas argues that, besides recognizing the creational design, such a classification of the animals reflects the society's intention to sustain creation's order and stability. Through its dietary practices, the human community makes a sustaining

---

42. The criteria for distinguishing between clean and unclean birds (11:13-19) are not stated, but carnivores or scavengers are an "abomination."

43. The state of impurity that results from a breach of boundaries varies in seriousness; hence the response required to remove the uncleanness also varies. Minor breaches could be repaired relatively simply by ritual bathing. More serious violations required more serious attention. G. Wenham (*Leviticus*, 216) has suggested that the purity laws in Lev. 11–15 may be structured on a sliding scale to reflect different levels of uncleanness, ranging from what is permanent and always to be avoided (Lev. 11—animals and food), to what is of more limited duration and may be ceremonially or ritually repaired (e.g., Lev. 15—the uncleanness of various genital discharges).

44. Her seminal study is *Purity and Danger* (London: Routledge, 1966). See also her *Natural Symbols: Explorations in Cosmology* (London: Barrie and Rockliff, 1970). For a critique of Douglas's work, see J. Sawyer, ed., *Reading Leviticus: A Conversation with Mary Douglas* (Sheffield: Sheffield Academic Press, 1996).

45. *Purity and Danger*, 40–57.

connection with what is "clean" in God's creational design, and resists what weakens or breaches creational boundaries.

The connection between the purity laws and the Priestly creational order to which Douglas has drawn attention reinforces the argument that Leviticus 11–15 is not just a list of irrational and arbitrary taboos.[46] In the Priestly perspective, discrimination between the "clean" and "unclean" is part of an intentional and purposeful theological construction of the world.[47] Indeed, Douglas has pushed the theological discussion to another level by suggesting that the impurity laws seek to maintain the principles of righteousness and justice on which the entire cosmos depends.[48] As she puts it, "Everything in the universe shows forth the righteousness of the Lord."[49] In this sense, the summons to purity and cleanness is a summons to emulate the holiness of God.

The connection between God's holiness and the summons to be holy in the mundane matters of common life is signaled at the outset of these purity laws. The dietary regulations conclude with a rationale for observance that repeats the root word *qādôš* ("holy") no less than five times:

> For I am the LORD your God; *sanctify yourselves (hitqaddištem)* there-fore, and be *holy (hĕyîtem qĕdōšîm)*, for I am *holy (qādôš 'ānî)*. You shall not defile yourselves with any swarming creature that moves on the earth. For I am the LORD who brought you up from the land of Egypt, to be your God; you shall be *holy (hĕyîtem qĕdōšîm)*, for I am *holy (qādôš 'ānî)*. (Lev. 11:44-45, NRSV)

This same language occurs in the keynote passage for human holiness in the image of God: "You shall be *holy (qĕdōšîm tihyû)*, for I the Lord your God am *holy (qādôš 'ānî)*" (Lev. 19:2).[50]

The purity laws thus teach a reverence for life that mirrors God's nature. But to be holy like God requires more than just maintaining prop-er distinctions between the clean and unclean. It also requires a God-like

---

46. Douglas's anthropological approach has been instructive for a number of biblical scholars and has now been widely appropriated as a heuristic tool in the standard literature on Leviticus. See, e.g., B. Levine, *Leviticus* (Philadelphia: Jewish Publication Society, 1989); Wen-ham, *Leviticus*; Milgrom, *Leviticus 1–16*; Kaiser, "The Book of Leviticus"; Jenson, *Graded Holi-ness*; W. Houston, *Purity and Monotheism* (Sheffield: JSOT Press, 1993).

47. On the theology of the Priestly construction of the world under the categories of "clean" and "unclean," see, e.g., Gammie, *Holiness in Israel*, 9–44; Nelson, *Raising Up a Faith-ful Priest*, 17–38.

48. M. Douglas, "The Forbidden Animals in Leviticus," *JSOT* 59 (1993), 3–23.

49. Ibid., 21.

50. On the connection between the purity laws and the summons to holiness in Leviticus 19. see further Milgrom, *Leviticus 1–16*, especially 729–36.

compassion towards those outside the boundaries, those who do not, for whatever reasons, "fit in." For example, Douglas suggests that some of the forbidden animals in Leviticus 11 may exemplify sufferers from injustice.[51] In the blindness of worms, the vulnerability of fish without scales, the ceaseless labor of ants, there is perhaps an analogy to human counterparts: the beggar, the defenseless widow and orphan, the laborer. The summons not to eat of such animals is not a license to avoid or shun them. It is a word of caution not to prey upon them. In her apt summation, "Holiness is incompatible with predatory behavior."[52]

In sum, maintenance rituals like those described in Leviticus 23 and Leviticus 11–15 enable the community of faith to sustain God's cosmic plan. They do so by ritually enacting the concerns and intentions of God in both the sacred and the common spheres of life. Besides making careful distinctions between the sacred and the common, the community of faith is summoned to a purposeful movement between the holy and the profane. The mandate is, as J. Milgrom has put it, "to advance the holy into the realm of the common and to diminish the impure and thereby enlarge the realm of the pure."[53] Such a mission means that ritual is never an end in itself, but is part of the grand creational design to realize on earth the compassion and justice of God.

Restoration Rituals

Rituals enable a community of faith not only to establish the founding vision of its origin and destiny and to maintain this vision across time through careful observance. They also empower the faithful to retrieve founding visions from neglect or abuse, to repair them, and to restore them to their proper role in the life of the community. In this capacity, restoration rituals serve to restore *both persons and worlds* to the cosmic design of God's creational intentions.

The ritual of restoration for the recovered leper in Leviticus 14 (already mentioned in connection with the daubing of blood on the priests[54]) is a good example of how individuals who have been excluded from society because of physical uncleanness may be restored to a full and normal life within the community. Another side of the restoration ritual shows up in

---

51. Douglas, "Forbidden Animals," 22. Douglas derives this highly suggestive theological explanation of the purity laws from approaching Leviticus as a form of ring composition. She interprets internal rhetorical and thematic connections between Lev. 11–15 and 21–22 as two parts of an expanding concentric circle whose center is found in Lev. 19 and whose climax occurs in Lev. 26.

52. Ibid.

53. Milgrom, *Leviticus 1–16*, 732.

54. See above, 152.

the ritual enactment of the Day of Atonement (Lev. 16). On this occasion both sinful people (vv. 17, 24, 30, 31) and a defiled sanctuary (vv. 16, 17, 20, 33) are cleansed and prepared for full communion with God. As the following paragraphs will show, the Day of Atonement thus seeks to restore to God's creational design not only the community of faith but also the entire cosmos, symbolized by the sanctuary.

Though the textual history of Leviticus 16 is complex,[55] there is broad consensus that the present form combines multiple traditions that were originally independent of one another. As it now stands, the chapter combines into one complex ceremony two distinct purgation rituals: the purification of the sanctuary through the sacrificial blood of "the sin offering" (*ḥaḥaṭṭā 't*; vv. 11-19); and the purification of the people through confession of sin and the banishment of the "goat for Azazel" (vv. 20-22; cf. v. 26).[56] Without severing the connection the text makes between these two rites, I wish to focus principally on the purgation and restoration of the sanctuary.

The key to the ritual outlined in Leviticus 16:11-19 is the meaning of the verb *kipper*, conventionally translated as "atone" or "expiate," which is repeated four times (vv. 11, 16, 17, 18). Milgrom[57] and Levine[58] have convincingly shown that the verb *kipper* in ritual texts regularly means "purge" or "purify," not "atone." More specifically, within the context of the *ḥaṭṭā 't* offering, the "sin offering" (cf. vv. 11, 15), *kipper* always has to do with purging or decontaminating some object or person that has been defiled by impurities. At the heart of Leviticus 16 is the concern to "purge" the sanctuary completely—inner sanctum (vv. 14-16a), outer sanctum (v. 16b), and outer altar (vv. 18-19)—"of the uncleanness and transgression of the Israelites" (v. 16).

The function of the *ḥaṭṭā 't* offering in purifying the sanctuary is tied to the Hebraic understanding of sin (*ḥāṭā'*). In the ritual world conceptualized by the priests, sin is not only a moral failing, it is also envisioned to be something like a physical substance. In this sense, sin is actualized as

---

55. For the major issues, see R. Rendtorff, *Die Gesetze in der Priesterschrift* (Göttingen: Vandenhoeck and Ruprecht, 1954), 59–62; Elliger, *Leviticus*, 200–210; K. Aartun, "Studien zum Gesetz über den grossen Versöhnungstag Lv 16 mit Varianten: Ein ritualgeschichtlicher Beitrag," *ST* 34 (1980), 73–109.

56. The latter of these two rites has been the subject of considerable scholarly analysis. Attention has focused both on the commonality of banishment rituals in the ancient Near East generally (cf. Milgrom, *Leviticus 1–16*, 1071–79; D. P. Wright, *The Disposal of Impurity: Elimination Rites in the Bible and in Hittite and Mesopotamian Literature* [Atlanta: SBL, 1987], 31–74) and on the specific meaning of the Azazel rite in Israel (cf. B. A. Levine, *In the Presence of the Lord* [Leiden: Brill, 1974], 53–114; *Leviticus*, 106–8, 250–53 [Excursus 4]).

57. Milgrom, *Leviticus 1–16*, esp. 253–69, 1079–84.

58. Levine, *In the Presence of the Lord*, 55–77.

impurity with power—in Milgrom's words, it is like "an aerial miasma that possessed magnetic attraction for the realm of the sacred."[59] Thus, when people sin or suffer serious impurity they defile not only themselves but also the sanctuary.

Milgrom has argued that this defilement follows a graded scheme: the more serious the sin or impurity, the more extensively the sanctuary is compromised.[60] A single individual's inadvertent sins or impurities defile the outer altar and courtyard area (cf. Lev. 4:22-35). Inadvertent sins by the high priest or the entire community defile the inner sanctum (cf. Lev. 4:2-21). Intentional unrepented sins defile not only the outer altar and the inner shrine, they penetrate to the inner sanctum of the sanctuary and the very throne of God. During the course of the year, inadvertent sins and their defilement may be purged as they occur through the ordinary sacrifices outlined in Leviticus 4–5. But because intentional sinners are barred from bringing an offering to the sanctuary (cf. Num. 15:27-31), the defilement effected by their offenses must await the special ceremonies conducted by the high priest on the annual "Day of Purgation."

From a theological perspective, Milgrom has effectively clarified one reason why the purging of the sanctuary was a matter of grave concern to the priests. A holy God will not reside in an unholy sanctuary. So if the sanctuary is not cleansed, God may leave, forsaking the community of faith to its own doom. Such a scenario is described by Ezekiel, a prophet of priestly descent, in Ezekiel 8–10. Having been shown the abominations taking place in the temple (8:10-16), Ezekiel looks on as God abandons the holy place and the city of Jerusalem to certain destruction (10:2, 4, 18). Thus the sanctuary is a "spiritual barometer" of the faithfulness of the community.[61] Its purity, its fitness as a residence for the holy God, is inextricably linked to the behavior of God's people. When the sanctuary is holy, God is present, and the destiny of the collective community is secure.

As a spiritual barometer, however, the sanctuary has theological significance far beyond the boundaries of the collective community. In the

---

59. Milgrom, *Leviticus 1–16*, 257.

60. Milgrom has developed this gradation scheme in several publications, most recently *Leviticus 1–16*, 257–58.

61. Ibid., 260. In Milgrom's view, the theology of the sanctuary's purgation is a fundamental part of the Priestly theodicy. It is a theodicy in cultic procedures rather than words or legal statutes; it may be described, on the analogy of Oscar Wilde's novel, as the "Priestly Picture of Dorian Gray": ". . . sin may not leave its mark on the face of the sinner, but it is certain to mark the face of the sanctuary, and unless it is quickly expunged, God's presence will depart" (260). See further Milgrom's article "Israel's Sanctuary: The Priestly 'Picture of Dorian Gray,'" *RB* 83 (1976), 390–99; reprinted in *Studies in Cultic Theology and Terminology* (Leiden: Brill, 1983), 75–84.

Torah's vision, as noted above,[62] the sanctuary symbolizes the realization on earth of God's creational plan for the entire cosmos. The heptadic patterning that structures the account of the sanctuary's design (Exod. 25–31) and of Moses' instructions for its erection (Exod. 35–40), the numerous verbal links between the completion of the sanctuary (Exod. 39–40) and the completion of creation (Gen. 1–2), and the conceptualization of the sanctuary as an orderly world that carefully demarcates the boundaries between the sacred and the common—all these point to the critical importance of the sanctuary in God's creational design.

From this perspective the defilement of the sanctuary and the potential departure of God threatens far more than merely the local community. It threatens the collapse of cosmic order. The ritual enacted on the Day of Atonement, therefore, engages the community of faith in an active repair and restoration of the sanctuary, not for its own sake alone, but for the sake of the world. When the sanctuary is holy, God is present, *and the world is secure*, because heaven and earth are joined in common pursuit of God's creational intentions.

Two particular emphases within Leviticus 16 support this theological linkage between a cleansed sanctuary and a world restored to its creational order. First, it may be recalled that the tabernacle mirrors the orderly separation and division between the common and the sacred that inheres in the creational design. When these boundaries are in place, the world enjoys order and harmony. When they are ignored or breached, the order of the world collapses and is replaced by chaos. The tabernacle reflects this orderly world by carefully marking the boundaries between the sacred and the common, the clean and the unclean, and by endeavoring to sustain them through holy rituals of worship *and* through holy behavior in the spheres of everyday life.

On the Day of Atonement, the community of faith acknowledges that these boundaries have been lost. The holy sanctuary has been compromised by the sins of the people. It must be cleansed from the outer court to the Holy of Holies before it is fit once more to mark the boundary and secure the intersection between the sacred presence of God and the common life of God's people. But it is not just the internal zones of holiness within the sanctuary that must be repaired. It is also the external boundaries between the holy sanctuary within the camp and the designated domains for chaos and disorder beyond the camp.[63] Towards this end the

---

62. See chap. 5, pp. 134–39.

63. On the significance of spatial categories in Lev. 16, see Gorman, *The Ideology of Ritual*, 72–73.

ritual of purifying the sanctuary is coupled with the ritual of dispatching the "goat for Azazel" to the wilderness (16:20-22; cf. v. 26).

Although the full meaning of the scapegoat ritual remains somewhat ambiguous, its primary implication seems clear enough. The sins of the people that have corrupted the sanctuary are banished to the wilderness. In a ritual world, the wilderness is the domain of chaos and disorder. On the Day of Atonement, as in the liturgy of creation, chaos is not removed or eliminated, but it is assigned its proper and restricted place in the grand design. The banishment of the goat to the wilderness secures not only the sanctuary but the creational boundary between order and chaos as well.[64]

A second indicator of the theological connection between the cleansing of the sanctuary and the restoration of the cosmic design is the rhetoric of the septenary system that connects the Day of Atonement ritual to the liturgy of creation. The cleansing of the sanctuary is a tripartite ritual involving a sevenfold sprinkling of blood in each of the sacred areas: the inner sanctum (Lev. 16:14), the outer sanctum (v. 16),[65] and the outer altar (v. 19).[66] Moreover, in the text's final form, the first time the people are addressed with instructions to observe the Day of Atonement is on the tenth day of the seventh month (vv. 29-31).[67] The seventh month represents a time of passage for the community and for the world. It is a liminal time at the point where one year ends and another begins.[68] In this seventh month, this "sabbath month," the community of faith is instructed to make the Day of Atonement a "sabbath of complete rest" (v.31: šabbat šabbātôn). Of all the holy days in Israel's liturgical calendar, only the Sabbath Day and the Day of Atonement require a complete cessation from all work (cf. Lev. 23:3; Exod. 35:2). The implication seems to be that on this momentous occasion, when both the community and the world stand at the juncture between past and future, undivided attention to restoring creation's

---

64. Cf. Levine, *Leviticus*, 252: "When the he-goat returned to the wilderness . . . a boomerang effect was produced: Evil was returned to its point of departure, to the wilderness!"

65. The text specifies only that the outer sanctum is to be purified the same as the inner sanctum: "and so he shall do (*wĕkēn yaʿ ăśeh*)." The implication is that there should be a sevenfold aspersion of the blood similar to that prescribed for the inner sanctum. The specifics for such aspersion in the outer sanctum are given in Lev. 4:6-7, 17-18. See further, Milgrom, *Leviticus 1–16*, 1034–35.

66. Cf. idem, 1038–39. When the aspersions of blood from both the bull (for the priest) and the goat (for the people) are totaled, the number is forty-nine, seven times seven.

67. Vv. 29-34 are usually regarded as a later appendix to the purgation rites. Milgrom speculates that they reflect the transition from an earlier period when the purgation of the sanctuary was an emergency procedure, to a subsequent time when the community began to observe this ritual on an annual basis (*Leviticus 1–16*, 1070–71).

68. Cf. Gorman, *The Ideology of Ritual*, 90–91.

ordering of the sacred and the common is fundamental for the journey that lies ahead.

Covenantal Holiness (Leviticus 17–26)

It is often noted that "holiness" is the keynote theme of Leviticus. In this book, various forms derived from the basic verbal root in Hebrew for "holy," *qādaš*, occur more than 150 times. Nowhere is this emphasis clearer than in the so-called "Holiness Code" of Leviticus 17–26. From the midst of the Priestly summons to communal behavior that unites people to God in worship, there emerges a call to "ethical holiness," a mandate to respond to one another in concrete expressions of God-like justice.

The conventional explanation for this "intrusion" has been that these chapters do not reflect true priestly interests. From Wellhausen until quite recently, the regnant critical assessment has been that the Holiness Code antedates the Priestly tradition. The concern with ethical and moral behavior seemed to Wellhausen and others very uncharacteristic of the Priestly tradition.[69] The conventional caricature of P argued that priests were preoccupied with the technicalities of ritual and had little or no interest in matters pertaining to ethics or morality.

But this view, which only thinly masks typical Protestant biases against ritual matters, has been seriously challenged. On the one hand, as J. Milgrom has insisted, priestly circles, both in Israel and in the ancient Near East generally, always had an ethical dimension.[70] They were never completely void of justice concerns, despite the caricature offered by the prophets and by many biblical interpreters.

On the other hand, I. Knohl has suggested that, however preoccupied with ritual esoterica the priestly circles may or may not have been, they nevertheless had the capacity and the openness to accept internal critique and correction. In support of this, Knohl argues that Leviticus 17–26 derives from a priestly "holiness school" that postdates the priestly circles who produced the bulk of the "Priestly Torah."[71] He locates its origins

---

69. In Wellhausen's view the Holiness Code has its origin in the J legislation of Sinai (Exod. 20–23) and is finally incorporated into the Priestly Code through multiple stages of revisions and modifications. The historical sequence is: Jehovist, Deuteronomy, Ezekiel, Law of Holiness, Priestly Code (*Prolegomena to the History of Ancient Israel*, 376–80). Wellhausen argued that in its original form the Holiness Code was a "work pervaded by a somewhat affected religious hortatory form, which harmonizes but little with the Priestly Code" (idem., 376).

70. J. Milgrom, *Leviticus 1–16*, 21–26.

71. I. Knohl, "The Priestly Torah Versus the Holiness School: Sabbath and the Festivals," *HUCA* 58 (1987), 65–117; idem, *The Sanctuary of Silence: The Priestly Torah and the Holiness School* (Minneapolis: Fortress, 1995).

between the years of Ahaz and Hezekiah (ca. 743–701 B.C.E.),[72] an era that coincides with the appearance of the classical prophets and the persistent prophetic condemnation of the cult's abandonment of social justice.[73] This priestly holiness school, in Knohl's opinion, represents an inner priestly response to the "moral refinement" of the cult that the prophets sought.[74]

Beyond the debate concerning the origin and redactional history of chapters 17–26, it is important to note their contribution as a distinctive literary unit to the covenantal liturgy at Sinai.[75] First, they direct God's instructions from the tabernacle to a new audience. Whereas chapters 1–16 contain instructions primarily for the priests, chapters 17–26 are addressed principally to the whole of the community. Apart from chapters 21–22, every chapter in this collection begins with a directive to speak to the people of Israel.[76] The opening words of 17:1-2 illustrate the focus that is characteristic of the entire unit: "The LORD spoke to Moses: Speak to Aaron and his sons and to all the people of Israel and say to them . . ."

The divine instructions contained in this collection cover a variety of issues (sexual behavior, neighborliness, worship, religious festivals, land tenure), but the summons to the community to exhibit holiness in every area of life remains consistent throughout the whole. The all-embracing standard of conduct that God requires is stated succinctly in Leviticus 19:2, the keynote passage in the book: "You shall be holy, for I the LORD your God am holy."

The heart of the summons to holiness occurs in Leviticus 18–20, a distinct literary unit located at the center of these instructions.[77] A formal

---

72. Knohl, *Sanctuary of Silence*, 209.

73. Ibid., 212–16.

74. Ibid., 216. At issue in the revisions proposed by Milgrom and Knohl is a reassessment of the longstanding assumption that prophets, not priests, were the custodians of ethical morality in ancient Israel. Against the regnant view, Milgrom has sought to demonstrate that throughout the Pentateuchal codes, "wherever Israel is exhorted to be holy, ethical precepts are involved" (*Leviticus 1–16*, 731). On the symbiosis between the cult and social justice advocated by the holiness school, see further Knohl, *Sanctuary of Silence*, 214–18.

75. On the need to attend to the inner unity of Lev. 17–26 and its structural connection to the Sinai pericope, see Blum, *Studien zur Komposition des Pentateuch*, 300–22. In a recent review of these matters, Crüsemann argued the case as follows: "The question of the inner unity of the text should be of equal importance to that of potential stratification. Careless preference for literary-critical operations over structural analysis and exegesis of content is methodological stupidit." (*The Torah*, 281).

76. Only the final injunctions in Lev. 26 lack such a specific introduction, and in this case the use of plural verbs (e.g., 26:1: "you shall make [*ta 'ăśû*] for yourselves no idols, and you shall erect [*tāqîmû*] for yourselves no carved images or pillars") makes clear that here too the address is to the people as a whole.

77. Cf. Gerstenberger, *Leviticus*, 245–304.

introduction (18:1-5) and conclusion (20:22-26) envelop instructions concerning sexual ethics (18:6-30) and other more broadly defined matters of social ethics (19:1-37). It is striking that these instructions admonish the community to a life of holiness that manifests itself in the world as ethical behavior, not as spiritual interiority or separatism. This is particularly clear in Leviticus 19 where each of the Ten Commandments is recalled as a foundational principle for ethical injunctions.[78] As B. Bamberger has observed, "The ethical component of holiness is not for the priestly writers of the Holiness Code a mere 'extra.'"[79]

Even more striking in this summons to covenant holiness is its grounding in the nature and character of God.[80] In chapters 19-20, the dominant refrain is the formulaic phrase "I am YHWH." This phrase recalls God's unparalleled self-disclosure to Moses (Exod. 3:15; 6:2), and God's absolute authority as the moral imperative behind the covenantal commission introduced in the Ten Commandments (Exod. 20:2; cf. Deut. 5:6). The following diagram shows the substance of these several exhortations to covenantal holiness, reinforced by the insistent assertion that to act ethically is to image the holy God.

Figure 6.1 clearly demonstrates that the summons to covenantal holiness is a summons both to *refrain from* and *engage in* certain behaviors, because to do so is to image God faithfully. Such is the message of the resounding motivational clause, "I am YHWH," which is repeated no less than twenty-six times in these three chapters. First, with respect to sexual relations, the community of faith is to avoid all illicit and incestuous relations that make common cause with the Egyptians and the Canaanites

---

78. Kaiser conveniently lists the parallels between Leviticus 19 and Exodus 20 ("The Book of Leviticus," 1131):

Ten Commandments	Leviticus 19
1 and 2	v. 4
3	v. 12
4 and 5	v. 3
6	v. 16
7	v. 29
8 and 9	vv. 11, 16
10	v. 18

For further discussion of the Decalogue in Lev. 19, see J. Morgenstern, "The Decalogue of the Holiness Code," *HUCA* 26 (1955), 1–28; B. Bamberger, "Leviticus," *The Torah: A Modern Commentary*, eds. W. G. Plaut, B. Bamberger (New York: Union of American Hebrew Congregations, 1981), 894; Gammie, *Holiness in Israel*, 33–34.

79. B. Bamberger, "Leviticus," 890.

80. Milgrom argues that throughout the Pentateuchal codes holiness is a question of *imitatio Dei*, the emulation of God's holiness (*Leviticus 1–16*, 730). In the Torah's vision, therefore, the life of holiness necessarily requires an emulation of the ethics associated with God's nature.

FIGURE 6.1.
Leviticus 18–20

"You *shall not do* as they do" (Lev. 18:3)

"I am YHWH your God"	(18:2)
"I am YHWH your God"	(18:4)
"I am YHWH"	(18:5)
"I am YHWH"	(18:6)
"I am YHWH"	(18:21)
"I am YHWH your God"	(18:30)

"You *shall be* holy, for I YHWH your God am holy" (Lev. 19:2)

"I am YHWH your God"	(19:3)
"I am YHWH your God"	(19:4)
"I am YHWH your God"	(19:10)
"I am YHWH"	(19:12)
"I am YHWH"	(19:14)
"I am YHWH"	(19:16)
"I am YHWH"	(19:18)
"I am YHWH"	(19:25)
"I am YHWH"	(19:28)
"I am YHWH"	(19:30)
"I am YHWH your God"	(19:31)
"I am YHWH"	(19:32)
"I am YHWH your God"	(19:34)
"I am YHWH your God"	(19:36)
"I am YHWH"	(19:37)

"You *shall not follow* the practices of the nations" (Lev. 20:23)

"I am YHWH your God"	(20:24)
"I am YHWH"	(20:26; cf. 20:7, 8: "I am YHWH/your God")

(18:6-23). These prohibitions are followed by a list of prescribed behaviors that are "God-like" (19:1-37), introduced by the central exhortation that undergirds the whole: "You shall be holy, for I the LORD your God am holy" (19:2). Like the Ten Commandments that inform these prescribed behaviors, this summons to covenantal holiness involves two fundamental duties for the community. They are to love God exclusively (vv. 4-8), and they are to manifest this commitment to God by engaging in acts of compassionate justice for all human beings (vv. 9-18).[81]

---

81. Gerstenberger notes that Lev. 19 places the Priestly concern for sanctification into a different context: "A specific sacrificial ceremony or cultic occasion is no longer the focus. At

This latter charge culminates in the admonition of verse 18: "You shall love your neighbor as yourself." What is often overlooked in this familiar injunction is the fact that "love of neighbor" is here only a summary expression for a comprehensive and unlimited commitment of compassion and justice. Beginning with verse 9, no less than eight words are used to describe the "neighbor" who is due unyielding attention by those who are summoned to covenantal holiness: "poor" (v.10: *ānî*), "alien" (v.10: *gēr*), "neighbor" (v.13: *rēa'*), "laborer" (v.13: *śākîr*), the "deaf" (v.14: *ḥērēs*), the "blind" (v.14: *iwwēr*), "poor" (v.15: *āwel*), "fellow citizen" (vv. 15, 17: *ămîtekâ;* NRSV: "neighbor/people"). Thus, "neighbor" is not just a peer with whom one may share social privileges. It is also the disadvantaged person on the margins of society, someone a community may be tempted to ignore for economic, political, or physical reasons.

One final feature of the "Holiness Code" requires attention. In its summons to ethical holiness, to behavior that both unites the community distinctively to God and images God-like justice in the real world of day-to-day living, the Holiness Code returns the covenantal liturgy to the concerns with which it began in the Decalogue and the Book of the Covenant. The epilogue to the Book of the Covenant, Exodus 23:20-33, instructs the community to know that justice and worship are critically important not only at Sinai, but also in the journey that lies ahead. Their commission is to be "a priestly kingdom and a holy nation" not just in the wilderness of Sinai but in the land of Canaan as well.

Leviticus 17–26 is similarly concerned with the commission to be holy *in* and *for the sake of* the land that Israel will inhabit. A repeating exhortation throughout these chapters links to covenantal holiness Israel's *possession* of the land as well as the land's *prosperity* under Israel's stewardship (18:24-30; 20:22-26; 25:18-24; 26:3-45).[82] If the community faithfully executes their covenantal commission, they will inherit the land according to God's promises (20:22, 24; 25:18), and the land itself will fulfill

issue is daily life as such, which is to be oriented commensurate with Yahweh's own holiness. One might say that just as the believer must submit to 'sanctification' in any preparation for a cultic encounter with Yahweh, that is, must avoid any deleterious forces, so also does Leviticus 19 insist that 'believers' entire lives' should consist of actions that please God and spurn evil. This view emphatically includes a person's ethical, social, and legal disposition, which perhaps plays a role in ritual sanctification as well" *(Leviticus, 282)*.

82. Blenkinsopp discerns a pentadic structure within the Holiness Code that emphasizes the connection between ethical and ritual laws and the possession of the land (*The Pentateuch,* 224–25). In this connection he isolates five exhortations: the four I have listed above, plus 22:31-33. Although I agree with his premise that land possession is an important theme throughout these chapters, the presence of this theme in 22:31-33 seems less clear than in the other four.

its creational capacities for productivity and sustenance (20:24; 25:19). But if the community forsakes this commission, they will defile the land by their behavior, just as inhabitants before them had done, and like their predecessors, the failed community of faith will be expelled (qā'āh, literally "vomited out") from the land they have corrupted (18:25, 28; 20:22). In sum, the community's commission to be "a priestly kingdom and a holy nation" is a charge to "redeem" the land (25:24) not to "defile" it.

Leviticus 26, the collection of blessings and curses that conclude the Holiness Code, make clear that the commission to be both priestly and powerful, both holy and ethically responsible, can be realized in the context of worship. The blessings of obedience are recorded in six promises: rain, peace in the land, removal of potential danger from wild animals, victory over enemies, fertility and productivity, and the indwelling presence of God (vv. 3-13). The curses of disobedience are also announced in six parts, although in considerably more detail: terror, drought and famine, wild animals, war, wholesale destruction, and exile from the land (vv. 14-39).[83]

The all important preface to the blessings and curses of Leviticus 26 occurs in verses 1 and 2. It is exclusive loyalty to God that informs the community in the matters of covenant holiness and insures that they attain the blessings of God. Towards this end, verses 1 and 2 recall the first four commandments of the Decalogue and their summons to love God absolutely. The particular emphasis of these opening verses, however, concerns the two principle avenues of worship through which loyalty to God may be enacted and sustained: the sabbath and the sanctuary.[84] The sabbath day marks a *sacred time* on earth in remembrance of the primordial order that God has ordained for the cosmos. The sanctuary marks a *sacred place* on earth where God's indwelling presence summons a community to concretize the creational design through covenantal holiness.[85] In the journey towards Canaan, the blessing of God resides with the people who realize their commission to become both a covenant community and a worshiping community.

---

83. For this structuring of the blessings and curses into reciprocal units of six parts each, see Kaiser, "The Book of Leviticus," 1178–83.

84. On the juxtaposition of injunctions concerning sabbath and sanctuary in the Holiness Code, see Knohl, *Sanctuary of Silence*, 15, 16, 196.

85. See further M. Weinfeld, "Sabbath, Temple and Enthronement of the Lord—The Problem of the Sitz im Leben of Genesis 1:1–2:3," *Mélanges bibliques et orientaux en l'honneur de M. Henri Cazelles*, ed. A. Caquot (Paris: Butzon & Bercker, 1981), 501–12.

Paradigms of Worship: The Ministry of Priesthood

The focus in this chapter has been on the book of Leviticus, commonly regarded as a "book of worship," and on its description of the priests, the rituals, and the ethical mandates that define this worship according to the Torah's vision. I wish now to suggest that this complex and peculiar portion of the covenantal liturgy at Sinai preserves an understanding of the ministry of priesthood that the Torah envisions to be vitally important for realizing God's ultimate intentions for the world. Before identifying salient features of this ministry, however, it will be instructive to review how the insights from cultural anthropology can provide the broad conceptual framework for understanding rituals and ritual texts.[86] We cannot appropriate Leviticus as a paradigm for worship unless our theological discernments are informed by an adequate understanding of how religious rituals function within society, both ancient and contemporary.

We begin with the fundamental observation that religion plays a vital role in maintaining and shaping society and culture. It offers perspectives on God (or divinity), the world, and humankind that have two capacities: to render life *as it is* apprehensible and meaningful; and to render life *as it may be or ought to be* conceivable and viable. C. Geertz has noted that religious perspectives typically exist within society alongside various alternative and competing perspectives for construing reality.[87] "Common-sensical" perspectives invite a simple, nonquestioning acceptance of the world as being just what it appears to be. "Scientific" perspectives deliberately expose the givenness of everyday life to doubt and systematic investigation. "Aesthetic" perspectives suspend naive acceptance and disinterested inquiry in favor of an eager "engrossment" and "absorption" in the things of the world "in themselves."

Against these major perspectives the "religious" perspective provides a particular way of seeing the world and of discerning the meaning of life. In contrast to the common-sensical, the religious perspective "moves beyond the realities of everyday life to wider ones which correct and complete them."[88] In contrast to the scientific, it explores the wider realities of life not with detachment, but with commitment; its goal is not analysis but encounter. And in contrast to the aesthetic, it seeks connection with the "really real," not merely with "sheer appearances"; its objective is to

---

86. See also the preliminary discussion in chap. 3, pp. 59–61.

87. For what follows in this and the succeeding paragraph, see C. Geertz, "Religion as a Cultural System," in *The Interpretation of Cultures: Selected Essays* (New York: Basic Books, 1973), 111–12.

88. Ibid., 112.

construe a world endowed with an "utter actuality," not merely with an "air of semblance or illusion."[89]

Geertz discerns that in the marketplace of competing perspectives, religion's distinctive capacity to persuade and convict is peculiarly generated and sustained in ritual. In the symbolic acts and embodied attitudes that comprise religious observance, religion offers not only models for what to believe about life and the world, but also models for the believing of it.[90] As he says:

> The acceptance of authority that underlies the religious perspective ... flows from the enactment of the ritual itself. By inducing a set of moods and motivations—an ethos—and defining an image of the cosmic order—a world view—by means of a single set of symbols, the performance makes the model *for* and the model *of* aspects of religious belief mere transpositions of one another.[91]

He makes the same point more evocatively by stating that "in a ritual, the world as lived and the world as imagined ... turn out to be same world."[92]

From this general anthropological framework for assessing religion's role in society, we can draw insight into the Torah's insistence that the rites and rituals of Leviticus are somehow central to the life of the covenant community gathered at Sinai. For this purpose, the work of F. Gorman, among others, is especially instructive. Drawing upon the theoretical insights of Geertz and others, Gorman has discerned that understanding the Priestly rituals in Leviticus and elsewhere in the Hebrew Bible requires "an imaginative construal of both the rituals depicted and the world within which the rituals take place."[93] He has shown that in the Priestly world-view, rituals of "founding," "maintenance," and "restoration" serve as a means of enacting creation theology. Such rituals, by recalling the Creator's purposeful design for the world, "gesture" or "perform" this design into reality through symbolic acts and attitudes. The intended effect is that all discordant understandings of the world are rendered inadequate as expressions of a transcendent truth that corrects and completes them.

Because Leviticus presents the priests as the custodians of those rituals, it invites reflection on the ministry of priesthood and its importance for

---

89. Ibid., 112.
90. Ibid., 114.
91. Ibid., 118.
92. Ibid., 112.
93. See the general discussion of Gorman above, 147–50. This particular citation is from Gorman's subsequent survey of contemporary discussions of ritual in "Ritual Studies and Biblical Studies: Assessment of the Past; Prospects for the Future," *Semeia* 67 (1994), 21.

the community of faith. By virtue of their calling and commission, priests are specially charged with the responsibility of administering the rituals that bind people and world into harmony with God's creational design. According to Leviticus 8–9 their ordination is a commission to stand in the breach between the holy and the common, between the pure and the impure. At this vital juncture, the priests are called both to uphold the foundational boundaries that sustain the world according to God's design, and to restore those boundaries when they are violated or ignored.

The objective of the priestly ministry, however, is not only to guard against the collapse of the sacred into the common. It is also to extend the claims of the holy onto the everyday so that the realm of God's presence on earth is enlarged and advanced. At the heart of priestly ministry, therefore, stands the abiding mandate *to secure a community of faith* in the midst of a fragile world and by so doing *to build a world* evermore attuned to God's cosmic purposes.[94]

As *agents of community,* priests administer the rituals that unite people to God in worship. Holy times of worship (for example, those in Lev. 23) are marked and observed so that a community's everyday life may remain connected to and defined by the sacred rhythms of creation's ordering. Places of worship are consecrated and purified (as described in Lev. 16) so that on earth there may always be a sanctuary where God's presence is visible and God's summons to become "a priestly kingdom and a holy nation" is palpable and evocative. Rituals for sustaining and restoring corporeal purity and wholeness (detailed in Lev. 11–15) keep a community ever mindful that it must take seriously its responsibility to keep itself physically as well as spiritually fit for worship in the presence of a holy God. In these various rites and rituals the priests serve as catalysts of community. Their ministry is to keep open the possibility that a faithful and forgiven people may yet realize its commission to image God on earth.[95]

In the Torah's vision, the ministry of priesthood cannot be fulfilled simply by uniting a community of faith to God in worship. The necessary imperative that shapes every community of worship is the summons to ethical holiness that binds people to each other with tangible expressions of God-like justice. The stewardship of this imperative is also the ministry of

94. Cf. R. L. Grimes, who defines "liturgical power" as a means by which people become attuned to an "ultimate frame of reference" that is understood to be of "cosmic necessity." As he puts it, "Liturgy is a way of coming to rest in the heart of the cosmos." It is how "a people becomes attuned to the way things are—the way they really are, not the way they appear to be" (*Beginnings in Ritual Studies* [rev. ed.; Columbia: University of South Carolina Press, 1995], 51).

95. On priests as "catalysts" of faithful and forgiven communities, see Nelson, *Raising Up a Faithful Priest*, 88–94.

priesthood. Priestly ministry seeks to build communities of faith in order that communities of faith may *build worlds* where justice, no less than piety, orders life in accord with the Creator's design.

Scholars particularly prone to dismissing "the priestly" should note that ritual observance inculcates ethical and moral behavior. That the Torah envisions an inner cohesion between worship and justice is suggested by the strategic placement of the "Holiness Code" within the priestly instructions preserved in Leviticus. Following the instructions for public worship (Lev. 1–16) the Holiness Code (Lev. 17–26) extends the priestly concern for holiness to the entire community. The mandate that Moses now delivers to all persons is stated succinctly: "You shall be holy *(qĕdōšîm tihyû)*, for I the LORD your God am holy" (Lev. 19:2). If the community of faith is to image God's holiness, it must do so not only with worship that is manifested in the quality of the offerings it brings to God's house (Lev. 22:17-33) but also with worship enacted through ethical behavior in the "common" areas that lie outside the boundaries of the sacred place. In the routines of everyday life—sexual relationships (18:6-23), neighborliness (19:9-18), family matters (20:9-21), land ownership (25:1-55)—the community's code of ethics must be a worthy embodiment of its sacred liturgies.

In his effort to appropriate the theology of biblical priesthood, R. Nelson has observed that ritual provides "the backbone of religion, for it can be carried on even when faith is weak." Indeed, ritual is empowered to sustain religious perspectives on God, the world, and humankind because, as he puts it, "a people actually learns what it believes from the way it worships."[96] The Torah's vision of the rites and rituals that give definition to the life of the covenant community invite studied reflection on the truth of this observation.

In ancient Israel, as in contemporary faith and practice, religious rituals aspire to a vision of the world that has more reality than what common-sense can grasp, or what science can prove, or what art can replicate. Rituals connect with and seek to embody the Creator's vision of a world that ultimately will not be limited by merely immediate or given realities. Wherever this vision is kept alive—whether in the secure confines of Sinai's holy mountain, the forbidding challenges of Canaan, or the politically controlled environment of Yehud—the Torah insists that the "very good" world of God's design may yet realize its full potential. Toward this end, the stewardship of rituals that build faith in God and effect justice in the world remains both an important legacy and a vital summons to the ministry of priesthood.

---

96. Ibid., 89

7.

AT THE BORDER:
THE EVER NEW,
EVER RENEWING SUMMONS
TO THE TORAH'S VISION

A T SINAI GOD COMMISSIONED ISRAEL TO BECOME BOTH A COVENANT community and a worshiping community. This commission, however, also carried with it the summons to *depart from* the sacred mountain, where covenantal obedience and ritual holiness might enjoy an untested harmony, and to *journey towards* the land of Canaan, where the obstacles to realizing God's designs in concrete terms will be significant indeed. In the wilderness, between God's promises and their fulfillment, Israel must take care not to let go of its distinctive identity. Hence the question: Will Israel *enter into Canaan* and live out, through its life and its liturgy, its commission to sustain and restore God's intentions for the created order; or will Israel become *immersed in Canaan* and so conform its special identity as God's people to the gods of the Canaanite culture?[1]

In addressing this question, the book of Numbers reports that those who departed Sinai organized themselves into concentric circles of holiness. At the center was the tabernacle, the central symbol of the presence of God. Encircling the tabernacle was the tribe of the Levites, special custodians of the holy tabernacle and all its appurtenances (Num. 1:50-53). Surrounding the Levites, in expanding circles, were the remaining tribes of Israel, with their respective tents facing toward the tabernacle (Num. 2:1-31). Whether encamped or on the march, Israel was to be a community of faith, a community that mirrored the truth of its commission. The center

---

1. Cf. T. Mann, *The Book of Torah: The Narrative Integrity of the Pentateuch* (Atlanta: John Knox, 1988), 139. Mann frames the discussion of Israel's passage *through* or *immersion in* the peoples of Canaan with reference specifically to the Balaam incident (Num. 22–24).

of both its life and liturgy was to be the summons to worship God in covenant holiness.

But just as in the Torah's creation liturgy, so also in the account of Israel's constitution as a people of God in the real world of Canaan, the Torah presents a quite candid picture. Both the world God creates and the community of faith God summons forth within it are indeed quite fragile. On the journey toward Canaan, a number of crises develop (Num. 11–14) that are no less threatening to God's creative designs than those that provoked an anguished God to send the flood in primeval days. Once again the Torah acknowledges the death of an old generation and the cleansing of a sinful community (Num. 21–25). Once again God summons forth a new generation of people (Num. 26–36). And once again God announces that the Torah's vision, as recapitulated by Moses in Deuteronomy, is critically important if a new generation is to realize its destiny as "a priestly kingdom and a holy nation."

The primary task of this chapter is to explore the ways in which Moses' final exposition of the Torah's vision summons those preparing to enter Canaan to remember that worship remains at the heart of what it means to be a people of God. The second part of the chapter concentrates on the structural and theological importance of the Decalogue (Deut. 5:6-21), particularly the Sabbath commandment, as the center for the presentation of Israel's constitutional polity in the land of Canaan (Deut. 12–26). This leads to the third part, which discusses the covenant liturgy in Moab (Deut. 29–32). As preface to those sections, the first part considers several perspectives in Deuteronomy that provide a hermeneutical key for interpreting and appropriating the book's role in conveying the Torah's vision to the people of God, both past and present.

The "Boundary Character" of Deuteronomy

In Deuteronomy the recapitulation of the Torah's vision is the product of a complex interaction of perspectives. The juxtaposing of these perspectives in the final form of the book contributes to what P. D. Miller has called the "boundary character of the book."[2] That is to say, in its present form Deuteronomy operates at the junction of a number of important perspectives. Key among them are three: the *literary*, the *historical*, and the *theological*.

1. From a *literary perspective*, Deuteronomy situates the people of God at the boundary between the ending of one era and the beginning of another. In the fortieth year of the journey from Sinai toward Canaan, a new gener-

---

2. P. D. Miller, *Deuteronomy* (Louisville: John Knox, 1990), 9.

ation pauses in the plains of Moab to receive Moses' parting words of instruction. The final scene of Deuteronomy records Moses' death and burial, thus anticipating the transition to new leadership in the land of Canaan under Joshua. But the first scene of Deuteronomy notes that Moses must "explain" (1:5; *bēʾēr*) to this new generation "all that the LORD had commanded him" to speak at Sinai (1:3). Between Sinai and Canaan, Moab symbolizes the critical juncture between past and future. It is the point in the journey when the normative vision of old must be reclaimed so it may be realized in the world that lies beyond the Jordan. At the very outset then, Deuteronomy presents itself as a message addressed to a people encamped at the border between vision and reality.

The present structure of Deuteronomy helps to delineate further the movement between past and future in Moses' presentation. A series of editorial superscriptions (1:1; 4:44; 6:1; 29:1; 33:1)[3] present Moses' address as a sequence of three speeches that focus the new generation of the people of God on their *past, present,* and *future.* Chapters 1–4 review Israel's *past* experiences with God, from the days of Horeb to the plains of Moab. Chapters 6–28 articulate afresh "the commandment—the statutes and the ordinances" (6:1) that are to guide the community in the *present* and in the near future. Chapters 29–34 announce the covenant provisions, accompanied by the blessings, that will sustain all *future* generations in the aftermath of Moses' death.[4] In short, Moses reminds the people gathered at Moab that their identity depends both on actualizing the vision bequeathed to them by the ancestors, and on preserving its legacy for all future generations.

2. The book of Deuteronomy is also shaped by and for different *historical* settings, in keeping with the long and complex process surrounding its origin and transmission. In general, three significant historical contexts provide alternate backdrops for understanding the book's message.[5] First, there is the setting given by the book itself. In the present form of

---

3. The significance of these superscriptions has been recognized and developed in varying ways by several studies. See especially, R. Polzin, *Moses and the Deuteronomist: A Literary Study of the Deuteronomistic History* (New York: Seabury, 1980); S. D. McBride, "Polity of the Covenant People: The People of the Book of Deuteronomy," *Int* 41 (1987), 231–36; N. Lohfink, "Der Bundesschluss im Land Moab: Redaktionsgeschichtliches zu Dt 28, 69-32,47," *BZ* 6 (1962), 32–34; G. Seitz, *Redaktionsgeschichtliche Studien zum Deuteronomium* (Stuttgart: W. Kohlhammer, 1971), 24–30.

4. For this particular use of the editorial superscriptions in sequencing Moses' speeches, see D. T. Olson, *Deuteronomy and the Death of Moses: A Theological Reading,* OBT (Minneapolis: Fortress, 1994), 17.

5. Different historical settings are widely recognized in Deuteronomy, but I am particularly indebted here to Miller's observations concerning the hermeneutical ramifications of these settings; cf. Miller, *Deuteronomy,* 3–5.

Deuteronomy, Moses addresses the people just before their entry into Canaan. The setting is the time between wandering in the wilderness and settling in the land. It is a time marked by promises received but not yet realized: land, prosperity, the stability offered by king and state—all are features of a founding vision that the people of God may anticipate with hope and confidence. Their expectation of imminent fulfillment rests in no small measure on the authoritative witness of their revered leader Moses, who, having received the instructions directly from God at Sinai, now prepares to deliver them directly to the people themselves.[6] In this setting, Deuteronomy conveys the Torah's vision as foundational, authoritative, and imminently attainable upon settlement in the promised land.

A second setting that informs this book is the period of the divided monarchy, specifically in Judah, most likely during the reigns of Hezekiah and Josiah. There are multiple connections between Deuteronomy 4:44—28:68 and Josiah's reformation efforts (2 Kings 22–23; cf. 2 Chron. 34–35), which were influenced by the discovery in 622 B.C.E. of a "book of the law" (*sēper hattorāh;* 2 Kings 22:8). These connections suggest that the bulk of the core teachings in Deuteronomy address—perhaps were created to address—this period in Israel's history.

Such a period is marked by contrasting features. On the one hand, the reigns of Hezekiah and Josiah are times of national prosperity and confidence. The land is securely in Judah's possession, the borders are expanding steadily, and the general mood of the population is one of optimism and abiding confidence, if not of superiority. Such enthusiasm can be detected throughout Deuteronomy. Numerous promises announce to Israel, for example, that God will "set you high above all nations" (26:19); that Israel "will rule over many nations, but they will not rule over you" (15:6); and that God "will make you the head, and not the tail; you shall be only at the top, and not at the bottom." (28:13).[7]

On the other hand, the very fact that most of the biblical record of Josiah's reign is devoted to his efforts to *reform* the ways of the southern kingdom suggests that this is a period also marked by disobedience, failure, and the threat of disintegration. Deuteronomy repeatedly admonishes the people to love YHWH with exclusive commitment and fidelity (for example, Deut. 6:4-5), and to avoid allegiance to all other gods, in whatever guise

6. Deut. 5:28 may be interpreted to mean that although the laws were given to Moses at Sinai, the people in fact receive them only in the plains of Moab, where they enter into a covenant with God that stands alongside the one concluded at Sinai (Deut. 28:69). Cf. M. Weinfeld, *Deuteronomy 1–11,* AB (New York: Doubleday, 1991), 1.

7. On the national resurgence during the period of Hezekiah and Josiah and its reflection in Deuteronomy, see Weinfeld, *Deuteronomy 1–11,* 50–53.

they may present themselves.[8] Such words indicate how the Torah's vision may function more as a corrective of present failure than as an announcement of future success.

A third setting is equally important in deciphering Deuteronomy's unique perspective on Israel's destiny. We noted above that the core of the Deuteronomic teaching (Deut. 5–28) addresses people in Judah during the time of the monarchy, when there was a king, a land, and a temple anchoring the Torah's vision in the reality of the people's existence. In 586 B.C.E., however, this scenario changes dramatically as the kingdom, the land, and the temple are lost, first to Babylonian exile, then to Persian domination. In the still influential hypothesis of M. Noth, the framework of the present book of Deuteronomy (chaps. 1–3 and parts of chap. 31 and 34) derives from an exilic editor who incorporated earlier forms of Deuteronomy into a larger compositional whole (the Deuteronomistic History: Joshua to 2 Kings) that chronicled the history of Israel from settlement to exile.[9] The details of this hypothesis and of the subsequent studies that have engaged it in substantive critique are not as important for present purposes as is the fundamental recognition that one of the historical situations addressed by Deuteronomy is the period of the exile.

The exile and its aftermath locate the people of God back in a "wilderness" setting, comparable to that experienced earlier in the journey between Sinai and the plains of Moab. Yet this new wilderness experience is radically different from the previous one. At Moab, Moses may be understood to have addressed a people awaiting with confident anticipation the imminent realization of the Torah's vision. In Babylon, and subsequently in Persia's Yehud, the reported words of Moses address a people defined not by the hope of the future but by the limitations of the present. In this setting, the Torah's vision is not only a *confident announcement* of a truth firmly rooted in history, but also an *impassioned plea to believe* in a future that seems to have no basis in present reality. It is more than a *corrective* offered to a people who already know the heady, if flawed, experience of living in possession of the divine mandate. It is an *exhortation to reclaim* a divine commission seemingly lost in the rubble of the failed promises of both God and Israel.

3. Finally, the book of Deuteronomy also operates at the junction of several different *theological* boundaries. Three major sources are typically posited for the theological perspectives that coexist in the present book:

---

8. Cf. Olson's suggestive discussion of Deut. 7–10 in terms of the temptations in Canaan to worship the gods of "militarism, materialism, and moralism" (*Deuteronomy and the Death of Moses*, 52–58).

9. M. Noth, *The Deuteronomistic History* (Sheffield: JSOT Press, 1981).

prophetic circles, priestly (Levitical) circles, and scribal/wisdom circles.[10] Though support for each perspective varies among scholars and during different periods within the history of scholarship, I prefer not to choose one as dominant. Rather (after looking at the three more closely), I will focus on how Deuteronomy holds the three perspectives together in a composite tension.

E. Nicholson has argued for a strong *prophetic* influence in Deuteronomy.[11] He points to concerns shared by Deuteronomy and the northern prophets, especially Hosea. He notes the observance of cultic law, the common adherence to holy war ideology, and the preference for charismatic ideals of leadership, exemplified prominently in a fundamentally critical attitude with respect to the monarchy. To these may be added the portrayal of Moses as a covenantal mediator/prophet *par excellence* (Deut. 18:15-22) and particularly the general ethical concern for justice issues, especially with reference to the socially and economically needy of society, a concern that is also characteristic of prophetic traditions.

G. von Rad has provided the formative hypothesis for identifying *priestly* tradents as responsible for the principal theological perspective in Deuteronomy. [12] He notes that the most distinctive feature of the so-called law code in Deuteronomy 12–26 is the way it is presented "homiletically." In Deuteronomy, old laws are not simply codified, as is true in comparable legal collections such as the Book of the Covenant; instead, they are "preached" in a way that brings them up to date and makes them applicable to new situations. These "sermons" on the law cover a wide range of topics, especially ritual/cultic concerns, but also various legal issues and holy war traditions. All such matters, von Rad argues, were likely promulgated within a liturgical setting, hence not by lay persons but by official religious spokespersons. He points specifically to the Levitical priests as the only persons who possessed both the access to the old sacral traditions and the requisite authority to interpret them freely.[13]

10. The information is surveyed in the standard commentaries. For a convenient summary, see Miller, *Deuteronomy*, 5–8; A. D. H. Mayes, *Deuteronomy* (Grand Rapids: Wm. B. Eerdmans, 1979), 103–8.

11. E.W. Nicholson, *Deuteronomy and Tradition: Literary and Historical Problems in the Book of Deuteronomy* (Philadelphia: Fortress, 1967).

12. G. von Rad, *Studies in Deuteronomy* (London: SCM Press, 1953); idem, *Deuteronomy: A Commentary* (Philadelphia: Westminster, 1966).

13. Von Rad suggested that the historical analogy for such Levitical preaching could be established from Neh. 8:7-8. There it is reported that when the law was read at the covenant renewal festival organized by Ezra, the Levites "helped the people to understand *(mĕbînîm)* the law," that is, "they gave the sense *(śôm śekel),* so that the people understood *(yabinu)* the reading." Although clearly descriptive of a later time than Deuteronomy, this text preserved,

M. Weinfeld has called attention to the *scribal/wisdom* perspective that informs Deuteronomy.[14] By isolating numerous verbal and conceptual parallels between Deuteronomy and Israel's wisdom traditions, he suggests that the origins of Deuteronomy may be found in the scribal circles of the Jerusalem court during the latter half of the seventh century B.C.E.. Such parallels are further enhanced by Weinfeld's comparison of Deuteronomy with ancient Near Eastern treaty forms, particularly the vassal treaties of Esarhaddon (dated 672 B.C.E.), which appear to provide the model for Deuteronomy's presentation of the covenant between God and Israel in the plains of Moab. Moreover, Israel's scribal circles had both an interest in and a familiarity with such international paradigms for monarchical leadership.

Of the many thematic affinities with wisdom traditions that Weinfeld identifies, none is more important for present purposes than the Deuteronomic concern for humane conduct and social morality. This humanitarian approach is distinctly manifest, Weinfeld suggests, in the way in which the Deuteronomic code emphasizes civil-secular and moral-social legislation rather than sacral-ritual legislation.[15] Such humanitarianism reflects a primary distinction between the wisdom orientation of Deuteronomy and the theological perspectives of other literary traditions (J, E, P) in the Pentateuch. With its unique focus on the social and moral aspects of Israel's laws, Deuteronomy in effect concludes (one may even say, *revises*)[16] the Torah's vision along distinctly secular and pragmatic lines.

In the ongoing debate concerning Deuteronomy's theology, the emphases identified with the three traditions are frequently reduced to two major areas: ritual-sacral issues and social-ethical-moral issues. The former is usually linked to priestly circles, in keeping with the general observations of von Rad; the latter to the prophets and scribes, in keeping with Nicholson and Weinfeld.

Some scholars have tried to prioritize Deuteronomy's "ethical" perspectives and "sacral" perspectives.[17] But there is wisdom in recognizing

in von Rad's opinion, a longstanding Levitical practice of cultic preaching (*Studies in Deuteronomy*, 13–14; cf. *Deuteronomy*, 23–27).

14. M. Weinfeld, *Deuteronomy and the Deuteronomic School* (Oxford: Clarendon, 1972); *Deuteronomy 1–11*, 55–60.

15. See especially, Weinfeld, *Deuteronomy and the Deuteronomic School*, 282–97; *Deuteronomy 1–11*, 19–34.

16. See, e.g., F. Crüsemann, who argues that Deuteronomic law (Deut. 12–26) is a "replacement" of the Book of the Covenant, not merely an expansion upon it (*The Torah: Theology and Social History of Old Testament Law* [Minneapolis: Fortress, 1996], 201–4).

17. Weinfeld, e.g., has cast these two theological perspectives in Deuteronomy as virtually polar opposites. In general, he understands P and Deuteronomy both to be reflective of preexilic historical circumstances. However, where institutions and laws are common to both, he argues that in most cases Deuteronomy is dependent on P. Thus the development that he

that these different theological perspectives are simply part of Deuteronomy's "boundary character." Indeed, one may see in Deuteronomy a major attempt to forge a synthesis between competing theological schemes.[18] Deuteronomy presents itself as the place in the Torah's vision, both canonically and historically, where the people of God are at a boundary: between Moab and Canaan, between past and future, between sacral and ethical perspectives. It offers the bridge between these various crossing points, not by eliminating one place of embarkment for another, but by insisting that each of these perspectives must contribute to the journey that lies ahead.

Deuteronomy provides the charter that guides Israel across the border and into the new land. This charter is not identical with priestly perspectives or prophetic/scribal perspectives, though it is clearly indebted to both. It is concerned with sacral matters and social justice issues, but it neither elevates nor diminishes the one for the other. Instead, in the Deuteronomic charter the community of faith is summoned to twin commitments, each with its distinctive and unyielding claim on people: the commitment to love God absolutely; the commitment to live justly with one another. Towards such a goal the book of Deuteronomy provides for an Israelite "polity" which, as S. D. McBride has suggested, is defined by a commitment to "theocentric humanism."[19]

Deuteronomy as Constitutional Polity

The key to Deuteronomy's model of theocentric humanism is its function as *tôrāh*. McBride has noted that the most distinctive feature of the Book of Deuteronomy is its self-conscious claim to be the authoritative *tôrāh* of

traces in Deuteronomy's theological perspectives is from the sacral to the social/ethical (*Deuteronomy 1–11*, 25–29). There is reason, however, to question whether Deuteronomy, either historically or canonically, represents a one-way development, away from a sacral perspective and toward a humanitarian or secular one. For a different view that posits a more complex understanding of the relationship between P and Deuteronomy, see I. Knohl, *The Sanctuary of Silence: The Priestly Torah and the Holiness School* (Minneapolis: Fortress, 1995).

18. See, for example, G. von Rad, who suggested that there was in Deuteronomy a "unifying tendency" with respect to different theological perspectives (*Das Gottesvolk im Deuteronomium* [Stuttgart: W. Kohlhammer, 1929], 66). R. Albertz has described Deuteronomic theology as a "large-scale mediating theology," and as a theology governed by a "wealth of syntheses" (*A History of Israelite Religion in the Old Testament Period: Volume I: From the Beginnings to the End of the Monarchy* [Louisville: Westminster/John Knox, 1994], 224–31).

19. S. D. McBride, Jr., "Polity of the Covenant People: The Book of Deuteronomy," *Int* 41 (1987), 244.

God mediated through Moses to Israel.[20] No other book of the Pentateuch refers to itself as *tôrāh;* thus Deuteronomy presents itself as a new and distinct literary genre.

To understand the importance of Deuteronomy's sense of itself as *tôrāh,* McBride draws on the observations of the first-century Jewish historian Josephus. Josephus conceived of Deuteronomy as a divinely sanctioned "polity" *(politeia)* or "constitution" that was to define Israel's identity and life in Canaan.[21] Building on this suggestion, McBride has described Deuteronomy as a "national charter," a kind of comprehensive "political constitution." Somewhat like the constitution of the United States, Deuteronomy conveys the normative, prescriptive legislation that governs the social, political, and religious existence of the people. In this sense, Deuteronomy's *tôrāh* is clearly related to the normal judicial practices associated with "law." But "Deuteronomic constitutionalism," McBride argues, goes well beyond the normal categories of jurisprudence. Deuteronomic *tôrāh* is *covenantal law;* it conveys the "divinely authorized social order that Israel must implement to secure its collective political existence as the people of God."[22]

D. Olson has sharpened this observation with the suggestion that Deuteronomy's *tôrāh* is best described as a program of "catechesis" (teaching and guidance in the essential matters of faith).[23] Like the "law," Deuteronomy's catechesis has the power to transform and shape behavior in accordance with its instructions. Unlike the law, however, Deuteronomy's instructions attain their power through rhetorical persuasion and conviction, not through enforcement. As Olson puts it, "A constitution is not so much taught as it is legislated and enforced. . . . Deuteronomy does not legislate as much as it teaches."[24] In short, what McBride describes as Deuteronomy's "constitutional polity," Olson might describe as the book's "constitutional catechesis." In both assessments, there is a common theme: as *tôrāh,* Deuteronomy presents itself as the authoritative basis for the religious and sociopolitical identity of the people of God in every new generation.

To return to McBride's suggestion that introduced this section: Deuteronomy's *tôrāh* provides the community of faith with a model for "theocentric

20. Ibid., 231–32. For references to Deuteronomy as *tôrāh* see 1:5; 4:8, 44; 17:18, 19; 27:3, 8, 26; 28:58, 61; 29:29 [MT 28]; 31:9, 11, 12, 24; 32:46. See also the phrase "this book of the torah" in 29:20 [MT 19]; 30:10; 31:26.

21. Ibid., 229. McBride cites Josephus's *Antiquities of the Jews,* 4.176–331, especially 4.184, 193, 198, 302, 310, 312.

22. Ibid., 233.

23. Olson, *Deuteronomy and the Death of Moses,* 10–14.

24. Ibid., 10.

humanism." Such a model embraces two distinct yet related commitments, one to God, the other to humankind. The Deuteronomic charter that is to guide both these commitments comprises "decrees" *('ēdōt)* and "statutes and ordinances" *(haḥuqqîm wĕhammišpāṭîm;* Deut. 4:45). This constellation of terms for *tôrāh* serves to introduce both the Decalogue (the "decrees" of 5:6-21, elaborated in chaps. 6–11) and the "constitutional matters," (the "statutes and ordinances," set forth in chaps. 12–26).[25] In the Decalogue, the primary summons is to love God with undivided fidelity. In the exposition of the "constitutional matters" the principal summons is to administer God's intentions faithfully within the body politic. In short, the Deuteronomic charter sets forth two complimentary goals for the community of faith: to love God, and to live as people who love God.

In the Torah's vision, the relationship between these two goals of the Deuteronomic charter invokes the memory of the Sinai covenant. At Sinai, religious imperatives (Ten Commandments) are followed by legal admonitions (Book of the Covenant). So also at Moab, the religious "decrees" of the Decalogue are amplified by the social and political concerns in the "statutes and ordinances" comprising Deuteronomy 12–26. Moreover, in Moab, as at Sinai, religious principles and political objectives are presented as derivative of an all-encompassing concern with the proper worship of God.[26] In Deuteronomy, for example, both the "decrees" and the "statutes and ordinances" begin with First Commandment concerns: "You shall have no other gods before me" (Deut. 5:7; cf. 12:1—13:18).[27] In sum, the community's experience in Moab is presented as a true recapitulation of the Sinai liturgy.

Nonetheless, at this critical juncture between Sinai and Canaan, the foundational concern with worship is enlarged and clarified in a number of distinctive ways. We will pursue these ways as they are manifested first in the Decalogue and then in the "statutes and ordinances."

The Decalogue: Deuteronomy 5:6-21; cf. Chapters 6–11

A comparison of the Decalogue accounts in Exodus 20:1-17 and Deuteronomy 5:6-21 shows that the two are quite similar in sequence and substance. Both move from commandments that summon exclusive fidelity to God (commandments 1–3) to commandments that order human relationships

---

25. McBride, "Polity of the Covenant People," 233–34. McBride notes that the word *'ēdōt* ("decrees") occurs only twice more in Deuteronomy (6:17, 20); in each case its referent is the decalogue of 5:5-21. The words *ḥuqqîm* and *mišpāṭîm* are standard Deuteronomic terms for the "statutory rulings" that Moses received after the Decalogue (cf. Deut. 5:1, 31; 6:1, 20; 11:32; 12:1; 26:16, 17).

26. See above, chap. 5, pp. 119–34.

27. See below, 189–91.

in accordance with the nature and purposes of God (commandments 5–10). Both present the sabbath command (commandment 4) as the center around which all commandments converge, the point of intersection between love of God and love of neighbor. In this respect, both Decalogues stipulate the centrality of worship in the life of the community of faith and acknowledge that it is principally worship that enables heaven and earth to attain their destinies in God's cosmic plan.

But it is precisely at the critical intersection between God and humankind envisioned in the sabbath command (Deut. 5:12-15) that the Decalogue in Deuteronomy diverges from its counterpart in Exodus. Of all the commandments, only the sabbath command shows significant variations in the two Decalogues. In the plains of Moab, this concern for sabbath once again emerges at the center of the community's preparation for crossing over into the world that God has prepared for them. Three distinctive features concerning the sabbath command in Deuteronomy underscore its importance at this point in the Torah's vision.

1. Though the sabbath command is the rhetorical center of the Decalogue in both Deuteronomy 5 and Exodus 20, the Deuteronomy text places greater emphasis on that centrality. The sabbath command is the rhetorical center of the Decalogue. This may be demonstrated on stylistic grounds in two ways, as N. Lohfink has shown.[28] First, motifs from the Decalogue's beginning (slavery in the "land of Egypt"—cf. v. 6) and ending ("ox and donkey," cf. v. 21) are present only in the Deuteronomic sabbath command (vv. 14, 15). The rhetorical effect is to suggest that the concerns of the entire Decalogue are drawn together in the command to keep the sabbath day.

Second, Lohfink has shown that in Deuteronomy the sabbath command structures the Decalogue into five blocks of alternating long and short statements, of which the third and central one is the sabbath command. This configuration may be illustrated as follows:[29]

This pentadic arrangement serves to reiterate that the sabbath command is not simply one of ten in the list. It is the pivotal center that connects the admonitions concerning YHWH (I–II) and the people (IV–V).

2. Within the structure of the sabbath command itself, the Deuteronomic version has a different beginning point than its parallel in Exodus.

28. N. Lohfink, *Das Hauptgebot: Eine Untersuchung literarischer Einleitungsfragen zu Dtn 5–11* (Rome: Pontifical Biblical Institute, 1963). For an English summary, specifically with reference to the structure of Deut. 5, see his "The Decalogue in Deuteronomy 5," in *Theology of the Pentateuch: Themes of the Priestly Narrative and Deuteronomy* (Minneapolis: Fortress, 1994), 248–64.

29. Lohfink, "The Decalogue in Deuteronomy 5," 257.

FIGURE 7.1

I	Worship of YHWH	5:6-10	long
II	Name of YHWH	5:11	short
III	**SABBATH**	5:12-15	long
IV	Parents	5:16	short
V	Moral commandments*	5:17-21	long

* Lohfink notes that commandments VI–X have been connected stylistically by the conjunction *waw* (vv. 18, 19, 20, 21 [2 times]) into a single block; ibid., 257.

In Exodus the admonition begins: "Remember *(zākôr)* the sabbath day and keep it holy" (Exod. 20:8). The summons is first to remember, then out of this memory, to sanctify the day. In Deuteronomy, the admonition begins differently: "Observe *(šāmôr)* the sabbath day and keep it holy" (Deut. 5:12). Here the summons is not to recollection but to obedience, out of which emerges the sanctification of the day.

In fact, the stress on obedience in Deuteronomy frames the entire sabbath command (5:12-15). Lohfink has noted that *šāmôr*, "observe," at the beginning of this command forms a parenetic inclusio with *la 'ăśôt*, "to keep," at the end (v. 15).[30] These twin exhortations provide the context for understanding the primary meaning and function of sabbath:

> 5:12   Observe *(šāmôr)* the sabbath day
> 5:14   so that *(lĕma 'an)* your male and female slave may rest as well as you
> 5:15   to keep *(la 'aśôt)* the sabbath day

As P. Miller has aptly observed, "In the case of Exodus, the community is called to remember and to obey out of that memory; in the Deuteronomic form, the community obeys to keep alive the memory of redemption and to bring about the provision of rest for all members of the community."[31]

3. The purpose of the sabbath in Deuteronomy—the provision of rest for all members of the community—brings into focus another difference

30. Lohfink notes that the verbs *šāmôr* and *la'ăśôt* are commonly used together in the "deuteronomic cliche vocabulary," occurring some 27 times in Deut. 5–28 alone (ibid., 252–53). See further *Das Hauptgebot*, 68–70.

31. Miller, *Deuteronomy*, 80; cf. "The Human Sabbath: A Study in Deuteronomic Theology," *PSB 6* (1985), 85–86.

between this Decalogue and the one in Exodus. In Exodus, the motivation for keeping the sabbath is grounded explicitly in God's creational design (20:11). The faithful are to remember the sabbath day because God "rested on the seventh day." To be in harmony with God and the created order, the people must follow God's example. To recall T. Fretheim's evocative expression: "sabbath-keeping is an act of creation-keeping."[32] In Deuteronomy, however, the motivation for sabbath observance is different (although the primary goal remains the same). Here sabbath observance is rooted not in God's creational act but in God's redemptive act of exodus deliverance (5:15). In this respect, the Deuteronomic sabbath encourages less the imitation of God's cosmic concerns than the imaging of God's earthly acts of compassion.

Though the motives are different, they are not mutually exclusive. In Exodus, humans image God by resting from work in order to prepare for ongoing acts of "creaturely creativity."[33] In Deuteronomy, humans image God by engaging in the work of liberation and freedom on behalf of those who are oppressed and enslaved. But the work of liberation and redemption is also creational. Just as the Exodus sabbath recreates the primordial harmony between God and God's world, so the Deuteronomic sabbath restores the world and all relationships within it to their created and intended states.

These three distinctions contribute to Deuteronomy's presentation of the sabbath as the principal commandment. Indeed, so central is the sabbath command in Deuteronomy that Lohfink has suggested calling this version of the Decalogue the "Sabbath Decalogue."[34] Herein resides the core of the founding vision that is to guide community life. At the center of the community's identity there is to be, as Miller has put it, an evolving "sabbatical principle"[35] that links the community with equal passion to love of God and to justice in the world. To those twin concerns of the Deuteronomic charter we now turn in the discussion of Deuteronomy 12–26.

The Statutes and Ordinances: Deuteronomy 12–26
The focus of the "statutes and ordinances" is different, though related, to that of the Decalogue (5:6-21). The Decalogue summons the community to

---

32. T. E. Fretheim, *Exodus*, 230. See the discussion of the Decalogue above, chap. 5, pp. 125–28.
33. See above chap. 4, 126–27.
34. Lohfink, "The Decalogue in Deuteronomy 5," 259.
35. Miller, "The Human Sabbath," 93; see further, "The Place of the Decalogue in the Old Testament and Its Law," *Inter* 43 (1989), 237; *Deuteronomy*, 138–39.

an exclusive fidelity to God. Its objectives are presented primarily in theological terms—love of God and love of neighbor—linked by observance of
the sabbath, a ritual of obedience that places worship at the critical intersection between God and humankind. In the "statutes and ordinances," the
focus is on constitutional matters, on the formation of the structures of
society, especially on the legitimate administration of these structures by
the proper human authorities. Thus, at the center of this collection are
instructions concerning the distribution of power among judges, kings,
priests, and prophets (Deut. 16:18—18:22). The objectives of the Decalogue
are presented primarily in theological terms, namely the sovereignty of
God; the objectives of Deuteronomy 12–26 are shaped more by political
concerns: authorizing human agents to administer God's cosmic intentions on behalf of all citizens in the body politic.

Even so, the present structure of the "statutes and ordinances" suggests
that the legitimate administration of justice in the body politic is itself
derived from the community's exclusive loyalty to God. In part, such a suggestion derives from the ordering of the stipulations in chapters 12–26,
which follows roughly the sequence of the Ten Commandments. Chapters
12–18 deal primarily with cultic concerns, serving as explication of the First
through Fourth Commandments. Chapters 19–25 focus more on issues in
the judicial and secular spheres, thus, broadly speaking, on the concerns of
the Fifth through Tenth Commandments. Thus the Decalogue and the
"statutes and ordinances" move in the same direction: from commitment
to God to responsibility to others.

Beyond the general sequencing similarities, however, it is of more
importance for the present study to note that chapters 12–26 invert the
rhetorical order of the Decalogue while continuing its emphasis on the
centrality of worship. In the Decalogue, concern for the sabbath is what
centers all commitments to God and humankind on the importance of
worship. In Deuteronomy 12–26, worship is what provides the context for
the intervening stipulations that order social behavior (see Figure .72). In
this respect the recapitulation of the Torah's vision in the plains of Moab is
similar to the rhetorical emphases that guide the Sinai pericope.[36]

Though not acknowledging the wide range of concerns addressed in
Deuteronomy 12–26, Figure 7.2 does show that all the stipulations, whatever their specific focus, are set within the framing context of worship. In the
paragraphs to follow, I will concentrate first on the framing context of worship, then on two manifestations of this central concern that Deuteronomic
polity summons into existence: the laws of release (14:22—16:17) and the
judicial administrators (16:18—18:22).

36. See chap. 5, pp. 125–28.

FIGURE 7.2

Deuteronomy 5:6-21	Deuteronomy 12-26

Admonitions concerning YHWH
(5:6-11)

Sabbath (5:12-15)

Admonitions concerning the people
(5:16-21)

Summons to the proper worship of God
(12:1—13:18)

The principle of social justice
(14:22—16:17)

The judicial structure and its
administrators
(16:18—18:22)

The practical details of social
justice (19–25)

Summons to the proper goal of worship:
the offering of the firstfruits in the ministry of stewardship (26:1-15)

1. *Worship as the Foundation and the Sustenance of Society (12:1—13:18, 26:1-15)*. The statutes and ordinances governing the community's social structures begin and end with concerns relating to the First Commandment: "I am the LORD your God . . . you shall have no other gods before me" (Deut. 5:6-7). Indeed, this first commandment and its summons to exclusive fidelity to God is a central concern that reappears throughout the varied collection of statutes and ordinances.[37] In 12:1—13:18 and in 26:1-15, this first commandment concern is explicated in terms of the *place* (12:1-28), the *object* (12:29—13:18), and the *times* (26:1-15) of worship. In this respect, the framing concerns of the Deuteronomic Code are quite similar to those that also envelop the Book of Covenant in Exodus 20:23-26 and Exodus 23:10-19.[38]

Both at Sinai and in the plains of Moab, the founding vision vouchsafed to the people by Moses identifies the central sanctuary as the "unique institutional locus"[39] of the community's social structures (Deut. 12:1-28). Whatever else they are to *do* or *be,* the community of faith must define themselves first by the proper worship of God in "the place that the LORD

---

37. Cf. Olson, who cites the following texts as evidence of the centrality of the First Commandment in Deut. 12–26: 12:30, 31; 13:2, 3, 6, 7, 13; 17:3; 18:20; 19:9; 20:18; 26:16-19 (*Deuteronomy and the Death of Moses*, 65).

38. See above, chap. 5, pp. 128–33.

39. McBride, "Polity of the Covenant People," 240.

your God will choose" (12:5; cf. vv. 11, 14, 18, 21, 26). Although tradition comes to identify the place of worship specifically with Jerusalem, both Exodus and Deuteronomy place the emphasis not on a specific locale but rather on the limitless freedom of God to choose the holy places where the divine-human encounter will occur. The community must know, as R. Cohn has put it, that "the holiness of place is never absolute," that as a symbol of the presence of God, the central sanctuary is envisioned to be "sacred but not ultimate."[40]

Corresponding to the emphasis on the central place of worship is the emphasis on the singular *object* of worship (12:29—13:18). The community is to give their allegiance to God and God alone. Whereas the Book of the Covenant cautions against the temptation to worship gods of silver and gold (Exod. 20:23), Deuteronomy broadens the admonition to warn against the many "voices" that will speak seductively, but misleadingly, on behalf of God.[41] False prophets (Deut. 13:1-6), friends and family members (13:7-11), even entire communities (13:12-18) may entice faithlessness with the same words: "Let us follow/worship other gods whom you have not known" (13:3, 7, 13). To such temptations, Deuteronomy responds by summoning the community to a singular commitment to the only legitimate object of their worship: "obey the voice of the LORD your God" (13:18).

Proper worship and singular fidelity to God are neither private nor casual concerns for the community of faith. Hence in Moab, as at Sinai, the community is instructed to observe regular *times* of public worship (26:1-15). Two liturgical occasions are specified, the offering of the first fruits (vv. 1-11) and the triennial tithes (vv. 12-15). Though a number of complexities surround the meaning of these two ceremonies,[42] one can at least say that in their present location they function effectively to return the Deuteronomic charter to its first concerns: the proper worship of God through personal commitments celebrated and publicly enacted for the benefit of the larger community.

---

40. R. Cohn, *The Shape of Sacred Space: Four Biblical Studies* (Chico, Calif.: Scholars Press, 1981), 79.

41. Cf. Olson, *Deuteronomy and the Death of Moses*, 69–70.

42. E.g., Deut. 26:1-11 does not specify clearly whether the offering of the first fruits is to be a regular offering or a one-time gift. The overall context seems to support the former rather than the latter, but the text itself is somewhat ambiguous. Moreover, the law of tithes (26:11-15) has a complex history, having already appeared in Deut. 14:22-29, which is itself a recontextualizing of pre-deuteronomic tithing laws (cf. Weinfeld, *Deuteronomy and the Deuteronomic School*, 217–24). Crüsemann has argued that instructions concerning the tithe in Deut. 14:22-29 and 26:12-15 provide a structural frame that is the key to the theological orientation of Deuteronomic law. In his judgment the triennial tithe, paid directly to socially underprivileged groups, serves to abolish the traditional state tax in favor of the "first known tax for a social program" (*The Torah*, 215–19).

In these three areas then—the place, the object, and the times of worship—Deuteronomy effectively recapitulates the Sinai experience. Beyond these shared concerns, however, the Deuteronomic charter places an additional emphasis on the *goal* or *purpose* of worship. Throughout the statutes and ordinances of Deuteronomy 12–26 there is a recurring emphasis on a special triad of relationships: God, humans, and creation.[43] The singular devotion that humans offer to God has more than a vertical (or heavenly) dimension to it. Worship of God is for the sake of the whole creation, enabling just and honorable relationships among humans and between humans and the world of nature. In other words, Deuteronomic polity envisions worship as an offering to God and a ministry to the world.

Both goals of worship are introduced in the framing concerns of Deuteronomy 12–26 and elaborated in the stipulations that follow. Deuteronomy 12:1—13:18 and 26:11-15 instruct the community to remember that the worship offered to God in fulfillment of the First Commandment must not neglect the equally binding instructions of commandments V–X. They are to love God *and* to care for their fellow human beings, particularly those who are most at risk in the body politic: children, slaves, dependent Levites, resident aliens, widows, and orphans (12:12, 18–19; 26:11, 12, 13). Moreover, proper worship of God enables a reverence not just for human life, but for all of life in God's creation. Harvest grain and firstborn animals are gifts that come from God and are to be returned to God. Sacred gift becomes sacred offering (12:6). The God who entrusts the land to human dominion is the God who demands a stewardship of compassion that reverences life in all its forms (cf. 12:23), while leaving none excluded from its bounty. Only by attending to this triadic relationship between God, humankind, and all of creation can the faithful person venture the bold confession of Deuteronomy: "I have neither transgressed nor forgotten any of your commandments. . . . I have obeyed the LORD my God, doing just as you commanded me" (26:13-14, NRSV).

2. *Social Justice and the "Sabbatical Principle" (Deut. 14:22—16:17).* Commitment to God begins and ends in the service of worship. Thus at both the beginning (12:1—13:38) and end (26:1-15) of the Deuteronomic charter for the future there is a summons to proper worship and a singular fidelity to God. But in Deuteronomic polity, what is offered to God in worship is, in turn, envisioned as a ritual of the stewardship of justice on earth. No society that seeks to attain the divine commission to become "a priestly kingdom and a holy nation" can ignore the centrality of justice for the body politic. In Moses' address to the community about to be constituted

---

43. Olson, *Deuteronomy and the Death of Moses*, 66.

in Canaan, the summons to love God *and* to live justly with one another takes concrete shape in the set of statutes and ordinances contained in Deuteronomy 14:22—16:17.

The framing context continues to be a concern for proper worship: 14:22-29 sets forth regulations concerning the tithing of crops and the first-born of the herds and flocks; 15:19—16:17 addresses the tithing of firstlings (15:19-23) and the three major religious festivals of Passover and Unleavened Bread, Weeks, and Booths (16:1-17). These framing prescriptions specify that such occasions for sacred worship are required interruptions in the ordinary calendar of life. They are to be observed "yearly" (14:22), "every third year" (14:28), "year by year" (15:20), in "the month of Abib" (16:1), "for seven days" (16:3; cf. vv. 13, 15), "on the seventh day" (16:8), after "seven weeks" (16:9), and "three times a year" (16:16). The observance of religious rituals throughout these regular cycles of days, weeks, and years reminds the community that their devotion to God is to be constant and abiding. They are to love God always.

And they are to live justly in the world. At the center of this set of statutes and ordinances are instructions (15:1-18) about what social justice requires in terms of release. Debtors are to be released from their financial burdens (15:1-6). The poor and needy are to be released from their plight through generosity and compassion (15:7-11). Slaves are to be released from the burden of perpetual enslavement with liberal provision for their success and prosperity as free persons (15:12-18).

These prescriptions for justice toward others are also to be observed regularly in the calendar of life. "Every seventh year" debts are to be forgiven (15:1). "In the seventh year" slaves are to be released from their bondage (15:12). Only the prescriptions concerning the poor and needy are not specifically scheduled. Here the attitude of the faithful is to be one of perpetual compassion and liberality. Whenever and wherever the poor are encountered, the faithful are to respond with a warm heart and an open hand (15:7, 11).[44] This requirement has the force of law; it is not merely an appeal for optional charity.[45] In short, Deuteronomic polity *requires* the community to commit with an enduring passion both to God in heaven and to acts of justice on earth.

Concerning this twin commitment to God and to justice, several observations are pertinent. First, the statutes and ordinances in Deuteronomy

---

44. On the significance of somatic and relational imagery in Deut. 15, see J. Hamilton, *Social Justice and Deuteronomy: The Case of Deuteronomy 15* (Atlanta: Scholars Press, 1992), 31–40.

45. Crüsemann, *The Torah*, 234.

14:22—16:17 function in the present arrangement of the text as exposition of the Sabbath Commandment (Deut. 5:12-15).[46] In a general way this connection is established through the repeated use of time references (days, weeks, years), recalling the primordial cycle of creation that culminates in the seventh day. More specifically, there are rhetorical links between the Sabbath commandment and Deuteronomy 15:1-18. As one "does *(la 'ăśôt)* the sabbath day" (Deut. 5:15), so one "does *(ta 'ăśeh)* a release of debts" (15:1). Just as the Fourth Commandment calls for a "sabbath to the Lord" *(šabbāt lyhwh)* on the seventh day (5:14), so is there a call for a "release to the Lord" *(šĕmiṭṭāh lyhwh)* every seven years (15:2).[47] In Deuteronomic polity, one may say that sabbath rest becomes sabbath release. The former enables a freedom "in time" for the regular worship of God. The latter secures a release "in space" to enable and encourage a justice on earth that will mirror divine compassion.[48]

Second, the Deuteronomic broadening of the Sabbath Commandment to address the larger concerns of social justice illustrates what P. Miller has aptly called the "sabbatical principle," a principle that provides the "touchstone for all actions on the part of the people as they seek to live in community and order their lives."[49] Specifically, Deuteronomy 15:1-18 is tied directly to Exodus 23:10-14, where the Book of the Covenant associates the law of the sabbath with the seventh year of fallow rest for the land. In Leviticus, the Holiness Code calls this seventh year of fallow rest a "sabbath to the Lord" (Lev. 25:2,4).[50]

But as Miller has noted, the force of the "sabbatical principle" creates a "trajectory" of concerns that goes beyond simply observing the sacred status of the seventh day or the seventh year.[51] Deuteronomy 15:1-18 extends the sabbatical principle to the economic sphere, specifically to concern

---

46. For this connection, see S. Kaufman, "The Structure of Deuteronomic Law," *Maarav* 1 (1978–1979), 105–58; G. Braulik, "Die Abfolge der Gesetze in Dtn 12–26 und der Dekalog," in *Das Deuteronomium: Entstehung, Gestalt und Botshaft*, ed. N. Lohfink (Leuven: Leuven University Press, 1985), 252–72. The basic arguments have been developed along theological lines especially by Miller (e.g., *Deuteronomy*, 128–40) and Olson (*Deuteronomy and the Death of Moses*, 73–78).

47. Cf. Miller, "The Human Sabbath," 93–94; "The Place of the Decalogue in the Old Testament and Its Law," *Int* 43 (1989), 237–38; *Deuteronomy*, 135.

48. With respect to the similarities between the sabbath commandment and the Deuteronomic laws of release, Miller observes that "The land was a provision for freedom in space, the sabbath a provision for freedom in time" (*Deuteronomy*, 135).

49. Miller, "The Place of the Decalogue," 237.

50. On the similarities and differences among the Book of the Covenant, the Holiness Code, and Deut. 15, see further, Crüsemann, *The Torah*, 226–34.

51. Miller, "The Place of the Decalogue," 237; "The Human Sabbath," 94; *Deuteronomy*, 138.

about economic justice for the poor and the disadvantaged of society.[52] In Deuteronomic polity, concern for economic justice is motivated by the same commitment to God that compels the faithful observance of the sabbath day. When engaging in acts of justice on behalf of the enslaved and powerless, the faithful community images God by offering to others the gift of compassion that they themselves have experienced: "Remember that you were a slave in the land of Egypt, and the LORD your God redeemed you; for this reason I lay this commandment upon you today" (Deut. 15:15, NRSV; cf. Deut. 5:15).[53] Conversely, to refuse help and compassion to the poor and needy is to act like Pharaoh, not like God: acts of economic injustice enslave; they do not liberate.[54]

Third, by grounding concerns for the poor and needy in the sabbatical principle, Deuteronomic polity stipulates that justice, no less than worship, is part of the "holy rhythm" that defines life in the community of faith.[55] The community's obligation to release from debt and from slavery is a regular and recurring one. It is a mandate for ministry to those in need that cannot be fulfilled with only sporadic or extraordinary acts of benevolence.[56]

Miller has observed that such a mandate of ministry summons the community of faith to resist common assumptions about the nature of human existence. It dispels the notions "that time is linear, not cyclical or repeatable and that the causal nexus of events cannot be broken or interrupted."[57] Deuteronomic polity insists that there is one way to break the seemingly

52. Crüsemann notes that Deut. 15 represents a radical attempt to eliminate the power of debt and lending from the social mechanisms that typically governed agrarian societies like Israel (*The Torah*, 227).

53. Miller observes that in Deuteronomy "all the places where the laws explicitly call for justice and compassion toward the weaker and powerless members of the community are directly tied to the Sabbath commandment by being motivated exactly the same way: 'You shall remember that you were a slave in (the land of) Egypt' (24:18,22)" ("The Human Sabbath," 93–94).

54. Cf. Olson, *Deuteronomy and the Death of Moses*, 76.

55. Cf. Hamilton, *Social Justice and Deuteronomy*, 107–13.

56. In this regard the social justice envisioned in Deut. 15 may be distinguished from that commonly attested in comparable legal literature from the ancient Near East. Hamilton has shown that whereas Deuteronomy mandates the community as a whole to be regularly concerned with matters of economic justice, Near Eastern analogies restrict such concerns to the king whose royal proclamations were typically designed to effect extraordinary, but temporary, measures on behalf of the economically dependent (*Social Justice and Deuteronomy*, 45–72). On the ancient Near Eastern parallels, see further, M. Weinfeld, "Sabbatical Year and Jubilee in the Pentateuchal Laws and Their Ancient Near Eastern Background," in *Social Justice in Ancient Israel and in the Ancient Near East* (Jerusalem/Minneapolis: Magnes/Fortress, 1995), 152–78.

57. Miller, *Deuteronomy*, 138; "The Human Sabbath," 94–95.

irreversible cycle of debt, poverty, and enslavement, and to forge a new beginning, free of old sins and failures. The sabbatical principle builds into the relentless movement of human life occasions to stop and recover. On the sabbath occasions of life, whether the seventh day, the seventh year, or the fiftieth year, the word of God in effect announces, "Stop and recover! Stop and recover freedom for slaves, stop and recover fertility for the land, stop and recover food for the poor, stop and recover property to its original owner."[58]

This mandate for regular renewal clearly recalls the exodus experience of God's compassionate deliverance, as has already been noted (for example, Deut. 5:15; 15:15). The fresh start offered by sabbath occasions is therefore linked in Israel's life and liturgy to the fresh start God provided at the beginning of Israel's history as a nation.[59]

But this mandate is also clearly linked to the holy rhythm of life that inheres in God's creational plan for the cosmos. It is not just to the beginnings of Israel's history as a nation that sabbath occasions look, for human history alone provides only a partial context for God's cosmic intentions. The new beginnings that may be effected on sabbath occasions extend to the whole of the created order. It is not only the poor and the disadvantaged who are redeemed; it is also the first offerings of the earth (14:22; cf. 26:1-15) and the firstlings of the herd and the flocks (14:23; 15:19). In sum, sabbath occasions envision the regular restoration of the world and its manifold relationships to their created order and character.[60] At its core, the holy rhythm that inseparably joins Israel's life and liturgy also summons the community of faith to reclaim and restore God's cosmic purposes through its ministry in the world.

3. *The Administrators of Social Justice (Deut. 16:18—18:22)*. The first half of the statutes and ordinances deals with the proper worship of God (12:1—13:38; cf. 26:1-15) and with the "sabbatical principle" of social justice that inheres in God's cosmic plan for creation (14:22—16:17). Deuteronomy 16:18—18:22 marks a shift in the focus of Deuteronomic polity. Here the concern is not with the *principles* of instruction that emanate from the soverign God of the cosmos, but with the *implementation* of these divine mandates by authorized human agents of power: judges, kings, priests, and prophets.

At the outset, it should be acknowledged that this section of the statutes and ordinances presents a composite picture of governance that is drawn

---

58. *Deuteronomy*, 138.
59. Cf. Hamilton, *Social Justice and Deuteronomy*, 113.
60. Cf. Miller, "The Human Sabbath," 94.

from different stages in Israel's history. Some of the practices appear to reflect judicial procedures in the pre-monarchical period;[61] others reflect monarchical systems of governance introduced in the ninth century;[62] and the final arrangement of the text is a product of Deuteronomistic editing during the time of the exile.[63] In this respect, the picture of Israelite governance, like much else in Deuteronomy, displays the book's "boundary character." On the one hand, it presents a portrait of governance that does not yet exist, a vision awaiting its implementation when the community crosses over into Canaan. On the other hand, it presents a critique of procedures tried and found wanting, hence a constitutional revision for a future world, beyond exile, when Deuteronomic ideals may be more successfully realized. In either scenario, these stipulations summon the community of faith to a *vision* of governance that is not yet a reality, but, nonetheless, is *meant to be*.

The Deuteronomic vision of human governance derives from and explicates essentially two of the Ten Commandments. First, these stipulations extend to the corporate level the values enunciated in the Fifth Commandment concerning the role and purpose of human authority in the family.[64] In the family, authority resides in the "reciprocal responsibilities"[65] of father and mother (cf. Deut. 5:16). In the larger context of community and nation, authority is to be distributed among four major groups of leaders—judges, kings, priests, and prophets—no one of which may claim exclusive power.[66]

---

61. E.g., the model for local administration by judges.

62. The appointment of specific judges and magistrates in each town (16:18-20) and a central court of justice (17:8-13) to augment local courts may reflect the judicial reforms introduced in Judah by Jehoshaphat (cf. 2 Chron. 19:5-11). See further, G. Macholz, "Zur Geschichte der Justizorganisation in Juda," *ZAW* 84 (1972), 314–40; M. Weinfeld, "Judge and Officer in Ancient Israel and in the Ancient Near East," *IOS* 7 (1977), 65–88.

63. Cf. Lohfink, "Distribution of the Functions of Power," 67–68.

64. Cf. Kaufman, "The Structure of Deuteronomic Law," 133–34; G. Braulik, "Zur Abfolge der Gesetze in Deuteronomium 16,18–21,23. Weitere Beobactungen," *Bib* 69 (1988), 63–82. This observation has been developed by others from a theological perspective, particularly Miller (*Deuteronomy*, 140–54) and Olson (*Deuteronomy and the Death of Moses*, 78–87).

65. For this model of "reciprocal responsibilities" as opposed to models of power that derive from unequal and hierarchical relationships, see P. Lehmann, "The Commandments and the Common Life," *Int* 34 (1980), 341–55; idem, *The Decalogue and a Human Future* (Grand Rapids: Wm. B. Eerdmans, 1995), 150–52.

66. On Deuteronomy's system for the distribution and balancing of power, see L. Hoppe, "Deuteronomy and Political Power," *TBT* 26 (1988), 261–66; M. Greenberg, "Biblical Attitudes toward Power: Ideal and Reality in the Law and Prophets," in *Religion and Law*, 101–12. For discussion of the ramifications of Deuteronomic polity with respect to Roman Catholic ecclesial systems, see N. Lohfink, "Distribution of the Functions of Power," in *Great Themes from the Old Testament* (Edinburgh: T. & T. Clark, 1982), 55–75.

Second, the mandate for the distribution of human power is itself an explication of the same First Commandment concerns that guide the entire collection of statutes and ordinances.[67] Sovereign power resides in God alone; all other agents of power are derivative. Their only authentic display of power is in obedience to the commandment that is primary to all others: "I am the Lord your God; . . . you shall have no other gods before me" (Deut. 5:6-7). The centrality of this commandment for each of the authorized agents of power in Israelite society is evident throughout this section of the Deuteronomic charter.

The stipulations concerning authentic administrators of power begins with the *judges* (Deut. 16:18—17:13). Both in their own lives and in the way they arbitrate disputes, judges are to pursue "justice and only justice" (16:20). Deuteronomic polity explains the requisites of this justice not with specific instructions for applying legal policies, but with exhortations to remember that any act or deed compromising one's exclusive fidelity to God is a perversion of justice. In general terms, judges are not to pervert justice by sacrificing impartiality in return for a bribe (16:19). Just as God accepts no bribes or gifts in exchange for guarantees of divine compassion (cf. Deut. 1:17; 2 Chron. 19:6-7), so human judges are to image God by being as fair and objective as possible.[68] Deuteronomy 17:2-13 extends this general concern to specific case decisions, both those that may be decided in the local courts (cf. 17:2-7) and those requiring the attention of the central judicial council (17:8-13). In both venues, justice obtains only when the decision rendered is in accordance with the mandate of the Torah: "You must carry out fully the *tôrāh* that they interpret for you; . . . do not turn aside from the decision they announce to you, either to the right or to the left" (17:11). Only thus can the judges' litigation remove the evil of infidelity from Israel's midst (cf. 17:7, 12).[69]

Second on the list of authentic administrators are the *kings* (17:14-20). In Deuteronomic polity they too may fulfill their divine mandate only through a singular focus on God. They are not self-appointed, but chosen by God (17:15). They do not impose themselves as outsiders; they emerge from within, as citizen-kings, authorized by God to lead as "one of your

---

67. Cf. Olson, *Deuteronomy and the Death of Moses*, 79.

68. For the connection between the prohibition against taking bribes and Israel's conception of God, see M. Goldberg, "The Story of the Moral: Gifts or Bribes in Deuteronomy?" *Int* 38 (1984), 15–25; cf. Olson, *Deuteronomy and the Death of Moses*, 81.

69. The phrase, "you shall purge the evil from your midst/from Israel (*biʿartā hārā miqqirbekā/miyyiśraʾēl*)," is found repeatedly in Deut. (17:7, 12; 19:19; 21:21; 22:21, 22, 24; 24:7), as a consequence of the enactment of the death penalty for a variety of crimes. In the present context, the crime is apostasy or infidelity. For further discussion on the possible background of the formula, see Mayes, *Deuteronomy*, 233–34.

own community" (17:15). Most importantly, their primary power derives not from their military expertise or their personal possessions (cf. 17:16-17),[70] but rather solely from their constant meditation on the instructions of the *tôrāh* (17:18). No other task is assigned to the king in Deuteronomic polity. His sole purpose is to "learn to fear the LORD his God, by keeping all the words of this law and these statutes" (17:19).[71] In this way, the king is portrayed as a "model Israelite,"[72] the embodiment of the Deuteronomic ideal of undivided allegiance to God.

At the center of the Deuteronomic system of governance are the *levitical priests* (18:1-14), potentially the most powerful administrators in the society.[73] They sit on the judicial council with the judge (17:9-12); they administer the sacrificial system (18:3-4); and, as custodians of the *tôrāh*, they are teachers of God's instructions to successive generations of Israel in times of peace (cf. 31:9-13) and of war (cf. 20:2-4). Indeed, all "extra-constitutional"[74] mediums of the divine will are categorically rejected as abhorrent and disloyal to God (18:9-14). Even the prophets, specially charged with the "word" of God, must meet strict standards for authentication (18:20-22). Of all the tribes of Israel, God has specially chosen the Levites "to stand and minister in the name of the Lord . . . for all time" (18:5).

Yet, for all their sanctioned authority, priests are totally dependent on God, the same as judges and kings. They have no land, no heritable allotments of property to secure their future. In this regard they reside in "perpetual exile."[75] They have no means of sustaining themselves, hence they

70. On the king's temptation to worship the "false gods" of "militarism, materialism, and self-righteous moralism," see Olson, *Deuteronomy and the Death of Moses*, 82–83.

71. Crüsemann notes that Deuteronomic polity understands the state to be defined principally by *tôrāh*. That Deuteronomy describes the powers of the king as "limited" by *tôrāh* is one clear indication of this (*The Torah*, 234–38).

72. Cf. Miller, *Deuteronomy*, 147–49. Miller contrasts the Deuteronomic image of the king with the model of the judge, who in Deuteronomy appears to image God. The distinction between judge and king likely reflects the Deuteronomistic concern with the abuses of kingship throughout the history of Israel.

73. The Deuteronomic picture of priesthood differs in important respects from what the Priestly tradition presents. Two of these differences are apparent in the present text. 1. Whereas Deuteronomy recognizes no special distinctions within "the whole tribe of Levi" (Deut. 18:1), the Priestly tradition distinguishes between the Levites who are descendants of Aaron and who minister at the central sanctuary, and the rest of the Levites who are assigned more subordinate duties (cf. Num. 3–4, 18). 2. In Deuteronomy the priests have no allotment of land (Deut. 18:1-2); in Priestly traditions the Levites are granted forty-eight cities to live in, but not own (cf. Num. 35:1-8; Josh. 21:1-42). For these and other questions relating to the history of Israelite priesthood, see A. Cody, *A History of Israelite Priesthood* (Rome: Pontifical Biblical Institute, 1969).

74. McBride, "Polity of the Covenant People," 242.

75. Olson, *Deuteronomy and the Death of Moses*, 83.

live from one day to the next in perpetual need. Nonetheless, they prosper, for God secures both their "inheritance" (18:1-2) and their daily sustenance (18:3-5). The priests' authority in the community, therefore, derives not from their sovereign power, but from their ministry of faithful servanthood "in the name of the LORD" (18:5, 7). As J. McConville has put it, the priests personify the Deuteronomic ideal that the community of faith "can only be prosperous in dependence" on God.[76]

Last in the list of divinely chosen administrators are the *prophets* (Deut. 18:15-22). They have no established institutional base of power in the bureaucracy. They have no official standing in the judicial, royal, or priestly venues of administration. Their authority derives from their link to the tradition of Moses, the prophet *par excellence* in Israel's history. In this regard their responsibilities in the governance of Israel are rooted in the liturgy of the Sinai experience (18:16-17). They are to be custodians of the "word" of God,[77] particularly those words of commandments and commission that first summoned forth this covenant people at the beginning of their journey towards Canaan. As with judges, kings, and priests, prophets have only derivative power. It is God who "raises up" the prophet (18:15, 18), God who commands the prophet to speak (18:18), and God who assesses the community's accountability to the prophet (18:19).

In sum, Deuteronomic polity recognizes the importance of human authority within the body politic. Judges legislate, kings govern, priests lead in the worship of God, prophets mediate God's word. In each case human governance consists of shared power and reciprocal responsibilities. It is a governance that derives from and witnesses to the sovereign claims of God: "You shall have no other gods before me" (5:7).

The delegation of legitimate authority is both necessary and important. If God's cosmic intentions are to be realized on earth, where divine plans and human interests often collide, the vision for "a priestly kingdom and a holy nation" cannot remain in the abstract. It cannot be only a utopian ideal, suitable for the sacred ground of Sinai but not for the land beyond the Jordan. Toward this end, Deuteronomic statutes and ordinances move to concretize the meaning of absolute fidelity to God. To love God absolutely means to extend cosmic standards of justice in specific ways to those who are particularly in need: the resident alien, the orphans, the

---

76. J. G. McConville, *Law and Theology in Deuteronomy* (Sheffield: JSOT Press, 1984), 151.

77. The emphasis on "word" repeats in vv. 18, 19, 20, 21, 22. See further Miller, who notes the theological importance of this "overarching category" in Deuteronomic polity (*Deuteronomy*, 152).

widows (cf. Deut. 14:22—16:17).[78] To love God absolutely means that in the practical details of social justice (cf. Deut. 19–25),[79] whenever a covenant community acts to prosecute or punish its citizens, to permit or prohibit certain behaviors, to include or to exclude persons from the ranks of its membership, it must act in every case specifically in accord with God's creational designs. It must never forget God's assessment that there is in all of life something that can be claimed as "very good."[80] In Deuteronomic polity, the gatekeepers who mediate between the ideal of loving God absolutely (chap. 12–16) and the requirements of living out this love concretely in the sociopolitical details of human life (chap. 19–25) are the divinely sanctioned judges, kings, priests, and prophets (16:18—18:22).

The Ever New, Ever Renewing Summons to the Torah's Vision

Just as the Sinai pericope reaches its climax with a service of covenant-making, so the "decrees and the statutes and ordinances" that Moses recapitulates in his final address lead to a renewed covenant liturgy in the plains of Moab. This liturgy is introduced by the superscription, "These are the words of the covenant" (Deut. 29:1 [MT 28:69]). It continues through chapter 32, following which another superscription, "This is the blessing" (Deut. 33:1), marks a new rhetorical section. While Deuteronomy 29–32 is a composite text,[81] the editorial superscriptions effectively unite its component parts under the "covenant" rubric.[82] Here, as in the Sinai pericope, the

---

78. On the transferral of the "beatific portrait" of social justice to the specific cases of the sojourner, the orphan, and the widow, see Hamilton, *Social Justice and Deuteronomy*, 135–38.

79. See above, 195–99.

80. On the major emphases in Deut. 19–25, specifically with reference to the focus on the "sanctification of life," note the following observation of McBride: "In short, this division [19:1—25:19] more than any other segment of the constitution shows us in sensitive detail just what it means for the covenant community to claim identity as a 'people holy to Yahweh your God' (7:6; 14:2,21; 26:19); for if holiness involves corporate apotheosis, setting Israel apart from all other nations, it does so by making sanctification of life at once the prime objective of the whole social order and the political prerogative of everyone who resides in Israel's midst" ("Polity of the Covenant People," 243).

81. Although there is considerable debate concerning the literary history of these texts, a general consensus holds that the Song of Moses in Deut. 32 is the oldest layer in this composition, to which has been added two prose supplementations, Deut. 29–30 and 31.

82. On the redactional function of the superscription in uniting Deut. 29–32, see N. Lohfink, "Der Bundeschluss im Land Moab: Redaktionsgeschichtliches zu Dt 28,69-32,47," in *Studien zum Deuteronomium und zur deuteronomistischen Literatur*, ed. G. Dartzenberg, N. Lohfink, vol. 1 (Stuttgart: Katholisches Bibelwerk, 1990), 53–82.

Torah's vision invites us to see that the message of the aggregate text is larger than the sum of its individual parts.

In its aggregate form, the covenant liturgy at Moab comprises three parts: chapters 29–30, 31, and 32.[83] Chapters 29–30 introduce the liturgy as an impassioned *speech* from Moses, modeled somewhat on ancient Near Eastern vassal treaties, summoning Israel to seize the moment and adopt the covenant God now offers them. Chapter 31 continues the ceremony by describing the transfer of leadership responsibilities from Moses to Joshua (31:7-8, 14-15, 23). With this transfer, the liturgy shifts its focus from the speech of Moses to the foundational *text*, the written *tôrāh*, that will guide the community in the aftermath of Moses' death (31:9-13, 24-29). Deuteronomy 32 concludes the ceremony with a liturgy of *song*. Like the rain that replenishes the earth, like the dew that distills on the grass (32:2), this song will imprint itself forever on the hearts of the community. Any earlier reference to the song describes it as a "witness" to the importance of the Israelites' maintaining covenant fidelity (31:19, 21), just as the written *tôrāh*, is a witness (v. 26). This song "will not be lost from the mouths of their descendants" (31:21). It will bring to fruition the work of the covenant.[84]

The covenant at Moab thus unites *speech, text,* and *song* in a liturgy of worship that focuses the community clearly on the choices that lie ahead. The intended goal of their journey, announced both at the outset of their encampment in Moab (cf. Deut. 5:21-31) and again in the parting words delivered to them by Moses (Deut. 33), is the blessing of God. But between the promise of blessing and its proclamation there are important choices to make. The choices are enunciated clearly in this covenant liturgy. They involve the community essentially in matters of life and death:

> I call heaven and earth to witness against you today that I have set before you life and death, blessings and curses. Choose life so that you and your descendants may live. (Deut. 30:19, NRSV)
> This is no trifling matter for you, but rather your very life; through it you may live long in the land that you are crossing over the Jordan to possess. (Deut. 32:47, NRSV)

---

83. Here I follow the helpful discussion of Olson, *Deuteronomy and the Death of Moses*, 129.

84. On the rhetorical power of the poetry and imagery of Deut. 32 to keep alive the memory of covenant, see the suggestive comments of H. Fisch: "Poetry is thus a kind of time bomb; it awaits its hour and then springs forward in harsh remembrance. . . . It will live in their minds and mouths, bringing them back, whether they like it or not, to the harsh memory of the desert sojourn. Once learned it will not easily be forgotten. The words will stick, they will be importunate, they will not let us alone" (*Poetry with a Purpose: Biblical Poetics and Interpretation* [Bloomington: Indiana University Press, 1988], 51).

This covenant liturgy suggests that in life-and-death decisions, worship is the primary context in which the community of faith attains sufficient clarity to choose wisely. In the paragraphs to follow I will explicate this observation by highlighting four aspects of this liturgy of covenant.

A Liturgy Summoned Forth and Sustained by the First Commandment

In keeping with the central concern that has guided Moses' speech from the outset, this covenant liturgy remains focused on the requirement of exclusive fidelity to God. It is both the history and the destiny of the covenant community to journey in a land where other gods may tempt them away from "the path that the LORD your God has commanded you" (Deut. 5:33). They are to resist such temptations at all costs, for other gods can only lead them to destruction and death (cf. 29:17; 30:6, 10, 20; 31:16, 18; 32:15-18, 37-39).[85]

God and God alone discloses the path that leads to blessing and fullness of life. God and God alone secures the journey along this path towards its intended destiny. Each refrain in this covenant liturgy (speech, text, and song) reviews this journey by tracing the community's movement with God from past to present to future. In each refrain the liturgy leads the community to recall God's *past acts of faithfulness* (29:2-9; 31:1-6; 32:4-14), the *present reality* of their own limitations and failures (29:16-28; 31:16-22, 27-29; 32:15-18), and the *future hope* that resides in God who is willing and able to sustain the relationship, despite their disobedience (30:1-14; 31:7-13 [cf. v. 23], 24-29; 32:36-43).[86] In sum, the liturgy asserts that the journey of faith is directed and sustained by God with a relentless compassion that will not be thwarted.

The summons to exclusive fidelity to God in obedience to the First Commandment is also a summons to reaffirm God's creational design for the cosmos. Heaven and earth have a stake in the covenantal relationship between God and humankind, for the well-being of the world is inextricably tied to humanity's faithful stewardship of God's compassion for the whole of the created order. Thus in each of the refrains of this liturgy, "heaven and earth" are summoned to witness the celebration of covenant-making (30:19; 31:28; 32:1). Their symbolic participation in the ceremony attests that they too are necessary partners in the process of attaining the goal of blessing and prosperity.

---

85. On these references and their explication of First Commandment concerns in the covenant liturgy, see Olson, *Deuteronomy and the Death of Moses*, 132, 151.

86. Olson has emphasized the importance of this threefold movement between past, present, and future, not only in the covenant liturgy, but also in the entire book of Deuteronomy (ibid., 16–17, 130–31).

A Liturgy Candid about the Fragility of Covenant Relationship

A central feature of the liturgy, in both word and song, is its candid rehearsal of the failures and limitations of the human community. Like a root that bears only poisonous fruit (Deut. 29:18 [MT 29:17]), like a child who grows fat and unruly (32:15), the human community is prone to abandon the covenant with God. At the same time that this liturgy reviews the history of the community's faithlessness, however, it also reiterates God's unyielding summons to the community to struggle towards obedience, to choose life over death (30:11-20; 31:9-13; 32:46). With its summons to obedience, the covenant liturgy at Moab reminds the community that as they prepare to cross the border into Canaan, they are in no way relieved of their moral responsibility: the commandments, statutes, and ordinances of Sinai remain in effect for the journey that lies ahead. In the words of Deuteronomy 29:1, the covenant that God makes with the community in the plains of Moab is offered "in addition to the covenant which he made with them at Horeb." At the border between Moab and Canaan, the Torah once again envisions the covenant relationship as a fragile bond of human faithlessness and divine summons.

There is, however, one important feature of the Moab covenant that distinguishes it from the mandates of Sinai. In its vision of the future, the Moab liturgy asserts that the chasm between human failure and divine expectation will be bridged by God. In the face of human fragility, God will act to sustain the covenant relationship:

> The LORD your God will circumcise your heart and the heart of your descendants, so that you will love the LORD your God with all your heart and with all your soul, in order that you may live. (Deut. 30:6, NRSV)

This clear echo of the Shema (Deut. 6:5) is a reminder that the liturgy at Moab is once again a summons to *love* God absolutely and to *live* with a fidelity to God that is consonant with God's intentions. But in view of the fragility of the human condition, the question that must be addressed in Moab is "How?" How can a community so prone to failure ever attain the obedience God requires? In response to this question, Moses envisions a "new" covenant[87] in which God will prepare the human heart to meet the divine expectations: God will "circumcise the heart."

The phrase occurs in only one other place in Deuteronomy. In 10:16 it takes the imperative form of a divine command: "Circumcise, then, the

---

87. On the dialectic in Deuteronomy between the "old" Horeb covenant and the "new" Moab covenant, see below 206-9.

foreskin of your heart and do not be stubborn any longer." The reference is to the physical act of circumcision that, according to Genesis 17:11, marks a "sign of the covenant." By recalling this act of covenant-making, Deuteronomy 10:16 exhorts the community to a relationship with God that is "marked" by obedience to God's covenantal demands. But whereas in 10:16 circumcision of the heart is a *command* that the people are to obey, in 30:6 it is a divine *promise* that the people are to receive as a gift.[88] What is envisioned here, in keeping with God's cosmic plan, is a new relationship based not exclusively on human fidelity and obedience—though both are clearly mandated and expected—but also on the promise of God's compassion and faithfulness. This transformation of the divine command to a promise, without yielding the former to the latter, opens the community at Moab to a future with God that they alone could never secure. In the sure assertion of Deuteronomy 32:36, the Lord "will have compassion on his servants when he sees that their power is gone."

An Inclusive Liturgy for Today

For all its focus on God's *past* acts of faithfulness and on the *present* reality of Israel's limitations and failures, the covenant liturgy at Moab is resolutely centered on the hope for the *future* that inheres in God's relentless compassion. It is therefore a liturgy that reminds the community of faith not only of its *frailty before God* but also of its *possibility with God*. Even with their limitations, this people may yet become the people God intends them to be (cf. Deut. 29:13). For such a goal do they gather at Moab: to participate in a liturgy of covenant-making that successive generations will reenact regularly (Deut. 29:10-15; 30:11-15, 15-20); to hear a foundational text that is to be read and reread with sabbatical regularity across the ages (Deut. 31:9-14, 24-29); and to sing and resing the story of God's abiding presence in their lives (Deut. 31:19-22; 32:44-47).

Two features of the hope that is announced in the Moab liturgy are particularly noteworthy. First, the vision of the Moab liturgy is that *the future God intends for the people of the covenant begins "today."* Even though the book of Deuteronomy locates the people of God at the "border" between Sinai and Canaan, between past and future, its rhetoric insists that this interim period is already the time when the future begins to take concrete shape.

One clear indicator of this focus on the present as a "future in the making" is the repeated use throughout Deuteronomy of the phrase "today" or "this day." It is present from the very beginning of Moses' address at Moab:

---

88. Cf. Miller, *Deuteronomy*, 207–8; Olson, *Deuteronomy and the Death of Moses*, 127.

"Hear, O Israel, the statutes and ordinances that I am addressing to you *today (hayyôm)*. . . . Not with our ancestors did the LORD make this covenant, but with us, who are all of us here alive *today (hayyôm)*" (Deut. 5:1, 3). But it attains its most prominent role in the climatic scene of this covenant liturgy. In chapters 29 and 30, "today" is repeated no less than twelve times,[89] marking the Moab liturgy as an occasion for actualizing in the present God's intentions for the future. The introduction to the liturgy emphasizes this point:

> You stand assembled *today*, all of you, before the LORD your God . . . to enter into the covenant . . . which the LORD your God is making with you *today*, in order that he may establish you *today* as his people. . . . I am making this covenant . . . not only with you who stand here with us *today* . . . but also with those who are not here with us *today*. (Deut. 29:10-15, NRSV)

The second feature of the hope announced in the Moab liturgy is that the covenant being actualized there is envisioned as *inclusive of all people, in all times and places*. Moses' opening summons (partially cited above) provides a list of persons invited to participate in this liturgy. Twelve phrases identify the persons with whom God desires "today" to be in covenant partnership: "all of you, . . . the leaders of your tribes, your elders, and your officials, all the men of Israel, your children, your women, the aliens who are in your camp, both those who cut your wood and those who draw your water" (vv. 10-11); and later, "you who stand here with us today, . . . [and] those who are not here with us today" (vv. 14-15). The list seems designed to include every conceivable person in the community: men and women and children, the socially titled leaders and officials as well as the socially inferior servants (water-bearers and wood-cutters), even resident aliens. Neither gender, nor age, nor social status is cited as a requisite for participating in this covenant. As P. Miller has observed, "To be a member of the community is to be drawn into the covenant."[90]

Moreover, the invitation is open-ended, extending to everyone in any age or place: those who are present at Moab "today" *and* those later generations "who are not here with us today" (29:14-15). The covenant is both for those whose good fortune it is to attain the promised land, *and* for those whose plight it is to suffer exile from the land (30:3-4). It is for those who are strong and courageous and live in the happy certainty of God's abiding

89. Deut. 29:10 [MT v. 9], 12 [MT v. 11], 13 [MT v. 12], 15 [MT v. 14] (twice); 30:2, 8, 11, 15, 16, 18, 19.
90. Miller, *Deuteronomy*, 209.

presence (31:23), *and* for those who are weak and wayward, for whom the hiddenness of God brings trouble and calamity (31:17-18, 21). In sum, the Moab liturgy proclaims that whenever and wherever God issues the invitation to covenant partnership, conventional boundaries of time and space will yield to the divine imperative.

An Interim Liturgy Awaiting Completion

At several places in this chapter I have emphasized the "border" or "boundary" character of the book of Deuteronomy. On literary, historical, and theological grounds, Deuteronomy invites reflection on what it means to be a community of faith at the crossroads—between past and future, between promise and fulfillment, between God's vision for a divine presence in the world imaged by "a priestly kingdom and a holy nation" and the actualization of this vision. The liturgy concluded at Moab functions within this tensive boundary situation. It is a liturgy for "today" that also sustains the community of faith during its journey into the future. It is a liturgy complete in itself yet incomplete because its goal is still to be achieved.

The liturgy concluded in Moab stands "in addition to the covenant that he [God] made with them at Horeb" (Deut. 29:1). In the Torah's vision, the community gathered at Moab participates in a liturgy that both recalls the experience of Horeb and "adds" to it in significant ways. It recalls the leadership of Moses in the journey from Egypt to Moab, and proceeds to announce his imminent departure and the new leadership that Joshua will now provide. It recalls the oral *tôrāh* of Moses that was inscribed on the stone tablets placed "in" the ark of the covenant (Deut. 10:1-5), and it provides for the periodic reading of the written *tôrāh* of Moses that is to be placed "beside" the ark of the covenant (Deut. 31:9-13, 24-31).[91] It reiterates the divine summons to obedience that was conveyed at Sinai through the Ten Commandments (Exod. 20:1-17) and the Book of the Covenant (Exod. 20:22—23:33), and it adds to those commands a divine promise of unmerited grace and compassion. With the gift of a "circumcised heart" (Deut. 30:6-8), the Moab liturgy announces that the future of the covenant partnership with God will be sustained more by the hope of fulfillment than by the dread of failure.

D. Olson has noted that this literary juxtaposition of the "old" Horeb covenant and the "new" Moab covenant introduces a theological trajectory that moves toward Jeremiah's promise of a still "newer" future covenant

---

91. On the theological significance of the juxtaposition of these two written forms of *tôrāh*, see Miller, *Deuteronomy*, 222–23; Olson, *Deuteronomy and the Death of Moses*, 135–36.

between God and God's people.[92] Jeremiah describes this future covenant in terms of God's promise:

> The days are surely coming . . . when I will make a new covenant with the house of Israel and the house of Judah. It will not be like the covenant that I made with their ancestors . . . a covenant that they broke. . . . But this is the covenant that I will make with the house of Israel after those days, says the LORD: I will put my law within them, and I will write it on their hearts, and I will be their God, and they shall be my people. No longer shall they teach one another, or say to each other, "Know the LORD," for they shall all know me, from the least of them to the greatest, says the LORD; for I will forgive their iniquity, and remember their sin no more. (Jer. 31:31-34, NRSV)

Olson notes that the covenants of Horeb, Moab, and Jeremiah offer three *different* perspectives on the partnership between God and the human community within the *same* Deuteronomic tradition.[93] The Horeb covenant places its emphasis on human obedience, thus on the primacy of human initiative in achieving the goal of covenant partnership. The Moab covenant shifts the focus away from human initiative—without relinquishing the requirement of obedience—and emphasizes the primacy of God's promise to sustain the covenant despite human failure. Still, the promise of God's relentless compassion and faithfulness is mediated in the Moab covenant through human teachers, foundational texts, and actualizing liturgies. In the new covenant envisioned by Jeremiah, God will again move to sustain the partnership with humankind. This time there will be no intermediaries; God will secure the covenant by writing its requirements and its promises directly on the hearts of the people. But that covenant is in the future: "after those days" (Jer. 31:33), a time not yet fully known.

Olson's observations invite us to see more fully that within the Deuteronomic tradition, the Moab liturgy is an *interim liturgy awaiting completion*. The Horeb covenant summons forth an ideal of human obedience that ought to be present in covenant partnership with God, but never really can be because of human failure and fragility. The Moab covenant, as Olson puts it, "does not so much command an ideal as tell the truth about what is real."[94] It reiterates the requirement of obedience, acknowledges the inevitability of human failure, and shifts the focus to the promise of God's sustaining grace as the human community continues to struggle towards

---

92. Olson, *Deuteronomy and the Death of Moses*, 152–56.
93. Ibid., 155–56.
94. Ibid., 155.

the goal of God's design. Jeremiah's covenant envisions the completion of this journey toward full covenant partnership with God. In some future time, there will be no further need for the liturgy of a covenant mediated by teachers, texts, and songs. In a time promised, but not yet present, covenant partnership will be a matter of the heart. In that day, the *ideal* of God's design will become *reality*. In the interim, however, the liturgy at Moab offers a practical and effective way of being the people of God. In Olson's words, "the strategy of the Moab covenant remains a viable, realistic, and hopeful alternative"[95] for living "today" toward the covenantal ideal.

Although Olson limits his assessment of the covenantal trajectory to the Deuteronomic tradition, the Torah's aggregate vision invites an even broader survey. In the Torah's vision, God's journey toward covenantal partnership with the human community begins not at Sinai/Horeb but at the creation of the world. From the very beginning the fragility of the human community is present (Gen. 3-6), and from the very beginning it is clear that the creational design can be finally sustained only through a cosmic covenant that signals God's relentless and unconditional commitment to the world and everything in it (Gen. 9).

The covenant at Sinai/Horeb is envisioned therefore as being enacted under the promise of God's cosmic commitment. It is a step toward the completion on earth of God's creational intentions. Thus, with T. Fretheim I have suggested that the liturgy of covenant-making can be properly understood as a liturgy of creation-keeping.[96] Even as the people of God struggle toward obedience in their micro-world, God is at work in the vast horizons of the cosmos to sustain a vision that can never be realized through human effort alone. At Sinai, as in the primordial past, the liturgy of worship is where this great cosmic-earthly drama is recalled and enacted.

In the Torah's vision, this ongoing liturgy of covenant-making/creation-keeping comes once more to center stage in the plains of Moab. Once more it is clear that the difficult passage from divine command to human obedience can finally be sustained only through God's relentless commitment to covenant partnership. Given Moses' review of the people's failures in the past (Deut. 1–4), it is appropriate that the Moab liturgy ends with a "renewed" articulation of God's promise to sustain the covenant in spite of the failings of the human partner (Deut. 29–32). In the Torah's vision, however, this Moab liturgy does not introduce so much a "new" covenant for "today" as it renews and extends God's ultimate creational intentions that

95. Ibid., 155.
96. See above, chap. 5, pp. 126–27.

are forever anchored in the cosmic covenant. The Moab liturgy asserts that wherever the community of faith finds itself at the border between "today" and the future days envisioned by Jeremiah, the interim task will always be to stay focused on the Torah's summons to love God and to live as people who love God.

It is fitting that the Torah's vision for the community of faith should reach its conclusion in Deuteronomy, where the people of God are poised at the border between old and new covenants. On the one hand, this border perspective portrays the ancient community of Hebraic faith on a journey between past and future. Their commission is to become "a priestly kingdom and a holy nation." This commission engages them in an ongoing liturgy that is constantly seeking, yet always falling short of, the full realization of God's creational design.

At the same time, the Torah's vision invites all who would be the people of God in any age, Jews and Christians, to understand themselves as a community living in the interim between past and future, between promise and fulfillment. For all the real differences between them, the "old" covenant remains tied, for Jews and Christians alike, to both the certainty of God's abiding presence and the frailty of humanity's obedience. And the promise of Jeremiah's "new" covenant, in which God's intentions for covenantal partnership are fully realized, remains a future hope, even as both communities remain—to use Olson's term—"Moab covenanters" who live "on the boundary yearning for the promised land but not yet there."[97]

For the journey that lies ahead, a journey across the border into the promised land, the Torah's vision for "a priestly kingdom and a holy nation" remains critically important. This vision requires the collaborative ministry of the *whole* community of faith, Jew and Christian in partnership together. It must never be reduced to the provincial or personal ascendancy of one faith community over the other, for God's creational designs can never be fulfilled by so limited a goal. In God's cosmic plan, "a priestly kingdom and a holy nation" is the key to realizing the creational design for the whole of the cosmos "on earth as in heaven." It is to the actualization of this vision that both Jews and Christians are summoned.

---

97. Olson, *Deuteronomy and the Death of Moses*, 156.

PART THREE

THE VISION THAT SHAPES
"ANOTHER WORLD TO LIVE IN"

8.

AT THE BORDER
OF A NEW MILLENNIUM:
IS THIS THE WAY
THE WORLD ENDS?

THUS FAR I HAVE ADVANCED TWO THESES. I ARGUED IN PART 1 THAT THE
Pentateuch is shaped in important ways by the imperial designs of the
Persian Empire. The text represents not only Yehud's internally generated
composite of ancient faith traditions, but also its acceptance of an externally imposed constitution that advances Persian hegemony and prosperity. Given the reality of Persian control, the canonization of the Pentateuch
stands as a reminder that Yehud's survival was the result of both stubborn
faith and political compromise. Whatever life Yehud constructed for itself,
it had to be viable in relation to Persia's power.

In Part 2, I argued that the Torah preserves a vision that, though shaped
by political realities, is not ultimately defined by them. This vision asserts
that God's intentions for the cosmos and for humankind can never be simply equated with status quo arrangements of power or politics. God's ultimate design is instead indelibly imprinted on creation itself. Creation's
liturgy summons humankind to worship and thus to a special partnership
with God that works to establish, sustain, and restore God's cosmic design.
Towards this end, the Torah envisions the community of believers as "a
priestly kingdom and a holy nation," commissioned to live out creation's
design faithfully at the border between the "givenness" of everyday realities
and the promise of wider ones that correct and complete them.

Part 3 now explores a third thesis. It argues that the Torah's vision has
the capacity not only to sustain the partnership between God and
humankind in the present, fragile world, but also to create imaginatively a
new world in which God's cosmic design may be more fully actualized.
The argument here turns on the assertion that the Torah's vision has a

215

rhetorical power to summon forth new horizons of meaning that help keep alive what C. Geertz has referred to as the vital distinction between the "real" and the "really real."[1]

In Yehud the "real" world was the observable world of everyday life as strategically defined by the Persians. Yehud's geographical boundaries, its political organization, its economic opportunities and obligations, its religious identity, all were shaped in important ways by the hard facts of Persian control. Yehud could not afford to be naive about this world, for any serious miscalculation could be decisively countered by Persian force. Nonetheless, the community of faith in Yehud could not simply accommodate itself unreservedly to the regnant powers, for to do so would be to lose the very essence of their identity as the people of God. The canonization of the Pentateuch in this historical context invites us to understand that in the midst of a Persian world, Yehud found in the Torah a foundational vision for another world in which the "really real" of God's creational design continued to shape life with a word of hope and promise.

I suggest that today's community of faith also finds itself at the border between the "real" and the "really real." At the edge of a new millennium the modern world is obviously no longer defined by Persian hegemony, but the contemporary forces that seek to define existence and proscribe faith are no less real and dominant. The gap between the world envisioned in the Torah and the world that actually exists in our everyday experience remains very large; indeed, one might justifiably argue that the gap is wider now than ever before.

T. S. Eliot has depicted this "gapped world" in his poem "The Hollow Men," a portion of which I cited earlier.[2] Penned in 1925, only two and one-half decades into the present century, this poem traces the lengthening shadow of the modern world that threatens to eclipse all assertions of faith. From Eliot's perspective it is a world in which the human quest for God has been reduced to little more than hollow souls groping for lost kingdoms. The full citation of the poem's final lines is instructive.

> Between the idea
> And the reality
> Between the motion
> And the act
> Falls the Shadow
>> *For Thine is the Kingdom*

---

1. C. Geertz, "Religion as a Cultural System," *The Interpretation of Cultures: Selected Essays* (New York: Basic Books, 1973), 112. See further the discussion above, chap. 3, pp. 60–61.

2. See above, chap. 3, p. 69.

Between the conception
And the creation
Between the emotion
And the response
Falls the Shadow
     Life is very long

Between the desire
And the spasm
Between the potency
And the existence
Between the essence
And the descent
Falls the Shadow
     For Thine is the Kingdom

For Thine is
Life is
For Thine is the

This is the way the world ends
This is the way the world ends
This is the way the world ends
     Not with a bang but a whimper.[3]

The threefold repetition of the poem's concluding assertion—"This is the way the world ends"—begs the question that our third thesis seeks to address. *Is* this the destiny of the world God has summoned into existence? Has the long course of human history so jeopardized the creational design that every idea, conception, and desire dies aborning, and every feeble effort at faith is muted in mid-sentence? My answer is to assert that the Torah preserves a vision of a world very different from the one Eliot has described. It is a vision of a world not yet realized, but one that remains nevertheless desirable and attainable.

But first I want to stress that the power of present hegemonies must not be ignored or minimized. Just as a Persian world shaped Yehud and determined the circumstances in which it received and embraced its own faith traditions, so the modern world has shaped us. In ways both direct and subtle, it has taught us how to read ancient religious texts like the Bible and how not to read them. In ways direct and subtle, it has rendered us at once both particularly needful of faith's vision and particularly immune to it.

3. T. S. Eliot, "The Hollow Men," in T. S. Eliot, *Collected Poems 1909–1962* (New York: Harcourt, Brace & World, 1970), 81–82.

Just as Yehud could not afford to be naive about the real powers that shaped its world, so we who stand at the end of a century and a millennium cannot afford to dismiss or ignore the powers that have left us in "this hollow valley" groping for "lost kingdoms."[4]

What are the powers that shape our world and define the context in which we must receive the Torah's vision, if indeed we are to receive it at all? Two contemporary works—one academic and rooted in the discipline of biblical studies, the other fictional and rooted in imagination—provide the particular focus on modernity that I wish to pursue here.

In *The Disappearance of God: A Divine Mystery,* Richard Elliott Friedman has traced the motif of God's hiddenness, not only within the context of the biblical witness, but also in terms of the profound legacy of that witness for the twentieth century.[5] We live in an age where God seems simply to have disappeared, not just from our intellectual conceptualizations (philosophical, scientific, even theological) but also in more immediate ways that we have come to know experientially and personally. The abiding and deepening sense of the absence of God, Friedman proposes, has been accompanied by a shift in the responsibility for life on earth from God to humans. I suggest that as we prepare to enter the next millennium, this pervasive sense of God's absence and humankind's responsibility for assuming more and more control over life on earth both requires and permits the Torah's vision to be embraced in new ways.

With *In the Beauty of the Lilies,* John Updike has offered a fictional account of an American family's relation to God through four generations, from 1910 to 1990.[6] What Friedman has emphasized from an intellectual perspective—the absence of God—Updike has chronicled in an imaginative construal of a particular family's journey from faith to loss of faith. But whereas Friedman sees the shift in the divine-human relationship more positively, as the invitation to greater human participation in the partnership with God, Updike is more focused on the burdens of faith, on the difficulty of believing in God when all else testifies that God is a non-factor. I suggest that the loss of God and the struggle to believe are what determine our current context for receiving the Torah's vision.

---

4. See Eliot's poignant images in stanza IV (ibid., 81): "There are no eyes here / In this valley of dying stars / In this hollow valley / This broken jaw of our lost kingdoms / In this last of meeting places / We grope together / And avoid speech / Gathered on this beach of the tumid river."

5. R. E. Friedman, *The Disappearance of God: A Divine Mystery* (Boston, New York, Toronto, London: Little, Brown and Company, 1995). Reissued as *The Hidden Face of God* (San Francisco: HarperCollins, 1997).

6. J. Updike, *In the Beauty of the Lilies* (New York: Alfred A. Knopf, 1996).

Obviously other perspectives could be added to these, and additional characteristics of our context could and perhaps should be identified. To analyze modernity is an exceedingly complex task, and I concede that what follows does not do the subject justice. Nevertheless, were a more comprehensive account of our present situation to be constructed, I am confident that the absence of God and the ceaseless yearning for faith would figure prominently in it.

The Disappearance of God

In keeping with current interest in the canonical presentation of the Bible's story, Friedman has observed that from the beginning to the end of the Hebrew Bible God steadily disappears.[7] At the outset, the Pentateuch portrays God as actively, visibly, at times extraordinarily present in the world. God speaks, acts, and in other ways directly intervenes to move the story towards its high point at Mt. Sinai. There, what is presumably the ultimate experience of God takes place. God personally descends on the mountain (Exod. 19:11, 18, 20), speaks audibly to the entire group of Hebrews encamped below (Exod. 19:19; 20:1, 22), appears in some actual form to selected persons (Exod. 24:9-11) and especially to Moses (34:5-8), and enters into a covenant relationship with the people that is initiated by God's personal gift of commandments (Exodus 20).

But after Sinai the presence of God steadily diminishes. As the Hebrew Bible unfolds the story, God gradually appears less and less, speaks less and less, and is less and less actively involved in the affairs of the world and of humankind. Friedman identifies a number of mileposts that mark God's steady retreat. For example:

—The last person to whom God is said to have been "revealed" is Samuel (1 Sam. 3:21).

—The last person to whom God is said to have "appeared" is Solomon (1 Kings 3:5; 9:2; 11:9).

—YHWH speaks to David and Solomon, but the words "And YHWH said to X" are never used with reference to any of the thirty-eight kings who come after them.

—The last appearance of the cloud and glory as signs of God's presence is at Solomon's dedication of the temple (1 Kings 8:10-11; 2 Chron. 5:14; 7:1-3).

7. With Friedman, a number of recent literary approaches that focus on the character of God have developed the argument that in the Hebrew Bible God is depicted as increasingly distant and silent. Cf. J. Miles, *God: A Biography* (New York: Alfred A. Knopf, 1995); F. Ferrucci, *The Life of God (as Told by Himself)* (Chicago, London: The University of Chicago Press, 1996).

—The last public miracle occurs in the story of Elijah at Mount Carmel (1 Kings 18).

—The last appearance of an angel in the Hebrew Bible is also in the Elijah story (2 Kings 1:3, 15); the last report of an angel acting on earth is in the days of Isaiah and Hezekiah (Isa. 37:36; 2 Kings 19:35; 2 Chron. 32:21).

—The last visible representation of divine presence is the temple in Jerusalem, and it is destroyed by the Babylonians in 586 B.C.E.[8]

Friedman traces these and other "last" manifestations of the divine presence throughout the entire Hebrew Bible, in narrative as well as poetic texts, until finally the journey winds its way into the "postrevelation world" of Esther and the last books of the Bible.[9] The Bible describes such a world as one where there are no more angels, no more cloud and glory, no more miracles, no more publicly visible signs or sounds of God's presence. The text does not say that God does not exist, or that God no longer cares about the world. Nevertheless, whether one reads the story from Eve to Esther critically or confessionally, there can be no denying that by the end of the Hebrew Bible, God is no longer depicted as present and involved in the same ways as in the beginning. Friedman puts the matter in the form of a challenge:

> For those who believe the Bible's story literally, take *this* part literally. For those who see it as myth, take this as part of the myth. But either way, come to terms with this: in the Bible God creates humans, becomes known to them, interacts with them, and then leaves.[10]

Why does God gradually disappear from the world, leaving creation alone to cope with diminishing evidence for the manifest presence of God? One might assume that the Bible's answer is to connect God's absence to human sinfulness: God withdraws from the world as a form of punishment for human transgression. Although the Bible clearly affirms that sin causes a separation between God and creation, this is not the full explanation for God's disappearance. Rather, the hiddenness of God is part of the very essence of God. As the book of Isaiah so tellingly puts it, God is "a God who hides himself" (Isa. 45:15).[11] Certainly God may hide because humans have sinned (cf. Isa. 59:2), but God may just as certainly choose to hide because to do so is consonant with God's own nature and purposes.

8. For these and other examples, see Friedman, *The Disappearance of God*, 19–26.

9. Ibid., 28. Friedman adopts the term "postrevelation world" from L. Wieseltier ("Leviticus," in *Congregation*, ed. D. Rosenberg [New York: Harcourt Brace Jovanovich, 1987], 30), who uses it specifically with reference to the book of Esther.

10. Ibid., 76.

11. On the critical assertions of this text concerning God's hiddenness, see S. E. Balentine, "Isaiah 45: God's 'I Am,' Israel's 'You Are,'" *HBT* 16 (1994), 103–20.

From this perspective Friedman asserts that divine hiddenness is encoded in the very nature of creation itself and as such is part of God's intentional design for the divine-human relationship. He finds the key for this design in the expression *histîr pānîm*, the phrase that describes the *hiding of God's face*, one of the critical metaphors of divine absence in the Hebrew Bible.[12] He points specifically to the imagery conveyed by this language in Deuteronomy: just before Moses' death, the Pentateuch announces that the future for the people of God will be a time of increasing divine hiddenness. "I will hide my face from them, I will see what their end will be" (Deut. 32:20).

The words "I will see what their end will be" suggest that God hides purposefully. Friedman indicates that it is part of the divine plan for God gradually to recede from direct intervention in the affairs of the world in order to encourage and promote a greater human responsibility for life on earth. God's disappearance from the stage of human history is therefore only half of the story the Hebrew Bible seeks to impart. The other half is the steady, intentional shift in the divine-human balance, because God determines that humans should have more and more responsibility for the fate of their world.[13] Thus when one goes back over the story that records the history from Eve to Esther, it becomes apparent that from beginning to end humans are expected and permitted to exercise an increasing role in affairs that once had been the exclusive prerogative of God: Noah builds his own ark (Gen. 6:14-22), Abraham questions God about divine justice (Gen. 18:22-33), Moses elicits "repentance" from God (Exod. 32:12-14), in the absence of direct communication between God and humans the prophets mediate God's words, and so on.

Of course, the shift in the balance of power between God and humans does not always work smoothly or without mishap. There is grief and loss to be experienced on both sides of the partnership. But as a whole, the Hebrew Bible affirms an ironic truth that derives from both the nature of God and the nature of humankind: the more God is distant, the more humans are free to become fully human, fully faithful. As Friedman puts it:

> The generation that is closest to the deity [the wilderness generation] is the most rebellious. The generations in which the deity is the most hidden [Ezra, Nehemiah, Esther] behave pretty well. One gets the

12. Friedman, *The Disappearance of God*, 69–76. On the phrase "hide the face" and other related expressions that comprise the vocabulary of divine hiddenness, see further, S. E. Balentine, *The Hidden God: The Hiding of the Face of God in the Old Testament* (Oxford: Oxford University Press, 1983).

13. Ibid., 30–59.

impression that closeness to the divine, though tempting, is not tolerable.[14]

Testimony to the disappearance of God and the shift toward human responsibility for life on earth is the legacy that the Hebrew Bible has bequeathed to both rabbinic Judaism and Christianity. Each has developed with a profound sense of the absence of God at the core of its consciousness, although they express this in different ways. And both, despite substantive and important differences in theological perspective, are founded on the belief that a reunion with God is not only possible but attainable.

Rabbinic Judaism, separated by more than a millennium from the time when God spoke directly to Moses at Sinai, looked to the oral teachings of the rabbis, codified in the Talmud (ca. 500 C.E.), as the vital link to God in a post-biblical age. The teachings of the rabbis were authoritative. On the scale of religious values, they were equal to the authority of the written Torah of Moses. Friedman observes that rabbinic teachings helped to construct a religion focused on the "divinely prescribed way of life rather than on divinity."[15] The central principle of that way of life—commonly referred to now as the "golden rule"—instructs the human community on the primary requirements for life in relation to other humans: "What is hateful to you, do not do to your neighbor." Clearly rabbinic Judaism does not neglect the importance of loving God, but in an age when God's presence was perceived to have seriously diminished, the rabbis believed that much of the responsibility for the affairs of humankind had been entrusted to humans.[16] In rabbinic Judaism, which prevails as normative for Judaism to this day, keeping the Torah is the vital link to reunion with the God who has disappeared.

Christianity's perspective on the disappearance of God is different. The New Testament asserts that in Jesus of Nazareth the Word of God has become flesh. Against the backdrop of the Hebrew Bible and its witness to the steadily diminishing presence of God in the world, the Christian doctrine of incarnation focuses on the most immediate contact God has had

14. Ibid., 101.

15. Ibid., 125.

16. Friedman illustrates with a story from the Talmud. On the occasion of a dispute among the rabbis, even God is overruled by rabbinic teachings. When informed of the decision by the rabbis, God is said to have responded not with anger but with amusement. In the words of the story: "He laughed. And he said, 'My children have defeated me. My children have defeated me'" (b. B. Mes. 59b). Friedman suggests that this story conveys an important perspective on how rabbinic Judaism coped with the legacy of the hiddenness of God: "The Torah is now in the hands of humans, and not even God can change it" (ibid., 124).

with humans since the garden of Eden.[17] And yet the New Testament's witness is that at the climactic moment in Jesus' life, the focus is once again on the absence of God. Jesus' last words from the cross are indelibly imprinted with the Hebraic sense of the hiddenness of God: "My God, my God, why have you forsaken me?" (Matt. 27:46; Mk. 15:34). This quotation from Psalm 22 invokes the abiding memory of a profound understanding of divine abandonment. At the same time, it recalls the fervent belief that God will not ultimately remain hidden from those who cry out for help (cf. Ps. 22:25). In the context of the Christian story, this belief is anchored to the resurrection of Jesus, whose reunion with God in a life after death provides the foundational model of salvation.

There are obvious differences in the way Judaism and Christianity address and respond to the legacy of the hiddenness of God. In Judaism, the Torah focuses the human community on the responsibility of obedience, for herein lies the path to reunion with God. In Christianity, the summons is to faith in Christ, whose redemptive ministry of grace and forgiveness holds the promise of salvation, eternal life with God. These differences notwithstanding, Friedman notes that both Judaism and Christianity mark the increased responsibility that accrues to humankind in the wake of God's diminished presence on earth. Both religions affirm that human beings must learn how to live responsibly in a world where God's direct control of affairs is less than it was in the past and not yet what it will become in the future. As he puts it, in this interim period between past and future, both Judaism and Christianity must be

> more concerned with humans' learning how to live, both with each other ("Love your neighbor as yourself") and in relation to their God ("Love the Lord your God with all your heart, and with all your soul, and with all your might").[18]

Friedman contends that the phenomenon of the hiddenness of God extends its legacy far beyond the formation of Judaism and Christianity. Now, nearly two thousand years after these great religions first began to wrestle with this issue, the twentieth century brings to closure a period when God's absence has been manifest in particularly acute ways. On the one hand, the ever expanding domains of science and technology have contributed to a diminished sense of God's importance or relevance in modern life. As more and more of the mysteries of the universe yield to scientific explanation, old religious claims for divinity are challenged as naive

17. Ibid., 128.
18. Ibid., 137.

and redundant. The human capacity to explain, to create, and to control life now seems to summon seekers of truth more convincingly to the computer terminal than to the church or the synagogue.

On the other hand, the twentieth century has also witnessed such profound catastrophes of suffering and death that the shift in the divine-human balance can hardly be embraced without deep ambivalence. After two world wars, the incomparable evil of the Holocaust, the seemingly unending eruptions of violence and barbarity throughout the world, to believe that humans have the capacity to master the universe for the betterment of all humankind is far less tempting today than it might have been even a century ago. In terms of sheer numbers alone, the quantity of suffering and loss piled on the scales of the twentieth century suggests that the balance between death and life is more precarious today than ever before. As we stagger toward the twenty-first century under the weight of such misery all around, Friedman pointedly wonders out loud, "Is there anyone who does not know that something is wrong here? that something is missing?"[19]

The evidence that many in the twentieth century have indeed noticed that "something is wrong here" is to be found in a variety of venues: art, literature, philosophy, drama, even theology. Friedman focuses especially on the notion of the "death of God," first as announced by F. Nietzsche at the turn of the century, then as explored in the various writings of the Russian novelist F. Dostoevsky, and finally as developed by theologians such as T. Altizer, W. Hamilton, and R. Rubenstein.[20] His exploration of the relationship among these various probes is both the most intriguing and the most compelling part of his presentation, and I regret that I cannot reflect on it more fully in this context. For present purposes it will have to suffice simply to note that concern with the disappearance or death of God is a substantial part of this century's philosophical, literary, and theological legacy.

This legacy has important consequences. A society that has lost all meaningful connection to divinity is a society exceedingly vulnerable. Friedman extrapolates the twentieth-century dilemma in two specific ways.[21] First, a world without God is a world vulnerable to fear and insecurity. If there is no Creator God to wield purposive power in the cosmos, then humankind is left to defend itself against the seemingly capricious forces of nature with no more than its own meager resources. To be faced with *both* the precariousness of our human existence *and* the loss of God is frightening indeed. Second, a world without God is a world of moral

19. Ibid., 208.
20. Ibid., 143–216.
21. Ibid., 208–14.

tumult. If there is no divine-human relationship whereby humans can know the deity's will and learn how to act in accordance with it—in Hebraic terms, no covenant relationship with God—then there is moral chaos. Where the connection between divinity and morality is absent, there can be no absolute standards of justice for either the weak or the powerful. Everything is relative. As both Nietzsche and Dostoevsky observed in different ways, "If God is dead, then all is permitted."[22] Faced with an existence defined by "moral cacophony," [23] humans must prepare to enter into Nietzsche's "world of the madman."[24]

The legacy of the twentieth century then, as Friedman reads it, is to have deposited humankind on the threshold of a new millennium bereft of God *and* tremendously vulnerable. However, he does not think such a situation should occasion as much pessimism as one might think. The biblical record portrays human responsibility as an integral corollary of the concept of God's disappearance. Indeed, the need for humans to assume an increasing responsibility for the affairs of the world is part of God's design in choosing to be a hiding God. God purposes to hide from humankind in order to "see what their end will be" (Deut. 32:20). The divine summons is for humans to "come of age"; humans must learn to live in a world where the immediate, visible, concrete signs of God's presence may be seriously diminished.[25] In such a world, the creature should not look to the Creator to solve every problem through divine intervention. In such a world, there is much that humans should and can do to sustain creation's design in the absence of God.

Friedman concludes his study by exploring the determinative role that humans may play in sustaining and restoring creation's design in God's absence. He concentrates on the intersection between science and religion, specifically on the parallels he discerns between the Big Bang theory of the origin of the universe and the understanding of creation in Kabbalah, a mystical movement in Judaism that developed beginning in the twelfth century.[26]

22. Ibid., 146, 158–62, 208.

23. Ibid., 213.

24. See further Friedman's general discussion of Nietzsche (ibid., 143–97). The specific quote noted above is from Nietzsche's *The Gay Science*, Book 2, section 76, as cited by Friedman (ibid., 209).

25. Friedman quotes D. Bonhoeffer, with whom the phrase "coming of age" is most identified (ibid., 215): "So our coming of age leads us to a true recognition of our situation before God. God would have us know that we must live as men who manage our lives without him" (*Letters from Prison* [New York: Macmillan, 1971], 360).

26. Ibid., 219–84.

Friedman suggests that the revolutionary developments in science during the twentieth century, which have in so many respects led the modern world away from traditional affirmations about God, may now in fact be positioning us for an intriguing and mysterious reunion with God. Simply stated, both Big Bang theory and Kabbalah assert that creation begins at a single point, from which it "bursts out," forming all that was to become the universe: stars, planets, stones, living things. Kabbalah goes on to claim that creation is a process that occurs within God. By this understanding, that which bursts forth from God, the emanations that comprise all the matter of the universe, retains a residue of the divine nature within it. The goal of creation is to return to the original unity with God that was fractured in the primordial beginning. In Kabbalah the key agent in bringing about this cosmic reunification with God is the human being. Endowed with the most developed state of consciousness in the created order, human beings—through deeds, words, and thoughts—are specially equipped for the task of *tikkun*, the "restoration, restitution, reintegration, mending" of the universe.[27]

As we move towards the year 2000 and a new millennium, Friedman suggests, humankind's long journey with the hidden God may be approaching a turning point. As the modern world has turned from religion to entrust itself more and more to science, science may have gradually prepared the way for a return to religious perspectives concerning the meaning of life. I find particularly intriguing the suggestion that the design of creation itself, whether interpreted scientifically or theologically, implies the possibility of a reunion between the cosmos and its originating source. Such a view is consonant with the thesis explored in this study, although I have been more concerned with the biblical summons to sustain and restore God's creational design as preserved in the Torah's vision than with the post-biblical reflections on creation found in Jewish mysticism.

At this point, however, what strikes me most about Friedman's analysis is his abiding confidence in the role that humans may play in determining the destiny of the universe. On this score his assessment appears to be thoroughly modern. It reflects and extends a major premise of modernity, namely that humans have the capacity to subdue and direct their own world. At the edge of a new millennium we are poised at a difficult but nonetheless exciting juncture in human experience. The time is ripe, Friedman suggests, for us to rebuild our universe and proceed on to the realization of our destiny. As he puts it:

> We may have to learn to get along without an immediate, visibly present, personal God. But this is bearable, and even motivating, if we

27. Ibid., 252–53.

understand that there lies the possibility of one day reencountering the deity. And in the interim we have the task of becoming worthy.[28]

It is precisely this "interim" period, however, that begs the question of whether humankind will be found worthy of the task it undertakes. Whereas Friedman examines life in the interim without divinity and finds hope in the human possibility to achieve reunion with God, others have come to different conclusions. To recall Eliot's assessment at the beginning of this century, in the gap "between the idea and the reality" life may not always be full of hope and opportunity; it may be only "very long."

Updike has imaginatively construed, in his story about Clarence Wilmot and his family, a life that is indeed very long. In Updike's fictional world of God's absence, the human plight is occasion for despair. Search as they will for the faith that rejoins them to God, the Wilmots seem destined to limp into the next millennium pathetically alone. To this journey and its implications for our present context for receiving anew the Torah's vision, we now turn.

In the Interim: The Burden of Faith in a God Inexorably Hidden

The despair that hangs over Eliot's assessment of the dawning of the twentieth century is even more sharply pronounced by William Butler Yeats in the poem "The Second Coming." Written in 1921 against the sobering experiences of World War I, this poem expresses the profound sense of loss that seemed at that time to define the widening interim between God's "first" and "second" comings to this tragically sad little world:

> Turning and turning in the widening gyre
> The falcon cannot hear the falconer;
> Things fall apart; the centre cannot hold;
> Mere anarchy is loosed upon the world,
> The blood-dimmed tide is loosed, and everywhere
> The ceremony of innocence is drowned;
> The best lack all conviction, while the worst
> Are full of passionate intensity.[29]

The journey through the twentieth century world, where "things fall apart" and "the centre cannot hold," is the journey of the Wilmot family

28. Ibid., 274.
29. W. B. Yeats, "The Second Coming," *The Collected Poems of William Butler Yeats* (New York: Macmillan, 1956), 184–85.

that Updike tracks through his novel *In the Beauty of the Lilies*. In his exploration of this family's struggles through four generations, from 1910 to 1990, Updike brings us to the threshold of a new millennium and invites us to look back and ponder what it means to live in a world that is judged to be full of "bombast and deviltry"[30] and "as empty of divine content as a corroded kettle."[31]

The patriarch of the family is Clarence Arthur Wilmot, a Princeton-educated minister who is struggling through his pastoral duties at the Fourth Presbyterian Church located on the corner of Straight Street and Broadway in Paterson, New Jersey. Clarence had been well trained in the mental gymnastics of balancing like a "trapeze artist" between traditional affirmations of undisturbed piety and seminary-induced questions that threaten to disassemble and subvert every unexamined faith assertion. But now, as Clarence sits in his book-lined study surrounded by defenders of the faith like Hodge and Warfield and "Teutonic ravagers" of the faith like Semler and Eichorn, Bauer and Wellhausen, the balancing act finally fails. The old certainties topple.

It is not just that the God of the Bible now seems to him little more than "an absurd bully, barbarically thundering through a cosmos entirely misconceived."[32] It is also the recognition that on any grounds whatever there seems to be insufficient reason for holding onto the idea of divinity. As far as Clarence can see, the theologian or philosopher must now concur with Nietzsche that there is no God, "God is dead."[33] With Darwin, the scientist and the mathematician now have good reason to conclude that "God is a non-factor—all the equations work without Him."[34] Faced with the evidence of God's "inexorable recession" from the world in which he ministered, Clarence comes to see the church and all its religious endeavors as just so much "flotsam and rubble, perishing and adrift."[35] At best, he is part of a "pathetic testimony to belief's flailing attempt not to drown."[36] At worst, he and fellow ministers have become co-conspirators in a "self-promoting, self-protecting tangle of wishful fancy and conscious lies."[37]

Clarence resigns from the ministry and becomes an encyclopedia salesman. Traveling door to door, this failed preacher of the gospel peddles leather-bound volumes of facts and pictures. For monthly installments of

---

30. *In the Beauty of the Lilies*, 23.
31. Ibid., 7.
32. Ibid., 5.
33. Ibid., 16–17.
34. Ibid., 74.
35. Ibid., 16.
36. Ibid.
37. Ibid., 19.

only $3.15, one could possess within two years all twenty-four volumes of *The Popular Encyclopedia*. With more than twenty-five thousand entries that offer all the information anyone could ever want about anything, the encyclopedia seems to Clarence to provide a twentieth-century substitute for the Bible. In his darker moments, when old memories of the truth he had once proclaimed from the pulpit intrude into his sales pitch, Clarence muses that the encyclopedia might be a modern-day blasphemy. It is "a commercially inspired attempt to play God, by creating in print a replica of Creation."[38]

Updike portrays Clarence's loss of faith as absent of struggle. When the moment of faith's defeat comes, Clarence yields passively. He simply lets go, and the "last particles of faith leave him."[39] The loss produces no more trace than "a set of dark sparkling bubbles escaping upward."[40] Once he surrenders, he is content to be done with God and to fall asleep peacefully on "the adamant bosom of the depleted universe."[41] Whereas Friedman calls attention to the human initiative to assume greater responsibility for a world in which God has disappeared, Updike's Clarence seems resigned to live out his days as a husk of his former self, "depleted but at last distinct in shape."[42]

Updike offers a carefully construed portrait of the tensive connection that exists between the loss of God and the hunger for God. As his narrator puts it, Clarence journeys through the world of God's nonexistence with

> . . . a clinging sense of lostness, as if within a series of ill-furnished, run-down classrooms he found himself in the wrong one, with an urgent appointment elsewhere, for which he was growing every minute more tardy.[43]

This "clinging sense of lostness" becomes Clarence's legacy to his children.

The relentless search for some vision that might offer meaning in a world where faith has been lost drives the Wilmot clan to the movies. In Updike's deft portrayal, the movies serve as the twentieth-century

---

38. Ibid., 101.
39. Ibid., 5.
40. Ibid.
41. Ibid., 42.
42. Ibid., 11. Cf. R. Woods, who observes that unlike Dostoevsky's Ivan in *The Brothers Karamozov*, Updike's Clarence does not struggle against the loss of faith. Clarence is spiritually passive in the face of God's absence. As Woods puts it, Clarence "passively permits the *is* to become the *ought*" ("Into the Void: Updike's Sloth and America's Religion," *The Christian Century* [April 24, 1996], 453).
43. Ibid., 104.

American substitute for God.[44] Where divine revelation and redemption have ceased, cinematic art and magic keep alive the hope that the world may still be imagined anew though the manipulation of the camera's lens. Clarence himself models what is to become the Wilmot fascination with the movies. From the tired days of his rejected sales pitches for the encyclopedia, Clarence seeks relief in "the incandescent power of these manufactured visions."[45] The great screen invites him into a church away from church, where the mysteries of life—joy and sadness, victory and defeat—can be addressed and resolved within a one-hour time period. In the world of the movie, the difficulty is not in yielding to cinematic illusion, it is rather in leaving the cinema's magic for the real world where life is not so carefully controlled. Thus, when the movie ends and the pale lights come on again, Clarence realizes that

> watching the 'movies' took no strength, but recovering from them did—climbing again out of their scintillating bath into the bleak facts of life, his life, gutted by God's withdrawal.[46]

In the post-God world of the twentieth century, the allure and the illusion of the movies continues to beguile the children of the Wilmot family. For Clarence's son Teddy, who settled early for a life of "plodding stoicism,"[47] the movies are a pleasant escape from lost belief, but hardly a lasting solution. He knows that the movies tried to say that "life was not serious; it was an illusion, a story, distracting and disturbing but at bottom painless and merciful."[48] Just the way actors move from movie to movie, with each new role offering the resurrection of an old character or the creation of yet another new one, so Teddy knows that for the price of a ticket one can buy into the dream that life offers endless possibilities for renewal. But he also knows that "the reel of your real life unwound only once."[49] On this reel there is often much pain to be lived through, some of it permanent. Teddy, like his father, simply resigns himself to the fact that "there was nowhere in mankind where he any longer fit—all around him, smooth

---

44. Cf. Muriel Spark (*Reality and Dreams* [Boston, New York: Houghton Mifflin, 1997]), whose major character, Tom Richards, is a film director who often wondered "if we were all characters in one of God's dreams" (7). Tom is prone to believe that through cinematic art he can turn dreams and fiction into reality. As he explains it to his crew members, "What we are doing . . . is real and not real. We are living in a world where dreams are reality and reality is dreams. In our world everything starts from a dream" (157).

45. *In the Beauty of the Lilies*, 107.

46. Ibid.

47. Ibid., 104.

48. Ibid., 148.

49. Ibid.

surfaces without a niche or handhold."[50] So he journeys on through life, "still curious about the world but with never any hope of changing it."[51]

Teddy's daughter Essie, more like her grandfather than her father, loves to hide herself in the movies where she has a way of "dreaming off into another world."[52] In the theater she feels safe, no matter what is going on in the real world outside that darkened sanctuary. Even when World War II intruded into the life of Essie and her parents and "sucked everything out of their peaceful world,"[53] it was the movies that defined what was real for her.

She becomes an actress. With a name change, collagen injections, diction lessons, and strategic sexual liaisons, she gives up her old identity and moves into the world of bona fide stardom. It is hard work, fraught with disappointment and failure, but she loves it. It is her route to immortality, not only because her movies can be preserved on celluloid film for eternal reruns, but also because acting gives her the illusion of being in direct contact with God. When she walks to the spot on the stage marked with tape and enters fully into the role she has been assigned, she believes she has entered a heavenly realm that is inaccessible to all but the precious few who share this craft.

> She felt, coifed and in costume and make-up, encased in a fine and flexible but impermeable armor; the bright island of make-believe, surrounded by scaffolding and wiring and the silhouettes of those many technicians who operated the equipment, was a larger container, a well-lit spaceship carrying her and the other actors into an immortal safety, beyond change and harm. A cosmic attention beat on her skin as when she was a child God had watched her every move, recorded her every prayer and yearning, nothing unnoticed, the very hairs on her head numbered.[54]

Her acting rescues her from the "fumbling reality" of everyday life and gives her entrance to a "reality keener and more efficient but not less true." It is like being lifted to heaven itself, and "she blazed with the miracle of it."[55]

The miracle of Essie's faith, although preserved for posterity on celluloid, could not be passed on to her son Clark. He drops out of school, moves from Los Angeles to Denver, and idles away his time as a ski instructor. LSD

50. Ibid., 153.
51. Ibid., 407.
52. Ibid., 239.
53. Ibid., 256.
54. Ibid., 335.
55. Ibid.

and PCP open cracks in his mind through which the illusory world of his mother's old movies plays on and on, but still he finds himself only a spectator of somebody else's drama, not an actual participant. "Who was this God everybody talked about but no one ever met?" "Where was the hidden miracle" that served his mother for religious faith?[56] He knows that his mother has a faith of sorts, even if only a manufactured, tinsel one, but he himself has nothing to believe in:

> . . . he knew only that he was going to die some day, and that was unthinkable—everything going out like a light bulb, and people and planets going on and on without him, even beyond the time when the sun exploded and became a cinder. He lay down at night into this charred and leaden eventuality."[57]

As his great-grandfather, Clarence, had passively let himself slide into unbelief, so Clark eventually lets himself succumb to belief in Jesse, the apocalyptic leader of the "Temple of True and Actual Faith." He joins the commune, changes his name to Esau (symbolic of his identification with the biblical son who had been cheated out of his birthright), and sets about preparing for the end of the world. As they head toward their own Armageddon, Esau and his fellow cult members become an odd company of believers. But then, as Updike's narrator observes, "A company of believers is like a prisonful of criminals: their intimacy and solidarity are based on what about themselves they can least justify."[58]

The cult ends in gunfire and destruction. Clark kills others even as he himself is killed. His mother, Essie, and his grandfather, Teddy, and other members of the Wilmot clan watch as the reports of Clark's demise flicker across the screens of their local television stations. In Bethesda, Maryland, Daniel Wilmot reflects on the Clark he had known:

> He struck me as a needy little guy, not quite knowing what was up. I told him what I thought was up, but I guess he needed more. That sounds pompous—of course he needed more. There's never an end to needing.[59]

With this recognition of the persistent human need for something more, Updike brings to a close his chronicle of the Wilmot family's journey through the twentieth century. At its ending as at its beginning, Updike's characters must limp alone through a world that inexorably remains "as

56. Ibid., 408, 409.
57. Ibid., 408.
58. Ibid., 426.
59. Ibid., 488–89.

empty of divine content as a corroded kettle."[60] For Friedman, such a world invites the confident faith assertion that in God's absence humans have much that they can and must do for the sake of the world. In Updike's construal, such a world invites only the plaintive petition "Have mercy." And this is addressed to the *Deus absconditus*.[61]

At the Border of a New Millennium: "Surely Some Revelation Is at Hand"

Is this the destiny of the world God has summoned into existence? At the border of a new millennium, can humankind expect anything more than a world empty of God and full of unending yearning? Friedman suggests that such a world need not evoke pessimism and despair, for now, as long ago when the community gathered at the border in Moab, we may be sure that God has a purpose in withdrawing from humankind: "I will hide my face from them, I will see what their end will be" (Deut. 32:20). Divine hiddenness, Friedman asserts, is a purposeful challenge and a promising opportunity. It is part of the divine summons to humankind to assume more responsibility for the maintenance of the world. Just as Noah and Abraham and Moses were expected and permitted to exercise an increasing role in the affairs of life on earth, so now at the close of the twentieth century, God continues to beckon the modern world to "come of age." Coming of age means learning how to manage life in this world without God's direct intervention. It means seizing the opportunity to live and act in such a way as to make a difference in the health of our species and in the destiny of our planet. Viewed scientifically, it means living in a world defined in terms of quantum physics, where "Big Bang" and "Big Crunch" theories suggest that the universe is expanding, vibrating, and radiating its birth pangs in unbounded oscillations. Viewed religiously, it means living in a world where creation itself endlessly yearns for reunion with its Creator. The religious summons and opportunity is to engage in cosmic reparation. In terms of Jewish mysticism, it is to commit to the task of *tikkun*, repairing the world for reunion with God.

Friedman suggests that at the close of the millennium religion and science have mysteriously joined forces in such a way as to bring us to a turning point in human experience. In biblical terms, the twentieth century has taught us, sometimes painfully, that to be created in the image of God "is to be enough like God to aspire to the divine, but not enough like God to achieve it."[62] And yet, scientific discoveries have taught us that as children

---

60. Ibid., 7.
61. Ibid., 108.
62. Friedman, *The Disappearance of God*, 99.

of the universe, we can nevertheless catch a glimpse of and be in touch with the underlying organizational design of the world. If humans cannot fully image God, they can at least assume, with confidence, the responsibility for preparing the universe for its ultimate and necessary reunion with the primordial center of its design.

Updike, however, is far less sanguine about the world that awaits us on the other side of the millennium. In his judgment, a world in which God is inexorably hidden is simply an empty world. One may pray for mercy, but the prayer will necessarily ricochet through an empty universe that is "bathed in the pitch-smooth black of utter hopelessness."[63] The pray-er may, indeed often must, persist in crying out to God. But in the end, the prayer will be utterly futile, a yearning voice "scratching at the air like a dog begging to be let in at the screen door."[64]

In such a world, the burden of sustaining faith and hope is too great. By trusting in the God made known through science or religion, one enters into commitments that merely confirm with varying levels of sophistication life's "ultimate nullity."[65] It is much simpler, and often a good deal more rewarding, Updike thinks, simply to buy a ticket for the "manufactured visions" of another world that can be embraced and discarded for little more than the price of admission. This is the witness of the Wilmots. This is the legacy of the twentieth century, where the charred remains of the "Temple of True and Actual Faith" symbolize the tragedy of a world in which, as Yeats put it, "the best lack all conviction, while the worst / Are full of passionate intensity."

In a fractured world where the center has not held, where "The blood-dimmed tide is loosed and everywhere the ceremony of innocence is drowned,"[66] Yeats went on to imagine that another world may yet be realizable. In his words, "Surely some revelation is at hand."[67] I cannot be sure of all that Yeats intended with this statement, yet it seems to me as much a query as an assertion. At the end of the twentieth century, when God seems increasingly hidden and humans seem destined to "survive by their sometimes good, but often bad devices,"[68] perhaps now, more than ever before, we have compelling reasons to hope that there is indeed some more revelation at hand.

63. Updike, *In the Beauty of the Lilies*, 10.

64. Ibid., 24.

65. Ibid., 108.

66. Yeats, "The Second Coming," 185.

67. Ibid.

68. This expression I take from R. Woods' insightful analysis of Updike's work: "The lord of Updike's fiction is the *Deus absconditus*, the deity who withdraws from history to let his people survive by their sometimes good but mostly bad devices" ("Into the Void," 457).

9.

ANOTHER WORLD
TO LIVE IN

A CRITICAL FEATURE OF RELIGION, AS SANTAYANA HAS NOTED, IS ITS power to propose "another world to live in."[1] But this claim for the religious perspective is precisely the claim that is in serious question as we prepare to cross the border into the third millennium. The crisis we face has been long in the making; T. S. Eliot's 1925 assessment of the human predicament still resonates. In many and varied ways the contemporary world exacts from us the concession that we remain, now as then, "hollow" people, groping sightlessly in the "valley of dying stars" for "our lost kingdoms."[2]

In this world of hollow souls—where an abiding sense of God's absence works to nullify faith even as it compels a restless yearning for the transcendent—is there some more revelation at hand? The Torah's vision, I believe, affirms that there is. In this chapter, I will recapitulate the discernments made earlier about this vision, then suggest specific ways they might address our present situation.

The Torah's Invitation
to a Counterimagination of the World

The Torah preserves a rich reservoir for imaginatively construing new realities about God, the world, and humankind. As Brueggemann has observed, "counterimagined worlds" offer alternatives to "presumed worlds."[3] They assert realities that extend the truth about God's intentions beyond those that current hegemonies may seek to promote as

1. G. Santayana, *Reason in Religion,* cited in C. Geertz, *The Interpretation of Cultures: Selected Essays* (New York: Basic Books, 1973), 87. See above, chap. 1, p. 36.

2. T. S. Eliot, "The Hollow Men," in T. S. Eliot, *Collected Poems 1909–1962* (New York: Harcourt, Brace & World, 1970), 81. See above, chap. 8, pp. 214-15.

3. See above, chap. 1, pp. 31-32.

ultimate. I suggest that a faithful counterimagination of the world that draws upon the truth of the Torah's vision will be informed by four principal discernments.

1. *The final horizon of faith's endeavors originates in, and returns to, God's design for creation.* The Torah asserts that God is Creator of the universe, hence that God's ultimate intentions can be discerned only when God's cosmic design is affirmed as faith's objective. If the community of faith commits to anything less than God's creational purposes, its identity and its vocation will be inadequate and incomplete.

God's primordial design declares that the world is created and ordered for good and purposeful intentions. In manifold ways, God endows creation with careful boundaries and directives that bind heaven and earth together in harmonious interplay. These boundaries and directives are vulnerable, by God's design, to both the best and the worst that humankind may contribute to the world. Even so, the Torah proclaims that a cosmic covenant ultimately secures God's intentions against human weakness and abuse. This "everlasting covenant," vouchsafed first to Noah (Gen. 9:16) and subsequently to Abraham, Sarah, and their descendants (Gen. 17:7, 13, 19), signifies God's relentless commitment to stay in relationship with creation, even when—indeed, according to the Torah's vision, *especially when*—the world of God's design is afflicted by violence and sorrow.

Creation's design is actualized by God in partnership with humankind at both the personal and the corporate levels. At the personal level, each human being, male and female, is commissioned to image God as a royal steward (cf. Gen. 1:26-28; 2:15). Each person is to exercise a God-like combination of "dominion" and "service" that enables all that is entrusted to them to attain its maximum potential. At the corporate level, this commission is realized in the covenantal summons to become "a priestly kingdom and a holy nation" (Exod. 19:6).

The venue for the covenantal enactment of God's design has a political dimension to it (kingdom, nation), but the politics of ordinary power are actualized by sacerdotal means (priestly, holy). In the Torah's vision, the covenant community is empowered for sacred service, not for mundane sovereignty.

2. *Encoded in God's creational design is a "sabbatical principle" that summons the faithful to worship.* The Torah envisions worship as a primary means by which the community attains clarity about God, the world, and human responsibility. In Genesis 1–2 the primordial foundation for the sabbatical principle is the seventh day, which invites the recognition and celebration of God's creative acts even as it prepares humankind to undertake the essential task of ongoing creaturely creativity. At Sinai the liturgy

of covenant-making portrays Sabbath observance as the critical juncture in life, the point where the imperatives to love God absolutely and to live in the world with absolute fidelity to God's purposes are joined with equal passion (Exod. 19–24). Both the Decalogue and the Book of the Covenant explicate Sabbath-keeping as an important means of creation-keeping: to keep the covenant is to enact the responsibilities of a partnership with God that places one in harmony with God's cosmic design.

The sabbatical principle extends to the tabernacle and its rituals. The heptadic patterning that undergirds the description of the tabernacle in Exodus 25–31 and 35–40 envisions the sanctuary as the completion of the work begun at creation. The verbal and thematic links between tabernacle and creation underscore the Torah's insistence that the sanctuary serves as one place on earth where God's primordial design for the cosmos may attain visible, concrete, and effective representation. Sabbatical imagery also undergirds the rituals that comprise worship in the sanctuary. Seven divine speeches convey instructions for sacrifice (Lev. 1–7). Seven acts complete the ordination to priesthood (Lev. 8). Seven principal festivals define the liturgical calendar, including the major fall and spring festivals of Unleavened Bread and Tabernacles, both of which stipulate a seven-day celebration (Lev. 23). In the seventh month, the Day of Atonement marks the ending of one year and the beginning of another, and does this with a seven-fold sprinkling of blood that purges the sanctuary and prepares the world for the indwelling presence of a holy God (Lev. 16). The constant ritual enactment of this sabbatical principal connects worship with the liturgy of creation. Thus worship becomes, in the Torah's vision, a primary means of constructing and maintaining the world of God's design.

The sabbatical principle extends still further to insist that worship inside the sanctuary be matched by a commitment to a life of covenantal holiness outside the sanctuary. The Holiness Code (Lev. 17–26) conveys this mandate through a summons to ethical and moral behavior that concretizes God-like justice in the real world of day-to-day living. The imperative is stated succinctly: "You shall be holy, for I the LORD your God am holy" (Lev. 19:2). Furthermore, the recapitulation of the statutes and ordinances in Deuteronomy envisions covenantal holiness as a constitutional imperative for the sociopolitical structuring of the community. In the economic sphere, Deuteronomic polity insists that the sabbatical principle works to secure cosmic standards of justice for the poor and the disadvantaged. The holy rhythm that defines life in the community of faith is also a summons to apply sabbatical regularity to forgiving the debts of the poor, freeing the enslaved, and providing for the needy with compassion and generosity (Deut. 14:22—16:17). The institutions of governance and those who administer them—judges, kings, priests, and prophets—are charged to demonstrate their love of God concretely by implementing social, political, and economic policies that secure and advance the Torah's concern for justice (Deut. 16:18—18:22). In sum, the sabbatical principle insists that justice, no less than piety, is imperative for a faithful stewardship of life in the image of God.

3. *In the Torah's vision, worship enables both a linguistic and a gestural construal of God's creational design.* The liturgy of covenant-making at Sinai and at Moab involves the proclamation and the reproclamation of statutes and ordinances. On these occasions the Torah understands that covenantal rhetoric—conveyed through speech, text, and song—has the capacity to speak new worlds into existence. In the wilderness of Sinai, such rhetoric has the decisive power to create "a priestly kingdom and a holy nation" where none presently exists. In the wilderness of exile, whether Babylonian exile or Persian occupation, the recapitulation of this rhetoric has the power to recreate such a community when present realities would seem to have rendered it both unimaginable and impossible. To recall once more Brueggemann's hermeneutic of imagination, the Torah's rhetoric has the capacity to evoke imaginative construals of alternative worlds that insist "the future is not yet finished."[4]

The Torah also asserts that the rituals of worship enable the construal of new worlds by symbolic gestures and acts, not just by words. Indeed, the book of Leviticus presents the rituals of worship as vitally important for the realization of the faith community's identity and vocation, a truth underscored by the placement of these ritual instructions at the very center of the Torah's vision. It is precisely these instructions, however, that too frequently have been ignored or discarded, especially in much of Protestant biblical study and theological reflection. But as I indicated earlier, a renewed interest in ritual and ritual theology invites and informs a reassessment of these important texts.[5]

Recent studies help to make clear that rituals serve a variety of purposes.[6] In closed, hierarchical societies, rituals may promote conventional behavior for the sake of decorum or ceremony. In such settings rituals can be an important and effective means of encouraging the surrender of personal or communal interests to the imperative of socially or politically defined necessities. Thus, as Durkheim noted, rituals may serve as instruments of

---

4. See above, chap. 1,pp. 73–75.

5. See above, chap. 3, pp. 147–50, 171–74; chap. 6, p. 32.

6. For a convenient typology of the "modes of ritual sensibility," see R. L. Grimes, *Beginnings in Ritual Studies*, rev. ed. (Columbia: University of South Carolina Press, 1995), 40–57.

social control.[7] For example, in Babylon or Persia, the Hebraic community of faith could be encouraged or required to participate in ritual activities that reinforced conformity to specific imperial attitudes and behavior. But in such settings, the conformity effected by rituals of social control would not necessarily be absolute. From the perspective of the dominator, consent is required, not belief. From the perspective of the dominated, consenting to externally generated values and ideas is not automatically the same as internalizing them.[8]

But rituals do not only serve as mechanisms for social control. As Turner, Geertz, and others have shown, when power relations between the dominator and the dominated are open for negotiation, rituals may serve not only to mirror society's values, but to alter them.[9] This is especially true of religious rituals, which typically claim an ultimate or transcendent frame of reference that tunes human actions to the way things really are, not the way they appear to be.

In the Torah's vision, the covenant community that receives the commission to become "a priestly kingdom and a holy nation" is shaped by rituals that are peculiarly empowered for just this sort of symbolic world-making.[10] "Founding rituals," such as the ordination of the priests (Lev. 8–9), establish a permanent paradigm by which the passage between the holy and the common may be sustained in everyday life. "Maintenance rituals," for example, the regular observance of holy days (cf. Lev. 23), keep the community reminded of the cosmic rhythm that sustains life in accordance with the Creator's design, even as the passage of ordinary time works to collapse the sacred into the mundane. "Restoration rituals," like those that mark the observance of the Day of Atonement (Lev. 16), empower the community of faith to retrieve founding visions from neglect or abuse, and to restore them to their rightful role in shaping both persons and world in accordance with God's creational designs. In each case, such rituals invite an embodied reflection[11] concerning the truth about the world of God's design. Such reflection typically connects with and acts

7. E. Durkheim, *The Elementary Forms of Religion* (New York: Free Press, 1965).

8. On the relationship between ritual, belief, and ideology, see the helpful analysis by C. Bell, *Ritual Power, Ritual Practice* (New York, Oxford: Oxford University Press, 1992), 182–96.

9. See ibid., 171–81, for the critique of the Durkheimian model of ritual as a means of social control by Turner, Geertz, and others.

10. On the designation "priestly kingdom and holy nation" as a peculiar example of Israel's summons to the process of world-making, see R. Hendel, "Worldmaking in Ancient Israel," *JSOT* 56 (1992), 16–17.

11. On rituals as gesturing forth new worlds through "enactment, embodiment, and a positioning of the self in the world," see F. H. Gorman Jr., "Ritual Studies and Biblical Studies: Assessment of the Past; Prospects for the Future," *Semeia* 67 (1994), 22.

upon a transcendent vision for the world that the status quo ultimately can neither eliminate nor control.

4. Finally, *the Torah envisions a truth about God and the world that successive generations of the community of faith have found to be especially pertinent for life at the border between past and future.* The present study has endeavored to substantiate this particular dimension of the Torah's vision in two ways. First, it has shown that in its final form, Deuteronomy's *tôrāh* has been shaped by and for multiple historical settings.[12] For the community encamped in the plains of Moab, Moses' recapitulation of the statutes and ordinances bridges the journey from the promises of Sinai to the opportunities and challenges of Canaan. For a subsequent generation in Judah, Josiah's rediscovery and promulgation of the "book of the law" invites a nation's repentance and reformation in accord with the abiding commandments and promises of *tôrāh*. For a generation consigned to live in the brokenness of Babylonian exile, the Deuteronomistic reclamation of *tôrāh* undergirds an impassioned plea to believe, despite all evidence to the contrary, that the future remains secure with God. Thus the microcosm of Deuteronomy shows *tôrāh* repeatedly clarifying for the community of faith the ever-renewing summons to become "a priestly kingdom and a holy nation."

Second, within the macrocosm of the Pentateuch's final form, the Torah's aggregate vision has been shaped by and for life in Yehud, where the community of faith must live at the intersection of external Persian directives and internal religious imperatives.[13] Persian policies and practices create the given world in which Yehud must exist. Strategic political and economic policies draw the geographic boundaries and control the financial resources that permit subject-citizens to live and work within the empire's domain. Symbolic and ideological mechanisms of control—creation stories, the codification of native law, the construction and maintenance of local cult centers—work to define and limit Yehud's self-understanding, at the same time securing and extending imperial objectives.

And yet, in this given world of Persian imperialism, the process that leads to the canonization of the Pentateuch works intentionally to preserve a vision of another world where the hope and promise of God's creational design remain vital and attainable. In the surety of this vision, the faith community in Yehud survives. Consigned to live at the border—between the realities that manage and extend the status quo and the enduring trust that rests in future possibilities, elusive but real—Yehud finds in the Torah's vision the foundation for building a new and viable self-identity.

---

12. See above, chap. 7, pp. 176–182.

13. See above, chap. 2, pp. 42–57.

The dynamics of life at the border may be construed in sociological terms. With A. van Gennep and V. Turner, one may understand the process as a stage in the rites of passage that involves initiation into a new status and a new way of being in the world.[14] Three distinct stages typically mark the passage: the *separation* of persons from their assigned roles in a given social structure; the margin or *limen*, a transitional stage when persons are "betwixt and between" assigned roles and new ones have yet to be actualized;[15] and the *reincorporation* of persons into society with new self-understandings and new roles. It is the liminal stage in this process that is critical, for here persons are shaped and fitted for the shift from what has been to what is yet to be. Liminality may be compared to being in the womb, awaiting the wonder of birth when a new person will enter the world specially prepared and uniquely shaped for life.

But liminality marks more than a change in a person's or a community's social status. It is the "generative center"[16] in the social drama of world-making. As Turner puts it, "The social world is a world in becoming, not a world in being."[17] It is not a world static and fixed, but a world constantly on the "threshold" (limen) of reconceptualization, rearrangement, renewal. For a world "in becoming," liminality marks the critical juncture for the emergence of what Turner calls "communitas," a special mode of relationship that does not depend on status quo arrangements of class, power, or social structure. Indeed, in Turner's view the bonds of communitas are "anti-structural," that is, they are "undifferentiated, egalitarian, direct, extant, non-rational, existential, I-Thou . . . (in Feuerbach's and Buber's sense) relationships."[18] Such I-Thou relationships engender new modes of thinking and acting that both disrupt ordinary structures and envision new ones that enable life to proceed in an orderly manner.[19] The custodians of structure regard "threshold people" (liminars) as dangerous and thus seek to hedge them in with restrictions and

---

14. A. Van Gennep, *The Rites of Passage* (Chicago: University of Chicago Press, 1960), especially 15–25. V. Turner's work on liminality can be consulted in a variety of publications: e.g., *The Ritual Process: Structure and Anti-Structure* (Ithaca, N.Y.: Cornell University Press, 1969); *Dramas, Fields, and Metaphors* (Ithaca, N.Y.: Cornell University Press, 1974); "Liminal to Liminoid, in Play, Flow, and Ritual: An Essay in Comparative Symbology," *Rice University Studies* 60 (1974), 53–92.

15. Turner, *Dramas, Fields, and Metaphors*, 232.

16. Ibid., 273.

17. Ibid., 24.

18. Ibid., 274.

19. Turner puts the matter as follows: "*Communitas* . . . is not structure with its signs reversed, minuses instead of pluses, but rather the *fons et origo* of all structures and, at the same time, their critique. For its very existence puts all structural rules in question and suggests new possibilities" (ibid., 202)

taboos. Consequently, in the interplay of this tension between structure and communitas, threshold people strain for openness in the midst of closure, liberation in the midst of confinement, new ways of thinking and being in the midst of settled identities.

Turner's work on liminality focuses primarily on sociological and cultural matters.[20] But clearly his perception of I-Thou relationships as the dynamic center of world-making has broad religious and theological ramifications as well. Particularly helpful in this regard is the work of C. Geertz, whose anthropological study of religion as a "cultural system" has been previously cited.[21] Geertz has shown that liminality may be construed not only as a social or cultural passage between structure and anti-structure, but also as a religious passage between the "real" world (the world "as lived") and the "really real" world (the world as "imagined"). In this interim between the world "as lived" and the world "as imagined," religious perspectives as well as social and political ones play a critical role in preparing persons for reentry into society.[22] As Geertz put it, religious perspectives, conveyed through linguistic, gestural, and material symbols, induce and sustain a "chronic inclination"[23] towards the birthing vision that enables persons to move resolutely "beyond the realities of everyday life to wider ones which correct and complete them."[24]

The Torah's vision of worship is a prime example of what it means for a faith community to sustain a "chronic inclination" towards the realization of a world beyond that which is merely given. If indeed persons, communities, and worlds move through liminal stages that permit and require new modes of thinking and acting, then surely our imminent crossing into a new millennium is a propitious time for reencountering the Torah's vision.

"Show Us in This World an Example of the World to Come"

With the ebbing of the twentieth century, the community of faith finds itself once more at a crucial stage in the rite of passage between past and

---

20. Turner does devote special attention to the phenomenon of pilgrimage as a liminal process in historical religions, e.g., Christianity, Islam, Judaism. See *Dramas, Fields, and Metaphors*, 166–230; *Image and Pilgrimage in Christian Culture: Anthropological Perspectives* (New York: Columbia University Press, 1978).

21. See above, chap. 3, pp. 60–61.

22. C. Geertz, "Religion as a Cultural System," *The Interpretation of Cultures: Selected Essays* (New York: Basic Books, 1973), 212.

23. Ibid., 96.

24. Ibid., 112.

future. Like our ancestors encamped in the plains of Moab, we stand at the border, looking backward to promises received and forward to the challenge of attaining them within the complexities of the world that lies ahead. If we are to heed the Torah's enduring summons to covenant fidelity, then we must know that we stand "today" before the jury of heaven and earth, like those assembled for Moses' parting instructions, with a momentous choice to make:

> I call heaven and earth to witness against you today that I have set before you life and death, blessings and cursings. Choose life so that you and your descendants may live. (Deut. 30:19)

The "today" of the world in which we must make the choice for life is shaped by different forces than those encountered in Moab or in Yehud. Ours is no longer a world defined by Canaanites or Persians but by modern powers like those that have been tracked by Friedman and Updike, Eliot and Yeats. Ours is a world that subtly empties life of the visible signs of God's presence even as it leaves hollowed souls yearning to believe that some more revelation must surely be at hand. So it is that our journey across the border into the next millennium confronts us anew with an old question: Where in *this world* may we find "a mind to understand, and eyes to see, and ears to hear" (cf. Deut. 29:4) that we may choose life over death?

Since this study is concerned with the Torah's vision, I believe it is fitting to address that question by turning to the wisdom of the great Jewish theologian, Abraham Heschel. In his book *The Sabbath: Its Meaning for Modern Man*, published in 1948, Heschel relates the following legend:

> at the time when God was giving the Torah to Israel, He said to them: My children! If you accept the Torah and observe my mitzvot, I will give you for all eternity a thing most precious that I have in my possession.
>
> —And what, asked Israel, is that precious thing which Thou wilt give us if we obey Thy Torah?
>
> —The world to come.
>
> —Show us in this world an example of the world to come.
>
> —The Sabbath is an example of the world to come.[25]

25. A. Heschel, *The Sabbath: Its Meaning for Modern Man* (New York: Farrar, Straus, 1948), 73.

I am struck by the fact that Heschel found meaning in this legend specifically within the world of 1948. Just three years after the incalculable horrors of World War II, when the world as given was broken and emptied of both reason and revelation by the killing of six million Jews, this Jewish scholar could find in obedience to Torah a way to think profoundly about the world to come. Heschel discerned that even in a world defined more by death than life, more by God's inexplicable absence than by God's presence, even in *this world*, the eyes of faith may see the signs for a new beginning.

For Heschel, the sabbath was the sign and the summons to believe that in God's design the immediate is not sufficiently empowered to defeat the eternal. Sabbath summons civilization, not the Jews alone, to remember and to share in that which is eternal in time. Sabbath is the occasion when we turn from the tyranny of the everyday to the holiness of the special day that empowers the sanctification of all time. In Heschel's words, sabbath is the occasion that prepares us to turn "from the world of creation to the creation of the world."[26]

I submit that the Torah's vision presents sabbath as the root symbol of the worship that summons and empowers the faith community, Jews and Christians alike, to its most distinctive way of being the people of God in the world. From a sociological perspective, one might say that it is worship, rooted in the sabbatical principle, that effects what Geertz calls the "chronic inclination" to remain committed to a transcendent vision of the "really real," even when present hegemonies seek to deny the reality of this vision or circumscribe its truth. From a theological perspective, one can argue that it is worship, informed by the wider realities encoded in the sabbath day, that enables a people to gain clarity on what it means to image God in the world as co-creators.

The daring assertion of the Torah's vision, however, does not encourage such neat and abstract lines of demarcation in the faith community's identity and vocation. To realize fully God's cosmic intentions, the faith community cannot disconnect its social and political obligations from its religious and spiritual ones. In the worship envisioned by the Torah, the summons to become "a priestly kingdom and a holy nation" leaves no part of the faith community's responsibility for the world unaddressed.

In sum, the Torah's vision of worship summons all who would embrace its truth to love God absolutely and to live in the world in such a manner that this love is manifest in concrete deeds and acts. Of the multiple ministries that are required to enact the Torah's vision of worship, this study has identified two that are critically important if God's creational design is to be fully realized.

26. Ibid., 10.

The first is the *ministry of prayer*, that dialogue with God that is a restless mixture of reverence and resistance. In the Torah's vision, the principal exemplars of such prayer are Abraham and Sarah, and especially Moses.

Abraham and Sarah (Gen. 15–17) epitomize both the problem and the promise of the people to whom God commits with an "everlasting covenant."[27] Abraham receives the promises of God for a life beyond the one he can discern with the naked eye, and he laments and laughs. On the one hand, the reality of his given circumstances drives him to protest and question the very idea that he may be included among those whose future will be secured by God's unconditional promises: "What will you give to me . . . I am childless . . . you have not given to me children" (Gen. 15:2-3); "How shall I know that I am to possess it?" (Gen. 15:8). On the other, given the evidence that God's promises may subvert status quo arrangements, he laughs (Gen. 17:17) and petitions God to conform divine plans to social convention (Gen. 17:18). In the Torah's vision, it is through this "father of faith," whose piety is shaped as much by doubt as by trust, that God chooses to extend to future generations the promise of the "everlasting covenant." Indeed, in the course of this discourse with Abraham, God's resolve to secure the partnership with humankind is strengthened, not weakened—a truth signified by the thirteen repetitions of the word "covenant" that occur in Genesis 17.

Sarah also models the piety of those whose conflicted lives invite and inform God's covenantal commitments. In the midst of the discourse in Genesis 15 and 17 that would establish God's covenant with humankind, the report of Sarah's barrenness (Gen. 16) is a candid reminder that divine intentions must often be implemented within a world of affliction and sorrow. Sarah asserts that *this world* also must be included and transformed by God's hopes and intentions if the covenant with humankind is to succeed. For those whose capacity for life has been inexplicably limited, God can be no detached observer. Sarah therefore confronts the promise of covenant with the truth of her aggrieved life: "*The* LORD has kept me from bearing children" (Gen. 16:2). Sarah's legitimate efforts to obtain by her own resources the child that God promises yet seems to withhold, ensnare an entire household in violence and abuse. It is a family matter. Even so, because its catalyst has been a divine promise, its ultimate resolution requires divine intervention. Sarah's plight introduces into the Torah for the first time the plea for justice: "May the LORD judge *(šāpaṭ)* between you and me" (Gen. 16:5). Within this web of human conflict, where those who would be addressed by God's promise seem destined for strife as well as blessing, Sarah's plea insists that divine justice, no less than human piety, is

27. See above, chap. 4, pp. 100–113.

required for the realization of the "everlasting covenant." Indeed, in this narrative it is Sarah's ministry of prayer that stands at the critical juncture between promise and fulfillment.

In the Torah's vision, it is Moses above all others who exemplifies the extraordinary ministry of prayer that sustains and restores God's covenantal intentions.[28] The Torah presents the eleven-month sojourn at Sinai as a liturgy of covenant-making that is empowered to recall and renew God's creational designs. Even so, within the aggregate vision of Exodus 25–40 the Torah candidly acknowledges that the sin and disobedience signified by the golden calf incident threaten to plunge the world of God's design into chaos and disorder. The community's temptation to yield to the seduction of manufactured gods (cf. Exod. 32:4,8: "These are your gods, O Israel") portends a crisis that may nullify the covenant and erase God's intentions with a finality not unlike that which biblical faith associates with the primordial flood (Gen. 6–9). At this critical juncture, between the promised future that God would secure and the given distortion in the world that would block its actualization, Moses engages God in the daring act of prayer.

On behalf of a people clearly guilty and deserving of punishment, Moses dares to question, to challenge, and to change God's announced plans for judgment. "Why" (vv. 11, 12: $l\bar{a}mm\bar{a}h$) would God move into the future without these people, even though their punishment is warranted, when such a decision would effectively annul the very vision that sustains creation's design? The question is buttressed with three bold petitions that instruct the Covenant-Maker in the protocols of covenant fidelity. Moses demands that God "turn away" (v.12: $\check{s}\hat{u}b$) from divine anger, "change" (v.12: $hinn\bar{a}h\bar{e}m$) the decision to punish, and "remember" (v.13: $z\check{e}k\bar{o}r$) the promises that have long secured God's covenantal intentions against the fragility and limitations of partnership with the human community. In this daring address Moses appeals to God to remember that the primordial vision vouchsafed first to Noah (Gen. 6:18; 9:11, 12, 13, 15, 16, 17) has been sustained by divine oath to Abraham, Isaac, and their descendants (v.13; cf. Gen. 15:5). If God's promises are now to survive the crisis of Sinai, Moses argues, God must once again act in accordance with God's unrelenting commitment to stay in covenant relationship with a sinful and undeserving people. The effectiveness of Moses' prayer is all the more dramatic for the simplicity with which its outcome is reported: "And the Lord changed ($wayyinn\bar{a}hem$) his mind about the disaster that he planned to bring on his people" (v.14).

---

28. See above, chap. 5, pp. 140–45.

The Torah's account of the liturgy at Sinai envisions Moses' prayer as a critical turning point in God's decision to reissue the commandments and restore the covenant relationship (Exod. 34). There is no mistaking the Torah's clear assertion that human sinfulness obstructs God's plans and suspends the realization of covenant possibilities for the duration of God's justified punishment. The Torah is equally clear, however, that even in the midst of judgment, a spurned and aggrieved God remains open and solicitous of new beginnings for partnership with humankind.

Moses' prayer models the ministry of intercession that works to create such new beginnings with God. The task before us is not simply to read and appreciate the intercessions of our forebears; an unthinking repetition of old testimonies of faith will not engage us meaningfully with the real needs of the present world any more than it did Clarence Wilmot. The urgent need rather is to identify contemporary situations in life where people are tempted to believe that God is a "non-factor." For these circumstances the Torah's vision provides a reservoir of prayers on which we may draw to imagine new ways of keeping God and people connected.[29]

When the community of faith engages in the ministry of intercession, it follows Moses into the breach between God's hopes and intentions for the world and the many and varied failings of humankind that render the world unfit for partnership with God. In this dangerous breach, it is the daring ministry of prayer to proclaim and insist that life with God remain finally open-ended, not settled or closed. The truth of the Torah's vision—which all those who would follow Moses' and Sarah's example may act upon—is that even east of Eden, where limitations and impossibilities seem to be the status quo, the ministry of prayer is peculiarly empowered to evoke from God change, new beginnings, new opportunities.

The second ministry that is crucial for enacting the Torah's vision of worship in a way that fully realizes God's creational design is the *ministry of priesthood*. For many in the Protestant tradition, the suggestion that God's creational design summons the faithful to a ministry of priesthood represents an enormous challenge. Our tradition of scholarship and theology has largely viewed anything associated with Israel's priesthood as the embodiment of everything distasteful in Roman Catholicism and Judaism.[30] Early Protestantism took root in the soil of the Reformation where the Pauline dualism of faith and works was foundational for the development of a theology that privileged gospel over law, prophet over

---

29. For further discussion of the way in which the ministry of prayer serves to keep the community in God and God in the community, see S. E. Balentine, *Prayer in the Hebrew Bible: The Drama of Divine-Human Dialogue,* OBT (Minneapolis: Fortress, 1993), 273–95.

30. See above, chap. 3, pp. 69-75, chap. 6, pp. 171-74.

priest, mind and spirit over body and flesh. In such a context it can hardly be surprising that the ceremonies and rituals identified with Israel's priests were typically ignored or denounced as irrelevant for authentic Christian existence.[31]

Critical biblical scholarship since the Enlightenment, especially in Protestant circles, has done little to change this negative assessment of the priestly. Sadly, Wellhausen's indictment of the priestly tradition as a "petty scheme of salvation" has enjoyed a wide influence in Christian Old Testament scholarship.[32] In Wellhausen's view, priestly religion can be dismissed as a "medium of worship" because it is fundamentally lifeless and misdirected. He described the priesthood thus:

> The warm pulse of life no longer throbbed in it to animate it; it was no longer the blossom and the fruit of every branch of life; it had its own meaning all to itself. It symbolized worship, and that was enough. The soul was fled; the shell remained, upon the shaping out of which every energy was now concentrated. A manifoldness of rites took the place of individualising occasions; technique was the main thing, and strict fidelity to rubric.[33]

Against this entrenched anti-priestly stance, the present study has endeavored to show that the Torah's vision presents the ministry of priesthood as an indispensable imperative in God's summons to the community of faith. In the Torah's vision the world of God's creation is ordered so that there might be a purposive and reciprocal movement between "earth and the heavens" (Gen. 2:4b; cf. Gen. 2:1). In priestly theology, this movement requires that both the boundaries and the gateways between the domain of God and the world of God's creation be carefully observed and sustained. When these boundaries and entrances are in place, God's design for the world may be actualized; creation and creatures are secure within the harmony of God's cosmic intentions. When they are ignored or transgressed, the order of the world collapses, and chaos threatens to undo creation. In

---

31. For a succinct and cogent survey of these matters, see F. Gorman, "Ritual Studies and Biblical Studies: Assessment of the Past; Prospects for the Future," *Semeia* 67 (1994), 14–20. See also J. Blenkinsopp's description of "the bad repute of the Israelite priesthood in the modern period" in *Sage, Priest, Prophet: Religious and Intellectual Leadership in Ancient Israel* (Louisville: Westminster/John Knox, 1995), 66–68. On the general issues surrounding the traditional designations "gospel" and "law," particularly with reference to reclaiming the importance of *torah* in Christian theology, see F. Crüsemann, *The Torah: Theology and Social History of Old Testament Law* (Minneapolis: Fortress, 1996), 1–6, 365–67.

32. See chapter 1 of J. Wellhausen, *Prolegomena to the History of Israel* (Gloucester, Mass.: Peter Smith, 1973).

33. Ibid., 78.

the Torah's vision, the vital task of marking and securing these boundaries is assigned to the priests. Their primary ministry is defined succinctly by God: "You are to distinguish between the holy and the common, and between the unclean and the clean" (Lev. 10:10).[34]

Distinguishing between the holy and the common, the clean and the unclean, involves a variety of responsibilities. Holy times of worship are marked and observed so that the daily routines of life may remain constantly connected to the sacred rhythms of creation's ordering (cf. Lev. 23). Purity laws and dietary regulations are observed so that life outside the Holy Place may conform with and mirror the integrity of the boundaries that uphold God's creational design (cf. Lev. 11–15). Of course, boundaries can and will be violated, and as a consequence, both persons and worlds may be defiled and rendered unfit for partnership with a holy God. Such defilement requires that priests extend their ministry through rituals that purify the unclean and sanctify the profane. Those distanced by sin or disease from communion with the clean and the holy may be restored to full fellowship with the people of God (for example, Lev. 14). A defiled sanctuary, which jeopardizes the presence of God on earth, may be purged and restored, thus inviting a new beginning with the Creator who desires to reside in the midst of a fragile world (for example, Lev. 16).

In the Torah's vision, the ministry of priesthood cannot be fulfilled only by marking boundaries and facilitating ritual observances of celebration and correction. Priests are themselves specially commissioned to live and work between the boundaries: between the holy and the common, between the clean and the unclean. They are therefore summoned to a liminal, a "threshold" existence. In the founding ritual for ordination that is preserved in Leviticus 8–9, the one charge given to the priests at the conclusion of their consecration is that they remain at the door of the tent of meeting for seven days (Lev. 8:35).[35] This sacred quarantine at the intersection between the holy and the common is paradigmatic for priestly ministry. Priests are to live and minister within the dangerous zone that divides and joins the things of God and the things of the world. They are to serve as both "insulators and connectors" for the whole community.[36] They are to

---

34. Priests obviously fulfilled a number of roles in Israel's society. For example, see the various functions described in Deut. 10:8-9; 31:9-13; 33:8-11; 1 Sam. 2:28; 1 Chron. 23:13. But their major responsibility lay in the realm of ritual, and in this respect the charge to distinguish between the holy and the common, the clean and the unclean, was clearly of primary importance. On the roles of the priests, see further: Blenkinsopp, *Sage, Priest, Prophet*, 80–83; R. D. Nelson, *Raising Up a Faithful Priest: Community and Priesthood in Biblical Theology* (Louisville: Westminster/John Knox, 1993), 39–53.

35. See above, chap. 6, pp. 150–53.

36. Nelson, *Raising Up a Faithful Priest*, 85.

insulate and safeguard worshipers from inappropriate contact with the holy, while providing the connection with God that makes life possible and full. They are to serve therefore as ministers of stability. Their charge is to effect a kind of "homeostatic balance" that binds together heaven and earth in the wholeness and harmony of God's cosmic design.[37]

Priestly theology knows well, however, that the harmonious union of heaven and earth cannot be attained through worship alone. For the full realization of the order with which God endows creation, there must be a corresponding ethic of justice and righteousness on earth. The mandate to image God as agents of justice is therefore an essential objective of the rites and rituals that define the ministry of priesthood. Nelson has suggested that "a people actually learns what it believes from the way it worships."[38] In terms of priestly theology, the truth of this observation is born out in the presentation of worship as a summons both to remember the holiness of God and to enact it: "You shall be holy, for I the Lord your God am holy" (Lev. 19:2).

The venue for worship commissioned by this objective lies in the "common" areas of everyday life no less than in the "holy" observances within the sacred place. Through its rites and rituals the ministry of priesthood enables a community of faith to construe and enact "another world to live in." In this world, justice, no less than piety, will be the measure of fidelity. The ministry of priesthood is at all times vitally important. But it is especially crucial in times when the community of faith finds itself staggering at the border: on one side, the mandate and the promises of its founding vision; on the other, the seductive appeal of culture's manufactured gods and values.

Whether in ancient Yehud or at the intersection of Straight Street and Broadway in any contemporary city, the summons for the people of God is to live faithfully inside the shadow that separates the "idea and the reality."[39]

Jacob Neusner has suggested that Judaism has the capacity to teach each of us, Jew and gentile alike, how to live faithfully and creatively inside the shadow of this world. Drawing upon the seminal insights of his teacher Abraham Heschel, Neusner invokes the prayers and rites of Jewish liturgy as acts of imagination that are empowered to transform ordinary human existence into metaphors of the sacred.[40] In the traditional

37. Ibid., 36.
38. Ibid., 89. See above, chap. 6, pp. 173–74.
39. Eliot, "The Hollow Men," 81.
40. J. Neusner, *The Enchantments of Judaism: Rites of Transformation from Birth Through Death* (New York: Basic Books, 1987).

language of Judaism, this transformation is termed "sanctification." Neusner prefers the term "enchantment," for in his assessment the change that is wrought in persons and communities through the practice of liturgy is as much a delight as a miracle. Through its rites of enchantment, Judaism transforms the givenness of life into a gift of God. Persons and communities are no longer what they once were, they are something more. They are empowered to see worlds not present and so therefore to live "as if" there is more to life than what appears to be. This daring act— living "as if" life is connected to a reality that is always more than what can be seen—stands at the very heart of Judaism. Neusner summarizes his fundamental thesis as follows:

> To be a Jew is to live both *as if* and also in the here and now. By *as if* I mean that we form in our minds and imagination a picture of ourselves that the world we see everyday does not sustain. We are more than we seem, other than we appear to be. To be a Jew is to live a metaphor, to explore the meaning of life as simile, of language as poetry and of action as drama and of vision as art. For Scripture begins with the judgment of humanity that we are "in our image, after our likeness"; and once humanity forms image and likeness, we are not what we seem but something different, something more. And for Israel, the Jewish people, the metaphor takes over in the comparison and contrast between what we appear to be and what in the image of, after the likeness of the Torah, we are told we really are.[41]

Living "as if" we and the world in which we exist are a metaphor for God's creational design begins with theology, not with politics: "Let us make humankind in our image, according to our likeness" (Gen. 1:26). Neusner understands that for such an assertion to be actualized, the work of faith must become an act of art. In his words, it must be

> . . . carried out alone by poetry, not by prose; alone by theater, not by ordinary speech; alone by dance, not by clumsy and ordinary shuffling; alone by the silence of disciplined sound we know as music, not by background noise and rackets; alone by the eye of the artist who sees within and beyond, not by the vacant stare of those who do not even see what is there.[42]

Neusner examines the variety of rites and practices that comprise the enchantments of Judaism and the art of faith. For our purposes here we

41. Ibid., 209.
42. Ibid.

may single out his discussion of sabbath, which forms the heart and soul of Jewish religion.[43] In the Judaic vision sabbath is a work of art. It celebrates the life with God and in God that is empowered to transform ordinary time into holy time. To observe its day of rest and renewal is to claim independence from the given world of time and space that typically reduces everyday life to one-dimensional preoccupations and commitments. It is to take leave of the commonplace and to celebrate and to participate in the enchantment that completes and perfects God's design for creation.[44]

Neusner asserts that modern civilization requires the Sabbath even more urgently than did those Jews who gathered at Sinai to enter into covenant partnership with God.[45] The commonplace virtues of this modern world may steadily seduce us to yield, with Teddy Wilmot, to a life of "plodding stoicism."[46] But the Sabbath reminds us that by God's grace the everyday is not all there is. With Heschel, Neusner would remind us that even in this modern world, the Sabbath stands as an impregnable cathedral, a holy shrine for the sanctification of life "that neither the Romans nor the Germans were able to burn."[47] From this place, in this enchanted world of Sabbath observance, those who embrace the invitation to share in what is eternal are wondrously empowered to turn "from the world of creation to the creation of the world."[48]

Throughout this study, I have focused principally on the Torah's vision and its legacy for Jewish faith and practice. But I have also repeatedly suggested that this vision is important for Christians as well. It is instructive to remember that the New Testament often turns to the figure of the Old Testament priest and to the idea of the ministry of priesthood as a model for the church.[49]

Of special significance in this regard is the Letter to the Hebrews, which seeks to convince Christians that the Aaronic priesthood provides important perspectives on the work and ministry of Jesus. Not only does it portray Jesus as the faithful high priest (Heb. 4:14—5:10) whose sacrificial death enables us "to approach the throne of grace with boldness, so that we may receive mercy" (4:16), it also describes Jesus' priestly mediation as an act of boundary-crossing that recalls the paradigm of the Day of

43. Ibid., 85–99.
44. Ibid., 89.
45. Ibid.
46. See above, chap. 8, pp. 228–29.
47. Neusner, *The Enchantments of Judaism*, 86. See Heschel, *The Sabbath*, 8.
48. Neusner, ibid., 95. See Heschel, ibid., 10.
49. For a cogent discussion of the importance of Israelite priesthood in the New Testament and in Christian ministry, see Nelson, *Raising Up a Faithful Priest*, 141–74.

Atonement (Heb. 9). Christ the priest enters into the Holy Place, into the very presence of God, and with the blood of his unique redemption he purifies the "heavenly things" (9:23) and reestablishes contact between God and humankind. This "excellent ministry" (8:6) of priestly mediation connects Jesus' followers to the new covenant promised by God in Jeremiah 31:31-34 (Heb. 8:6-13; 9:15).

Whereas Hebrews focuses primarily on the priestly role of Christ, 1 Peter describes the ministry of priesthood that belongs to the Christian community. Addressed to the "exiles" and "resident aliens" dispersed throughout Asia Minor (cf. 1:1, 17; 2:11), this letter seeks to encourage those whose minority status has lead them to question their identity as the people of God.[50] The incentives for reassessment used by 1 Peter are drawn from the Old Testament.[51] The author addresses these Christians as Sarah's "daughters" (3:6), members of a "chosen race" (2:9), "God's people" (2:9-10; cf. Isa. 43:20-21), who are born of "imperishable seed" (1:23). Redeemed by the blood of Christ, they are summoned to a life of holiness just like their ancestors in Israel: "for it is written, 'You shall be holy, for I am holy'" (1 Pet. 1:6; cf. Lev. 11:44). The particular metaphor for their identity and vocation is none other than the Torah's vision of "a priestly kingdom and a holy nation." Citing the LXX translation of Exodus 19:6, 1 Peter 2:9 urges these exiles to realize their legacy as "a royal priesthood" (*basileion hierateuma*). Christians do not have a priesthood in the strictest sense of the Old Testament's description; 1 Peter's exhortation is that the community of faith exercise a collective ministry of "spiritual sacrifices" (cf. 2:5) that proclaims and extends the salvation of God in Christ.

It is true that in Hebrews, 1 Peter, and elsewhere, the New Testament stresses that Jesus' priesthood and ministry are superior to what is offered in Judaism. Moreover, within Christianity different denominations have particular theological and ecclesiological perspectives that may heighten the perceived discontinuity between Old Testament and New Testament models for the community of faith. I do not wish to deny the significance of these differences or to minimize their importance in shaping the history of the church. However, in view of the long history of Christian neglect and disparagement of "the law," and the sad rupture between Christian and Jewish communities of faith that this has too often created and sustained, I suggest that a reconsideration of the Torah's vision holds the promise that what unites us in God's design is greater than what divides us.

---

50. For the importance of these images in I Peter, see J. H. Elliott, *A Home for the Homeless* (Philadelphia: Fortress, 1981).

51. For further discussion, see Nelson, *Raising Up a Faithful Priest*, 155–68.

As the sons and daughters of Abraham and Sarah, Jews and Christians alike stand at the threshold of a new millennium very much as a border people. We are in transition "betwixt and between" the promises of God and their ultimate fulfillment. In this interim period our common task is to live in this world "as if" there is still more to come. Whether in Moab or Yehud, Asia Minor or the modern world, the Torah's vision has continued to summon the community of faith to become "a priestly kingdom and a holy nation." Here again, the task before us is not simply to replicate by rote the rituals that our forebears found meaningful in their world. We are summoned to be "a priestly kingdom and a holy nation" in *this* world. To fulfill that mandate we must return again and again to the priestly paradigms for ministry. There we may find the sacred deposits of faith that enable us to imagine new ways of embodying and gesturing into reality those alternative worlds that sustain God's creational intentions. As exiles and resident aliens in a world that too often seems "as empty of divine content as a corroded kettle,"[52] could it not be that the Torah's vision of a community gathered in worship may yet bind us together in a common ministry of imaging God on earth? With Abraham and Moses, Jeremiah and Jesus, that ministry will have as its objective the full realization of the new covenant promised by God. The "days are surely coming" (Jer. 31:31) when this new covenant, announced by Jeremiah and mediated by Jesus, will secure God's creational design for the whole of the cosmos "on earth as in heaven." On that day God and all of creation will enjoy the full rest and celebration of Sabbath, for it will finally be the case that the world as envisioned and the world as lived have become one and the same. But until that day, the Torah's vision bequeaths to Jew and Christian alike a new and ever renewing summons to faithful stewardship of the covenant partnership with God.

With Moses we are reminded that at the border between promise and fulfillment, the choices we are called to make are matters of life and death. Faithful stewardship requires of each of us that we "choose life" so that we and our descendants may live (Deut. 30:19). With Paul we are reminded that the choices we make redound throughout the cosmos, for we know that "the whole creation has been groaning in labor pains until now"; it "waits with eager longing for the revealing of the children of God" (Rom. 8:22, 19). While we hope and trust in that which we do not see, faithful stewardship requires that we wait and work for the vision with patience and commitment (cf. Rom. 8:25).

---

52. Updike, *In the Beauty of the Lilies*, 7 (see above, chap. 8, 226, 230-31).

INDEX OF ANCIENT SOURCES

INDEX OF AUTHORS